Life & Letters at Bath

IN THE EIGHTEENTH CENTURY

Beau Nash. *From the portrait by Hoare.*

Life & Letters at Bath

IN THE EIGHTEENTH CENTURY

A. BARBEAU

First published 1904
This edition published 2009
Reprinted 2020

The History Press
97 St George's Place, Cheltenham,
Gloucestershire, GL50 3QB
www.thehistorypress.co.uk

British Library Cataloguing in Publication Data.
A catalogue record for this book is available from the British Library.

ISBN 978 1 84588 602 8

Typesetting and origination by The History Press
Printed in Great Britain by TJ International Ltd, Padstow, Cornwall.

Contents

Illustrations

Oliver Goldsmith
From the portrait by a pupil of Sir Joshua Reynolds

Marshal Wade
From the picture by Hogarth

Ralph Allen
From the drawing by William Hoare, RA

William Warburton
From the portrait by Charles Phillips

Henry Fielding
From Basire's engraving of the portrait by William Hogarth

Thomas Gainshorough
From the portrait by himself

Sir Thomas Lawrence
From an engraving by Worthington

The Old Bridge
From the drawing by John Claude Nattes

Preface

Among the pleasant premonitions of the *entente cordiale* between France and England is the increased attention which, for some time past, our friends of *Outre Manche* have been devoting to our literature. That this is entirely of recent growth is not of course to be inferred. It must be forty years since M. Hippolyte Taine issued his logical and orderly "Histoire de la Littérature Anglaise"; while other isolated efforts of insight and import— such as the "Laurence Sterne" of M. Paul Stapfer, and the excellent "Le Public et les Hommes de Lettres en Angleterre au XVIIIe Siècle" of M. Alexandre Beljame of the Sorbonne— are already of distant date. But during the last two decades the appearance of similar productions has been more recurrent and more marked. From one distinguished writer alone—M. J.J. Jusserand—we have received an entire series of studies of exceptional charm, variety, and accomplishment. M. Félix Rabbe has given us a sympathetic analysis of Shelley; M. Auguste Angellier, what has been rightly described as a "splendid work" upon Burns; while M. Emile Legouis, in a minute examination of "The Prelude," has contrasted and compared the orthodox Wordsworth of maturity with the juvenile "semi-atheist" of Coleridge. Travelling farther afield, M. W. Thomas has consecrated an exhaustive volume to Young of the "Night Thoughts" ; and, incidentally, a flood of fresh light has been thrown upon the birth and growth of the English novel by the admirable "Jean-Jacques Rousseau et les Origines du Cosmopolitisme Littéraire" of the late Joseph Texte—an investigation unquestionably of the ripest scholarship and the most extended research. And now once more there are signs that French lucidity and French precision are about to enter upon other conquests; and we have M.A. Barbeau's study of a famous old English watering-place,—appropriately dedicated, as is another of the books already mentioned, to M. Beljame.

At first sight, topography, even when combined with social sketches, may seem less suited to a foreigner and an outsider than it would be to a resident and a native. In the attitude of the latter to the land in which he lives or has been born there is always an inherent something of the soil for which even trained powers of comparison and a special perceptive faculty are but imperfect substitutes. On the other hand, the visitor from overseas is, in many respects, better placed for observation than the inhabitant. He enjoys not a little—it has often been said—of the position of posterity. He takes in more at a glance; he leaves out less; he is disturbed by no apprehension of explaining what is obvious, or discovering what is known. As a result, he sets down much which, from long familiarity, an indigenous critic would be disposed to discard, although it may not be in itself either uninteresting or superfluous. And if, instead of dealing with the present and actual, his concern is with history and the past, his external standpoint becomes a strength rather than a weakness. He can survey his subject with a detachment which is wholly favourable to his project; and he can give it, with less difficulty than another, the advantages of scientific treatment and an artistic setting. Finally, if his themes have definite limits—as, for instance, an appreciable origin, growth, and termination—he must be held to be unusually fortunate. And this last, either from happy guessing or sheer good luck, is M. Barbeau's case. All these conditions are present in the records of the popular pleasure resort of which he has elected to trace the story. It arose gradually; it progressed through a century of unexampled prosperity; it sank again to the level of an ordinary county town. If it should ever arise again, it will be in a different way. The Bath of the Eighteenth Century—the Bath of Queen Anne and the Georges, of Nash and Fielding and Sheridan, of Anstey and Mrs Siddons, of Wesley and Lady Huntingdon, of Quin and Gainsborough and Lawrence and a hundred others—is no more. It has gone for ever. To borrow an apposite expression from M. Texte,—it is an organism whose evolution has run its course.

In such circumstances one may well marvel—as one always does after the event—why no one was clever enough to hit upon so promising a subject before. But while M. Barbeau is to be congratulated upon the happy task he has selected, we may also congratulate ourselves that he has performed it so effectively. In his earlier and more preliminary pages, the old "Queen of the West" lives again, with its ill-paved streets and stone houses, its crush of chairs and chariots, its throngs of smirking, self-satisfied promenaders. One sees the clumsy coaches depositing their tousled and tumbled inmates in queer travelling costumes at the "Bear" or the "White Hart," after a jolting two-or-three-days' journey from Oxford or London, not without the usual experiences, real and imaginary, of suspicious horse men seen at Hounslow or masked footpads on Claverton Down. One hears the peal of four-and-twenty bells which greets the arrival of fresh visitors of importance; and notes the subservient town-waits who follow them to their lodgings in Gay Street or Milsom Street or the Parades, where they will, no doubt, be attended incontinently by the Master of the Ceremonies—a very pretty gentleman, to be sure, whether his name be Wade or Derrick. Next day will probably discover them in chip hats and flannel, duly equipped with bowls and bouquets, at the King's Bath, where, through a steaming atmosphere, you may inspect their artless manoeuvres (as does Lydia Melford in "Humphrey Clinker") from the windows of the Pump Room, to which rallying-place they will presently repair to drink the waters, in a medley of notables and notorieties, members of parliament, chaplains and led-captains, noblemen with ribbons and stars, dove-coloured Quakers, duchesses, quacks, fortune-hunters, lackeys, lank-haired Methodists, bishops, and boarding-school misses. Ferdinand Count Fathom will be there as well as my Lord Ogleby; Lady Bellaston and Mr Thomas Jones; Geoffry Wildgoose and Tugwell the cobbler; Lismahago and Tabitha Bramble; the blushing Miss Anville and the caustic Mrs Selwyn. Be certain, too, that you will encounter Mrs Candour and Lady Sneerwell, Sir Benjamin Backbite and his uncle Mr Crabtree, for this is their "fitting environment"—in fact, they were born in Bath. You may follow this worshipful procession to the Public Breakfasts in the Spring Gardens, to the Toy-shops behind the Church, to the Coffee-houses in Westgate Street, to the Reading Rooms on the Walks, where, in Mr Leake's sanctum at the back, if you are lucky you may behold the celebrated Mr Ralph Allen of Prior Park, talking either to Mr Henry Fielding or to Mr Leake's brother-in-law, Mr Samuel Richardson, but never—if we are correctly informed—to both of them together. Or you may run against Mr Christopher Anstey, of the "Guide," walking arm-in-arm with another Bath resident, Mr "Pliny" Melmoth. At the Abbey Church, where there are daily morning services, you shall listen to the silver periods of the excellent Bishop Hurd, whom his admirers call fondly "the Beauty of Holiness"; at St James's you can attend the lectures, "more unctuous than ever he preached," of Bishop Beilby Porteus; or you may succeed in obtaining a card for a select hearing, at Edgar Buildings, of Lady Huntingdon's chaplain, Mr Whitefield. With the evening you may pass, if you are so minded, to Palmer's Theatre in Orchard Street, and follow Mrs Siddons acting Belvidera in "Venice Preserv'd" to the Pierre of that forgotten Mr Lee whom Fanny Burney put next to Garrick; or you may join the enraptured audience whom Mrs Jordan is delighting with her favourite part of Priscilla Tomboy in "The Romp." You may assist at the concerts of Signor Venanzio Rauzzini and Monsieur La Motte; you may take part in a long minuet or a country dance at the Upper or Lower Assembly Rooms; you even may lose a few pieces at the green tables; and, should you return home late enough, may watch a couple of stout chairmen at the door of the "Three Tuns" in Stall Street, hoisting the seasoned *bon vivant* Mr James Quin into a sedan after his evening's quantum of claret. What you do today you will do tomorrow, if the bad air of the Pump Room has not given you a headache, or the waters a touch of vertigo; and you will continue to do it for a month or six weeks, when the lumbering vehicle with the leathern straps and crane-necked springs will carry you back again over the deplorable roads ("so *sidelum and jumblum*"—one traveller styles them) to your town-house, or your country-box, or your city-shop or chambers, as the case may be. Here, in due course, you will begin to meditate upon your next excursion to The Bath, provided always that you have not dipped your estate at "E.O." or been ruined by milliners' bills; that your son has not gone off with a sham Scotch heiress or your daughter been married (by private licence) to a pinchbeck Irish peer. For all these things—however painful the admission—were, according to the most credible historians, the not infrequent accompaniments, or sequels of an unguarded sojourn at the old jigging, card-playing, scandal-loving, pleasure-seeking city in the loop of "the soft-flowing Avon."

And all these things—save and except a few vagrant variations of our own—are duly recorded in M. Barbeau's conscientious chronicles—chronicles which, let us hasten to add, comprise much more than a mere picture of that quotidian Bath programme which King Nash and his successors had ordained and established. The author goes back to the origins; to the too-much-neglected Celia Fiennes; to Pepys, and Grammont's "Memoirs"; to the days when hapless Catherine of Braganza, with the "*belle* Stewart" in her train, made fruitless pilgrimage to Bladud's spring as a remedy against sterility. He sketches the biography of that arch-quack and *poseur*, the first Master of the Ceremonies; he gives a minute account of the marriage of Sheridan to his beautiful "St Cecilia", Elizabeth Ann Linley. A special chapter is allotted to Lady Huntingdon and the Methodists, not without levies from the clever "Spiritual Quixote" of the Rev. Richard Graves of Claverton. Other chapters are occupied with Bath and its *belles lettres*; with "Squire Allworthy" and his literary guests; with the historical Frascati vase of Lady Miller at Batheaston, which stirred the ridicule of Walpole. The closing pages treat of Bath musical, artistic, scientific;—of its gradual transformation as a health resort;—of its ultimate and foredoomed decline and fall as the watering-place *par excellence* of Great Britain and Ireland.

But we must dispense with further introductory intrusion. In the words of OLIVER GOLDSMITH—whom M. Barbeau may be proud to have for a predecessor—it is impolitic to tire the reader with a long preface, when his unfatigued attention is wanted to a serious performance. Let us content ourselves with adding here that M. Barbeau's skilful and scholarly book is fully furnished with all the requisite references to authorities; that it has an exhaustive Bibliography, and a copious Index. These attractions its present publisher has endeavoured to enhance by a series of portraits and views of localities. Nothing remains; therefore, but to quote that latter-day and somewhat Alexandrine Bathonian, Mr Cyrus Angelo Bantam of "Pickwick," and bid the reader—who, on this occasion, may fitly be apostrophised as "gentle"— "Welcome to Ba-ath!"

AUSTIN DOBSON
EALING, *September* 1904.

I

Bath to the Last Years of the Seventeenth Century

i

To the north-east of Somersetshire, twelve miles above Bristol, on the banks of the lazy Avon, which rolls its heavy waters towards the neighbouring sea, an amphitheatre of green hills arises as if to embrace and encircle in its verdure the pleasant white city of Bath. Gay and cheerful, built of stone and not of the usual English brick, the little town unfolds itself in the narrow valley, filling it entirely; then, overflowing, it throws out its terraces boldly to climb the steep slopes, stage after stage. In the middle, rising from the depths of the hollow, an Abbey in the Tudor style, massive and heavy in spite of its large windows,[1] dominates the mass of small houses, and rears its stunted tower aloft in the haze in a some what unaspiring fashion. It evokes the long ecclesiastical past of the monastic and episcopal borough,[2] which we see in retrospect nestling in a bend of the river, behind its feudal walls. But the other churches are nearly all modern, as are the streets and the buildings. Almost the whole place obviously dates from the eighteenth century. There is no disparity in the buildings, no confusion in the plan, no (or very few) relics of bygone times, obtruding themselves among modern structures,[3] scarcely anything, in fact, of what in most modern towns indicates a slow development patiently pursued from age to age. In this city of yesterday, or of the day before yesterday, the Abbey is but an isolated monument of ancient times, like those *thermae,* more ancient still, the ruins of which have lately been excavated. All the rest betrays a brusque metamorphosis, a development at once sudden and orderly, which seems to have been in no wise determined by ordinary political, commercial, or industrial causes. It was a pleasure-city that was improvised here, and its sumptuous aspect has outlived its fortune. Its wide, straight streets, its uniform or symmetrical façades, its houses, arranged in architectural groups, its regular squares, its long monumental lines, its pediments, its colonnades, the constant recurrence of classic motives, give it a grandeur that is somewhat academic and pompous, relieved, however, by the trees and lawns of its parks and gardens, and diversified by the perspectives skilfully introduced in a happy and varied site. The general aspect is characterised. now by the grandiose dignity of the New Town of Edinburgh, now by the somewhat artificial elegance of certain German "Residences." The spectacle of modern life in this setting—the busy life of a prosperous provincial centre, the decorous life of retired professional men and persons of independent means, attracted by the amenities of the place and the climate—comes upon one with something of a shock. The eye instinctively wanders over the wide pavements, seeking the costumes of a bygone age, embroidered coats and flounces, long waistcoats and *paniers;* it would not be surprised if it encountered emblazoned sedan-chairs at the corners of the streets. On this stage, prepared for a very different society, it is the present occupants and their habits that seem out of place. Only the eighteenth century, we feel, could ever be at home here; these scenes were a theatre it arranged according to its own taste, for its use and pleasure, and in which it figured in its utmost brilliance, if not in its most serious and estimable aspect. The theatre is empty; the actors have long deserted it, the play, already forgotten, can never be revived. But literature makes it possible to resuscitate some of the former, to reconstitute the main lines of the latter, and by means of this dual memory to animate scenery that has remained almost intact.

ii

Though the eighteenth century laid out Bath, made it a favourite place of residence, and stamped its own impress so strongly upon it, it neither created nor discovered the town. We know that before its metamorphosis it already boasted a long and respectable history, which it will not be necessary to set forth at length here, though we may briefly recall its most important points.[4]

Few towns in Great Britain seem to have been founded at so early a date as Bath, and, like Rome, its origin is surrounded by legend. A tradition, which was accepted till quite recently,[5] connected it with one of the old mythic Kings by Geoffrey of Monmouth and the "Roman de Brute." Bladud, son of Hudibras, and afterwards the father of King Lear, was its reputed founder.[6] Heir presumptive to the throne, he was suddenly attacked by leprosy, and consequently banished from the Court; in the course of his wanderings he came to a remote part of what is now Somersetshire, where his destitution was so great that he was forced to hire himself out as a swineherd. He found after a time that he had given his disease to the animals he was tending, but was greatly surprised to see them plunge into the hot—water springs of the district, and emerge completely cured. He followed the example of his charges, was cured like them, returned to his father, and on the spot where the miracle had taken place he founded baths, built a temple of

General view of Bath, from the Claverton Road
From the drawing by John Claude Nattes

Minerva in which fires were kept perpetually burning,[7] and finally a town, where he afterwards reigned in great splendour.[8] Such, stripped of its details, which are very circumstantial, was the legend which, in spite of the raillery of Rochester[9] and Powell,[10] was piously believed in Bath down to the beginning of the last century, is still popular in the city, and was parodied by Dickens in "Pickwick." It is a developed and embellished version of another, simpler and more ancient, to be found in that inexhaustible repertory of (so-called) British fables, the "History of the Kings of Britain" by Geoffrey of Monmouth.[11] It was repeated after him by Wace ("Roman de Brut," II 1667–1677), Layamon ("Brut," 11. 2834–2895),[12] Higgins, one of Sackville's collaborators ("Mirroure for Magistrates," part 1., ix.), Leland ("Commentarii de Scriptoribus Britannicis," cap. vi.), Spenser ("Faery Queen," book ii., canto x., v. 25 and 26), Camden ("Britannia," vol. ii., "Belgae," p 107). Geoffrey merely relates that at the time of the Prophet Elijah, Bladud, a great magician, skilled in all the arts of Greece, created the hot springs by his enchantments; he says nothing of the leprosy and the pigs. In any case, Bath, as we learn from a physician of the sixteenth century, is supposed to have been founded in 890 BC,[13] or in 863, the date given on a commemorative tablet placed in the Baths.[14] It would be idle to insist on greater accuracy.

The first historic evidences we have concerning Bath, though neither so precise nor so venerable as the legend assign a very respectable antiquity to the city. Ptolemy mentions it under the name of Ὕδατα θερμά[15] "The Itinerary of Antoninus" under that of Aquae Solis;[16] and the antiquities discovered on the spot show that the Roman settlement here must have followed closely on the conquest of Britain by A. Plautius, or, at latest, on the expedition of P. Ostorius Scapula in the year 50. The new masters of Britain, attracted by the hot springs they esteemed so highly,[17] founded a city around them, constructed baths, temples and buildings of all sorts, and settled there in large numbers, protected from attack by the ramparts which afterwards served as a base for the mediaeval walls. For three centuries Aquae Solis seems to have been what it became again later on, a town of luxury and pleasure, a little British Baiae. Judging (as we must do, in default of documentary evidences) from the remains of every kind, fragments of statues, coins, pedestals, altars, *bas-reliefs* and inscriptions, the colony must have been comparatively rich and populous. It is supposed that the sites of several public buildings and of a temple of Minerva[18] have been discovered; Roman villas sprang up in the surrounding country; the baths, though they have not been completely excavated, and it is not possible to estimate their exact extent, "must have occupied from six to seven acres, and included all the requirements to be found in the grand baths of ancient Rome."[19]

There is no doubt that the abandonment of Great Britain by the Roman legions in 411 considerably diminished the prosperity and importance of Aquae Solis. Deserted by a portion of its population, the town further suffered from the general confusion that followed the departure of the Romans, the incursions of the Picts and Scots, and finally, the Saxon conquest.[20] Under the new name of Akemanceaster,[21] soon replaced by that of Bath,[22] it formed part of the district of Hwiccia, afterwards incorporated in the Kingdom of Mercia.

Two centuries passed before the foundation of a monastery by King Offa (775) somewhat restored the fortunes of the ruined city.[23] It now became a religious centre; the monastery was enlarged and enriched by various sovereigns, and in 973 King Edgar was crowned in the Abbey;[24] the memory of this ceremony was perpetuated at Bath by a custom, vestiges of which still lingered in the seventeenth century, the annual election of a "king" by the citizens.[25] Devastated afresh by civil war a few years after the Norman conquest[26] the town was restored to prosperity by Jean de la Villette of Tours (Joannes de Villula), chaplain and physician to William Rufus, who, when in 1088 he was appointed Bishop of Somerset, transferred the episcopal seat from Wells to Bath, rebuilt the Abbey, and restored the baths. During the four centuries that followed, Bath owed nearly all its importance to this Benedictine Abbey; the cloth industry introduced by the monks also made a certain amount of progress.[27] The municipal system developed as in other English towns;[28] Bath was represented in Parliament as early as the reign of Edward I, but the population does not seem to have exceeded from one to two thousand persons. In 1499 Bishop King undertook the reconstruction of the Abbey, a task which was interrupted shortly afterwards by the Reformation, and by the consequent suppression of the monasteries in 1539. The restoration of the church was not resumed until the reign of James I.

Throughout this period we find but little trace of the thermal waters which had been the origin of Bath, and were to revive her fortunes. They were, however, neither forgotten, nor entirely abandoned. In the twelfth century a canon of St. Alban's praised them in Latin verse,[29] and a little hospital was built in 1138 for the lepers they attracted. In the fifteenth century we find the ecclesiastical authorities intervening to restore order and decency at the baths.[30] But it was not until the middle of the sixteenth century that these natural riches once more commanded a certain attention and favour. This revival is noted by Leland, who in 1542 speaks of the baths as very much frequented,[31] and by Doctor Turner, physician to Edward VI, who, comparing the English baths to those of other countries, deplores the shamefully neglected state of the former (1562).[32] Ten years later Dr Jones wrote the first medical book specially devoted to the waters of Bath, [33] and in 1616 a visit from a loyal patient, Anne of Denmark, wife of James I,[34] attests the confidence once more inspired by these long-forsaken springs, which the poet Massinger declared a few years later, somewhat hyperbolically, to be "far-famed," and comparable to those of Spa.[35] This confidence spread, bringing to the baths an increasing number of visitors among them many aristocratic and notable persons, in spite of the discomforts and frequent disorders of the place.[36] But it was not until after the Restoration that a visit paid by Queen Catherine of Braganza, accompanied by Charles I and the Court,[37] attracted such an unprecedented concourse of persons to Bath that the vogue of this watering-place was permanently established, while at the same time the value of the waters was increased by a new medical use to which they were put. The King's physician, Sir Alexander Frayser, recognising in them properties identical with those of the Bourbon Springs, recommended them for drinking (a purpose for which they had already served, see Jones, "Bathes of Bathes Ayde," lib. iv, fol. 28), and thenceforth sent all the patients he had formerly despatched to Bourbon to Bath. "From this period," says Wood, "the drinking of the hot waters of Bath may be very justly said to have been established; and from the same period the trade of the city began to turn from the woollen manufacture to that of entertaining the strangers that came to it for the use of the hot waters."[38] This visit of Charles II's was of further importance to Bath, for it inaugurated a new era. The character of the town was transformed; the new Bath, the Bath of the eighteenth century, began to manifest itself.

iii

It was during the interval between this royal visit of 1663 and the end of the century, that Bath, while continuing to attract invalids, gradually became a centre of pleasure as well as a place of healing. There, where people had formerly gone from necessity, many now began to assemble for amusement. Others followed them in increasing numbers. "Men and women flock hither from all Great Britain, in quest of health but also of pleasure,"[39] we are told as early as 1672, and "thousands of persons go to spend a few weeks there without troubling about either drinking or bathing, simply to divert themselves in good company."[40] Long before Queen Anne's visit in 1702,[41] we may consider that the transformation was in progress, and that Bath was on the way to become a sort of general casino for the whole kingdom, a periodical rendezvous for polite society, and a holiday resort common to all sorts and conditions of men. How was this rapid metamorphosis brought about?

We must note in the first place that if our town took on a new character, it was not alone in this development, and that rival towns, Epsom and Tunbridge Wells in particular, attracted many visitors at the same time, and enjoyed a similar reputation.[42]

Fashion had not yet decided between them; but from this time forth all of them (and this was the novelty) became little social centres, playing a part of unparalleled brilliance in the annals of country towns. It is significant that all were watering-places. For the first time a concourse of persons in good health "consented to follow the sick to those places of spleen, and live with those whose disorders are ever apt to excite a gloom in the spectator."[43] A strange fancy, as Goldsmith remarks, and one that was both sudden and swiftly propagated. It was an age when the polite world inclined to the imitation of everything foreign, and we might reasonably ask if the caprice was a French importation, which would explain its sudden apparition and its rapid diffusion.

Such, however, was not the case. Between the French and English watering-places of this period we can trace only those inevitable resemblances which arise from the nature of things. In both, patients had necessarily to observe a somewhat similar *régime*, and to seek distractions, which were, of course, conversation, walking, music, dancing and gaming; transient relations were established between chance acquaintances, in a society so limited, the members of which were continually meeting, and charlatans and rogues looked about for gulls. How could it have been otherwise? These are traits common to the watering places of all periods and all countries, and are in no sense characteristic. But the things that distinguish Bath and Tunbridge at the period of which we are writing were to be found neither at Forges, nor at Bagrières, nor at Bourbon, nor at any other place in France, or even in Europe.[44] I mean the social brilliance, the organisation of pleasure, the number and variety of the visitors, the universal attraction exercised by the spot, all those points in fact, which, in spite of the difference of age and manners, recall the health resorts of antiquity, such as Baiae and Puteoli. The expansion of the English watering- places and their final development are phenomena that may be accounted unimportant, but they are certainly original and spontaneous, owing nothing, directly at least, to continental influences. Yet from these they are derived, though indirectly. We must seek their origin in the new manners of the Court and of the nobility, introduced by the Restoration; or rather, in the contrast between these manners and such as obtained in contemporary provincial England. Charles II and his adherents had brought back with them from France a system of fashionable life, strangely modified, it is true, and that not to its advantage. The stories told and the descriptions given by Hamilton suffice by themselves to show us the place occupied in this strange Court by fêtes, intrigues, gallantry and gambling, the unedifying fashion in which its members sought compensation for the Puritanical rigours of the past.[45] But this fashionable life in all its corruption, which had become necessary to aristocratic Society, was only to be had in London, and the summer drives people from London. Unable to enjoy it elsewhere, and refusing to be deprived of it, even for a time, society's sole resource was to found colonies, as it were, in the shires; the fashionable watering-places were these colonies. "At this time," says Goldsmith, "London was the only theatre in England for pleasure or intrigue ... In this situation of things, people of fashion had no agreeable summer retreat from the town, and usually spent that season amidst a solitude of country squires, parsons' wives, and visiting tenants, or farmers: they wanted some place where they might have each other's company, and win each other's money, as they had done during the winter in town."[46] This desire will seem natural enough if we consider how greatly provincial England differed from the capital in those days of slow and difficult Communication[47] and how boorish manners continued to be in the country. A great gulf separated the polished, refined, and witty courtier, depraved, irreligious and immoral, from the rustic squire, healthier in his moral tone, but as illiterate, as ignorant, as coarse as the humblest of his peasants, speaking the same jargon as these,[48] and ill-disposed to all, that came from that distant London where he himself had never ventured.[49] The Squire Western of "Tom Jones," though of a later date, gives a hint of what the rural landowner of the period often was.[50] The courtier, accustomed to the splendours and refinements of Whitehall or St James', was reduced to the society of persons of this stamp; they soon disgusted him, and drove him to look about for some favourable spot, where he might resume his usual mode of life and rejoin his favourite company.

Where was he to find this necessary and much-desired rallying-ground? The watering-places offered themselves for the purpose under the most propitious conditions. In the first place, necessity brought a certain number of sufferers together in them, who were not so ill as to be obliged to resign every kind of pleasure, and who naturally sought to enliven their enforced retirement and inactivity by all possible means. This nucleus of a society, and the diversions it offered, were already attractive. Then the visits of the Court to Tunbridge and Bath brought together for a time a company that was dispersed as a rule, and suggested the possibility of meeting there again later on, there and not elsewhere, for only watering-places such as these were adapted for the reception of large numbers of temporary visitors, and could offer them conditions of sufficient comfort. Finally, with such advantages as are proper to cities, Tunbridge, Epsom and Bath, villages or little towns, combine the pleasures of the country; they are half urban, half rustic; in them the citizen finds the degree of change that he enjoys when he goes to the fields, the charm of fashionable amusement and of country surroundings; this combination drew an ever-increasing crowd of strangers, bathers, and mere idlers, to the springs.

A further attraction for the gentry and the rich *bourgeoisie* at Bath or Tunbridge was the presence of the nobility.[51] The increase in public wealth, which had given leisure to a numerous and enlightened class,[52] had further inspired in it a taste for polite pleasures and courtly manners, an ambition to belong to the world of fashion. Just as the Court modelled itself upon the Sovereign, the gentry modelled itself upon the Court, and was in its turn imitated by the class immediately beneath it. A world of fashion below and apart from the nobility began to appear in England and naturally looked about for a domain in which it might appear without too many disadvantages, and learn the secrets of good breeding. Where was this domain to be found? In London? A prominent position was very difficult to achieve there, in an exclusive and inelastic society. In the country towns? A few local families held undivided sway in these. The watering- places were much more favourable ground for such ambitions; in these there were facilities for approaching persons of quality and taking them as models, even for being brought into contact with them by sharing their pleasures. A periodical journey to Bath might take the place of a journey to London for those who wished to study fine manners; it was often a much more successful method of gaining admittance to exclusive circles.

iv

From the reign of Charles II to that of Anne these various causes were only beginning to operate, and gradually to fill the new summer resorts; they did not produce their full effect till the eighteenth century, when they were supplemented by an improved organisation of the watering-places, more especially of Bath, in view of their new destinies, and by a methodical organisation of the social system. The Bath of the eighteenth century, as it appears to us in the writings of Pepys, Hamilton, and one or two contemporaries more obscure, is a some what colourless entity a second-rate town, primitive pleasures, scanty company. The old borough of the middle ages retained its narrow streets, unpaved and unlighted.[53] A certain number of houses, it is true, were built of freestone, and made a good appearance, but the descriptions of the interiors are far from seductive. "The floors of the dining-rooms were uncarpeted, and were coloured brown with a wash made of soot and small beer, in order to hide the dirt. Not a wainscot was painted. Not a hearth or a chimney-piece was of marble. The best apartments were hung with coarse woollen stuff, and were furnished with rush-bottomed chairs."[54]

On leaving these indifferent lodgings many of the visitors went to the baths. These were taken very early in the morning, and occupied a long time. "Up at four o'clock," says Pepys in his Journal, "being by appointment called up to the Cross Bath.[55] And by-and-by, though we had designed to have done before company come, much company come; very fine ladies ... Carried away, wrapped in a sheet, and in a chair home; and there one after another thus carried, I staying above two hours in the water, home to bed" ("Diary," June 13, 1668). Pepys also tells us that the Cross Bath was reserved for the gentry the others being "full of a mixed sort, of good and bad." Celia Fiennes, writing some dozen years

The King's Bath
From the drawing by John Claude Nattes

The Queen's Bath
From the drawing by John Claude Nattes

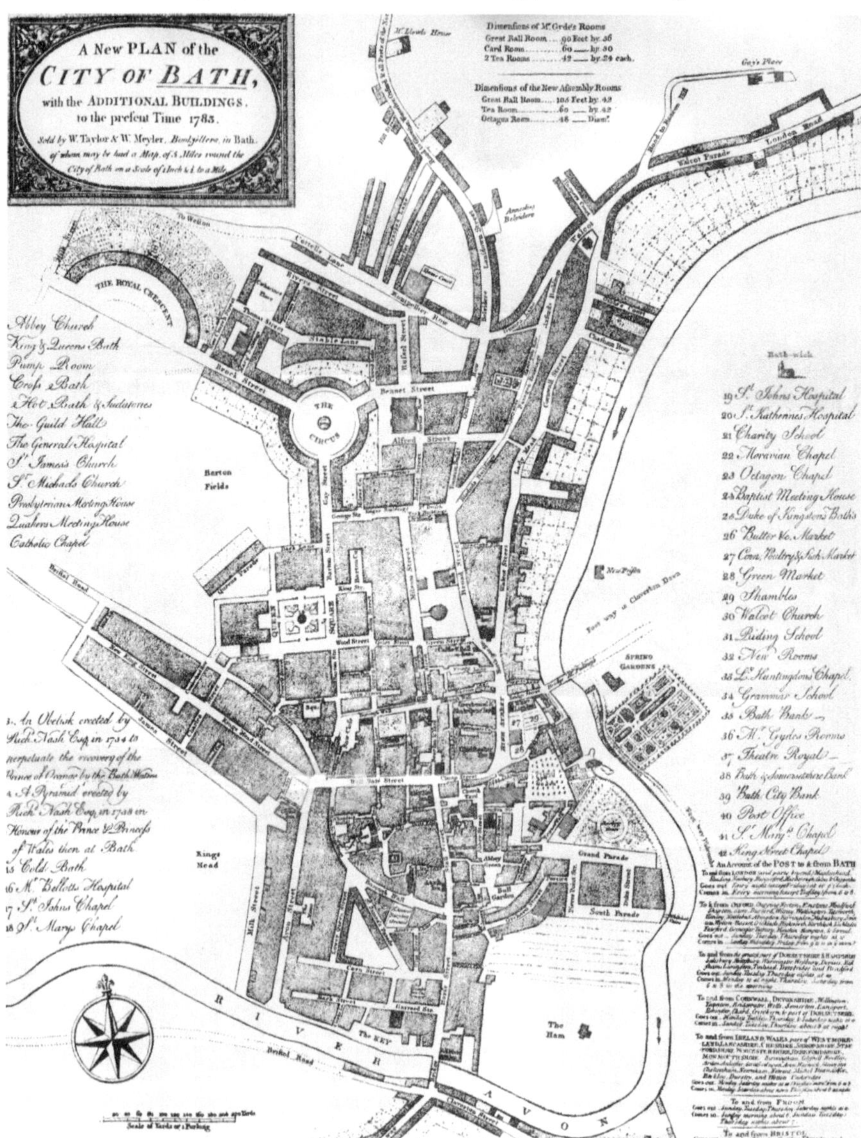

Plan of Bath, 1783

later, describes the costume of the bathers: "The Ladyes goes into the bath with garments made of a fine yellow canvas, which is stiff and made large with great sleeves like a parson's gown; the water fills it up so that its borne off that your shape is not seen, it does not cling close as other linning which looks sadly in the poorer sort that go in their own linning. The gentlemen have drawers and waistcoats of the same sort of canvas, this is the best linning, for the bath water will change any other yellow" ("Diary," p 13). It was in the Cross Bath that Charles II's two famous mistresses, the Duchess of Cleveland and the Duchess of Portsmouth, bathed in 1674; as also, at a later date, Queen Mary, wife of James II. It was customary for the daughters of the chief citizens to attend ladies of distinction at the Cross Bath,[56] and for musicians to serenade them; but as the bathers took to accompanying the instruments with songs, making a tumult, the municipality intervened and forbade all music thenceforth.[57] The bath, and the subsequent rest enjoined by the physician, occupied but a few hours. The amusements available to fill up the rest of the day were on the whole meagre and primitive. The chief of these was walking in a neighbouring meadow[58] and playing bowls, which was not only an amusement but an opportunity for betting.[59] Or visitors might spend their time among the shops of a little fair,[60] or in the arbours, where hydromel and Spanish wines were served.[61] They also amused themselves by throwing small coins into the King's Bath and letting little boys dive for them.[62] If some leader of fashion like the Chevalier de Grammont happened to be in the place there would be horse-racing.[63] The company, as Hamilton tells us, was easily amused, and seized upon everything for diversion. At rare intervals there were balls at the Town-hall,[64] a cock-fight,[65] or a dramatic entertainment in some chance place.[66]

But these were occasional amusements, and the great resources of pleasure-seekers were then, as always, gambling and gallantry. Gaming was universal, and was practised in the most diverse forms.[67] It had developed to such an extent that a class of persons had sprung up called rooks, "men who always carry money about them to enable them to lend to losing gamesters, for which they receive a gratification which is nothing for such as play deep, as it is only two per cent, and the money to be repaid the next day."[68] As to gallantry, this commodity the Court had imported from London; the liberty of watering-places was favourable to it, and it reigned unchecked.[69] These two indefensible attractions persisted throughout the greater part of the eighteenth century, even after the transformation of Bath, and the methodical organisation of its pleasures by the strange personage we are now about to meet, who suddenly brought to a single centre the wandering currents of fashion that were setting now to one, now to another, little town.

1 It has been called "the lantern of England."

2 From the twelfth century to the Reformation, Bath was a Bishopric, which was then transferred, or rather brought back, to Wells, to which the dignity belonged before the Norman Conquest. The Bishop was Abbot of the Monastery of Bath. The see is still known as the diocese of Bath and Wells.

3 There are one or two (see C. E. Davis, "Ancient Landmarks of Bath"); but they are rare for such an ancient town.

4 The classic work on this subject is Warner's "History of Bath."

5 The Rev. G.N. Wright, author of a "Historic Guide to Bath," published in 1864, upholds it, though he prunes it a little.

6 What follows is an abstract of the very long narrative of Wood, the local architect and historian, who, in the eighteenth century gave the legend its most, complete form ("Description of Bath," vol. i. chap. ix.). The principal points were given as early as 1697 by Peirce, in "Bath Memoirs," chap. viii. pp. 172–75.

7 This last touch, reported by Geoffrey of Monmouth ("Historia Regum Britanniae," lib. ii. cap. x.), was no doubt borrowed from a passage in Solinus, an author widely read in the Middle Ages ("Polyhistor," xxii.).

8 The history of Bladud does not end here. We learn further from Geoffrey of Monmouth, and all who followed him down to Wood inclusively, that in his old age this prince practised magic, which he had learnt at Athens with philosophy and other sciences, and that in an attempt to fly through the air he fell to the ground and perished miserably.

9 The famous John, Earl of Rochester, coming to Bath, the story of Bladud and his Pigs became a subject for his wit, and this proved the cause of striking it out of the inscription placed against one of the walls of the King's Bath (Wood, chap. ix. p. 76).

10 The famous marionnette-showman mentioned several times in the *Tatler* and *Spectator*. One of his pieces was called "Prince Bladud," and was given at Bath (*cf* Wood, *ibid.*). On April 20, 1778, we find that another piece was given at Bath, "Bladud, or Harlequin at Bath" (Geneste, "Some Account of the English Stage," vol. vi. p. 38). The tradition, probably discredited by ridicule, was revived by Wood.

11 Book ii. chap. x.

12 Bladus fut molt de grant puiçance
Et sot assés de nigromance.
Cil fonda Bade et fist les barns
Onques n'i orent esté ains,
De Bladu fu Balda nomée
La seconde letre l'ostée.
Ou Bade ot par le bain cest nom
Por la mervillose façon.
Les bains fist chauz et saluables
Et al poeple mult profitables.

13 Jones, "The Bathes of Bathes Ayde" (book ii. fol. ii.).

14 The inscription is recorded by Misson ("Mémoires et Observations," p. 26).

15 "Geography," lib. ii. cap. iii.

16 "Britannia," *in fine*.

17 The waters are sulphureous and chalybeate, and are recommended for a great variety of diseases (gout, paralysis, dyspepsia, etc.) See Freeman, "The Thermal Waters of Bath."

18 Or rather of Sul Minerva. Sul was no doubt a native divinity, whose cult was confounded with that of the Roman Minerva. The antiquities of Bath have been dealt

with in works too numerous to mention here. We will only mention "The Antiquities of Bath," by the Rev. R. Warner, and "Aquae Solis, or Notice of Roman Bath," by the Rev. H. M. Scarth. The first description is to be found in Leland.

19 C. E. Davis, "The Baths, Ancient and Modern," in the "Hand book to Bath," p. 150.

20 The Battle of Deorham (577) which gave the west of England to the Saxons, was fought in the neighbourhood. It is possible that the destruction of the Roman buildings dates from this period. The fine fragment of Anglo-Saxon poetry generally known as "The Ruin," which describes a devastated city (in Grein, "Bibliothek der angel-sachsischen Poesie," vol. i. p. 238), seems to refer to Bath. (See an article by Mr Earle in the "Proceedings of the Bath Natural History and Antiquarian Club," 1872, pp. 259–70).

21 The Anglo-Saxon termination *ceaster* (city, from the Latin *castra*) is the same ,we find in Chester, Manchester, Winchester, etc. As to the first part of the word, Mr. Earle sees in it a British word, Akeman made up of a transcription of the Latin *aquae* and of the Celtic root *man* = place, which still exists in Welsh ("Bath Ancient and Modern," chap. iv. p. 42).

22 See the history of this new name in the "New English Dictionary" article "Bath," sb[2] . Some Anglo-Saxon coins of the eleventh century are inscribed Bathan (Earle, "Bath Ancient and Modern," p. 68).

23 A convent had been founded in 676 (*cf* Leland, "Itinerary," ii. fol. 38).

24 Leland, *ibid*. fol. 39.

25 "And at Whitsunday-tide, at the whych time men say that Eadgar there was crownid, there is a king elected at Bath every year of the Townesmen in the joyful remembraunce of King Eadgar and the Privileges given to the toun by hym. This King is festid, and his Adherents by the richest Menne of the Toun." Leland, *ibid.*

26 By Geoffrey of Coutances, the partisan of Robert Curthose in the rising in favour of the latter in 1087.

27 See Leland, vol. ii. fol. 38. Chaucer indicates the reputation of Bath in this connection:

A good wife was ther of bisyde Bath
Of clooth-making she hadde swich an haunt
She passed hem of Ypres and Gaunt.

"Canterbury Tales," Prologue, 445, 447–49.

The monks introduced a shuttle in the arms of their monastery. This industry was still very flourishing at the close of the seventeenth century: "The Clouthing Trade flourished so exceedingly that in the Parish of St. Michael without the North Gate, there were no less than sixty broad Looms at the Time of the Restoration." (Wood, "Description of Bath," i. p. 217.)

28 See King and Watts, "Municipal Records of Bath."

29 Neckam, "De laudibus divinae sapientiae, Distinctio tertia," 11. 275–88.

30 Bishop Bekyngton, in 1449.

31 "This Bath [the Cross Bath; the others are enumerated afterwards] is much frequented of People diseased with Lepre, Pokkes, Scabbes and great Aches, and is temperate and pleasant, having 11 or 32 Arches of.Stone in the Sides for men to stonde under yn

time of Reyne. Many be holp by this Bath for Scabbes and Aches." ("Itinerary," vol. ii. fol. 6.)

32 '"We ... would be ashamed that any straunger, whych had sene the bathes in foren landes should looke upon our bathes ... because we do so lightly, regard so hygh and excellente giftes of All mighty God ..." ("A book of the Properties," etc, p. 2) He suggests various reforms. He is, he tells us, the first Englishman who ever wrote of the thermal waters . . . "I wot of no man had, written one word that ever I could read, wherfor if that I write not so perfitly of it, as sum perfit idle overseers would that I shuld have done, I trust that an honest man will pardon me, because I had no help of any writers that wrote of it before me" (Preface). At about this same period, the Bath springs are also mentioned by the Italian Bacci in his "De Thermis, Lacubus, Fluminibus et Balneis totines Orbis," lib. iv cap. ix. p. 256. Guidott, ("Discourse of Bath," 2nd ed. p. 49) tells us that it was the English Ambassador at Rome, Sir Edward Came, who revealed the existence of these baths to the Italian, and that they were quite unknown to foreigners before this. Sir Philip Sidney, in a letter to his friend Languet, speaks of a visit paid by his father and his uncles to Bath in 1577; he does not say if they went for their health.

33 "The Bathes of Bathes Ayd;" a somewhat obscure title, as Mr Earle remarks, mentioning in this connection the Welsh origin of the author ("Bath Ancient and Modern," chap. viii. p. 119). This work was the earliest of a long series which is still continued. The principal treatises are given by Freeman, "Thermal Baths," p. ix. *et seq.*

34 One of the Baths was called after her, and still retains the name of the Queen's Bath.

35 "Parliament of Love" (1624), ii. 2, 113.

36 Queen Henrietta Maria thought of trying the Bath waters, but decided in favour of Bourbon, a decision on which she had reason to congratulate herself if we are to believe Wood: "About the time that the Queen went there" [to Bourbon], he says, "all kinds of disorders were grown to their highest Pitch in Bath, insomuch as the streets and public ways of the City were become like so many Dunghills, Slaughter-Houses, and Pig-Styes ... The Baths were like so many Bear Gardens, and Modesty was entirely shut out of them; People of both Sexes bathing by Day and Night naked; and Dogs, Cats, and even human creatures were hurl'd over the rails into the water, while People were bathing in it" (*op. cit.* pp. 216–217). Many of the distinguished visitors of the seventeenth century left some material trace of their sojourn, notably bronze rings fixed in the baths to which visitors held on as they walked.

37 In 1663 the Queen hoped to find the waters remedial in sterility. "The queen's physicians, men of great prudence, sagacity and wisdom, as they always are, having duly weighed and considered that the cold waters of Tunbridge had not succeeded in the preceding year, concluded that it would he advisable for her to try the warm baths at Bristol. This journey was therefore fixed for the next season; and in the confidence of its proving effectual, this excursion would have afforded her much pleasure, if the most dangerous of her rivals had not been one of the first that was appointed to attend the Court ... Miss Stewart, more hand some than ever, was appointed for this excursion, and began to make magnificent preparations. The poor Queen durst say

nothing against it, but all hopes of success immediately forsook her."—("Mémoires de Grammont," chap. xiii.) The same chapter contains some account of the diversions of the Court at Bath.—See also Pepys' "Diary," August 11 and 25, 1663.

38 Wood, "Description of Bath," chap. xi. p. 216.

39 Caroli Claromontii, "De Aere, locis et aquis terrae Angliae." *Cf* Defoe referring to the same period in "Moll Flanders," pp. 125, 126.

40 "Mémoires et Observations," by Misson, p. 25 (1698). The same author says: "In winter Bath is melancholy enough; but in May, June, July, and August, there is a great concourse of fine folks who enrich and embellish it."

41 Mary of Modena spent a season there in the interval, and James II a few days, in 1687.

42 "It was now a Rumbling Time of the year, and the gentlemen being most of them gone out of town, Tunbridge and Epsom and such Places were full of People."—(Defoe, "Moll Flanders," p. 323.) As early as 1673 Shadwell painted the society of Epsom in one of his comedies, "Epsom Wells"; as to Tunbridge, which was visited by Charles II and Catherine of Braganza before Bath ("Mémoires de Grammont," ch. xiii.), it long divided the favour of fashion with the latter, even in the eighteenth century. The earlier vogue of Epsom and Tunbridge is probably to be explained by their proximity to London, but when once the fashion of watering-places was established, the distance of Bath from the capital became an advantage, as it offered a greater change of society and habits, and allowed of greater freedom.

43 Goldsmith, "Life of Nash," Globe edition, p. 519.

44 The contrast was noted later by Diderot: "A sojourn here [at Bourbon] is not attractive ... Those who have been once rarely return ... If the inhabitants had any notion of their own interests ... they would make it a place capable of charming the healthy as well as the sick ... This is what the English have done at Bath and at Cambridge [*sic*, for Tunbridge], whither husbands go to find distraction from the humours of their wives, and wives from the humours of their husbands, and where, while taking the waters, folks laugh and talk and dance and arrange amusements still more agreeable.—("Voyage à Bourbonne.") The Abbé Le Blanc wrote in the same strain towards the middle of the century: "Those who think the Bath springs are like those of Bourbon, where only the infirm, the paralytic, and valetudinarians are to be found, make a great mistake. Indeed, Bath is of all places in England the one where people enjoy the best health, and turn it to the best account."—("Lettres d'un François" no. hxxviii. vol. iii. p. 310.)

45 "Mémoires de Grammont." *Cf* Macaulay, "History of England," book i., chaps. ii. and iii.; Taine, "Histoire de la Littérature anglaise," book iii. chap. i.; Beijame, "Le Public et les Hommes de Lettres en Angleterre," chap. i.

46 "Life of Nash," Works, Globe edition, p. 519. The last suggestion is notable, the gambling passion being universal in England at that period and long afterwards (*cf* below, chap. iv.). It is significant that the first attempt made to organise fashionable life at Bath was due to a professional gambler, Webster, and that this attempt was resumed and completed by another gambler, Nash.

47 See Macaulay, "History of England," Edinburgh edition, chap. iii. pp. 290–300.

48 See Macaulay's admirable description of the country gentleman of the time (*ibid.* pp. 249–54).

49 "In that age it was but seldom that a country gentleman went up with his family to London. The county town was his metropolis."— (Macaulay, "History of England," chap. iii. p. 265.)

50 The Sir Roger de Coverley of the *Spectator* was a very different person, but he was a baronet who had mixed in the fashionable society of the Restoration, and who continued to divide his time between London and the country.

51 "There is a concourse not only of the Nobility and Gentry, but of the commonalty too from all parts of the Nation hither."—(Brome, "Travels" [1700], p. 38.)

52 See Lecky, "History of England," chap. ii.

53 It had not increased in size, nor probably in population. A plan of Bath, published at Bristol in 1694 by J. Gilmore, differs very little from the Elizabethan plan in the British Museum (Sloane MSS no 2596). "The town is very small," said Misson in 1698, "at the most four or five hundred paces long, and three hundred wide".—("Mémoires et Observations," p. 25.) "The streets," says Pepys, "generally narrow".—("Diary," June 12, 1668.) A manuscript of Wood's quoted by Warner ("History of Bath," v., i. p. 220) gives 1700 as the approximate date when for the first time "the citizens applied for an Act of Parliament to oblige one another to pave the streets of the town, to enlighten them in the right time, and to raise money by tolls to amend the highways."

54 Macaulay, "History of England," chap. iii. p. 272 of the Edinburgh Edition. This is an abridgment of a long passage of Wood's "Description of Bath," vol. ii. preface. *Cf* Fleming, a musician of Bath, who, no doubt, spoke of traditions he had heard on the spot: "Bath, in the year 1670, was one of the poorest towns in England … the houses were very indifferent, there being only one that had a sash window … Accommodations were but indifferent, few houses were capable of receiving a family of condition."—("Life, etc, of Timothy Ginnadrake," vol. iii. p. 16.) Towards the close of the century there was a marked improvement. "The houses are indifferent, the streetes of a good size, well pitched. There, are severall good houses built for lodgings that are new and adorned, and goud furniture."—(Celia Fiennes, "Diary," p. 12.)

55 So called from an old cross which was there even in Leland's time; it was replaced by a handsomer one in memory of the visit of Mary of Modena in 1687.

56 Wood, "Description of Bath," vol. ii. chap. xii. p. 437.

57 "They [the municipality] assembled together to put an end to a custom which then prevailed of smoaking Tobacco in the bathing Cisterns, singing songs and making such Disturbances in them as rendered the Baths like so many Bear-Gardens."—(Wood, *op. cit.* vol. i. chap. xi. pp. 219–220). If we are to believe the author of "A Step to the Baths" (1700), decency was no better observed than order "is perform'd all the wanton Dalliances imaginable" (p. 13), but this malicious little pamphlet is not to be too implicitly accepted. Others give more favourable testimony. *Cf* C. Fiennes "There is a sergeant belonging to the Baths that all the bathing-time walkes in galleryes and takes notice order is observed, and punishes the rude, and most people of fashion sends to him when they begin to bathe then he takes particular care of

them, and complements you every morn, which deserves its reward at ye end of the season."—("Diary," p. 12.)

58 Pugh, "Bathon. et Aquisgr. Therm. Compar.," p. 81; "A Step to the Bath," p. 15; C. Fiennes, "Diary," p. 14.

59 A plan of Bath published at Bristol in 1694 shows two bowling-greens. In "A Step to the Bath" we have a lively description of a game of bowls: "About five in the Evening we went to see a great match at Bowling; there was Quality, and Reverend Doctors of both Professions, Topping Merchants, Broken Bankers, Noted Mercers, Inns of Court Rakes, City Beaux, Stray'd Prentices and Dancing Masters its Abundance. Fly, fly, fly, said one; Rub, rub, rub, rub, cry'd another. Ten Guineas to Five I uncover the Jack, says a Third. Damn these nice Fingers of mine, cry'd my Lord, I slipt my Bowl and mistook the Bias. Another swearing he knew the ground to an inch, and would hold Five Pounds his Bowl came in. But in short, the Citizens won the Courtiers money, and the Courtiers swore to be Reveng'd on their Wives and Daughters (p 14)."—*Cf.* Pugh, p 82–83.

60 "There is music, gaming, walking and a perpetual little Fair," (Misson, "Mémoires et Observations," p. 25. *Cf* C. Fiennes, "Diary," p. 17, and "A Step to the Bath," p. 14). Hamilton tells us that at Tunbridge there was also a long row of shops for the sale of jewellery and hosiery, where gambling went on as at the fairs.

61 "Mémoires de Grammont," chap. xiii. "Some," adds Pugh, "met together 'dudum invalescente apud nos Turcarum consuetudine, ad sorbillandum quem vocabulo barbaro coffee dicunt, ferventem liquorem'" (p 84).

62 Pepys, June 13, 1668; Pugh, p 85.

63 "Mémoires de Grammont," chap. xiii

64 In 1670 and the years immediately following dancing was only practised on the grass. "There was neither ball-room, or. places of amusement. When a party was made to dance, they repaired to the Bowling-green, open and exposed to the weather. In this situation it continued for a series of years until the Duke of Bt [Beaufort], whose seat is about £4 miles from Bath [Badminton], took upon him to conduct the company to the Town Hall. Ten couple at that time was thought to be great assembly"—(Fleming, "Life … of T. Ginnadrake," vol. iii. pp. 6–7). The balls seem to have become more brilliant in 1700 (*cf* "A Step to the Bath," p. 15).

65 "Mémoires de Grammont," chap. xiii. The plan mentioned above (p. 16, *note* 1) shows an arena reserved for this sport, then a very fashionable amusement.

66 The town archives contain this brief mention in 1673 "1s. to the players at the Towne Hall" (Penley, "The Bath Stage," chap. iii. p. 16), and Gilmore's plan shows a stable transformed into a theatre. This is all the information we have as to the dramatic performances at Bath between the Restoration and the year 1705, when the first theatre was built.

67 Note this picture, for instance: "From hence we went to the Groom-Porters, when they were labouring like so many Anchor Smiths at the Oakes, Backgammon, Tick Tack, Irish Basset and throwing of Mains. There was Palming, Lodging, Loaded Dice, Levant and Gammoning with all the Speed imaginable; but the Cornish Rook was too hard for them all" ("A Step to the Bath," p. 54).

68 " Mémoires de Grammont," chap. xiii.

69 The Duc de Cominges, French Ambassador, wrote as early as 1663 of Tunbridge Wells: "They should be called the Wells of Scandal, for they have gone nigh to ruining all the women and girls of reputation (I mean such as had not their husbands with them)."—(Quoted by M. Jusserand, "A French Ambassador," p. 217.) In "A Step to the Bath," p. 74, a friend tells the narrator some scandalous story, of an absolutely insipid and uninteresting nature, about each person they meet. Men and women are alike represented as absolutely corrupt, and as delighting in Bath for this reason. Such malignant judgments must of course be discounted, but the watering-places seem certainly to have had a bad reputation. See chap. iv. below.

II

The King of Bath – Organisation of fashionable life (1730–1761)

A visit paid by Queen Anne and the Prince Consort, George of Denmark, in 1702, was the occasion of unusual festivities, and of an unprecedented influx of visitors. The municipality was eager to atone for certain incivilities shown to Anne some ten years earlier at the command of her royal sister.[1] They accordingly approached her immediately after her accession, begging her to honour Bath with her presence again, and prepared a most sumptuous reception for her.[2] A hundred young men belonging to the town, armed and dressed alike, and two hundred women and young girls on horseback, went to meet the Sovereign at the boundary of the county, and brought her to the gates of the city by a road specially constructed for the occasion. These and similar rejoicings attracted more visitors to the little town than it had ever yet received The pumps that supplied the thermal waters could not satisfy all who came to drink, and lodgings were so scarce that a guinea a night was paid for a bed; many persons of quality had to put up with a lodging in one of the neighbouring villages. Thanks to a repetition of the royal visit the following year, there was the same influx;[3] and the inhabitants, delighted at the reviving and increasing vogue of their city, at last set to work to embellish it, and to make it more accessible and more agreeable to strangers.[4] A certain Captain Webster undertook the amusements, and organised balls at the Town Hall, the tickets for which cost half a guinea each. In accordance with a custom mentioned above (see chap. 1. p. 18), he had been elected King of Bath; he was, apparently, a professional gambler.[5] There are no indications of his having been a person of much influence. He died shortly afterwards, and was succeeded by an extraordinary person, whose life Goldsmith did not disdain to write,[6] and who demands a much larger share of our attention—Richard Nash, nicknamed Beau Nash.[7] He is known to us chiefly through the intermediary of Goldsmith, and, thanks to Goldsmith, his memory is certain of an immortality due rather to fortune than to merit. The biography published by the famous writer a year after the death of Nash seems at first somewhat out of proportion with its subject by its extent and elaboration; but the ease and variety of the narrative, the liveliness of the anecdotes, the precision of the drawing and the grace of the style, make us forget the relative poverty of the matter. It is most agreeable reading, and the moral reflections in which the author excels make it instructive to boot.[8] Goldsmith writes as if he had known Nash personally,[9] and declares that his biography is based on papers left by Nash, and on others equally authentic, a statement less open to controversy.[10] He quotes from many letters, and from certain other documents,[11] and, save for a little excusable partiality, and perhaps an occasional indulgent reticence, he appears as an exact biographer and a faithful painter. Besides, we have no complete and continuous life of Nash but his; all the later notices are founded upon it, or even copied from it word for word.[12] It is possible to check it occasionally by contemporary documents, with which it will be found to be in constant agreement, but it contains nearly every thing that is to be found elsewhere, and continues to be our sole authority on many points. The sketch of Nash's career which follows is accordingly based upon it throughout, save where some other authority is expressly quoted.

He was born at Swansea in 1674, and belonged to a family of modest means. At Oxford, where he went at an early age, he worked very little, and was indeed rusticated at the age of seventeen in consequence of some intrigue.[13] The army attracted him as the profession in which his taste for gallantry could be most easily

King's and Queen's Baths
From the picture by Robins

indulged, a further temptation being the uniform, as he was already very fond of dress. He accordingly bought an ensign's commission, which he sold again on finding out that a red coat, unsupported by money or interest, was not enough to make him irresistible to the fair sex, and that certain duties he considered very irksome counterbalanced the charms of a military career. He then entered himself at the Temple as a law-student, but was no more industrious here than he had been at the University; he thought only of pleasure, and indulged in all the luxury possible to one with his limited means. Goldsmith says that, although very poor, he dressed sumptuously, that he spent the little money he had in a lordly fashion, and that, though the gilding was not thick, he contrived to spread it over a large surface. He was an agreeable companion, naturally obliging, and polite, always well dressed and well mannered. One or two fashionable young men took him up, and when the Inns of Court gave their customary entertainment to William III. he was chosen to manage the festivities, acquitting himself so well on the occasion that the King marked his satisfaction by offering him a knighthood, which he had the good taste to decline.[14] The success of this entertainment increased the number of acquaintances already made by Nash among the idle and pleasure-loving. He continued to lead his frivolous and dissipated life among them, a sort of inferior Will Honeycomb, entirely absorbed in his amusements and his toilette. He lived mainly by expedients, counting upon the profits of the gaming-table for his expenses, and rarely paying a creditor. Luck seems often to have favoured him, although, unlike many of his associates, he appears to have played fairly.[15] Cards and dice were, no doubt, the attractions that drew Nash to Bath at the time of Queen Anne's visit, among the many other adventurers who flocked thither to seek their fortunes.[16] He soon attracted attention. A certain well-known physician had written a pamphlet against the efficacy of the Bath springs, and boasted of having "put a toad in the waters."[17] Nash retorted that, if authorised to do so, he would counteract the poison of the toad as that of the tarantula is counteracted, by music. He started a subscription for an orchestra, which had a great success; the number of visitors increased sensibly, and Captain Webster having died at this juncture, the new comer was chosen to succeed him. Master of the Ceremonies and King of Bath, Nash revealed remarkable aptitudes for functions which agreed so well with his tastes, and made so suitable a sequel to his past career. He took his office seriously from the first, and determined to avail himself of the power it gave him, to impose upon the mixed society of the place the tone and habits he himself admired, to make it subject to a rigid etiquette, to clothe it in uniform elegance; in short, to render Bath the temple of fashion and of good manners. Such an attempt presented serious difficulties, the greatest of which, no doubt, lay in the differences of origin and education that divided the *habitués* of Bath. How was he to attenuate these differences or cause them to be overlooked? How direct and control people in their pleasures? How make them all accept a sort of social dictatorship? Nash speedily found the means to all these ends. Though a man of mediocre intelligence, he possessed all the qualities necessary to exercise influence over a society which in many respects was no whit superior to himself. He had acquired in the society to which he was accustomed, ease of manner, a playful and animated address, and imperturbable assurance. He was perfectly acquainted with the laws of precedence, he danced well,[18] and though he was not particularly attractive in person,[19] excelled in the art of dressing with care and taste. We may add that his brusque sallies might pass for wit in default of anything better. Such were his talents; and he was "the favourite of those who had no others." He was already the friend of certain persons of rank, who treated him with familiarity, and with whom he allowed himself considerable freedom;[20] people of more obscure birth admired him greatly on this account, and esteemed it an honour to enjoy his friendship. His adroitness was such that he soon carried his prestige and new-born authority to incredible limits. The amusements of Bath differed very little from those in vogue under Charles II. They were marked by the same rusticity and lack of refinement. The men smoked in the ball-rooms and danced in their thick boots; the ladies did not even lay aside their aprons. A sort of shanty had been reserved for gaming, and this went on without intermission. The aristocracy, now more numerous than formerly, preserved a sort of feudal haughtiness, and refused to hold any sort of inter course with the middle classes at the public entertainments.[21] This was due, no doubt, in some degree to pride of caste, but still more to differences of education.[22] The first step taken by the new Master of the Ceremonies was, as we have seen, to bring musicians to Bath by means of a subscription. Other subscriptions enabled the authorities to repair the neighbouring roads and thoroughfares. The Pump Room was rebuilt and put under the care of a special functionary; a theatre was begun,[23] and, at Nash's instigation, one Harrison built the first Assembly Rooms,[24] to which gardens were added. The completion of these rooms brought about an effacement of distinctions, and a fusion of coteries hitherto strictly separate; every one came to them, just as every one went to walk in the shady alleys.[25] At the same time, the evident tendency of Bath to develop, induced many speculators to set about building on all sides, and it was not long before an architect of talent, the elder Wood; began the construction of those squares in the to and of those colonnaded terraces on the surrounding hills which delight the eye to the present day.[26]

Meanwhile the King of Bath continued to organise fashionable society, not altogether without occasional revolts on the part of his subjects. With much ingenuity he arranged a succession of pleasures and pastimes which awaited the visitor when he rose in the morning, and led him on without fatigue to the end of the day. Every hour had its appointed occupation; the interval between the morning bath and the evening dance or play was filled up by regular gatherings in the Pump Room, at concerts, and on the public promenades. The idle crowd readily accepted a programme of life marked out for its adoption. Private parties were voted unfashionable, and discontinued; and all meals, even to the early morning breakfast, were taken in company at the Assembly Rooms.

Occupations and amusements being thus established, the Master of the Ceremonies made them subject to a severe etiquette, and it was in this connection that he met with most opposition. His authority was recognised as very considerable, since he was allowed to have "the government of all the Publick Assemblies, and an absolute power vested in him to rebuke whoever may, through Inadvertency, infringe in the least upon the Bounds of Decency and good Manners."[27] This authority Nash exercised in the first place by persuasion, and afterwards by audacities which often came, very near to impertinence, or worse. Thus one day at the Baths, to which ladies came in full dress and with elaborate coiffures, Nash heard a visitor address a compliment he considered rather too broad to one of the bathers; the only reproof that occurred to him was the somewhat primitive one of throwing the gallant into the water, clothes and all. It cost him a duel and a wound in the arm, but his authority seems to have been strengthened by this curious proceeding.[28]

A reform in costume next engaged his attention, and here again we find another instance of the boldness, to call it by no harsher name, with which he insisted on the observance of his decrees. He had forbidden ladies to appear at the assemblies in white aprons. The Duchess of Queensberry having come to a dance one day in hers, he tore it off and threw it away, saying that such articles were suitable only for Abigails. The thing was done with such an air that "the good Duchess acquiesced in his censure, and with great good sense and good humour begged his Majesty's pardon!"[29] The men resisted more stoutly when the Master of the Ceremonies attacked their sword and high boots. He had recourse to ridicule to banish the boots. He composed a lampoon against those who wore them,[30] and had a little piece performed by the marionettes in which Punch, made love to his mistress in boots and spurs, and refused to take off his boots even on his wedding-night. "Why, madam, you may as well bid me pull off my legs!" he cried. "I never go without boots. I never ride, I never dance, without them, and this piece of politeness is quite the thing at Bath. We always dance at our town in boots, and the ladies often move minuets in riding-hoods." It was impossible to resist such delicate satire. Only very occasionally did some rebel venture to appear booted at an assembly. In such a case Nash never failed to walk up to the delinquent and ask him if he had not forgotten his horse.[31] There was a more obvious reason for getting rid of the swords, for they constituted a permanent danger. Scarcely a day passed without some insolence on the part of the chairmen, which excited gentlemen to draw their swords and engage in brawls; these terrified the ladies and often ended disastrously.[32]

A still graver inconvenience was caused by the frequency with which gambling quarrels resulted in duels. Nash, though he had begun by fighting himself, determined to suppress these, and whenever the rumour of a challenge reached his ears he at once caused the two adversaries to be arrested. A nocturnal encounter between two professional gamblers, in which one of them was run through the body, took place very opportunely to give weight to his objections. The wearing of swords was definitely forbidden,[33] a trifling change apparently, but one which had consequences of great importance. Young gentlemen did not resume the sword they had laid aside in Bath when they returned to London, and this

The Pump Room (Exterior)
From the drawing by John Claude Nattes

abandonment of weapons in daily life at once attested and favoured a notable softening of manners.[34]

Public entertain being the real domain of the Master of the Ceremonies, we may suppose that Nash worked with all his might to multiply these and make them attractive, but here again he insisted upon the strictest regularity. There were two balls a week, on Tuesdays and Wednesdays. They began at 6 o'clock and ended at 11 o'clock, that invalids might not be tempted to sit up late. On the stroke of 11 the band ceased to play, and on one occasion, when the Princess Amelia, daughter of George II, asked Nash for one more dance after this signal, she was told that the laws of Bath were as immutable as those of Sparta, and that a single infraction would break down all their authority.

These laws of Bath gradually became more and more extensive and precise. In 1742[35] the following code was hung up in the Pump Room. It is no less curious in the prescriptions it makes than in its very unwarrantable pretensions to wit. As Goldsmith remarks: "Were we to give laws to a nursery, we should make them childish laws: his statutes, though stupid, were addressed to fine gentlemen and ladies, and were probably received with sympathetic approbation." These fine ladies and gentlemen were accordingly duly informed:

1°. That a visit of ceremony at first coming, and another at going away, are all that is expected or desired by ladies of quality and fashion,—except impertinents.

2°. That ladies coming to the ball appoint a time for their footmen coming to wait on them home, to prevent disturbance and inconveniences to themselves and others.

3°. That gentlemen of fashion never appearing in a morning before the ladies in gowns and caps show breeding and respect.

4°. That no person takes it ill that any one goes to another's play or breakfast, and not theirs—except captious by nature.

5°. That no gentleman give his ticket for the balls to any but gentlewomen.—NB. Unless he has none of his acquaintance.

6°. That gentlemen crowding before the ladies at the ball show ill-manners, and that none do so for the future—except such as respect nobody but themselves.

7°. That no gentleman or lady take it ill that another dances before them—except such as have no pretence to dance at all.

8°. That the elder ladies and children be content with a second bench at the ball, as being past, or not come to perfection.

9°. That the younger ladies take notice how many eyes observe them.—NB. This does not extend to the Have-at-alls.

10°. That all whisperers of lies and scandal be taken for their authors.

11°. That all repeaters of such lies and scandal be shunned by all company—except such as have been guilty of the same crime.—NB. Several men of no character, old women and young ones of questioned reputation, are great authors of lies in these places, being of the sect of levellers.

We can but smile at ordinances of such a nature, and Nash's efforts to regulate the lives of a handful of idle folks in their smallest details strike us as strangely puerile. But we must not forget that all this had undoubtedly some serious and lasting influence on the nation at large. Periodically, at stated seasons, Bath, thanks to Nash, drew together very diverse classes of society, each equally ignorant of the other, and brought them into daily and hourly contact, on a footing of transient equality, submitting them all to the same social discipline. In this single assembly-rooms, common to the whole kingdom, all sorts and conditions of men elbowed each other. A good education was the only passport required. It is true that an exaggerated value was attached to etiquette and ceremony; but, after all, this was only in the interest of elegance and politeness. Nash, as Goldsmith well says, "was the first who diffused a desire of society and an easiness of address among a whole people, who were formerly censured by foreigners for a reservedness of behaviour and an awkward timidity in their first approaches. He first taught a familiar intercourse between strangers at Bath and Tunbridge,[36] which still subsists among them. That easy and open access first acquired there, our gentry brought back to the metropolis, and thus the whole kingdom by degrees became more refined by lessons originally derived from him." Ideas enlarged by the intermixture and reciprocal action of different classes upon one another, politeness taught by precept and by example—these are points where we may say that the frivolous and mediocre Nash collaborated in the work carried on elsewhere by Steele and Addison.[37]

In any case he took his part very seriously, and showed himself no less proud than jealous of the fantastic sway he exercised. We have already seen how arrogantly he refused an extra dance to a princess of the blood, and how he thought himself within his rights in snatching from a duchess an ornament that displeased him. On the same principle he affected a special costume and special habits. He wore a white hat, a waistcoat always unbuttoned,[38] and a costume rather too rich for good taste, a mixture of the fashion of the day and that immediately preceding it.[39] He set off to Tunbridge Wells in a coach drawn by six dapple-grey horses, with an escort, lackeys and outriders, and spent his revenues right royally.

Whence came these revenues, we may ask, for we know that the future Master of the Ceremonies arrived at Bath without any fortune, after living a life of shifts and expedients. He complained one day to Lord Chesterfield of his bad luck at play: "Would you think it, my Lord, that bitch Fortune, no later than last night, tricked me out of £500. Is it not surprising," continued he, "that my luck should never turn—that I should thus be eternally mauled?" "I don't wonder at your losing money, Nash," says his lordship," but all the world is surprised where you get it to lose."[40] Cards and dice must have been his principal means of subsistence, and indeed the brief allusions made to him by his contemporaries show him to have been very assiduous at the gaming-tables.[41] Goldsmith describes him as a skilful but honest player (a character by no means common at the period), always ready with good advice to novices, endeavouring by every means to check the fatal passion in some,[42] and generous enough, occasionally to refuse a gain which would have been disastrous to an unlucky opponent.[43] He was able to recoup himself in other directions, as we see in the matter of the game of EO, an invention destined to elude certain legislative measures of 1739 and the following years, and extremely profitable to the banker, who took 2½ per cent. on all sums lost or gained.[44] This game of EO was established at Tunbridge Wells, but the inventor, quarrelling soon afterwards with his impresario, determined to ruin the latter by revealing the frauds he had committed to ensure the advantage of the banker. Nash, being advised of the matter, intervened, put an end to the quarrel, and made no difficulty about accepting a quarter of the profits of the bank thenceforth. He established the same game at Bath, where also he retained a good share of the profits.

But this state of things did not last long. The law of 1745[45] effectually put a stop to public gambling in England, and the blow was all the more crushing to Nash, because his partners had, it appears, cheated him no less than the public. He attempted to wrest from them what he considered his due, but failed, and then appealed to the law, only to be nonsuited. These desperate expedients revealed to the public his participation in illicit profits, and he himself, with sin effrontery, was careful to give an exact account of the whole affair in pamphlets which he caused to be distributed.[46] The result was not favourable to his reputation; he began to lose his credit and influence; his enemies accused him of other ill-gotten gains; he replied by new pamphlets that failed to silence his adversaries.

The foregoing episodes are far from redounding to Nash's honour. But it must be confessed that the society which so promptly punished him for his faults had hardly the right to be very severe. It will be but just to point out those characteristics by which he had commended himself to this society, and had long enjoyed its affection and even its esteem.

Goldsmith tells us, and occasionally allows us to see for ourselves, that, though he could not pretend to wit, Nash had considerable vivacity, and that his sallies were often amusing.[47] He had the manners of a man of the world, was a skilful flatterer, and very obliging. In London, and perhaps at Bath at the beginning of his career,[48] he had applied these qualities and talents to intrigue and gallantry, and had led a very dissolute life. But his royalty changed him; he set an example of regularity, and ranged himself on the side of virtue, which he was always ready to defend if necessary.[49] In that motley society, which gave every facility for intrigue, he made it his business to enlighten feminine ignorance, to prevent imprudent marriages, to arrest the erring on their downward road,[50] and this often at considerable risk to himself.[51] The part of affectionate counsellor which Fielding makes him play to one of the characters in "Tom Jones" seems to have been quite in keeping with actual facts. "Child," said he to Mrs Fitzpatrick, "I am sorry to see the familiarity which subsists between you and a fellow who is altogether unworthy of you, and I am afraid will prove your ruin … I never advise old women; for if they take it into their heads to go to the Devil it is no more possible than worth while to keep them from him. Innocence and beauty are worthy a better fate, and I would save them from his clutches," etc.[52] Anxious to save persons, he also tried to save reputations. We have seen above that evil-speaking was forbidden in the laws promulgated by him. An idle prohibition, no doubt, but one which attests a desire to stamp out slander in a spot where it reigned unchecked.

Another trait that did Nash honour was his charity, sometimes thoughtless and indiscriminate, but always untiring. Even when he was a student at the Temple, having one day heard some one say that a sum of ten pounds would make him happy, he could not resist trying the experiment, and, he even tried it again on another occasion with a sum twenty times larger.[53] These were mere sudden impulses of generosity, but throughout his life he showed great compassion for real, and even for fictitious miseries. He exerted himself personally to find out cases of hidden distress, and was assiduous in relieving them, giving away in charity as much as he spent on himself, and weeping over misfortunes he was unable to repair.[54]

Not content with thus preaching by practice, he was an active and indefatigable beggar on behalf of his poorer brethren, often making rich visitors to Bath co-operate in good works somewhat against the grain.[55] By the influence he thus exercised, he was able to contribute indirectly but largely to the foundation and endowment of a hospital that still exists at Bath, and is an honourable monument to his memory.[56]

The Pump Room (Interior)
From the drawing by John Claude Nattes

The year 1738 marks the apogee of Nash's glory. The Prince of Wales having given him a snuff-box, all the nobility followed suit and made him similar presents. A full-length portrait of him was placed in the Assembly Rooms between the busts of Newton and Pope, and gave occasion for a famous epigram.[57] The crowd of flatterers who had long been fawning round him increased, as did also their baseness; authors humbly dedicated their works to the King of Bath.[58] The poor man, intoxicated by all this homage, fairly lost his head. He became more affected in his manners and speech,[59] and more eager to disseminate his own jests and stories, which scarcely deserved repetition; he himself may have prepared a collection of these.[60] His imperturbable assurance and freedom of manner degenerated into impertinence, and he thought himself at liberty to wound anyone, so long as he addressed some witticism, or what he considered such, to them. Some of the sallies attributed to him are merely the audacities of an ill-bred person.[61] This affectation and rudeness diminished his popularity, and the gambling transactions which soon came to light also dealt it a very heavy blow. We must further remember that old age was approaching, and it was strange to see this wrinkled dandy still attempting to discuss fashions, lead dances, take part in and direct the surrounding dissipation.[62] Nash lived some ten years longer with diminished but still considerable authority,[63] ruined by the suppression of gambling, and subsisting on a pension of ten guineas a month granted him by the Corporation.[64] He died in 1761, at the age of eighty-seven, and the city, which had neglected him in his old age, gave him a sumptuous funeral.[65] He was buried in the Abbey, and pompous epitaphs were composed in his honour.[66]

Such was the career of this strange personage, a man of mediocre parts, it is true, but one who nevertheless had a considerable influence upon a section of English society. His sole ambition was to be the reputed arbiter of fashion in a limited circle; in this he succeeded for a time, and his frivolous sovereignty satisfied his aspirations, just as it afterwards sufficed the famous Brummell under different conditions.[67] Nash had at least moulded the society of Bath to suit himself, he had regulated its pleasures, its manners, even its morals; he had made a little watering-place of no special importance into a capital of fashion, to some extent. After his death the town long remained what he had made it, retaining the customs he had imposed upon it, and the character he had given it. He had successors[68] who endeavoured to imitate him in every respect, but who never succeeded in acquiring an authority in any way comparable to his;[69] the dependents of the public,[70] they became its servants, instead of assuming and keeping the direction thereof.[71] Nash was, indeed, the first and the last King of Bath,[72] and his memory, somewhat embellished and purified by distance, is still living and popular in the city that was his realm.[73]

1 "Queen Mary, the wife of William III, not being on very friendly terms with her sister Anne, took offence at the attentions paid by the civic authorities to her sister, and ordered the, burgesses of the municipal council to abstain from such demonstrations in future. They obeyed reluctantly, with many apologies to the princess." (*Cf* Warner, "History of Bath," iv., chap. ii. pp. 207–9.)

2 For a detailed account of this visit, see Warner, *ibid.*

3 Wood, vol. ii. p. 221. The good effect of the waters upon the Prince's health induced the second visit, but he died shortly afterwards; the Queen obstinately refused to return to Bath after this, even at the urgent advice of her physicians ("Some Memoirs of John Radcliffe, MD," pp. 65–8).

4 "Thatched coverings were exchanged for such as consisted of stone and tile, low and obscure windows were made into sashes, and handsome rooms were built for people to drink the water and assemble in. These improvements encouraged strangers to come here." … (MS by Wood, quoted by Warner, "History of Bath," book v. chap. i. p. 220.)

5 At least, if Goldsmith was right in identifying this Webster with the one spoken of by Lucas in his "Lives of Gamesters." Lucas's book gives no information on this point. Fleming, a musician of Bath, who seems to have been very well posted in local tradition, says merely: "At that time, a Captain Webster resided here, who had a thirst for gaming, and introduced it to a great degree; he was a man of spirit and address. After the duke relinquished his undertaking (*cf supra*, p. 19, *note* 5), the captain took upon him to conduct the amusements" ("Life … of T. Ginnadrake," vol. iii. p. 17).

6 "The Life of Richard Nash of Bath, Esq," published anonymously in October, 1762. A second edition, dedicated to the Municipality of Bath, with slight corrections and additions, appeared in December of the same year. A receipt given by Goldsmith shows us that Newbery the bookseller paid him fourteen guineas for the work (Forster, "Life of Goldsmith," p. 243).

7 This term, *Beau,* was still taken in good part; it had been applied quite recently to well-known persons, such as Sir George Hewitt, the original of Etherege's "Sir Fopling Flutter"; Wilson, who was killed in a duel by the future financier, Law; Fielding, the husband of the Duchess of Cleveland in her old age; and Edgeworth, spoken of in the *Tatler* (No 246). As late as 1786, the actor Bernard mentions a certain Sir John Oldmixon, who, "from the refinement of his dress and manners, bore the peculiar appellation of the 'Bath Beau,' and upon all points of good breeding was looked up to as an oracle. This distinction in the metropolis of fashion he was not slightly proud of; it acknowledged him as the legitimate successor of the dynasty of Nash" ("Retrospections of the Stage," vol. ii. chap. i. p 31). *Cf* a passage in Madame d'Arblay's "Diary," concerning one Beau Travell (vol. i. p. 176, Ward edition).

8 Goldsmith and Nash, if we may compare two men so unequal in merit, had certain traits in common, such as kind-heartedness, a generosity of a somewhat reckless kind, combined sometimes with neglect of strict obligations, carelessness and prodigality in the midst of a life of shifts and expedients, unfailing good humour, and certain puerile vanities, such as a love of fine clothes. See in this connection Mr Forster's shrewd and discriminating remarks ("Life of Goldsmith," book iii. chap. v. pp. 243–46). Perhaps these points of resemblance had something to do with the biographer's interest in his hero.

9 "I shall beg leave to give some other instances of Mr Nash's good nature on these occasions, as I have had the accounts of himself" ("Life of Nash," p. 532 of the Globe edition of Goldsmith's Works. It is to this edition I shall refer throughout this chapter, unless some other is expressly mentioned). He also speaks of seeing him at Bath: "One night, when I was in Wiltshire's room, Nash came up to a lady and her daughter, etc (*ibid.* p. 532); and in London: "I have known him, in London, wait a whole day at a window in the Smyrna Coffee-house, in order to receive a bow from the Prince, or the Duchess of Marlborough, as they passed by where he was standing," etc (*ibid*, p. 544). Of the two last assertions, the first is extremely questionable as Nash died in l76 and there is no record of a journey made by Goldsmith to Bath before the year 1762. As to the second, it is even less admissible, if the Duchess of Marlborough mentioned by Goldsmith was, as it is natural to suppose, the famous Duchess, who was, we know, Nash's friend. She died in 1744, when Goldsmith was barely sixteen, and had not yet left Ireland. Did the biographer invent these touches, to give colour and interest to his page, or, using as he did the notes and papers of another man (George Scott), did he simply transcribe this other's personal souvenirs, without troubling to modify them?

10 Preface, p. 514. The introduction to the second edition is still more explicit: "We have the permission of George Scott, Esq (who kindly undertook to settle the affairs of Mr Nash for the benefit of his family and creditors), to assure the public that all the papers found in the custody of Mr Nash which anyways respected his life, and were thought interesting to the public, were communicated, to the editor of these volumes; so that the reader will at least have the satisfaction of perusing an account that is genuine, and not the work of imagination, as biographical writings too frequently are." This George Scott is again mentioned by Goldsmith in a footnote as

"a person to whom we are indebted for many anecdotes respecting the life of Mr Nash." (This note is omitted from the Globe edition, but appears in the Gibbs edition, vol. iv. p. 54.)

11 As, for instance, circulars (p. 530), dedications (p. 545–48), Wood's work (p. 533), and manuscript notes of Nash's own preserved at Bath (Gibbs edition, vol. iv. p 54 and 132, *notes*). I may add that in his description of Bath, Goldsmith quotes several passages from Wood almost word for word, without acknowledgment; from the same work ("Description of Bath," first edition, I 742), he takes 'the story of Sylvia (pp. 533–538), but here he mentions the author.

12 The article in the *Gentleman's Magazine* of I 763 commended as excellent by the "Dictionary of National Biography" (see under *Nash*), is a mere abstract of Goldsmith's "Life." The same may be said of the articles in the *London Magazine* (1762), the *Universal Magazine* (1762), the *Biographical Magazine* (1776), and *Blackwood's Magazine* (1840), as well as of the modern works mentioned.

13 According to the *Saint James' Chronicle*, quoted by the *London Magazine* of October 1762, p 515, without any indication as to date of issue, he decamped from the University in a fit of disgust, just after receiving his quarter's allowance, leaving all his debts unpaid.

14 It is to this period of his hero's life that Goldsmith ascribes various anecdotes which give an idea of the sort of jokes that were looked upon as amusing in those days! Nash bet on one occasion that he would ride through a certain village naked, on a cow, and won his wager. Another time he stood wrapped in a blanket at the door of York Cathedral when the congregation was coming out, also to win a bet. One day, some friend invited him on board a man-of-war, and made him drunk as she weighed anchor. He was obliged to make a long voyage, and even to take part in a naval engagement, in which he declared he was wounded.

15 This, at any rate, was the opinion of Goldsmith, who pronounced him "generous, humane, and honourable" in his profession ("Life of Nash," p. 526 and attributed his success to his skill. I have found no evidence to the contrary anywhere, save in the violent diatribe of the "Court Tales" which I shall quote further on (p 37, *note* 4), where he is denounced as a "common sharper." The musician Fleming credits him with a different source of revenue. He relates that certain persons having accused him of mending his fortunes by highway robbery and other criminal methods, a deputation of friends waited on him, begging him to give an explanation on this point. With some embarrassment accordingly he exhibited some twenty love-letters received within an hour, containing £50 sterling. The writer adds this extraordinary comment "Prejudice vanished and Nash reassumed his character and self."—("Life of T. Ginnadrake," vol. iii. pp 18–21.)

16 "Wherever people of fashion came, needy adventurers were generally found in waiting. With such Bath swarmed; and among this class Mr Nash was certainly to be numbered in the beginning, only with this difference, that he wanted the corrupt heart too commonly attending a life of expedients, for he was generous, humane, and honourable, even though by profession a gamester."—(Goldsmith, "Life of Nash," p. 525.)

17 This physician, whose name Goldsmith does not give, was Dr John Radcliffe. I can find no trace of the pamphlet, and the "Memoirs of the Life of Dr John Radcliffe" merely say (pp 63–5) that he advised Prince George of Denmark not to take the waters. But the "Letter from a Citizen to his Excellency Dr R., 1705," accuses him of having said: "firstly, That you will put a *Toad* in our *Waters*; secondly, That you will spoil the Trade of the Bath Waters, by G—d you will; thirdly, that you will bring our *Lodgings* to half a Crown a week" (p 7); adding (on p 9) "Tunbridge has been your Favourite formerly, next Bath, and now Tunbridge again." The writer defends the waters, and vaunts their properties. He does not mention Nash.

18 The author of a little book dedicated to Nash compliments him on his grace in English country dances, and adds "I don't mention your dexterity in French dances, because you don't affect dancing them."—("Characters at the Hot Well," Dedication.)

19 Such at least was Goldsmith's opinion, to which all who have seen one of the numerous portraits of him that have come down to us will subscribe: "Nature had by no means formed Mr Nash for a *beau garçon*. His person was clumsy, too large and awkward, and his features harsh, strong and peculiarly irregular" (p 531). The author of the little book mentioned in the preceding note naturally judges somewhat differently: "A man about five foot eight inches high; of a diameter exactly proportioned to your height, that gives you the finest shape; of a black, brown complexion that gives a strength to your looks suited to the elastic force of your fibres and muscles. You have strength and agility to recommend you to your own sex, and great comeliness of person to keep you from being disagreeable to the other." ("Characters at the Hot Well," Dedication.) He returns to the charge a little further on to mention "the very agreeable oddness of your appearance, your black wig, scarlet countenance, and brown beaver hatt."

20 Nash's relations with the aristocracy naturally increased very much at Bath. We find from Lady Bristol's letters that he was received at her house ("Hervey Letter-Books," May 4, 1723, vol. ii. p. 280), and invited by the Duchess of Marlborough (*ibid.* p. 383, September 23, 1718) etc. Some letters from the Duchess to Nash are quoted by Goldsmith ("Life of Nash," pp 537, 538). The "Jests of Beau Nash" are dedicated to Lord Chesterfield, his "protector and friend."

21 Goldsmith, "Life of Nash," p. 520.

22 *Cf* Lecky on this point "The power of the nobility was supported by great wealth of the kind which carries with it most social influence, and by a superiority of education and manners which distinguished them far more than at present from the average Country gentleman"—("History of England," vol. vii. chap. xxi. p. 184.)

23 In 1705 (Wood, *op. cit.* vol. ii. chap. xii. p. 223).

24 In 1708 (*ibid.* p. 225).

25 "But when proper Walks were made for exercise and a House built for assembling in, Rank began to be laid aside, and all Degrees of People, from the Private Gentleman upwards, were soon united in Society with one another."—(Wood, *op. cit.* part iv, chap. ix. p. 411.)

26 See chap. x. below. It was in 1728 that he began to build Queen's Square.

27 "An Undertaking. so nice and delicate," continues Wood, "that till the Humours of the Place are, by the various Ceremonies of Initiation, perfectly known, no monarch can discharge it so as to induce People to submit to his Decrees."—(*Op. cit.* part iv. chap. xi. p. 455.) Fleming observes that "the magistrates of the city found he was necessary and useful, and took every opportunity of paying the same respect to his fictitious royalty that is generally paid to or claimed by real power."—("Life of … T. Ginnadrake, vol. iii. p. 61.)

28 Thicknesse, who gives the anecdote with great detail ("New Prose bath Guide," pp 26–8), and says he had it from Nash himself, adds that by this double stroke (the immersion and the duel) "he shewed himself a Man of Pleasantry as well as Spirit, Two excellent Qualities for a Prince who presides over the Pleasures and Pastimes of Youth." Nash evidently sought an opportunity for a duel which should establish his courage and increase his prestige.

29 The last clause of the sentence, which was added to the second edition, is omitted in the Globe edition (p. 523).

30 Goldsmith gives this little piece. It is called "Frontinella's Invitation to the Assembly":
Come one and all to Hoyden Hall,
For there's the assembly this night;
None but prude fools
Mind manners and rules,
We Hoydens do decency slight.
Come trollops and slatterns,
Cocked hats and white aprons,
This best our modesty suits,
For why should not we
In dress be as free
As Hogs Norton squires in boots?

31 The eccentric Lord Peterborough resisted. "Lord Peterborough has been here some time, though by his dress one would believe he had not designed to make any stay, for he wears boots all day, and as I hear, must do so, having brought no shoes with him. It is a comical sight to see him with his blue ribbon and star and a cabbage under each arm, or a chicken in his hand, which, after he himself has purchased at market, he carries home for his dinner."—(Letter from Lady Hervey, June 7, 1725, in the Countess of Suffolk's "Correspondence," vol. 1. p. 181.) The rules of the New Assembly Rooms (1771) reiterate the injunction: "That no gentleman in boots or half-boots be admitted into any of these rooms on ball-nights, or public card or concert nights."—(Nightingale, "Beauties of England and Wales," vol. xiii. p 419.)

32 "It was the Insolence of the Chairmen that gave rise to the first of these Laws; it having been usual with those turbulent people to provoke gentlemen to draw their Swords upon them, and then, by defending themselves with their Chair Poles, the Danger of Murder frighted the Ladies to such a Degree, that the Publick Assemblies for Diversion seldom ended without the utmost Confusion."—(Wood, *op. cit.* part iv. chap. ix. p 413.)

33 There are various allusions to this prohibition in Sheridan's "Rivals": "We wear no swords here" (iii). "A sword seen in the streets of Bath would raise as great an alarm as a mad dog" (v. 2).

34 *Cf* Lecky: "Between 7720 and 1730 it was observed that young men of fashion in London had begun in their morning walks to lay aside their swords, which were hitherto looked upon as the indispensable signs of a gentleman. Beau Nash made a great step in the same direction by absolutely prohibiting swords within his dominions, and this was perhaps the beginning of a change of fashion which appears to have been general about 1780, and which has a real historical importance as reflecting and sustaining the pacific habits that were growing in society."—("History of England," vol. ii. chap. v. p. 198.)

35 Goldsmith seems to attribute these rules to the very first stage of Nash's sovereignty, but Wood declares that they were not established and posted up till the date here given, after a general council.—("Description of Bath," chap. x p. 412.)

36 Though Bath was his proper domain, Nash occasionally appeared at Tunbridge Wells, where his influence was also recognised. "Mr Nash always stayed at Tunbridge till the first ball-night, at the beginning of a season, was over, and I daresay he did so to let the public see how unwieldy and awkwardly the business went on without a Regulator" (Thicknesse, "Valetudinarian's Bath Guide," p. 66). *Cf* Burr, "History of Tunbridge Wells," chap. xiv. The various watering-places accorded him a sort of general suzerainty: "Nor will, I hope, be thought improper that I give you the patronage of the frequenters of the Hot Well too. Kings, Sir, are as much sovereign in their principalities as in their kingdoms; their power is equal, though their titles are not so, Sir, and though with respect to the greater number of your subjects you are King at Bath, you may be styled Prince at the Hot Well, Duke at Tunbridge, Earl at Scarborough, not to mention your Lordships of Buxton, and your own kindred famous place of resort, St Wenefride's Well" ("Characters at the Hot Well," Dedication). Epsom, on the other hand, seems to have had a special ruler of her own (*Cf Tatler*, no 36), perhaps in imitation of the King of Bath.

37 Inasmuch, at least, as these enjoined social pleasures, distinction of manners and of language, "propriety, good-breeding, and those forms of daily politeness which contribute so much to the dignity and amenity of life" (A. Beljame, "Le Public et les Hommes de Lettres," p 306 see all the chapter devoted to Addison). I do not, of course, forget that the counsels of the *Spectator* had another end in view, and that the exterior refinement commended therein corresponds, in the minds of the authors, to an inward refinement of heart and intelligence of which Nash had no idea.

38 "Life of Quin," p 8.

39 Goldsmith, "Life of Nash," p 526. *Cf:*—"Being His Majesty's birthday, Nash gave a ball at Lyndsey's [one of the Assembly Rooms]; he wore his gold-laced clothes on the occasion and looked so fine that, standing by chance in the middle of the dancers, he was taken by many at a distance for a gilt garland."—(Lord Chesterfield to Lady Suffolk, November 2, 1734, in "Letters to and from Henrietta, Countess of Suffolk," vol. ii. p. 114.)

40 "Life of Nash", p 551

41 "Nash lost fivety pound a Saturday at Harrison's, and as they say, broke all the windows according to custom" (Letter from Lady Bristol, September 20, 1725, in the "Letter of John Hervey, first Earl of Bristol", vol. ii. p. 203). "Poor Nash is almost undone, for 'tis allowed by all that he has lost £1400" (*ibid.* p 332). "He concluded his evening as usual by basset and blasphemy" (Chesterfield, letter quoted above, p 36, *n.* 3).

42 See, for instance, the story of the Duke of B. (Bolton?) ("Life of Nash," pp 526–527). It is true that, by exception, it ended to Nash's advantage. It is no doubt the same story as that given in the *Gentleman's Magazine* of 1732 (p 62), on February 9: "A certain Duke paid £5000 to Beau Nash, and agreed to allow him £400 a year for life, *in lieu* of £10,000 he was to pay in case the nobleman should lose at hazard above £2000 at one sitting; which he did in October last at Newmarket."

43 *Ibid.* pp. 526–27. Goldsmith quotes several instances of young men whom Nash tried to dissuade from gambling, or to warn against unscrupulous adversaries. A similar trait is mentioned in "Bath Characters," p 97. I have found but one testimony to the contrary, and this comes from a very suspicious source, the "Court Tales," a collection of scurrilous anecdotes. The accusation was probably unfounded, for we should otherwise find some hint of it in the numerous passages of letters, memoirs, and journals in which Nash is mentioned. But it may be quoted by way of a contrast in dark tones to the portrait which Gold smith perhaps drew rather too flatteringly: "Nessus [the name is translated as N-s-h in the key at the end of the volume), a common Sharper, who to the Scandal of the Quality of the Island, was admitted into their Cabinets when he ought to have been sent to the Gibbet. The fellow was an odd Composition of Cowardice and Impudence, of Pleasantry and Nonsense; and had he not been too much a Rascal would have made a finished Coxcomb. But a Rogue has something too horrible in him to make a Subject for Satyr, and instead of making a jest of Nessus, one cannot think of him without trembling; So many Bubbles has he reduc'd to Beggary, so many Heirs sent to the Armies, so many Heiresses to the Stews; yet in all Publick Places who but *Nessus* for the Marshal of their Pleasures? *Nessus* is Treasurer to the Ball, and Banker to the Basset. *Nessus* raps at my Lady's Bed Chamber, and enters it as freely as if he was to dress her; *Nessus* calls for Chocolate, and cries Damn him., if it is not ready, for he has Fifty Visits to pay, and the Ladies will be all stirring else. *Nessus* kisses the Wife and cocks at the Husband; lives with the Women as Horner did [Horner in Wycherley's "Country Wife," a seducer by profession, who lulls the vigilance of husbands by a cynical stratagem, and makes them introduce him themselves to their wives, and encourage his intimacy with them], because the Husbands are in hopes that he'll be contented with cheating them. He had the Reputation of Courage till he was kick'd out of a Coffee-House for want of Half-a-Crown to pay an old Debt and denying it rather than discover his Indigence. For with all his Bubbles, Nessus is himself a Bubble, and spends on a common Strumpet what the less common ones lavish on him" (pp 93–94). The writer goes on to describe an intrigue with a certain Maura, whom Nessus finally despoils of 400 crowns at play: "not having Money enough to pay him, he had the Gallantry to take her Necklace in pawn for it; and at the next Assembly, his own dirty Mistress

appear'd with it, to the terrible Mortification of *Maura* and the wonderful Delight of the whole Company" (p 95).

44 According to the definition given by the New English Dictionary, the game seems to have been very like Rouge et Noir: "EO. A game of chance, in which the appropriation of the stakes is determined by the falling of a ball into one of several niches marked E and o respectively."

45 This law condemned all persons who lost or won at play or in bets a sum of £10 at one coup, or £20 in twenty-four hours, to pay a fine five times the value of the amount for the benefit of the poor. Wood gives the statute in detail ("Description of Bath," part iv. chap. vii. p 391).

46 I have been unable to trace any of these pamphlets. I only know them by Goldsmith's extracts.

47 See also a little collection of anecdotes, called "The Jests of Beau Nash." Many of the witticisms recorded are pointless, others rude rather than subtle, others simply unmannerly. Can it have been that Nash's air and tone in delivering them gave point to some and made others pass? Here are two or three specimens which are by no means the worst in each genre. "When drams were more in vogue than they are at present, a gentleman called for a glass of brandy at the Smyrna [Coffee House], because, he said, he was very hot. 'Bring me one, waiter,' says another, 'for I am very cold.' 'It is a strange. thing,' said Nash, 'that people can't find an excuse for their foibles without insulting the good sense of the company. There, bring me a dram, Boy, for I like it'" ("Jests," p 3). "A gentleman once told Nash that he was both the butt and the fool of the company. 'No, Sir,' says Nash,' I am the butt, and you' 'What?' says the gentleman. 'You are to supply the deficiency,' says Nash"—(*Ibid.* p 56). "An author came into a bookseller's shop where Nash was reading and offered a poem to sell. The bookseller refusing to give the money he asked, he turned short round and said he would carry it home, for that he did not care how much wit he had in hand. 'True,' says Nash, 'and I think you should always keep some in hand, my friend, for I fancy you have but little in head'" (*Ibid.* p 39).

48 Without deciding upon the authenticity of the adventures attributed to him in the "Court Tales" (see above, p 49, *note* 42), I may observe that the pamphlet dates from 1717.

49 Though [his life] was passed in the very midst of debauchery, he practised but few of those vices he was often obliged to assent to. Though he lived where gallantry was the capital pursuit, he was never known to favour it by his example, and what authority he had was set to oppose it."—("Life of Nash," Preface.)

50 "Many persons now alive … owe their present happiness to his having interrupted the progress of an amour that threatened to become unhappy or even criminal, by privately making their guardians or parents acquainted with what he could discover" (*ibid.* p 532). The writer gives several instances.

51 Goldsmith mentions one case in which he was involved in a duel, the dismissed suitor having found out who had baffled him.

52 "Tom Jones," xi. 4. Cf Anstey:

"For Him not enough at a Ball to preside,
Th' unwary and beautiful Nymph would he guide;
Oft tell her a tale, how the credulous Maid
By Man, by perfidious Man is betray'd."
("New Bath Guide," pp 76–79.)
See also "Bath Miscellany," 1741, p 23.

53 "Life of Nash," pp 518 and 538.

54 *Ibid.* pp 538–42, where various instances of his charity are recorded. *Cf.* Thicknesse: "Mr Nash made it his Business to inquire for Persons in Distress, and in particular for such as had known better days : and thought himself obliged when any Information was given him, that would justify his going in Person to unfortunate People, whose distress was only suspected, and who from Delicacy, are frequently ashamed to make their own Condition known … " ("New Prose Bath Guide," pp 99–100). *Cf* also an article of the *London Magazine* of 1745, p 345, or again these feeble verses in the "Bath Miscellany," p 22:

No Orphans' Tears are shed in Vain
At his too friendly Gate
Their Parents' loss they will sustain
Whilst he commiserate.

The Wretched Living thus he saves
In hospitable way,
And even when Dead, provides 'em Graves
To lay their senseless Clay.

55 Goldsmith tells how one day, when Nash was collecting for the hospital in the Assembly Rooms, a certain lady not famed for her generosity (the Duchess of Marlborough), finding it impossible to escape him, said: "You must put down a trifle for me, Nash, for I have no money in my pocket." "Yes, madam," says he, "that I will with pleasure if your grace will tell me when to stop"; then, taking a handful of guineas out of his pocket, he began to tell them into his white hat—"One, two, three, four, five—." "Hold, hold," says the duchess, "consider what you are about." "Consider your rank and fortune, madam," says Nash, and continues telling: "six, seven, eight, nine, ten." Here the duchess called again, and seemed angry. "Pray compose yourself, madam," cried Nash, "and don't interrupt the work of charity—eleven, twelve, thirteen, fourteen, fifteen." Here the duchess stormed, and caught hold of his hand. "Peace, madam," said Nash, "you shall have your name written in letters of gold, madam, and upon the front of the building, madam. Sixteen, seventeen, eighteen, nineteen, twenty." "I won't pay a farthing more," says the duchess. "Charity hides a multitude of sins," replies Nash, "twenty-one, twenty-two, twenty-three, twenty-four, twenty-five." "Nash," says she, "I protest you frighten me out of my wits. L—d, I shall die." "Madam, you will never die with doing good; and, if you do, it will be the better for you," answered Nash, and was about to proceed; but perceiving her grace had lost all patience, a parley ensued, when he, after much altercation, agreed to stop his hand, and compound with her grace for thirty guineas. The duchess, however,

seemed displeased the whole evening, and when he came to the table where she was playing, bid him, "Stand farther, an ugly devil, for she hated the sight of him." But her grace afterwards having a run of luck, called Nash to her. "Come," says she, "I will be friends with you, though you are a fool; and to let you see I am not angry, there is ten guineas more for your charity. But this I insist on, that neither my name nor the sum shall be mentioned."

56 In the list of the second subscription for the hospital (1742), appended to a charity sermon preached by Warburton, we find Nash acting as intermediary for the most distinguished subscribers: The King, per Mr Nash, £200; the Prince of Wales, do.; the Princess of Wales, £50," etc. The same form appears against the names of many members of the aristocracy, of the Bishop of Worcester, etc. Nash himself is put down for £100 (Warburton, A Sermon preached ... at Bath on Sunday, October 24, 1742, p 29). See also the list of the first subscription in Wood, part ii. pp. 275–78.

57 Goldsmith says the municipality caused the picture to be placed there, but the *Gentleman's Magazine* gives a somewhat different version in its heading to the well-known verses: "On Mr Nash's present of his own picture at full length fixt between the Bustos of Mr Pope and Sir Isaac Newton in the Long Room at Bath:

Immortal Newton never spoke
More truth than here you'll find;
Nor Pope himself e'er penn'd a joke
Severer on mankind.

The picture plac'd the busts between,
Gives satyr its full strength,
Wisdom and wit are little seen
But folly at full length.

Such is the text given by Goldsmith in his second edition (in the first only the second quatrain is given, with *statue* instead of picture), and reprinted in 1777 in the "Miscellaneous Works" of Chesterfield, published four years after the death of the latter. It had already appeared in the *Gentleman's Magazine* of February 1741, p 102, but anonymously, and the *London Magazine* of 1745, which quotes it (p 345), merely ascribes it to "no bad Poet." Goldsmith attributes it to Chesterfield, as does also Graves in his "Festoon" (p 36); the Festoon version substitutes *more cruel* for *severer* in the fourth line and *all its length* for its *full strength* in the sixth. But there is another version, in which the last strophe (identical save that the second line is altered to: *Adds to the thought much strength*) is preceded by the following five:

The old Egyptians hid their Wit
In Hieroglyphic Dress,
To give men Pains to search for it
And please themselves with Guess.

Modern to tread the self-same Path,
And exercise our Parts

Place Figures in a Room at Bath,
Forgive them, God of Arts!

Newton, if I can judge aright,
All Wisdom doth express;
His Knowledge gives Mankind new Light,
Adds to their Happiness.

Pope is the Emblem of true Wit,
The Sunshine of the Mind,
Read o'er his Works for Proof of it,
You'll endless Pleasure find.

Nash represents Man in the Mass,
Made up of Wrong and Right,
Sometimes a Knave, sometimes an Ass,
Now blunt and now polite.

This version of six strophes is to be found in an earlier work by another writer, Jane Brereton's "Poems on Several Occasions" (vol. ii. pp. 121–22), published in 1744, four years after her death. Which is the true version, and who is the author of each? The best way of harmonising the publication and the evidences is, I think, to accept Chesterfield as the author of the two stanzas quoted by Goldsmith. Jane Brereton must have borrowed the last and watered down the rest into twenty rather feeble lines, and this modified version, with its identical finale, was then ascribed to Chesterfield. Such is Mr Reeve's conclusion (*Notes and Queries*, 5th series, vol. x. p 429). It may, however, be pointed out that the epigram first appeared in the *Gentleman's Magazine*, to the best of my knowledge. Now Jane Brereton was a regular contributor to this publication. Cave, the owner of the *Gentleman's Magazine*, and afterwards the posthumous publisher of Jane Brereton's work, may have received it directly from her.

58 See in Goldsmith several examples of their dithyrambs (pp 545–48). It is true that they were all obscure writers.

59 The *London Magazine* of 1745 mentions "his monstrous white Hat, motly distinguish'd Garb, and uncouthly affected or broken Manner of Speech" (p 345).

60 " … A certain gentleman … wrote Mr Nash a poem ninety feet long, requesting the Publication of his Jests. This naturally gave Offence to a Man of his extreme Modesty; however, Good-Nature soon got the better of Resentment, and he promised to gratify the Gentleman's curiosity, and for that Purpose had strung together a Number of excellent Jests, which, have very fortunately fallen into our Hands" ("Jests of Beau Nash," Preface, ii.-iii.).

61 Smollett, in "Roderick Random," chap. lv., takes his hero to the Assembly Rooms at Bath accompanied by a young lady, who was slightly deformed. The visitors began to ridicule the newcomers, and "the celebrated Mr Nash, perceiving the disposition of the assembly, took upon himself the task of gratifying their ill-nature still further,

by exposing my mistress to the edge of his wit. With this view he approached us, with many bows and grimaces, and after having welcomed Miss Snapper to the place, asked her, in the hearing of all present, if she could inform him of the name of Tobit's dog. I was so much incensed at his insolence that I should certainly have kicked him where he stood, without ceremony, had not the young lady prevented the effects of my indignation, by replying with the utmost vivacity, 'His name was Nash, and an impudent dog he was.' This repartee, so unexpected and just, raised such an universal laugh at aggressor, that all his assurance was insufficient to support him under their derision; so that after he had, endeavoured to compose himself by taking stuff and forcing a smile, he was obliged to sneak off in a very ludicrous attitude while my Dulcinea was applauded to the skies, for the brilliancy of her wit, and her acquaintance immediately courted by the best people of both sexes in the room." Goldsmith accepts this anecdote as historic. It appears in a slightly different form in "The Jests of Beau Nash" (see below, chap. vii.). He adds that the evening before, Nash had asked the same lady (who, as we have said, was slightly deformed), whence she had come. Upon her replying, "Straight from London," he exclaimed: "Confound me, madam, then you must have been damnably warped by the way." *Cf* the following from a letter attributed to Quin, the actor: "A young lady was asked to dance a minuet. She begged the gentleman would be pleased to exquise her, as she did not chuse to dance; upon this old Nash call'd ont so as to be heard by all the company in the room: 'G— d—m you Madam, what business have you here, if you do not dance?' Upon which, the lady was so affrighted she rose and danced. The ress't of the company was so much offended that not one lady more would dance a minuet that night ... This man by his pride and extravigancies has outliv'd his reasion; it would be happy for thiss city that he was ded" ("Life of Quin," chap. xiii. p 53). Although the letter is certainly apocryphal, the incident does not seem to have been an invention. The date is given as one day in October 1760. For Quin's supposed attempts to supplant Nash, see "Life of Quin," chap. xiii., and beginning of chap. xiv.

62 Even in 1731 Lord Orrery wrote thus to Lady Kaye: "In my mind he [Nash] seems to labour under the unconquerable distemper of old age, and though he attends the balls as usual, his dancing days are over." ("Historical Manuscripts Commission, Eleventh Report," v. p 327.) He retained, however, the ease and distinction of his manners to the last. "Beau Nash, when my father saw him at Bath, was nearly in his ninetieth year, and I remember his describing him in manners as the finest old gentleman that he had ever seen. He reminds me, said my father, of the oldest of the old French *régime*."—(Angelo, "Reminiscences," vol. i. p 232.)

63 "Would you see our law-giver, Mr Nash, whose white hat commands more respect and non-resistance than the crown of some kings, though now worn on a head that is in the eightieth year of its age. To promote society, good manners, and a coalition of parties and ranks; to suppress scandal and late hours are his views and he succeeds better than his brother monarchs usually do."—(Lady Luxborough to Shenstone, February 15, 1752, "Letters," p 297.)

64 "Bath Corporation Minute Book," February 17, 1760.

65 At the expense of the Corporation, which voted a sum of 50 guineas for the purpose (*Ibid.* February 14, 1761).

66 The following is on his tomb: Adeste, O Cives, adeste Lugentes!—Hic silent Leges,—Ricardi Nash, Armig.—Nihil amplius imperantis.—Qui diu et utilissime.—Assumptus Bathoniae.—Elegantiae Arbiter.—Eheu!—Morti (ultimo designatori)—Haud indecore succubuit. Ann. Dom. MDCCLXI, Aetat. suae LXXXVII.—Beatus ille qui sibi imperiosus!

If social virtues make remembrance dear,
Or manners pure on decent rule depend,
To his remains consign one grateful tear,
Of youth the Guardian, and of all the Friend.

Now sleeps Dominion; here no Bounty flows:
Nor more avails the festive scene to grace,
Beneath that hand which no discernment shows,
Untaught to honour, or distinguish place.

67 Brummell was no doubt a more accomplished type of dandyism than Nash had been, and one who made a more brilliant figure to contemporary eyes. There is, however, a certain similarity between the two, notably as regards the amazing assurance of each, the rude sallies which was their substitute for wit, their vanity and their impertinence (see on this subject Brummell's biography by Captain Jesse, and Barbey d'Aurevilly's pamphlet, "Du Dandysme et de G. Brummell").

68 The first was a certain Collett, who resigned his office in 1763 (see Fleming, "Life … of T. Ginnadrake," iii. pp 126–128). An Irishman who had dabbled a little in literature, Samuel Derrick, author of "Letters Written from Leverpoole," etc, followed him, and reigned, not without some opposition, till 1769 (see "Life of Quin," chap. xiv.). A list of the other Masters of the Ceremonies down to our own times would be without interest. When another set of Assembly Rooms were opened (the *Upper Rooms*) there were sometimes two at the same time.

69 The imitation extended to costume. Derrick, second in succession to Nash, was careful to wear a white hat like his, and to leave his waistcoat unbuttoned ("Life of Quin," xiv. p 58). In spite of this, none of Nash's successors made their decisions respected as his had been, and the private entertainments he had forbidden soon told unfavourably on the regular gatherings in the Assembly Rooms (see Warner, "Literary Recollections," vol. ii. pp 2 *et seq.*).

70 "The place of Master of the Ceremonies ceased to be a place of independence at the decease of Mr Nash; Mr Ctt was appointed his successor but as he received certain emoluments from his office, did not act with the same authority as his spirited predecessor" (Fleming, "Life … of T. Ginnadrake," vol. iii. P 126). The same statement appears a little later in the "Tour Thro' Great Britain," ed. 1778 (vol. ii. p 233).

71 Warner, speaking of their remonstrances, adds: "Alas! enforcement expired with Nash" ("Literary Recollections," vol. ii. chap. xiii. p 5).

72 The modern novelists and dramatists who have introduced Nash in their works have generally represented him in a very favourable light. *Cf* the novels quoted below, in

chap. vii, and in particular, Douglas Jerrold's comedy of *Beau Nash*, where the author portrays him as an eccentric and bizarre, but sympathetic person, who thus sums up his functions at the end of the piece: "I'm a King, to be sure, and think the best of all governments is that of peace and good-will. 'Tis true I declare war against nothing but meanness—scandal—and ill-temper. If I mix with knaves,' tis to make knaves fall. Certain my kingdom isn't large, but I shan't with my brother of Macedon weep for new empires—so I can keep all within my little realm happy in themselves, and at charity with all the world beside."

73 The whole of this chapter has been devoted to showing the influence of Nash on the development of Bath in the eighteenth century. It is only fair to say that others contributed to this development, especially the two Woods, the architects, and Ralph Allen, the friend of Pope, who applied his large fortune to the material advantage of Bath. (See chapters ix. and x. for these persons. Wood the elder died in 1754, Allen ten years later.)

III

Life at Bath: Amusements

To give the idle the means of diverting themselves by putting all kinds of social distractions at their disposal, and, on the other hand, to subject all these amusements to the laws of a rigid etiquette, and to ensure not only their regular succession, but their elegance, was the double task attempted and accomplished by Nash. Throughout his reign and long afterwards, Bath, and the other watering-places that followed her lead, were the theatres of carefully regulated pleasures, where every hour had its fixed occupation, where almost every movement was foreseen and even directed.[1] "The course of Things," says a contemporary review, "is as mechanical as if it went by Clockwork."[2] Persons of fashion accepted all this, approving a concentration of amusements that made distractions more accessible even than in London, the regular order in which they presented themselves, the ready-made programme[3] that relieved pleasure-seekers from the strain of invention, and finally the decorum and ceremony that invested frivolous pastimes with an imaginary dignity. Besides this, the whole system had been set in motion, and "you cannot well be a free Agent, where the whole Turn is to do as other People do; it is a sort of Fairy Circle; if you do not run round in it, you cannot run at all, or are in everybody's way."[4] Let us follow in thought one of those who ran round this fairy circle.

First of all, he had to get there; and we may remind our readers that during the first half or two-thirds of the eighteenth century, a journey to Bath was a costly undertaking, not to be accomplished without considerable fatigue and annoyance. The roads were very bad, the communication between the different regions of Great Britain slow and difficult.[5] It was on horseback[6] or in their private carriages that persons of quality came to the waters, accompanied by a retinue calculated not only to do honour to the master, but to prevent or repulse the attacks of highwaymen.[7] Towards the middle of the century it took the stage-coaches three whole days (two during the special summer service) to travel the hundred odd miles between London and Bath,[8] and it was not until 1784 that, at the initiative of a citizen of the latter town,[9] the first mail-coach seen in England, reduced the journey, to fourteen hours.[10] A journey to Bath was consequently a matter of considerable trouble and expense, but these very conditions induced visitors to make a stay of some length in the city. We must further take into account that there was no other summer resort in Great Britain. Neither the seaside, where bathing was very rarely indulged in,[11] nor the Scotch and Welsh mountains, ignored, despised and for the most part inaccessible, were adapted for holiday retreats; and the difficulty and expense of travelling kept many from continental journeys.[12] The Englishman who wanted change of air and scene naturally thought at once of the watering-places, especially of Bath, instead of hesitating as he does now between the thousand attractions of Europe and of the world.

Let us suppose, then, that our traveller has arrived safely at the gates of Bath. As soon as his advent is made known, the bells of the Abbey ring a peal in his honour.[13] Such is the custom, which makes Bath a sort of Ringing Island. The invalids, however, do not complain, for "the Pleasure of knowing the name of every Family that comes to town recompenses the inconvenience. Invalids are fond of news, and upon the first round of the bells everybody sends out to inquire for whom they ring."[14] The visitors pay the ringers for their welcome, and then repair to their lodgings or inn,[15] where they are serenaded by singers and musicians who come to the door.[16] When they were thus duly installed to music, the Master of the Ceremonies made his appearance to call upon them.[17] They handed over their subscriptions to the Pump Room, the public promenades, the Assembly Rooms, the circulating libraries;[18] they at once began to live the life of Bath. We will follow them throughout the occupations of one of their days.[19]

They began it by bathing at an early hour, between six and nine in the morning.[20] The baths were some times taken by the doctor's orders, but more often as a diversion. There were five in all, but only two were fashionable and frequented by the *beau monde*, the King's Bath and the Cross Bath.[21] The town had not spent much in arranging or decorating them they were open to the sky, badly kept, and surrounded by buildings; they were approached by narrow passages, and niches in the walls afforded the only shelter obtainable from wind and rain.[22] The ornamentation of one consisted of a sort of octagonal tower in the centre, containing seats for the bathers, a stone balustrade, and a seated statuette of King Bladud in a hollow of the wall; the other boasted a little monument with a dome and columns, erected to the memory of Queen Mary of Modena, on which paralysed persons hung up their crutches after their cure.[23]

Both baths were inconvenient, very small,[24] by no means scrupulously clean;[25] but such as they were, invalids made the best of them in their quest for health, and idlers in their desire for amusement.[26] The crowd that thronged these narrow spaces offered a gay and animated picture.

Men and women bathed together, keeping more or less apart, the men in drawers and jackets,[27] the women in brown linen costumes and chip hats.[28] The ladies were carried from their lodgings to the baths in this costume, in sedan chairs, "hermetically closed," says a French traveller, "when the occupants were old, ugly or prudish, and artistically penetrable when they were finely formed."[29] They were provided with a little wooden tray that floated on the water in front of them, and held handkerchief, snuff-box and patches,[30] and thus they walked about in the water, either alone, or attended by a guide.[31] Musicians played all the time; conversation, compliments and jests were exchanged between the bathers.[32] An hour soon passes, and the bathers return to their sedan-chairs to be carried home; but the whole company will meet again almost immediately in the Pump Room.

This Pump Room, opened in 1706 and enlarged in 1751, is the morning rendezvous of both sick and sound.[33] The visitors assemble there in *déshabille* to drink the three glasses of hot water generally ordered,[34] to listen to the band, and to watch the bathers in the King's Bath just below the windows.[35] The crowd, the noise of the orchestra, and the hubbub of voices was somewhat bewildering to new comers, but they soon got used to the tumult.[36] The conversation generally turned upon the trifles of the day, and the latest scandals, real or supposed. Sheridan, beginning to dream of the School for Scandal, had an idea of laying the scene of his piece in this very Pump Room,[37] and in Lady Teazle's malicious speeches and Mrs Candour's evil insinuations we certainly have an echo of what he himself had heard there every day.

Breakfast then separated the company, the ladies going home, the men to the coffee-houses,[38] where the London papers awaited them;[39] but fashionable visitors very often ordered what were called public breakfasts in the Assembly Rooms or elsewhere, to which they invited their friends, and sometimes even a crowd of strangers.[40] Then came the daily service at the Abbey, which, by a bizarre contrast, was attended by a considerable portion of this frivolous society.[41]

The service was over about twelve, and in the interval before dinner, some went to the parades, others to ride, drive or walk, to look at the novelties in the shop windows, to take part in the lotteries held in the booths,[42] or to read in the booksellers' shops.[43] Dinner was served from two to three o'clock, and was followed by further gatherings, first at the Pump Room, and afterwards on the fashionable promenades. It was at these that all the refinements of dress and the elegances of fashion were displayed on the Parades.[44] Tea was afterwards taken at the Assembly Rooms, and the evening closed with visits,[45] gambling, a ball or a theatre.

The balls, which took place twice a week, on Tuesdays and Fridays,[46] were naturally the chief diversion which Bath had to offer to her visitors, and where indeed, even in London, was it possible to see a spectacle more brilliant in its way than those large, brightly lighted and gaily decorated rooms, thronged with all the *élite* of English society.[47] A curious ceremonial obtained at these balls, coupled with that gravity the English have long been supposed to preserve when they take their pleasure.[48] We have seen how the time and order of the dances, the costumes of those who took part in them, and all matters of precedence were regulated by Nash. At six o'clock the ball began with minuets.[49] The first couple advanced; the company seated round the room kept silence, and watched the dancers. At the end of the minuet, the lady was at once conducted to her seat, and the Master of the Ceremonies led forth a second lady, with whom the gentleman danced a second minuet. After this second couple came forward, and went through the same proceeding, and so on for about two hours, each gentleman dancing with two ladies in succession. Only two persons performed at a time, as we see. They were the cynosure of all eyes, and many a novice accepted the invitation given her with fear and trembling.[50] "Que de choses dans un menuet!" How many difficulties too! Happy the squire and dame who acquitted themselves to the satisfaction of the critical company who watched them![51] After the minuets came the country dances, which followed each other in the same manner, (the ladies of rank dancing first, in order of precedence), and went on till 11 o'clock, with an interval for tea. Looking back from this distance, the whole entertainment seems oddly chilly and formal[52] just as the music by which it was accompanied sounds thin, monotonous,[53] melancholy, almost sad indeed to modern ears;[54] Nash's subjects judged very differently, and were grateful to him for the quasi-solemn character he gave to their pleasures. The order, the decorum, the measured pomp, that distinguished the festivities of Bath were the pride and boast of the place.

For a long time the theatrical entertainments which alternated with the balls were far less brilliant and fashionably attended. The Bath theatre did not become really interesting till about 1750, but thenceforth for many years it shone with a vivid and sustained lustre, taking rank immediately after the London stage, and resolving itself into a nursery of actors for the metropolis. Several of the greatest

A Long Minuet as danced at Bath
From the drawing by H. Bunbury

English players of the eighteenth century acted at Bath; some were almost entirely formed there, and some, like the celebrated Mrs Siddons, prepared the way there for a triumphant return to the capital that had scorned them at first. As the only literary amusement among the diversions we are now passing rapidly in review, the theatre of the little town has a special claim to our attention.

ii

The Bath theatre boasted a considerable history at the beginning of the eighteenth century.[55] To say nothing of the mysteries and moralities which, according to tradition, were performed in one of the parishes of the town, the municipal archives note the visits of numerous actors from the days of Elizabeth onward.[56] Between the years 1569 and 1612 we find that thirty different companies visited Bath, some only once, others on several occasions, giving about a hundred performances, and receiving subsidies from the municipality. The registers, though they are silent as to the plays, record the names of the various companies; among them we find inscribed in 1592 and 1593, Lord Strange's Players,[57] in 1597 the Lord Chamberlain's Players, in 1604 the King's Players, in other words the company to which Shakespeare belonged, under different names.[58] It is possible, therefore, that the great poet acted at Bath, and the hypothesis is confirmed by two of the Sonnets,[59] which seem certainly to point to the city of the hot springs, even if they are not actually inspired by personal recollections of the town.

After 1612, the local archives cease to record the visits of actors. This is merely an omission, no doubt, for the public taste for the drama had by no means diminished under James I, or during the first years of his successor. There is the same dearth of information during the period that followed the civil war and the Puritan domination. In the municipal registers, however, a performance given at the Town Hall in 1673 is mentioned,[60] and the plan of Bath by J. Gilmore, which dates from 1694, shows a stable transformed into a theatre.[61] It was not until 1705, three years after Nash's arrival, that the first theatre was built at Bath. Several persons of rank contributed to the expense, and allowed their coats of arms to be painted in the interior, as a memorial of their liberality.[62] But the building, was small and inconvenient, the seats rising one above the other to within four feet of the ceiling; there was only a single box above the entrance, with seats for four persons.[63] Of the pieces that were performed in this wretched building, and of the players who acted them, during the first forty years, we know scarcely anything, and the absence of all records concerning them is perhaps significant.[64] The play was often ordered, and no doubt paid for by some private individual;[65] on one of these occasions, Lord Chesterfield records an audience of seventeen persons all told.[66] The slender profits of such a limited audience were not calculated to attract good actors; they were indifferent and probably few in number, and the success of their performances was far from brilliant.[67] The theatre was sold to make place for a hospital,[68] and the players were transferred to one of the Assembly Rooms (that of Simpson), where we learn from Wood that a "cellar" was reserved for them, that is to say a room under the ballroom. It does not appear, however, that the spectators were more comfortable in this new place, which was occasionally abandoned for a room in an inn,[69] nor that the performance was any better.[70] The repertory, when we begin to find it more or less well known (1745), was not ill-chosen. Shakespeare is well represented by *Othello, The Merchant of Venice, Richard III, Romeo and Juliet*; other tragedians and comedians who figure after him are Otway, with the *Orphan*,[71] Farquhar with the *Constant Couple*, Mrs Centlivre, with the *Gamester*, Steele with the *Conscious Lovers*, Addison with *Cato*, Gay with the *Beggar's Opera*, Garrick with *Albumazar and A Miss in her Teens*, Lee with *Theodosis*, Southerne with *Oroonoko*, Lillo with *George Barnwell* etc. [72] But the performances were rare,[73] and there were long intervals between them.

Such was the state of dramatic art in Bath when, in 1747, a London actor named Hippisley conceived the idea of building a theatre worthy of the town![74] He drew up an address to the "Nobility, Magistracy and Gentry at Bath," in which he reminded them that "theatrical Performances, when conducted with Decency and Regularity, have always been esteemed the most rational Amusements by the Polite and Thinking Part of Mankind," and pointed out that "in a Place during its Seasons honour'd with so great a Number of Persons eminent for Politeness, Judgment and. Taste … might reasonably be expected (next to London) the best Theatre in England."[75] He accordingly proposed to build a new theatre by subscription, and to reinforce the actual company by a sufficient number of good actors. The idea was favourably received, and when Hippisley died very shortly afterwards (1748), the enterprise was taken in hand by a certain John Palmer, a brewer and chandler, who carried it out successfully. The new theatre was opened at the end of October, 1750, with the First Part of Shakespeare's Henry IV[76] A prologue in somewhat turgid verse promised a varied repertory:

Shakespeare with Energy shall warm the Heart,
And Jonson the true Comic Force impart;
Lee in high pompous verse shall nobly swell,
And Addison in patriot Thoughts excel;
Ev'n laurell'd Dryden with the rest shall vie
And Otway's Lines imperil the melting Eye.
When plaintive Rowe shall paint the Nymph's Distress,
Each heaving Bosom shall her grief express
Nor shall we fail to add the Changeful Scene
With hum'rous Farce and motley Harlequin.[77]

These promises were faithfully carried out, and in the incomplete list that has come down to us of pieces given at the new theatre, we find most of the tragedies and comedies that found favour at Drury Lane or Covent Garden at this period.[78]

Shakespeare, who had recently come into great favour again in London, has the place of honour. It was with his Henry IV, as we have seen, that the theatre was opened, and his name was never very long absent from the bill.[79] If an actor of talent was found to interpret him, certain of his pieces were given six or seven times in a season, a very good average for a town where, the public, after all, was not very numerous.[80] Other authors who were granted a place, though a less prominent one, on the stage, were Ben Jonson, with Every Man in his Humour, Beaumont and Fletcher, with Rule a Wife and have a Wife and Philaster, Milton with an adaptation of Comus, Dryden with the Spanish Friar, Otway with Venice Preserved (several times), and The Orphan, Rowe with Jane Shore (very frequently), and The Fair Penitent, Southerne with Oroonoko and Isabella. Several

Henderson
From the portrait by Gilbert Stuart

of the comedians of the Restoration, and their direct successors,[81] were popular, as also Goldsmith with She Stoops to Conquer, Sheridan with The Rivals, A Trip to Scarborough, The School for Scandal, The Duenna and The Critic (these latter were given at Bath as soon as they had appeared in London), and many authors more or less forgotten now.[82] The repertory is varied and well chosen; it also shows a high level of literary excellence. To appreciate this, we need but compare the majority of the works contained in it, already classics, or destined to become such, with the insipid operettas and inferior vaudevilles, that alone find favour in those resorts of modern times which most nearly approach the Bath of the eighteenth century.

They were interpreted by good actors too. These were recruited throughout the kingdom by the managers,[83] and summoned from Bath to London. First, Henderson, considered by many the best actor of his day after Garrick, and then the greatest tragic actress England has produced, Mrs Siddons.

It was in 1772 that Henderson made his début at Bath in the part of Hamlet. Garrick, to whom he had been presented in London, had not considered his voice or his elocution powerful enough for the London theatres, but had recommended him to Palmer.[84] This distinguished patronage piqued the curiosity and excited the interest of the public A brilliant audience assembled to witness his first appearance,[85] and accorded him unanimous applause.[86] He was no less favourably received in Richard III, after which he essayed most of the other great parts, tragic or comic, nearly twenty in the same season, and always with the same success.[87] The strain was great, but he did not complain, for by this variety he found himself happily constrained to enlarge and diversify his methods.[88] He practised in this manner for five years.[89] At last, in 1777, he appeared at the Haymarket, and immediately after at Drury Lane, then under Sheridan's management. He was most favourably received, and as the incomparable Garrick had just retired from the stage, he at once took and retained the first place among English actors.[90]

It is often difficult to form any very definite opinion as to the talent of actors of a past generation. Their art is purely personal, and leaves no monument. All the evidences of it that remain to us may frequently be reduced to a few vague indications, a few anecdotes concerning the effect they produced upon their audiences on certain occasions. But in the case of Henderson, we are rather more fully informed. We know that he had not the same natural advantages as Garrick, or even as Quin, that he was below the average in height, that his face was not remarkable for mobility or expression, that his voice was not rich in modulations, On the other hand, he had all the qualities that are to be acquired or perfected by study; a perfect comprehension of his parts, a clear and careful elocution, a delivery that gave full effect to every detail.[91] "In the variety of Shakespeare's soliloquies, where more is meant than meets the ear, he had no equal."[92] His best parts were Shylock and Sir John Falstaff; in the latter he was generally considered to rank next to Quin.[93] He had, besides, a great talent for mimicry, which he exercised so imprudently that it several times got him into trouble.[94] On the whole, his name figures honourably beside those of Quin, Mackim, Munden and Elliston.

The year following the departure of Henderson for London witnessed the first appearance at Bath of the actress whom the English still account the greatest of all who have shed lustre on the stage. In the same theatre where Henderson had established his reputation, Mrs Siddons gloriously vindicated hers, which had been compromised in London. It was at Bath that the novice who had been so coldly received at Drury Lane conquered the public, and it was thence that she returned to the capital.

After a few unsuccessful months at Drury Lane, she had been dismissed by Garrick.[95] Henderson happened to see her in 1776, at the Birmingham theatre; and declaring that "she was an actress who never had had an equal, nor would she have a superior,"[96] he at once recommended her to Palmer.[97] The impresario's company was complete at the time, but the recommendation took effect two years later, when she made her début in Vanbrugh's Provoked Husband,[98] subsequently appearing in all the great tragic parts, and also taking. the subordinate characters in comedy, in which she was never very successful.[99] She was then twenty-three. She tells us herself how she was received, in a note which is also interesting because it shows the hardships of the actor's lot, at this time. "I now made an engagement at Bath," she says in her Memoranda. "There my talents and industry were encouraged by the greatest indulgence, and I may say with some admiration. Tragedies, which had been almost banished, again resumed their proper interest; but still I had the mortification of being obliged to personate many subordinate characters in co the first being, by contract, in the possession of another lady. To this I was obliged to submit, or to forfeit a part of my salary, which was only three pounds a week. Tragedies were now becoming more and more fashionable. This was favourable to my cast of powers; and whilst I laboured hard, I began to earn a distinct and flattering reputation. Hard labour indeed it was, for, after the rehearsal at Bath, and on a Monday morning, I had to go and act at Bristol on the evening of the same day,[100] and reaching Bath again, after a drive of twelve miles, I was obliged to represent some fatiguing part there on the Tuesday evening. Meanwhile I was gaining private friends as well as public favour; and my industry and perseverance were indefatigable. When I recollect all this labour of mind and body, I wonder that I had strength and courage to support it, interrupted as I was by the cares of a mother, and by the childish sports of my little ones, who were often most Unwillingly hushed to silence, from interrupting their mother's studies."[101] A hard school, as we see, but one in which the actress' talent grew daily, and also her popularity with the public.

She had to conquer this, which had become somewhat indifferent to tragedy since Henderson's departure.[102] Though she was at once appreciated by certain connoisseurs, she had to win the favour of the general public gradually; but this she did at last so completely that the theatre only filled on the evenings when she was acting,[103] and that all the ordinary arrangements for seating the audience had

Mrs Siddons
From the picture by Gainsborough

to be altered for her benefit performances.[104] She was, indeed, remarkable from the very first. Taylor, Garrick's friend, who saw her in January 1779, wrote: "I have attended to her with the most critical attention I was master of, and I declare my opinion of her to be all that my ideas can reach."[105] The elder Sheridan, the first time he saw her act again (for he had already seen her in London), went to tell her how surprised he was that she should be content with the provincial stage.[106] She did, not, indeed, remain much longer in the provinces, for in the summer of 1782, proposals were made to her for a return to Drury Lane, then under the management of the younger Sheridan. "In the summer of 1782 I received an invitation to revisit Drury Lane. After my former dismissal from thence, it may be imagined that this was to me a triumphal moment," she writes.[107] She accepted, and announced that on May 21, 1782, on the occasion of her benefit, she would give a recitation setting forth her three reasons for leaving Bath. These reasons were her three children, whom she led forward on the stage, declaring that it was only anxiety for their future that induced her to quit a town to which she owed so much. They were, she said, the

> ... little magnets, whose influence draws
> Me from a point where every gentle breeze
> Wafted my bark to happiness and ease—
> Sends me adventurous on a larger main, etc.[108]

It is not within the scope of this study to follow Mrs Siddons in her long career, and to retrace the well-known traits of her dramatic talent.[109] Descriptions and anecdotes abound of her triumphs on the stage, the extraordinary pathos of her renderings, the unparalleled effects she achieved. The gayest farces played by the best comedians failed to raise a laugh after a tragedy in which she had appeared.[110] At a performance of Macbeth, the public refused to listen to anything after her, and insisted upon the dropping of the curtain when she had made her last exit;[111] more than once, the actors with whom she was playing were so moved that they were unable to reply to her.[112] All agree that in the midst of these successes she remained simple, modest, and amiable, deserving of the eulogy of Johnson, who declared her to be one of those rare beings whom the two great factors of human corruption, praise and money, had failed to pervert.[113] Nor did she forget the little provincial theatre where her star had risen, and she returned several times[114] to give a series of performances at Bath.

Henderson and Mrs Siddons were far from being the only recruits the Bath theatre furnished for London during the reign of Palmer and his successors.[115] Besides a number of forgotten actors, of whom Edwin and Miss Wallis (afterwards Mrs Campbell) were perhaps the most notable, it gave Middleton[116] and Elliston[117] to the capital, and later was the cradle of Macready's and of Kean's[118] reputation. Elliston, immortalised by Lamb's delightful essays, appeared between 1796 and 1804 at the Haymarket, at Covent Garden, and at Court, without severing his connection with his provincial company. No better evidence could be given of the high estimation in which the Bath theatre was held by actors. Frequented by the most distinguished and discriminating public, a public whose opinion almost invariably forestalled that of London,[119] it came to be looked upon as a sort of preparatory school for the leading theatres of England.[120] It was also a kind of succursal to the London theatres, for if Bath sent actors to London, the most famous of the London actors did not disdain to act occasionally at Bath. We have already seen that Henderson and Mrs Siddons often revisited it. After them came many who had no sort of anterior connection with the city, the Kembles, the Cookes, the Mundens, the Bettys, Mrs Jordan and a hundred others.[121] During the early years of the nineteenth century, these tours, or short engagements of famous actors, became an established custom that had a disastrous effect. The public deserted the regular performances, wearied of the local company, and only troubled itself to attend the theatre when some passing "star" was to be seen.[122] This brought about a decadence which became complete some twenty years later; we shall not trace its successive stages which were of later date than the period with which we are mainly concerned. The vicissitudes of the Bath stage have only a narrow local interest from the time when this stage lost its independent and personal existence. It enjoyed such an existence for half a century. Through out this term, it had life of its own; it was a luminary and no mere reflection. Even if we look upon it during its most brilliant period merely as a kind of conservatoire, its history has its importance in connection with that of dramatic art in England.

1 See the description of the life at Tunbridge in Prévost's "Mémoires d'un Homme de Qualité," vol. v. pp 144–46.

2 English Magazine, December 1737, p 684.

3 "I think Bath a more comfortable place to live in than London; all the entertainments of the place lie in a small compass, and you are at your liberty to partake of them or let them alone just as it suits your humour."—(Mrs Delany, letter to Swift, April 22, 1736, published in her "Autobiography," vol. i. pp 553–54.)

4 English Magazine, December 1737, p 684.

5 See Macaulay, " History of England," chap. iii (pp 290–300 of the Edinburgh edition), and Lecky, vol. vii. chap. xxi. Here are some contemporary evidences as to the Bath roads, which might easily be multiplied "Having Din'd we proceeded on our Journey, but with a great deal of difficulty; for the Road was so rocky, unlevel and narrow in some places that I am persuaded the Alps are to be passed with less danger … we were jolted so cursedly, that I thought it would have made a Dislocation of my Bones …" etc. ("A Step to the Bath," p 12, 1700). "The news you tell me of the many difficulties you found in your return of the Bath gives me such a kind of pleasure as we usually take in accompanying our friends in their mixed Adventures for methinks I see you labouring through all your inconveniences of the rough roads, the hard saddle, the trotting horse and what not " (Pope to H. Cromwell, November 12, 1711, "Pope's Works," Elwin and Courthope ed.,

vol. vi. p 126). "After four days journey in very bad roads I arrived here a good deal tired" (Mrs Montagu, "Letters," December 27, 1740, vol. i, p 72).

6 See, for instance, the journal of Celia Fiennes, recently published under the title of "Through England on a Side Saddle in the Time of William and Mary," London, 1888.

7 We know how frequently novelists turned to account these adventures, which were, in fact, of frequent occurrence. There is scarcely an English novel of the eighteenth century that does not describe an exploit of the sort. See, for instance, "Tom Jones," book xii, chap. xiv; "Humphry Clinker," June 23 and 26; "Roderick Random," chap. liv. In this last work, it was on the journey to Bath that the hero so bravely defended the carriage attacked on Hounslow Heath. Claverton Down, at the very gates of Bath, was infested by footpads. (Cf Goldsmith's "Life of Nash," p 545.)

8 "Stage-coaches, between Bath and London, in three days, set out Mondays and Thursdays from the following inns etc … There are coaches that go in two days from April to Michaelmas and set out both from Bath and London Wednesdays, Mondays, and Fridays" ("Tradesmen's and Travellers' Companion," 2nd ed., pub. about 1750). We learn from the same source that there were regular services between Bath and Bristol, Bath and Oxford (two days), Bath and Exeter (three days), Bath and Salisbury (one day).

9 John Palmer, an enterprising person, whose name we shall meet with again when we deal with the Bath theatre, and who was Member of Parliament for Bath from 1801 to 1808.

10 The length of the journey had been reduced, indeed, before this date, for in 1776 we find Johnson leaving Bath on May 3 at 11 in the evening, and arriving in London at 7 the next evening. Mrs Thrale, "Letters to and from Johnson," vol. i. p 321. See the Bath Chronicle for February 24, 1785, on the inauguration of the mail. The length of the journey was afterwards curtailed; in the "Pickwick Papers" Dickens makes his hero (in 1827) arrive at Bath at 7 in the evening, having left London at half-past seven in the morning (chap. xxxv.).

11 Bathing in the sea only became general in England towards the middle of the century. See Lecky, "History of England," vol. ii., chap. v. p 199.

12 This state of things changed in the last third of the century. See Lecky, vol. vii. chap. xxi. p 230.

13 "The Etiquette is that whoever enters Bath with a Set of Horses, their Arrival must be announced by the Clappers of Four and Twenty Bells, while Two Hundred miserable Sick are to be tortured by them." ("The New Prose Bath Guide," p 91.) Cf Wood, "Description of Bath," part iv., xi. p 427; Goldsmith, "Life of Nash," p 524; Anstey "New Bath Guide," v. p 2; Smollett, "Humphry Clinker," J. R. April 24.

14 Goldsmith, "Life of Nash," p 524.

15 The Bath inns were famous for their comfort and luxury, especially the Bear, where Anstey makes his characters put up, and the White Hart. This latter, established before the eighteenth century, still existed in the time of Dickens, and the owner bore the name of Pickwick (cf "Pickwick Papers," chap. xxxv.).

16 Goldsmith, "Life of Nash," p 524; Wood, "Description of Bath," part iv., xi. p 417; Smollett, "Humphry Clinker, April 24 and 25. The custom is mentioned as early as 1700: "In the morning we were saluted by the whole Fraternity of Cat-Gut Scrapers" ("A Step to the Bath," p 12).

17 "Humphry Clinker," April 26.

18 Wood, part iv., chap. xi. p 417.

19 These occupations remained uniform and unvaried down to the close of the eighteenth century. There will therefore be no impropriety in taking various items, as we shall now do, from authors of different periods. In the successive editions of the "Tour through Great Britain," which appeared at considerable intervals (1724 to 1778), the description of life at Bath remains almost identical throughout.

20 Goldsmith, "Life of Nash," p 524.

21 After the discovery of the Roman baths in 1755, the Duke of Kingston built a private bath on the site, which was roofed in and more comfortably arranged than the others, and to this public favour was soon transferred. "They are now the only Place where Persons of Condition or Delicacy can bathe decently," said Thicknesse in 1778 ("New Prose Guide," p 25. They were very small: "To purify myself from all such contamination, I went to the Duke of Kingston's private bath, and there I was almost suffocated for want of free air; the place was so small, and the steam so stifling" (Smollett, "Humphry Clinker," April 28). Other baths were built at a later date.

22 See Wood, part iii, chap. iv. pp 257–65. Cf also "A Description of Bath" (1734), p 11, and the complaints of Dr Sutherland: "The avenues which lead to the Slips are dark narrow passages, less conspicuous far than the entrances to the meanest inns. The Slips resemble rather cells for the dead than dressing-rooms for the living. Their walls and floors are composed of the same materials, cold stone, and eternally sweating with the steam of the baths, dark as dungeons, and in their present condition incapable of being warmed. From these dressing-rooms we descend by narrow steps into open unseemly ponds. As Pliny the Younger said of old of the bath at Claudiopolis, so may we truly say of 'The edifice seems rather sunk into the earth than raised above the ground.' Irregular walls incrusted with white washing of lime, freestone sand and the heat of hot water, now bound our cisterns, exposed to wind and rain, as well as to the gaze of every footman … In as many words, our baths answer exactly that character which Baccius gives of the Italian baths of his day. 'Tum stupharum ipsarurn vitio quae, angustae ac tenebrosae, carent omni commoditate, et omni delicia, ac noxiae idcirco multis, invisae potius quam gratae et utiles'" ("Attempts to Revive Antient Medical Doctrines," pp 10–11).

23 Just in the midst a marble cross there stands
Which popish minds with pious awe commands,
Devoid itself of power to cure our woes,
Yet deck'd with monumental crutches, shows
What mighty cures that wondrous pool has done.
("Description of Bath," p 12)

24 The Cross Bath was only 20 feet long by 19 feet wide; the King's Bath, the largest, of all, was about 60 long by 40 wide. It communicated with a smaller tank, the Queen's Bath.

25 See Smollett's severe indictment of the baths as regards convenience, cleanliness and hygiene, in a medical treatise, "Essay on the External Use of Water" (p 34–36), and cf "Humphry Clinker," April 28, and passim. Several of Smollett's strictures appeared in an anonymous satire of 1737, called "The Diseases of Bath," where the subject is treated (ll. 356–81) with the same realism as in "Humphry Clinker." The description of the Pump Room here (ll. 335–56) also agrees with that given by Matthew Bramble in Smollett's novel.

26 "The Bathing is made more a Sport and Diversion than a Physical Prescription for Health" (Defoe, "Tour thro' Great Britain," ed. 1724, vol. ii., letter iii. pp 51–52. Diseases of the stomach, rheumatism and paralysis were the maladies chiefly treated at Bath. The waters were also recommended for female ailments and sterility. See Freeman, "Thermal Waters of Bath."

27 In the series of engravings by Rowlandson called "The Comforts of Bath," published in 1798, the bathers are represented with three-cornered hats on their heads (plate 7).

28 "The ladies wear jackets and petticoats of brown linen, with chip hats in which they fix their handkerchiefs, to wipe the sweat from their faces … " ("Humphry Clinker," Lydia Melford, April 26). In 1724, Defoe merely says "dress'd in your Bathing Cloths, that is, stript to the Smock" (vol. ii. pp. 51–52). The 1748 edition of the "Tour thro' Great Britain" adds "The greatest Decency is preserv'd here by both Sexes, and while Mr Nash lives, must always be so" (vol. ii. p 295). The statement is repeated in all the editions down to the death of Nash, and in that of 1769, with the omission of the second part of the sentence. On the other hand, Thicknesse apologises for being unable to repeat with decency "all the transactions which I have seen in the baths, without mentioning those I have heard" ("Valetudinarian's Guide," chap. x. p 55). The more favourable evidence seems to have been true on the whole, allowing for occasional exceptions. Habitual, or even frequent disorders, would certainly have been denounced in the satires, often very outspoken, which were directed against Bath.

29 Chantreau, "Voyage dans les trois Royaumes d'Angleterre, d'Ecosse et d'Irlande," 1792, p. 232.

30 " … The women that tend you present you with a little floating wooden Dish like a Bason, in which the Lady puts her Handkerchief, and a Nosegay, of late the Snuff-Box is added, and some Patches; tho' the Bath occasioning a little Perspiration, the Patches do not stick so kindly as they should." (Defoe, op. cit. ed. 1724, vol. ii. p 51. I may note here for the convenience of reference that each volume of this edition has a double pagination.) The Abbé Prévost also mentions this little basket floating on the water, fastened to the waist of the bather by a ribbon, and containing the handkerchief and snuff-box ("Pour et Contre," no. 38, p 176). It is mentioned as early as 1700 in "A Step to the Baths" p 53.

31 Goldsmith, "Life of Nash," p. 525.

32 "Here [at the Cross Bath] the Ladies and Gentlemen pretend to keep some distance, and each to their proper side, but frequently mingle here too, as in the King and Queen's Bath, tho' not so often; and the place being but narrow, they converse freely, and talk, rally, make Vows, and sometimes Loves; and having thus amus'd themselves an Hour or two, they call their Chairs and return to their lodgings." (Defoe, ibid. pp 51–2). The remark is suppressed in the later editions.

33 After successive enlargements, it was. demolished in 1791 and replaced by the existing building. The inscription from Pindar upon it, transmitted from the original Pump Room (ἁ ριστον μέ ν ὕδωρ) was suggested, it is said, by Dr. Johnson.

34 Goldsmith, "Life of Nash," p. 525.

35 "Right under the Pump Room windows is the King's Bath, a huge cistern where you see the patients up to their necks iii hot (" [Humphry Clinker," April 26).

36 "The noise of the music playing in the gallery, the heat and flavour of such a crowd, and the hum and buzz of their conversation, gave o the headache and vertigo the first day; but afterwards all these things became familiar and even agreeable" (Ibid.).

37 Sheridan's first rough draft of certain features in his great comedy was called "The Slanderer; a Pump Room Scene."

38 There were also certain coffee-houses for ladies only (cf Mrs Montagu, "Letters," vol. i. p 72, December 27, 1740). One of these seems to have been situated near the Pump Room ("Life of Nash," p 252). To certain of these young girls were not admitted, as the conversation turned upon "politics, scandals, philosophy," and other subjects above their capacity, as Lydia Melford's aunt said ("Humphry Clinker," April 26).

39 And also those of Bath, for the town very soon had its own journals, which compared not unfavourably with the London gazettes; the principal of these local papers were: the Bath Journal, founded in 1742; the Bath Chronicle, founded in 1757 (both are still in existence); and the Bath Advertiser, 1755–1768.

40 Goldsmith, op. cit. p 525. Wood, part iv., chap. xii. p 439. Cf a description of one of these breakfasts in Anstey, "New Bath Guide," xii. In "Humphry Clinker," again, a parvenu gives "a general tea-drinking" (Jeremy Melford May 30).

41 The same practice obtained at Tunbridge:

You all go to Church upon hearing the Bell,
Whether out of Devotion yourselves can best tell.
("Tunbridgiale," p 10))

The congregation seems occasionally to have failed in devoutness:

Now for pure worship is the church design'd,
O that the Muse could say to that confin'd!
Ev'n there by meaning looks and cringing bows,
The Female Idol her Adorer knows.
Fly hence, Prophane, nor taint this sacred place,
Mock not thy God to flatter Celia's face.
("A Description of Bath, 1734," p 10.)

As early as 1700 we are told: "A Sunday, we went to Church to the Abby ... ; 'tis crowded during Divine Service as much as St Paul's, in which time there is more Billet Deaux (sic) convey'd to the Ladies than Notes to desire the Prayers of the Congregation at B.'s Meeting House, and as the Ingenious Doctor in his Discourse told the Audience; He was afraid most of them came more out of Custome and Formality than in Devotion to the Sacred Deity, or a suitable Reverence to the Place of Worship, which was very True I am confident, and the Ladies were the only, Saints several came there to Adore ("A Step to the Bath," p 15), The Gentleman's Magazine of 1760 relates this anecdote (p 536): "Not long since at Bath the Subscription Books were opened for Prayers at the Abbey and gaming at the Rooms. In the evening of the first Day, the Numbers stood as under, and occasioned the following Thought:

The Church and Rooms the other day
Open'd their books for pray'r and play;
The priests got twelve—Hoyle sixty-seven,
How great the odds for Hell 'gainst Heaven.

42 Defoe, op. cit., ed. of 1724, ii. p. 52.

43 Goldsmith, op. cit. p 525. Wood, part iv., chap. xii. p 439. The Bath reading-rooms were famous: "We can offer you friendly book sellers, who for five shillings for the season will furnish you with all the new books" (Lady Luxborough, "Letters … to Shenstone," p 296, February 29, 1752). Smollett's Lydia Melford waxes enthusiastic over them: "The booksellers' shops … are charming places of resort, where we read novels, plays, pamphlets, and newspapers for so small a subscription as a crown a quarter; and in these offices (offices of intelligence as my brother calls them) all the reports of the day and all the private transactions of the bath are first entered and discussed" ("Humphry Clinker," L. M. April 26). Another Lydia, she of the Rivals, gets her stock of fashionable novels from them (act i. scene ii.), though they are energetically denounced by her aunt and Sir Anthony (ibid. infra).

44 Materials for a complete history of English costume in the eighteenth century might be gleaned from various local productions, but as the Bath fashions only reflected those of London, it is useless to linger over details that have no special local character.

45 Bath differed in this respect from the other watering-places "I told you in my former letters that Epsom and Tunbridge does not allow visiting, the Companies there only meet on the Walks, but here visits are received and returned" ("A Journey to England," 1722, vol. ii. letter viii. p 127).

46 There were two sets of Assembly Rooms, which were patronised alternately, one built by Harrison in I 708, and enlarged several times, the other opened in 1728 by a certain Thayer. They were called after their successive owners (Harrison, Mrs Hayes, afterwards Lady Hawley, Gyde, Simpson in one case; Thayer, Mrs Lindsay, Wiltshire, in the other). In 1771, the architect Wood built a set of larger and more luxurious rooms in the upper town, and a strong rivalry sprang up between these, known from their position as the Upper Rooms, and Harrison's older structure, the Lower Rooms. These latter gradually declined, and were burned down in 1820.

47 Wood says these assemblies were marked by "a real splendour, perhaps equal to that of the most Brilliant Court of Europe" (part iv., chap. xii. p 443), and Thicknesse pronounces them "one of the most pleasing Sights that the Imagination of Man can conceive; and what we are convinced, no other part of Europe can boast of ..." ("New Prose Guide," pp 36–7). These judgments are no doubt partial, coming as they do from inhabitants of Bath; yet it would hardly have been possible to meet such brilliant society anywhere in England save at Court. A German traveller, who had been present at one of these balls in 1775, begins his description thus: "Ich habe am Montage Abends einen Ball beygewohnt, und bin überzeugt, dass er alles was man von der Art prächtiges sehen kann, weit hinter sich zurucke liess." ("Bemerkungen eines Reisenden," vol. iii. letter lxvi. p 85.)

48 "It is always remarked by Foreigners, that the English Nation, of both Sexes, look as grave when they are dancing, as if they were attending the Solemnity of a Funeral. This Charge is in general true; and ... we strongly recommend the Ladies to remove this Nations Charge, and to consider that the Features and Countenance ought to be in Unison, and as perfectly in Tune with the Body, as the Instruments are which direct its motions. And that that sort of bewitching Look bordering on the Smile, which always accompanies Cheerful Conversation should never be omitted in the Dance ... We are aware that the Ladies think Gravity of Countenance a necessary Attendant on Modesty and Sentiment; but till they can prove that a cheerful pleasing Smile is incompatible with Virtue, Prudence or Discretion, we must beg leave (while we allow them all imaginable Praise for such ill-placed Precaution) to assure them, that they cannot bestow on mortal Man, a more pleasing nor a more innocent Mark of their Public Favour, than by shewing their Features under the Advantage of a Smile," etc. ("New Prose Guide," pp 37–9). It is odd that such counsels were considered necessary.

49 The order of the programme is given by Goldsmith, "Life of Nash," p 522.

50 "About six in the evening all the Company made the best appearance they cou'd at Harrison's room; at seven the ball began, where the most extraordinary thing of all was Betty [her daughter], to make the greatest compliments she cou'd to the day, danced 4 minuets; the first time she trembled and was so out of countenance I thought she would not have been able to go thro' with it; but the second time she performed very well ..." (Lady Bristol to Lord Bristol, May 29, 1723, in the "Hervey Letter-Books," vol. ii. 741). Cf Thicknesse: "How many fine Women do we see totter with Fear, when they are taken out to dance? And is it possible that such who cannot walk firmly should be able to dance gracefully?" (" New Prose Guide," p. 38.)

51 Minuets fell into disfavour towards the end of the century. In 1813 the Master of the Ceremonies, King, vainly attempted to revive them (Nightingale, "Beauties of England and Wales," vol. xiii. p 421).

52 "I cannot fancy that the amusement was especially lively," says Thackeray in "The Virginians," describing a ball at Tunbridge Wells in the eighteenth century (chap. xxvi.). The crabbed Matthew Bramble was naturally of the same mind: "I sat a couple of long hours, half stifled in the midst of a noisome crowd, and could not

help wondering that so many hundreds of those that rank as rational creatures, could find entertainment in seeing a succession of insipid animals describing the same dull figure for a whole evening on an area not much bigger than a tailor's shop-board," etc. ("Humphry Clinker," M. B. May 8). See also Bunbury's later caricatures, "The long Minuet as danced at Bath."

53 The same air was repeated, it would seem, for each minuet:
"Now why should I mention a hundred or more
Who went the same circle as others before
To a tune that they play'd us a hundred times o'er?"
(Anstey, "New Bath Guide," xi. pp. 119–21.)

54 We are reminded of Thacker charming passage touching these old-world airs: "Then after the minuets came country dances, the music being performed by a harp, fiddle and flageolet, perched in a little balcony and thrumming through the evening rather feeble and melancholy tunes. Take up an old book of music, and play a few of those tunes now, and one wonders how people at any time could have found the tunes otherwise than melancholy. And yet they loved and frisked and laughed and courted to that accompaniment. There is scarce one of the airs that has not an amari aliquid, a tang of sadness. Perhaps it is only because they are old and defunct, and their plaintive echoes call out to us from the limbo of the past, where they have been consigned for this century. Perhaps they were gay when they were alive, and our descendants, when they hear—well, never mind names—when they hear the works of certain maestri now popular, will say: 'Bon Dieu, is this the music which amused our forefathers?'" ("The Virginians," xxvi.)

55 For all this preliminary period consult Penley, "The Bath Stage," chaps. i. to iii, and King and Watts, "Municipal Records of Bath," chap. xiii.

56 See Penley, op. cit. chap. iii. pp 11–14, for textual extracts from the registers.

57 It is hardly necessary to explain that companies of actors very commonly bore the name of some prince or nobleman whose patronage they enjoyed.

58 Mr Sidney Lee, following various authorities, assigns the dates 1593, 1597, and 1603 to those itineraries of Shakespeare's tours in the provinces which included Bath ("Life of Shakespeare," chap. iv. p 40 note). It should be noted, however, that it is not absolutely certain that Shakespeare was already a member of the troupe in 1593.

59 Sonnets cliii. and cliv.

60 Penley, op. cit. p 16.

61 *Cf* above, p 16 note.

62 Wood, "Description of Bath," part iv. chap. xii. p 445.

63 Fleming, "Life of … T. Ginnadrake," vol. iii. p 33. Mainwaring, "Annals of Bath," p 37.

64 According to Fleming (op. cit. p 35), the manager. in 1730 was a certain Hornby, an actor. Genest ("Some Account of the English Stage," vol. ii. p 340) mentions a performance of Farquhar's Recruiting Officer in 1708; in 1728 the Beggar's Opera was given (letter from Gay to Swift. March 16, 1728, in Swift's "Works," Bohn's edition, 1864, vol. ii., p 16). It is probable that strolling companies who visited Bath occasionally. The Tatler (no 16, May 17, 1709) mentions one such

which played Alexander the Great (probably Lee's Rival Queens, which bore this sub-title.) We must also remember that Powell brought his famous puppet-show to the city (Tatler, ibid., and nos 44 and 45; cf above, chap. i. p 4). The Bath Journal, which announces dramatic performances, was not founded till 1744, and the (incomplete) collection of this paper, which is preserved at the offices, begins in March 1745.

65 No 16 of the Tatler, quoted above, speaks of two rival ladies, one of whom bespoke a tragedy, the other a performance of marionnettes for the same day. The custom of ordering special performances lasted for a long time (see the Bath Journal, theatrical notices, October 27, 1746, November 30, 1747, October 29, 1750, etc.)

66 "The Countess of Burlington bespoke the play, as you may see by the inclosed original bill; the audience consisted of seventeen souls, of which I made one." (Letter from Chesterfield to Lady Suffolk in "Letters to and from Henrietta, Countess of Suffolk," vol. ii. p 117, October 35, 1734.) A few days later another piece drew a larger audience: "Mrs Hamilton bespoke the play at night, which we all interested ourselves so much to fill, that there was as many people turned back as let in." (November 2, ibid. p 118). In 1721, Lady Bristol wrote to her husband "For plays, there is hardly ever company enough to make it [the house] warm." ("Hervey Letters," September 18, vol. ii. p 647.)

67 This is what Defoe says in 1725: "In the afternoon there is generally a play—though the decorations are mean, and the performance accordingly—but it answers, for the company here make the play, to say no more" ("Tour through Great Britain," vol. ii., letter iii., p 52). The criticism is suppressed in the edition of 1769; in that of 1778, after praising the theatre as "elegant and commodious," he adds that the theatre possesses. "a company of comedians little inferior to those of London" (vol. ii. p 225).

68 In 1738 (Wood, chap. vi. pp 288 and 290).

69 In February and March 1746–1747 (the double date after the first months of the year indicates Old and New Style), a series of performances took place at the Globe (Bath Journal, no of February 25, and the five March numbers). In 1747–1748 another series was held at the George (ibid., nos of February 15, March 7 and April 7).

70 "The present Playhouse, or rather Play Room, is so small and incommodious that tis almost impossible to have things better done in it than they are. The Profits arising from the Performance as now conducted will not support a larger or better company of actors" (address by Hippisley, quoted by Wood, part iv., chap. 3, pp 444–445).

71 Given in another hall in Kingsmead Street (New Theatre), which seems to have remained open a very short time (Bath Journal, February 12, 1749–1750).

72 The dates of these various performances are indicated its the Bath Chronicle in various numbers between 1746 and 1755.

73 About twenty-five in six years.

74 The law of June 24, 1737, forbidding theatrical performances save in a limited number of privileged theatres, does not seem to have been very rigorously applied.

Performances continued to take place at Bath, at any rate, and the new theatre was inaugurated without difficulty (Wood, op. cit. pp 444–5). It was not until 1768 that the law was passed (8 Geo. III. c. 10) which made Bath a theatre royal (the first out of London).

75 Wood, op. cit. p 444.

76 The theatre is often called the Orchard Street Theatre from the street in which it was situated. It is now the Masonic Hall. The other theatre remained open for some years, till Palmer bought out the owners (Derrick, "Letters," vol. ii., letter xxxv., p 169). It had not improve with time. A Frenchman who visited it in November 1750 borrows from it a typical example of the bad acting he deprecates in many English players "You know that I was at Bath eight months ago, when you were here. I have never yet told you how astonished I was to see your little theatre forty feet under the ground. It is quite a pretty little catacomb, though naturally somewhat stunted in its proportions. But when the curtain went up, and the stage began to vomit forth the actors, I was reminded of the band of robbers in Gil Blas' cavern. Their manner of acting did not break the spell, nor even the young actress in male attire who appeared between the two pieces, and recited a complimentary address. There was no lack of silver braid on her grey doublet, though they had been sparing of satin for her pink vest. Everything that the coarsest affectation could invent in the way of offensive grimaces to spoil a pretty face was successfully made use of by the little person; I was never more shocked" (Clement, "Les cinq Années littéraires," vol. iii. p 543).

77 Quoted by Penley, op. cit. p 29.

78 It will be unnecessary therefore to give a detailed list year by year. To judge of the general character of the repertory, it will suffice to note the summary list given in note 4 below, of the pieces played from 1772–1782, a period made memorable by the co-operation of Henderson and Mrs Siddons. A poem of 1753, "The Bath Comedians," passes all the actors then at Bath in review, distributing praise and criticism. Several seem to have been respectable, but none eminent performers.

79 "We have also friendly Othellos, Falstaffs, and Richard the Thirds, and Harlequins, who entertain one daily for half the price of your Garricks, Barrys and Riches" (letter from Lady Luxborough, February 29, 1752, quoted by Kilvert, "Remains," p 97). Of course Shakespeare's plays were given at Bath as in London with strange modifications. In 1802, when, acting on Kemble's advice, the manager of the Bath theatre suppressed a witches' dance that had been introduced in Macbeth, the audience clamorously demanded it, and forced him to re-instate it. It was not finally deleted till 1828 (Genest, vol. vii. pp 596–97).

80 In the incomplete list of pieces given during the season of 1772–1773 in which Henderson first appeared (Genest, vol. v. p 380 et seq.) we find Hamlet (seven times), Macbeth (six times), Much Ado about Nothing (six times), King Lear (four times), Henry IV (three times), Richard II and Twelfth Night. This varied repertory was increased during successive seasons down to 1782 (the date of the departure of Mrs Siddons, who came to the theatre in 1778) by the addition of Othello, The Merry Wives of Windsor, Cymbeline, The Merchant of Venice,

Romeo and Juliet, Measure for Measure and Henry V. (See Genest, vols. v. and vi., passim.)

81 Buckingham (The Rehearsal); Wycherley (The Country Wife and the Plain Dealer); Congreve (Love for Love); Farquhar (The Beaux' Stratagem); Vanbrugh (The Provoked Wife and The Provoked Husband) Steele (The Conscious Lovers).

82 See Genest for a list of the pieces given season by season, taken from playbills and other documents. I have taken all my examples from between 1772 and 1782, but the general character of the repertory remained unchanged till the end of the century, and after.

83 John Palmer, already mentioned, and the son who acted as his assistant. Every year he visited the principal theatres of England to engage new members for his company. His journeys had another and very different result. He had been struck by the slowness and difficulty of postal communications. The service was carried on by a sort of cart with a single horse, which took two days to get from Bath to London, and further, was frequently attacked and robbed by highwaymen, as it carried only its solitary driver. It occurred to Palmer to replace this kind of vehicle by the fast carriages he used for transporting his actors from Bath to. Bristol, in which latter town he also managed the theatre. He proposed mail-coaches, a new system of relays, etc. Addressing himself to the Government, he managed, not without some difficulty, to see Pitt, and won him over to his plan. It was adopted, and Palmer became Superintendent and Comptroller-General of Posts, with a salary of £1500 a year, and a percentage on the profits realised. He was afterwards Member of Parliament for Bath. (See "Ralph Allen, John Palmer and the English Post Office," a pamphlet by Mr Murch.)

84 Davies, "A Genuine Narrative of the Life and Theatrical Trans actions of Mr John Henderson," p 5. Garrick's friendly interest is further attested by the congratulations and counsels he addressed to Henderson after his début ("Correspondence," January 5, 1773, vol. i. p 509), and by another intervention between him and Palmer, for which Henderson returns thanks (ibid. vol. ii. p 15, November, 1774). Garrick also wrote to various persons at Bath on his behalf: "Mr Garrick has done me great services by writing of me to several of his friends here" (Henderson, "Letters," pp 82–3, December 25, 1772). The relations between them cooled towards the beginning of 1775. (See below, p 79, note 94.)

85 Under the name of Courtney, which he soon discarded. "When it was buzzed about in the Rooms, in the walks, and all over the city of Bath, that a new actor was arrived from London under the patronage of the great Roscius, all people of whatever rank were, eager to see the phenomenon. The house was soon filled, and he had the satisfaction to act Hamlet to a very brilliant audience ..." (Davies, "Genuine Narrative," p 7.)

86 See the detailed account of this first performance by a spectator (Ireland), in Henderson, "Letters," etc., pp 67–8. Cf a letter in the Bath Chronicle of October 15, 1772, where the writer pronounces "the character of Hamlet performed inimitably well," and mentions "such showers of deserved applause as hath not been heard these thirty years in the absence of Mr Garrick."

87 Henderson, "Letters," p 87. More than thirty during the same season, says Davies ("Genuine Narrative," p 9).

88 "The continual practice I am in here is of great advantage to me—I once thought it a hardship to be forced upon so many characters. I think so now no longer, being convinced that every part I play, however unsuited to me, does me good. In London it would do me harm for this reason: there are computed to be thirty different audiences in London, here there are but two; and those who see me to a disadvantage one night, see me to an advantage the next." ("Letters," p 141, October 24, 1772.)

89 Negotiations between him and Garrick at the end of 1774 had come to nothing, and differences arose between the two actors (see "Garrick's Correspondence," vol. ii. pp 39–45, letters from Henderson, Taylor and Garrick, January 9 to February 2, 1775).

90 "Henderson excited great attention when he first appeared in London ... In a short time he became so popular and attractive that he excited great jealousy among his theatrical compeers" (Taylor, "Records of my Life," vol. i. chap. xxxi., p 337). "He was, I conceive, the best general actor since the days of Garrick ..." (Ibid. p 381). Cf Genest, vol. v. pp 594–95 for Henderson's début in London. He often came back to act at Bath.

91 "Nature has not been beneficent to him in figure or in face; a prominent forehead, corpulent habit, inactive features, and not a quick eye; nevertheless he has great sensibility, just elocution, a perfect ear, good sense, and the most marking pauses (next to your own) I ever heard; in the latter respect he stands next to you, very near you. His memory is ready to. a surprising degree ... " (Letter from Cumberland to Garrick, not dated, but written probably in 1774; "Garrick's Correspondence," vol. ii. p 366.) Mrs Siddons said of him: "He was a fine actor, with no great personal advantages indeed, but he was the soul of feeling and intelligence" (Campbell, "Life of Mrs Siddons," vol. i. p 82). See also Davies' "A Genuine Account," etc., p. 45, and Genest, vol. vi. pp 403–6.)

92 Genest, loc. cit.

93 Genest, vol. v. p 601. Cf Davies, p. 53, and Taylor, "Records," vol. i. chap. xxxi. pp 377–9.

94 Garrick, who one day heard him mimic Barry, Woodward and Love, contemporary actors, insisted that Henderson should also imitate him, which Henderson did at last with some reluctance, reproducing certain faults of Garrick's so perfectly that the latter was greatly incensed (Henderson, "Letters," pp 101–102).

95 In 1775–1776. For an account of this unfortunate début see Campbell, "Life of Mrs Siddons," chap. ii., and Genest, vol. v. p 96. Was the public at fault? Perhaps, but it is more probable that the young actress did not at once reveal the powers she afterwards manifested. She herself accused Garrick of ill-will towards her. "Instead of doing me common justice ... [he] rather depreciated my talents" (Campbell, loc. cit. p 62).—She was questioned about her transactions with Garrick, and she said, "He did nothing but put her out; that he told her she moved her right hand when it should have been her left. In short, said she, I found I must not shade the tip of his

nose" (Walpole to the Countess of Ossory, December 24, 1782, "Letters," vol. viii. p 320).

96 Campbell, op. cit. vol. i. pp 82–83.

97 ibid. p 78.

98 October 24, 1778. The Bath Chronicle, which had announced her début for the 22nd, does not mention it in the following number. But a performance of *Percy*, (on November 3) drew forth the following compliments: "Mrs Siddons' performance of Elvira, in the tragedy of Percy, has established her, in the judgment of the town, as the most capital actress that has performed here these many years" (no. for November 5).

99 Genest gives the list for the season of 1778–1779 (vol. vi. pp 117–118). There were twenty-three pieces. The season lasted about eight months.

100 It will be remembered that Palmer was manager of the Bristol Theatre too. His company played alternately in the two towns.

101 Campbell, "Life of Mrs Siddons," pp 80–81.

102 "The theatre for some time was sufficiently cool on the nights of its greatest ornament. Tragedy, although the most exalted delight of refined nature, is seldom sought by those who are merely in search of amusement; when a rage is once excited, it is followed not for its object; but its vogue" (Boaden, "Men of Mrs Siddons," chap. ii. p 17). The biographer adds: "Palmer for a considerable time troubled Mrs Siddons only on his Thursday nights, when the Cotillion balls carried off everything that could move to the Rooms; and that eye was frequently bent on vacancy that ere long was to fascinate all ranks and ages of life." The list of performances given by Genest contradicts the first part of this statement.

103 Boaden, ibid. pp 168–69.

104 Cf Genest, vol. vi. pp 203, 234, 235.

105 Taylor to Garrick, January 14, 1779, "Private Correspondence of D. Garrick," vol. ii. p 332.

106 "While at Bath for his health [he] was strongly solicited to go to the play to witness the performance of a young actress who was said to distance all competition in tragedy … He found, to his astonishment, that it was the lady who had made so little impression on him some years before in the Runaway, but who, as Garrick had secretly declared, was possessed of tragic powers sufficient to delight and electrify an audience. There prevailed at that time and long afterwards a very disagreeable clause in the articles of the Bath company, by which they were obliged to perform also at Bristol, and in consequence, by some mistake in their frequent and hurried journeys, the stage clothes of this admired actress were not arrived on the night Mr Sheridan saw her, and she was obliged to perform in one of the dresses she usually wore in private life. But no disadvantage of dress could conceal her transcendental merit from an eye so penetrating as that of Mr Sheridan, and after the play was over he went behind- the scenes to get introduced to her, in order to compliment her … Mr Sheridan said 'I am surprised, Madam, that with such talents you should confine yourself to the country; talents

that would be sure of commanding in London fame and success.' The actress modestly replied that she had already tried London, but without the success that had been anticipated; and that she was advised by her friends to be content with the fame and profit she obtained at Bath, particularly as her voice was deemed unequal to the extent of a London theatre. Immediately on his return to London he spoke to the acting-manager of Drury Lane, strenuously recommending her to him." (Miss Lefanu, "Memoirs of the Life and Writings of Mrs F. Sheridan," chap. xi. pp 380–382.)

107 "Memoranda," quoted by Campbell, "Life of Mrs Siddons," p 89.

108 Address, quoted at length by Penley, "The Bath Stage," p 62.

109 See on this subject, Russell, "Representative Actors," pp 225–234.

110 Genest, vol. vi. pp 252–253.

111 Campbell, "Life of Mrs Siddons," vol, ii. p 337.

112 Mrs A. Kennard gives several instances in her "Mrs Siddons," pp 156–157.

113 Boswell, "Life of Johnson," 1783, vol. iv. p 172.

114 1799, 1801, 1807, 1808.

115 The younger Palmer gave up the management in 1785 on account of his official occupations, and handed it over to two partners, Keasberry and Dimond.

116 Appeared at Bath first on January 31, 1788, and went on to Covent Garden the same year.

117 First appeared at Bath April 14, 1791. He afterwards belonged to the theatre from 1793 to 1804.

118 First appeared at Bath in 1814 and 1815.

119 " ... The judgment of a Bath audience was regarded as a pretty sure presage of the decision of the metropolis" (Macready, "Reminiscences," vol. i. p 91).

120 "The Bath audience had long maintained the character of being the most elegant and judicious in the kingdom; and the 'School' which gradual formed under their influence and the exertions of Mr Palmer obtained the pre-eminence in the eyes of the Dramatic Tyro and the London critic. It is well known that for many years, the very name of Bath was a guarantee for a man's good taste in his profession; while on the score of genius, it is acknowledged to have contributed more largely to the metropolitan boards than Dublin and York put together" (Bernard, "Retrospections" vol. i. p 34). The writer refers to the time when Henderson was playing at Bath. Genest again, writing in '8 when the theatre had lost a good deal of its prestige, says : "Bath has long been considered as a nursery for the London theatres—the managers of course get all the performers who have distinguished them selves on the Bath stage" ("Some Account of the English Stage," vol. vii. p 565). Not only actors but dramatists courted the suffrages of Bath. Even after the brilliant success of The School for Scandal at Drury Lane, we find Sheridan coming to superintend the rehearsals of his piece at Bath, and spending a fortnight in arranging the preliminaries As the actor Bernard, who gives us all these details, very justly remarks: "This was no slight compliment to the judgment of the Bath audience, who were to conform or cavil at the verdict passed upon the merits of his composition in London.' Mary

Linley, writing an account of the first performance of the Rival, at Bath to her sister, Mrs Sheridan, says: "I waited the success of Sheridan's play at Bath; for let me tell you, I look upon our theatrical tribunal, though not in quantity, in quality as good as yours," etc. (letter quoted by Moore, in "Memoirs of Sheridan," vol. i. chap. iii. pp 139–40).

121 Genest, passim. Penley, "The Bath Stage," chapters xv. and following.

122 Penley, *ibid.*

IV

Society in Bath

At balls and theatres, in the baths and the Pump Room, on the Parades and at the gaming-tables, the same company re-assembled on appointed days and at fixed hours, a very numerous company,[1] which included nearly every visitor to the town. Throughout the reign of Nash it may be said that there was but a single society at Bath. Cliques, coteries, and private circles seem scarcely to have existed, or at any rate to have been reduced to a minimum; a transient equality and familiarity reigned, bringing together persons of widely different callings and conditions.[2]

Unique, but heterogeneous and varied, this society reveals the chief elements in its composition at a glance: the aristocracy of the kingdom, which was the nucleus, the classes immediately below this, eager to imitate their superiors, and, as far as possible, to mix with them; the mere pleasure-seekers, the curious, and then the motley tribe that lived, honestly or otherwise, at the expense of the other groups. The mixture was strange enough; even in the early years of the century an anonymous writer notes with amusement the assembly of "Quality, and Reverend Doctors of both Professions, Topping Merchants, Broken Bankers, Noted Mercers, Inns of Court Rakes, City Beaus, Stray'd Prentices, and Dancing-Masters in Abundance"[3] Seventy years later one of Smollett's characters adds to the list "ministers of State, judges, generals, bishops, projectors, philosophers, wits, poets, players, chemists, fiddlers and buffoons."[4]

This is a pretty comprehensive summary, applied only to the one sex, but, as we shall see in the course of our study, it is far from complete. To fill in the picture, let us hear the evidence of a Frenchman, given between the two dates: "We shall find there," says the Abbé Prévost; "at all times, Beauties of all ages who come to show off their charms, young Girls and Widows in quest of Husbands, married Women who seek Solace for the unpleasant Ones they possess, Players making or becoming dupes, Musicians, Dancers, Actors, growing rich on the pleasure for which others pay, and sharing it with them; finally, Dealers, in all kinds of Jewels, delicacies, and gallantries, taking advantage of a kind of enchantment which blinds every one in these realms of enjoyment, to sell for their weight in gold trifles one is ashamed of having bought after leaving the place."[5]

The only persons lacking in this gallery, as in the others, are the invalids; or at least, if these appear, "they have none of those illnesses which spoil enjoyment." "They are much deceived,", says another French traveller,[6] "who think that the waters of Bath are like those of Bourbon, where only infirm, paralytic or valetudinarian persons are to be found. On the contrary, this is the place in all England to enjoy good health, and to turn it to account."[7]

Among people so well inclined to make a good use of their time a general gaiety naturally prevailed, and, above all, a freedom of intercourse and a familiarity which surprised strangers coming from the capital, where every one was so grave, cold and reserved. "Taking all things into consideration, the charms of the place are surpassed by that of the society, for it is difficult to imagine anything more agreeable than the easy and familiar mode of life that everyone adopts."[8] Good manners and a decent coat were the essentials, and with these a stranger was at liberty to accost any one he chose, and might count upon a civil reception.[9] Even the ladies were no longer "reserved and inaccessible, but gentle and easy in their intercourse with strangers … A party of Englishwomen taking tea is generally a rather dull assembly. The most gallant of men are shy of presenting themselves to such a company. They speak very little, unless slander loosens their tongues. At Bath, on the contrary, the Tea-Parties are extremely gay."[10]

There was universal good-humour, sociability, and apparent forgetfulness of rank, and station, for it was an understood thing that no temporary familiarity was to have any sequel, that it was to end with the visit to the wells, and that, once back in London or in their respective counties, the friends of a season would become strangers to each other again.[11] Scott's reflections of a century later already applied to these resorts "The society of such places is regulated by their very nature, upon a scheme much more indulgent than that which rules the world of fashion, and the narrow circles of rank in the metropolis. The titles of birth, rank or fortune are received at a watering-place without any very strict investigation, as adequate to the purpose for which they are preferred: and as the situation infers certain degree of intimacy and sociability for the time, so to whatever height it may have been carried, it is not understood to imply any duration beyond the length of the season. No intimacy can be supposed to be more close for the time, and more transitory in its endurance, than that which is attached to a- watering-place acquaintance."[12]

The royal family itself did not disdain to mingle in this varied company. If the successors of Queen Anne did not follow her example and come themselves to the waters, the Princess Amelia, daughter of George II, passed some time there in 1728, and again in 1752.[13] It was to her that Nash refused another dance after the prescribed hour, a decree to which she submitted with a very good grace. The Prince of Orange came also (in 1734), and was no less condescending; Nash, delighted with the present of a snuff-box made him by the Prince, responded by having an obelisk set up commemorating his visit.[14] Four years later a second obelisk was raised in honour of a visit from the Prince and Princess of Wales, and for this Pope was called upon to write an inscription.[15] These august persons were not the last royal visitors; others of equal rank succeeded them throughout the whole century, and at the beginning of the next.[16]

Lord Chesterfield
From the portrait by William Hoares

The English nobility, who had contributed so much to the vogue of the city of Bladud, remained even more faithful to her. The newspapers of the town, the local publications of all kinds, the private correspondence of the day dated from the city, are studded with the famous names of the British aristocracy. The arrival of great persons is announced, their words and actions, often of no great importance, are chronicled. All the Peerage, with very few exceptions, passes before us; in default of other evidences, the numerous escutcheons carved on the stone of the Bath houses would have sufficed to preserve the memory of the great families who inhabited them.[17] It would be idle to attempt to enumerate them all, but we. have already encountered some of these persons of quality; and others will present themselves in due course. The rest we must pass over, save one or two who have a special claim to our attention.

Lord Chesterfield takes a prominent place among these and Bath had no more constant and assiduous guest. Strange to say, political reasons first attracted him to the town. In 1737 the opponents of the Ministry had chosen Bath as a rendezvous and centre of operations.[18] They turned to account the visit of the, heir to the throne, whose first child had just been born. "An event so interesting to the nation afforded a favourable opportunity of assembling his friends, and concealing business under the appearances of festivity and joy. The royal and much beloved pair received the homage of the numerous concourse of people of every rank, who flocked thither to make use of a liberty they were restrained from in the capital.[19] Sumptuous entertainments were given by the Corporation, under the direction of the famous Nash. Lord Chesterfield did the honours of the place, and his servants were employed to attend."[20]

Was the conspiracy a very formidable one? Be this as it may, it was ineffectual, and Walpole, who had withstood more redoubtable attacks, remained in office. The provisional seat of operations pleased Chesterfield, however, and from this time forward he rarely failed to pay one or more visits to Bath in the course of the year. A great deal of his correspondence is dated from Bath, notably a number of the famous letters to his son.[21] He gives but few details of the life he is leading, dwelling mainly on subjects of general interest, or on his health, which he was trying to re-establish with the help of the waters. But we may be sure that such a lover of good company and of social pleasures found himself in a thoroughly congenial atmosphere at Bath. We find him amusing himself at the Assembly Rooms,[22] and attending Lady Huntingdon's Methodist Chapel out of curiosity;[23] interesting himself in the foundation of a hospital;[24] joking with Nash, patronising him,[25] and turning an epigram on him the while;[26] and losing at play with unscrupulous adversaries.[27] Far from being "biffé de la société"[28] ("blotted out from society") on account of his deafness, as he declared he was, he evidently retained a brilliant place therein, and in his old age the younger generations modelled themselves upon him, as a perfect type of the politeness, the fine manners, and the wit of the past.[29]

Horace Walpole, the son of the Minister against whom Chesterfield conspired at Bath, spent three months in the town in 1766. It seems to have given him very little pleas and he spent his time regretting his dear Strawberry Hill. The waters were good for his health, but nothing else found favour in his eyes, neither the mountains which her "run against one's nose,"[30] so that one "cannot stir out of the town without clambering"; nor the new buildings, "that … look like a collection of little hospitals";[31] nor the old, which are "detestable"; nor the public rooms, which he avoids, or if he ventures into them pronounces "insupportable."[32] "These watering-places," he cries, "that mimic a capital, and add vulgarisms and familiarities of their own seem to me like Abigails in cast gowns, and I am not young enough to take up with either."[33] He also found himself obliged to return to society, of which he professed himself weary, all London having transported itself from the banks of the Thames to those of the Avon. "We have all kind of folk here—Lord Chatham, the Chancellor [Lord Camden], the Dowager Chancellor [Lord Northington], Lady Rockingham, Lady Scarborough, Lord and Lady Powis, Lord and Lady Spencer, judges, bishops, and Lady Vane."[34] At last Walpole can bear it 'no longer'; he declares that "three months in a fair seems to me a century," and flies, even at the risk of having to come, again.[35]

Walpole mentions several politicians. Among them there were three who had more than a mere passing connection with the town. The former Chancellor, Lord Northington,[36] had been for many years one of the dandies of the Assembly Rooms, and one of the frequenters of the Bear.[37] He was afterwards Recorder of the town and from 1747 to 1757 he represented it in Parliament. Lord Camden[38] had also been Recorder of Bath before becoming Attorney-General. But the proudest boast of Bath from the political point of view was that it had been represented in Parliament by the elder Pitt (afterwards Lord Chatham). Very popular at Bath, which he often visited,[39] he was on terms of close friendship with an influential person of whom we shall have more to say later on—Ralph Allen[40] in 1757 the freedom of the city was conferred upon him.[41] The same year, having resigned his seat at Okehampton, he offered himself as a candidate at Bath,[42] was unanimously elected,[43] and in 1761 re-elected under similar conditions.

Two years later, however, an incident took place which made the relations between the distinguished statesman and his constituents less cordial. In 1763, Pitt opposed the peace with Spain, declaring that the conditions proposed were unsatisfactory. The Municipality of Bath, on the other hand, sent the King an address of congratulation upon the peace, certain awkwardly chosen expressions in which seemed to convey a pointed contradiction to the terms used by Pitt on the subject. Letters were exchanged between the member and Allen, chairman of the Town Council, slightly haughty on the one hand, courteous but firm on the other, in which each maintained his opinion. Pitt kept his seat three years longer, till he was created Earl of Chatham; but he sold his house at Bath that same year, and his further relations with Allen and his colleagues were very much colder than formerly.[44] The visits paid to Bath at different times by other politicians of various degrees of celebrity, Marlborough,[45] Bolingbroke, Peterborough, Wilkes, Burke, the younger Pitt,[46] or warriors such as Clive,[47] Wolfe, and, later on, Nelson, call for no special remark. They serve, however, to justify Thackeray's statement that "scarce a character one can mention of the early last century but was seen in that famous Pump Room where Beau Nash presided." Religious reformers like the Wesleys and their disciples, artists like Gainsborough, Lawrence, and the Woods, and above all a host of writers, demand more detailed attention for what they brought to Bath, and what they took thence, the influence they exercised on this special centre, the impression they received and translated for us. They must be considered apart and in detail. But before returning to them, we will finish the rapid review we are making of this motley throng, in which certain more or less curious groups are still conspicuous.

The most ancient, the only one which existed before the fashionable days of Bath, though the vogue of the city had, of course, tended to increase its numbers and importance, was naturally the medical group. A watering place, the rallying point of sufferers, real and imaginary, necessarily attracts those who profess to heal. At an early date their number was legion; so much so that even in 1709 Steele jestingly demanded that the authorities should not allow more than two to each patient in the town.[48] One of them, Guidott, writing in 1725, found even then eighteen contemporaries or immediate predecessors notable enough to warrant his giving their biographies; and among these eighteen several were persons of some celebrity, while several had been attracted from a considerable distance by the British springs: a Dr Jorden (d. 1598), who had studied at Padua; a Dr Bave, of Cologne; a Dr Maplet, principal of a college at Oxford; a Sir Edward Greaves, afterwards physician in ordinary to Charles II, and others.[49] These doctors had the best houses in Bath, and several of them received their patients as boarders; one of them, called Peirce, complacently describes the facilities his house afforded for visiting the baths.[50] It was he who received the Court of Charles II.[51] In addition to these members of the Royal College, there was, of course, a goodly array of quacks; the same Guidott mentions a certain Seneschall who acquired a swift notoriety by two devices, the practice of alchemy, and the wearing of a fur coat in the height of summer.[52] May we trust Steele's account of the eagerness of these various healers to secure patients? "The physicians here," he says, "are very numerous, but very good-natured. To these charitable gentlemen I owe that I was cured in a week's time, of more distemper than I ever had in my life; they had almost killed me with their humanity. A learned fellow lodger presented me a little something at my first coming, to keep up my spirits; and the next morning I was so much enlivened by another, as to have an order to bleed for my fever. I was proffered a cure for the scurvy by a third, and had a recipe for the dropsy gratis before night. In vain did I modestly decline these favours, for I was awakened early in the morning by an apothecary, who brought me a dose from one of my well-wishers. I paid him, but withal told him severely that I never took physic. My landlord hereupon took me for an Italian merchant that suspected poison; but the apothecary, with more sagacity, guessed that I was certainly a physician myself."[53]

The gentle Steele's satire is harmless enough. But another writer, Smollett, who was also a doctor,[54] treats his brethren more savagely. Taking the hero of one of his novels to Bath, he brings him into contact with "a class of animals who live in this place, like so many ravens hovering round a carcass, and even ply for employment like scullers at Hungerford Stairs. The greatest part of them have correspondents in London, who make it their business to inquire into the history, character and distemper of every one that repairs to Bath for the benefit of the waters; and if they cannot procure interest to recommend their medical friends to these patients before they set out, they at least furnish them with a previous account of what they could collect, that their correspondents may use this intelligence for their own advantage. By these means, and the assistance of flattery and assurance, they often insinuate themselves into the acquaintance of strangers, and, by consulting their dispositions, become necessary and subservient to their prevailing passions. By their acquaintance with apothecaries and nurses, they are informed of all the private occurrences in each family, and are therefore enabled to gratify the rancour of malice, amuse the spleen of peevish indisposition, and entertain the eagerness of impertinent curiosity."[55]

The Bath AEsculapius is certainly painted in very lurid colours here. But we must not accept Smollett's statements quite implicitly. Not only was he a writer who believed humanity to consist mainly of the rogues he was fond of describing, but it is very possible that in this case he was satisfying some personal grudge. There is a very plausible tradition to the effect that Smollett thought of settling at Bath to practise, but that he failed to attract patients; he would not have forgiven his successful rivals.[56] He did not see, or, at any rate, he did not show us, side by side with the contemptible charlatans, learned and honourable practitioners such as Moysey, for instance, for whom Chesterfield shows so much affection and esteem in his correspondence;[57] Hartley,[58] a man of great originality and penetration, whose "Observations on Man" suggesting novel solutions for various psychological and metaphysical problems, were long famous; and Oliver, the correspondent of Pope;[59] Cheyne, of whom Pope declared that there lived no honester man nor truer philosopher,[60] and later, Henry Harington and Edward Falconer, whose professional skill was equalled by their wide culture and lofty character.[61] Giving little occasion for ill-natured remarks, and showing themselves to be hardly distinguishable from the best of their *confrères* in London, these doctors and others of the same class were passed over by the satirists. But we need not pity the invalids of Bath too deeply; it would be a waste of sympathy. If they occasionally became the prey of the "ravens," of whom Smollett writes with such indignation, it was by no means of necessity, but through their own folly or imprudence.

The occasional visitor had perhaps more difficulty in defending himself against certain other birds of prey more formidable than these charlatans, that swarm of rascals of every kind, professional gamesters, "knights of industry," and miscellaneous adventurers, to whom the fashionable watering-places afforded a magnificent field for their operations, and who came from the four quarters of the horizon to swoop down upon a wealthy society, constantly renewed, easily accessible, and offering spoils no less abundant than easy of capture.

The professional gamesters formed the main body of this army. Hamilton notes their existence even in the time of Charles II,[62] and each year saw them return at an appointed season[63] often, in confederate bands. As time went on, they multiplied and became more assiduous. What, indeed, was Nash himself in his early days but one of them? He never, in fact, ceased to be of the confraternity, for all his life long he practised their trade, a profitable calling, subject to few fluctuations in a town where the passion for play was general, and where, to quote Mrs Montagu, the only questions one ever heard were, in the morning, "How d'ye do?" and in the after noon, "What is trumps?"[64]

The gambling mania was by no means peculiar to the watering-places, though the general idleness of these resorts of course fostered it. It spread from London,

Catherine Hyde, Duchess of Queensberry
From the portrait by Charles Jervas

where it never raged more furiously than during the first fifty or sixty years of the eighteenth century. It was already general under the Restoration, and, growing steadily, it reached its apogee under the first two Georges. This was the time of the heyday of White's famous Chocolate House, and of all the lesser gambling-houses which suddenly sprang up round it.[65] Of these metropolitan hells, the Assembly Rooms of Bath and Tunbridge at once became annexes, frequented with a like assiduity by a *clientèle* that was largely identical. The place occupied by dice and cards in the. daily life of Bath at this period is almost incredible. Goldsmith, in his "Life of Nash," gives us an idea of it which is amply confirmed by contemporary letters, journals, and other documents.[66] What endless references they contain to good or bad luck at lansquenet or faro, to persons suddenly ruined or enriched, to successful or detected swindlers! Throughout the century, but above all during the first half of it, gambling went on at Bath as in London, that is to say, immoderately and incessantly. Unscrupulously, too, we are bound to add. "Nor shall I speak dishonourably of some little artifice and finesse used upon these occasions; since the world is so just to any man who is become a possessor of wealth, as not to respect him the less for the methods he took to come by it."[67] Novices are charitably warned that "those who love Play must understand it in a superlative degree, if they expect to gain anything by it at Bath, where there are always ingenious Men, who live by their great Talents for Play; for however great an Adept a man may think himself at the Games of Whist, Billiards, etc., he will always find Men, and Women too, here, who are greater, and who make it a Rule to divide the many Thousands lost every year at Bath among themselves only ..." [68] Good advice, no doubt, but no more effectual than the efforts and counsels of Nash,[69] or the daily spectacle of ruined victims.[70] In all that was written at Bath or upon Bath, nothing is of more frequent occurrence than allusions to dishonest players, or even more, or less circumstantial accounts of their exploits.[71] As these exploits were very monotonous, the anecdotes dealing with them are uninteresting and not worth recording.[72] Sometimes, however, we catch a glimpse of some brutal and even murderous quarrel as the sequel to the discovery of a cheat. For instance, a certain detected trickster was thrown out of a first-floor window by his victims;[73] another had his hand pinned to the table by a fork, his adversary remarking coldly: " Sir, if you have not a card hidden under that hand, I apologise."[74] Duels arising out of the same causes were also frequent, in spite of all Nash's endeavours to avert them.[75] Most of those, the records of which have come down to us, were fatal to one or the other of the adversaries.[76] Gambling was also the direct cause of suicide in many cases;[77] one that stands out tragically from he rest was that of the daughter of General Braddock,[78] the "Sylvia" whose sad story was told by Wood and by Goldsmith.[79] Young, beautiful, virtuous, remarkable for her qualities both of mind and heart, the fortune bequeathed her by her father made her the object of the most horrible machinations. Hemmed in on every side by intrigue, the fatal passion was gradually instilled into her, till, stripped of her last penny, she hanged herself in despair.

The passion of women for play (they were quite as eager as the men) was not always such a tragic spectacle; but the depth and extent of the evil are apparent enough even in the ironical banter of a Steele, for instance, on the subject of the fair gamblers of Bath: "I must own that I receive great pleasure in seeing my pretty countrywomen engaged in an amusement which puts them upon producing so many virtues. Hereby they acquire such a boldness as raises them near the lordly creature man. Here they are taught such contempt of wealth as may dilate their minds, and prevent many curtain lectures. Their natural tenderness is a weakness here easily unlearned, and I find my soul exalted when I see a lady sacrifice the fortune of her children with as little concern as a Spartan or a Roman dame ... But I am satisfied that the gamester ladies have surmounted the little vanities of showing their beauty, which they so far neglect as to throw their features into violent distortions, and wear away their lilies and roses in tedious watching and restless lucubrations ... It is to me an undoubted argument of their ease of conscience that they go directly from church to the gaming-table; and so highly reverence play as to make it a great part of their exercise on Sundays."[80] When in "The Virginians" Thackeray shows us Madame de Bernstein, formerly Beatrix Esmond, and the group surrounding her at Tunbridge, creatures who, like herself, seem to have but two pleasures and two occupations in life, gambling and scandal-mongering, he does not paint mere fancy figures, but the types of a real and numerous class. But the majority of those who composed it did not wait, like Beatrix, till they had grown old before confining their interests to the calumnies of the Pump Room or the emotions called forth by cards and dice. Round Harrison's and Dame Lindsey's tables all ages assembled, as well as all sexes and all professions.

There are other ways of losing one's money, and not one's money only. These were all practised at Bath, where they had been introduced by adventurers of various kinds. If we are to credit Smollett, these generally operated in confederate gangs. He makes some one explain to his Peregrine Pickle, that "there was at London one great company of adventurers who employed agents in all the different branches of imposition throughout the whole kingdom of England, allowing these ministers a certain proportion of the profits accruing from their industry and skill, and reserving the greatest share for the benefit of the common stock, which was charge able with the expense of fitting out individuals in their various pursuits, as well as with the loss, sustained in the course of their adventures. Some, whose persons and qualifications are by the company judged adequate to the task, exert their talents in making love to ladies of for tune, being accommodated with money and accoutrements for that purpose after having given their bonds, payable to one or other of the directors, on the day of marriage, for certain sums proportioned to the dowries they are to receive.[81] Others, versed in the doctrine of chances and certain secret expedients, frequent all those places where games of hazard are allowed; and such as are masters in the arts of billiards, tennis, and bowls, are continually lying in wait in all the scenes of these diversions, for the ignorant and unwary. A fourth class attend horse-races, being skilled in those mysterious practices by which the knowing ones are duped."[82]

The Comforts of Bath
From a drawing by Rowlandson

The picture might be supplemented from the pages of the same writer and of others by the addition of other types—persons, for instance, who fix themselves upon rich old men and extort from them wills in their own favour by flattery or threats,[83] and those again who traded upon the vices of their fellows in various fashions, blackmailing among the rest.[84] But this would be beyond our purpose. Such practices are common to all ages and all countries, as are the wretches who indulge in them. It was only natural that the latter should have been very numerous, and the former very prevalent, in places so favourable to their growth as Bath or Tunbridge in the eighteenth century.

In addition to these industries, that of the fortune-hunters in pursuit of dowries seems to have been one of the most flourishing. It is significant that Fielding, Smollett, and Anstey all send one of their least estimable characters to Bath in search of a wife.[85] The other sex was not behindhand, and furnished adventuresses in quest of husbands, like Defoe's Moll Flanders; occasionally, impostors were themselves imposed upon.[86] But all the candidates for matrimony were not of this despicable order. As Bath was the town of all others in England where "young Ladies ... have the best opportunity to improve and shew their Persons to advantage, as well as to have their prudent conduct observed,"[87] marriages were arranged and carried out there,[88] sometimes preceded by the romantic episode of an elopement.[89] The observations of a French traveller upon Tunbridge are even more applicable to Bath: "Mothers take care to make their daughters appear to the greatest advantage there, with all the luxury of dress and ornament within their means, and even beyond them. The young men on their side are very well dressed, and do their utmost to outshine each other; and all this sometimes with intent to deceive on one side or the other, if not, as sometimes happens, on both."[90] It is to one of these Bath marriages that the world owes the birth of Lord Byron: his father, a widower in quest of an heiress who would enable him to pay his debts, met Miss Gordon of Gight, the owner of £23,000, at Bath. He married her in 1785, and she became the mother of the poet.[91]

To intrigue, gallantry and moral, licence the watering. places were even more favourable than to marriage. No where in England were manners so dissolute, or liaisons so easily formed, nowhere was vice so public or so unblushing. At the very genesis of the summer gatherings in these resorts (in 1663), the French Ambassador, Cominges, declares that they might be christened "the Waters of Scandal."[92] "Never," says Hamilton, "did Love behold his Empire so flourishing as here. Those who had been attacked by him before coming hither felt their ardour redoubled, and those who seemed the least inclined to the passion lost all their austerity, and became different, beings." The stories he goes on to relate of Prince Robert, Miss Hughes and Lady Muskerry bear out hi assertion. The French Academician, Pavillon, also observes that

Ces Eaux portent au Cœur de si douces vapeurs
Qu'une belle en buvant, presque sans qu'elle y pense
Guérit en un moment de toutes ses rigueurs
Et le galant de sa souffrance.[93]

The foregoing passages refer to Tunbridge Wells, and were written before the fashionable supremacy of Bath was established, but the same society frequented the two towns and led the same life in each.[94] We have seen that Charles II and his Court passed from one to the other, halting in London only to "rest and renew their strength."[95] It is very certain that they did not reform on the road. Rochester and Durfey chose it, the one as the scene of a ribald tale,[96] the other as that of a licentious comedy.[97] An anonymous author, writing in 1700, says that the town is as "eminent for wickedness as London, bating its magnitude"; coming thither from London is a plunge "out of the frying-pan into the fire."[98] This the writer proceeds to show by taking his hero on the Parades, and causing him to hear scandalous and very dull stories, about all the persons he meets there.[99]

Nash succeeded in introducing a little decorum into the society he governed, in making it show a little more regard for appearances. It was probably all he desired, and he would have been ill-advised to pose as a reformer. At any rate, he did not prevent certain sections of the community from indulging their usual habits during the greater part of the century. Loose women,[100] ladies of doubtful reputation,[101] procurers and procuresses,[102] the profligate of both sexes throng as heretofore to the convenient rendezvous, where, as a local writer ironically remarks, "no pleasures sully and no freedoms stain."[103] Young men even came here to take a course, as it were, in profligacy, like that 'prentice Don Juan described in the *Spectator*,[104] who, after practising in accordance with a carefully drawn up programme at Astrop, Bury, Epsom, Scarborough and Tunbridge (all watering-places, as we see), considers a season at Bath the last training necessary before approaching London. "It is here that successful libertines come from all quarters to establish their reputations;"[105] and if Smollett gives a true picture of things in "Peregrine Pickle," they had no difficulty in so doing.[106] The idea of corruption seemed to be naturally associated with the name of Bath. Perhaps one of the most significant evidences of this is the announcement Goldsmith thought it necessary to prefix to his "Life of Nash." Being about to describe the famous watering-place to his readers, he warns them at once that his work "is neither calculated to inflame the reader's passions with descriptions of gallantry, nor to gratify his malevolence with details of scandal." These were evidently expected from any book which dealt with life at Bath. But Goldsmith declared it his intention to pass over "the amours of coxcombs and the pursuits of debauchees"; one of his hero's merits was that "he practised but few of those vices he was often obliged to assent to," and that "though he lived where gallantry was the capital pursuit, he was never known to favour it by his example."

These are strong expressions, and they agree with the evidences to be gleaned elsewhere. But without any desire to attenuate their import, I may observe that they probably applied' only to a limited section of the temporary population. If Bath had really been the sink of iniquity they would lead us to suppose, the excellent persons we have seen there, and others we shall presently meet, would never have visited, and, above all, revisited the town; they would have turned away from it in disgust. The very suspicion of contagion would have kept away or put to flight the respectable county families who were regular visitors to the town. Finally, the letters and memoirs in which Bath is so constantly mentioned would be filled, if not with indignant denunciation at least with scandalous anecdotes and allusions. But, on the contrary, these are conspicuous by their absence,[107] nor is local literature more explicit in this respect.[108] May we conclude, with a contemporary, that, appearances were a good deal worse than facts, and that the evil behind them was really inconsiderable?[109] We will not go quite so far as this, but we may not unreasonably conclude that moralists, novelists and observers, without actually perverting truth, neglected those aspects thereof which appealed but slightly to their indulgent or indignant curiosity. Though corruption may have been more public, more insolent and more leniently regarded here than elsewhere, it cannot have been general, even at the beginning of the eighteenth century. The pictures drawn by the Bath comedies and novels in the second half suggest that it had sensibly decreased here, as, perhaps, throughout England. This is certainly the impression produced, not only by Mrs Sheridan's "Journey to Bath," and her gifted son's Rivals, but even by Smollett's "Humphry Clinker," as compared with his "Roderick Random" or "Peregrine Pickle," while Miss Austen's novels give it in a much higher degree.[110] But with these we reach and even overstep the threshold of the nineteenth century; it was just the period when Bath was losing its distinctive characteristics. We are bound to admit, even if we accept all extenuating pleas, that morality was not one of them.

Frivolity was, however, one, and one of the most strongly marked. To be convinced of this, we have but to study the thousands of short pieces, madrigals, epigrams, pamphlets and miscellanies which echo the daily life and conversation, inane and empty trifles, valueless in proportion to the slightness of the intellectual effort that produced them.[111] They make it evident that in these places of amusement, only trifles were of interest; every serious subject was banished from Pump Room and Parades, and reserved for other times than the Bath season.

A certain amount of reading was nevertheless indulged in. There were reading-rooms which provided newspapers and new books. Here the men met to discuss the latest political intelligence, or the little incidents of the day.[112] In the Rivals (act i. scene ii.), Lydia's maid brings from one of these libraries novels by Smollett and Sterne, the "Memoirs of a Lady of Quality,"[113] and other works now forgotten.[114] Lydia, hearing her aunt approaching, hides the volumes, replacing them by more serious works. We see then that novels were popular at Bath; even French ones were not unknown; those of Crébillon *fils,* at any rate.[115] But it is probable that, outside the small group of famous men who gathered round Ralph Allen,[116] and the curious coterie over which Lady Miller presided,[117] there was little desire for literary or scientific knowledge, and little interest in higher subjects generally.[118] "I think," says Mrs Montagu in 1740, "one may live here at as small expense of wit as in any place I ever was in in my life, and by all rules of economy, the disbursement bearing proportion to the receivings, one ought to lay out very little."[119]

Mrs Montagu does not tell us what it was that took the place of wit or ideas in conversation, but one can easily imagine; long commentaries upon the trifles of the day or hour, conventional phrases, compliments, scandal. Occasionally, some tragic adventure, some duel, suicide, or abduction occurred opportunely, and kept tongues wagging for days together. Or some little difference would arise between two fractions of society, and in this assembly of persons without a real occupation of any kind, roused excitements and emotions out of all proportion to their cause. One at least of these differences, the most violent on record, must be briefly reported, not because of its importance, which was nil, but because it clearly shows the native brutality that lay beneath the surface of an apparently polished, and highly disciplined community.

The quarrel broke out in 1769, on the death of Nash's second successor. The next heir of the King of Bath had been one Collett, an amiable person, an accomplished dancer, and an opponent of games of chance. He was not, however, a very successful ruler, and he resigned his office at the end of two years.[120] Derrick, an Irishman of good family and of some literary pretensions,[121] was elected to succeed him, thanks to the influence of a certain lord and two or three ladies,[122] but having omitted a name in the invitation to some festivity,[123] and having further incurred ridicule for his diminutive stature,[124] a violent campaign was organised against him, in which Quin, the actor, took a leading part.[125] Superseded for a time by a Frenchman,[126] he was reinstated in his office after a reconciliation with Quin. But at his death, five years later, war broke out afresh, and more violently than before in his kingdom.

The Comforts of Bath
From a drawing by Rowlandson

As soon, in fact, as Derrick fell ill, two parties had been formed to lay claim to his inheritance. The one supported the candidature of a certain Major Brereton, who had acted as Vice-President during Derrick's illness; the other wished to appoint Plomer, the manager of the balls at Bristol.[127] Circulars at once began to fly about, pamphlets to pass from hand to hand, attacks and retorts to be exchanged, meetings to be held. As the election was made by the subscribers to the balls and entertainments, Plomer's friends hastily beat up seventy recruits, and caused them to appear on the lists at the Assembly Rooms. Brereton's adherents protested against this proceeding; then, in alarm, offered Plomer money to desist. A third rascal, Jones,[128] hoping to get the post, appealed to the Lord Chamberlain as the only person who had a right to appoint a superintendent of public amusements. Meanwhile, Derrick died, upon which Brereton's supporters held a meeting the very same day, and declared their candidate duly elected; their opponents held a meeting in their turn, and proceeded to elect and proclaim Plomer. The whole town was divided into hostile camps. Then began a fresh shower of addresses, broadsheets, pamphlets, epigrams, and even poems, some serious, some violent and scurrilous, some ironical.[129] But the contest was not carried on solely by such means; arguments and broadsheets were reinforced by fisticuffs. When Plomer made an attempt to appear in the Assembly Rooms, one of his adversaries pulled him out by the nose. A fortnight after this beginning of hostilities, the great encounter took place. The two parties, men and women, assembled in force in the rooms. A friend of Plomer's rose to speak; his voice was drowned in hisses and shouts; altercations raged from one end of the place to the other; abuse was followed by blows, whereupon a general engagement followed, in which the women were well to the fore, tearing each other's dresses, laces, and hair.[130] The uproar was only quelled by the arrival of the Mayor with the officers of justice, and even then he had to read the Riot Act three times.

It seems probable that the combatants felt somewhat ashamed of their prowess, for the affair ended here. Passions cooled; the two candidates were persuaded to withdraw for a consideration, and a certain Captain Wade was elected by common agreement.[131] A few years later, however, Brereton obtained the post once so hotly contested; but other Assembly Rooms had just been opened in the Upper Town,[132] with another Master of the Ceremonies; and a rivalry of a less martial kind sprang up between the Upper and Lower Rooms, which lasted till the decline and closure of the latter in 1820.[133] A much more romantic affair occupied all Bath in 1772; but this deserves to be related at some length, not only because of the idea it gives of the society of the day, but above all because the hero of the story was one of England's great writers and great orators, Richard Brinsley Sheridan.

1 Eight thousand families (persons?) at a time, we are told, even in 1722 ("A Journey through England," vol. ii., letter viii. p 127); nearly seven thousand persons, writes Lady Bristol on September 16, 1723, adding on the 23rd of the same month "Our company increases daily" ("Hervey Letters," vol. ii. pp 330 and 337). Forty years later, it was computed that the town could lodge about 12,000 strangers (Wood, vol. ii. p 351).

2 A certain trace of exclusiveness makes its appearance now and again, nevertheless. Fielding writes as follows "Though the people of quality at that time lived separate from the rest of the company and excluded them from all their parties, Mr Fitzpatrick found means to gain admittance ("Tom Jones," xi. 4; Bath is the scene of the narrative). Such statements are rare; and even in this instance the novelist makes his adventurer find his way without much difficulty, into the circle he describes as exclusive. Derrick wrote in 1762: "There is no place in the world where a person may introduce himself to the first people in Europe as in the rooms at Bath" ("Letters," xxxi. p 5).

3 "A Step to the Bath," p 14.

4 Humphry Clinker," Jeremy Melford, April 30.

5 "Pour et Contre," no. 38, pp 173–4 (1734). The whole number is given up to a description of the English watering-places, "perhaps of all places in the world those in which pleasures are most lavishly multiplied and continue with least interruption." The Abbé Prévost gives Bristol, Bath, Tunbridge, Scarborough, Epsom, Acton and Islington as almost equally famous, merely remarking that the waters of Bath alone are drunk in all seasons. But as early as 1745 another French traveller, the Abbé Le Blanc, returning from the waters of Bath, says he did not go to "those of Scarboroug (sic), Tunbridge, or Epsom, because they are no longer fashionable, and if one goes to drink the waters without being ill, one should at least choose those where one is sure of finding the best company."—"Lettres d'un François," lxxxviii., vol. iii. p 309.

6 "Pour et Contre," loc. cit.

7 "Lettres d'un François," loc. cit. p 310.

8 "Pour et Contre," loc. cit. p. 174.

9 "Here [at Tunbridge] you have all the Liberty of Conversation in the World, any Person that looks like a Gentleman, has an agreeable Address, and behaves with Decency and Good Manners, may single o whom he pleases, that does not appear engaged, and may talk, rally, be merry and say. any decent thing to them" ("The Foreigner's Guide," 4th ed. 1763, p 210).

10 Lettres d'un François," lxxxviii., vol. iii. pp. 312–3. "Their tea," he adds, "is made with arrack, lemon and sugar. This is what they call Arrack Tea, and is known everywhere else as Punch." Writing to Crébillon the younger, the Abbé Le Blanc goes on to discuss at some length the special dispositions of English ladies at Bath "They are indeed different beings here and in London, and that which causes this remarkable difference is the wearisome uniformity of their ordinary life. In the first place, as Women they seek compensation here in a month of liberty for the constraint and melancholy imposed upon them by the yoke of habit during the rest of the year in the capital. Manners may differ, but the Sex is everywhere the same. Women like to enjoy their rights, and if they are deprived of these by the injustice or the caprice of Men, by fashion or by prejudice, they make use of every means at their command to recapture them at the first opportunity ; even in' the countries where they are treated as slaves, they discover how to rule their masters. Secondly, the women of this country have an additional reason for wishing to make use of their liberty. Their melancholy temperament, which often restrains them from pleasure, must make them more keenly alive to it when they once give themselves up to it. A coquette yields herself readily to it when ever it presents itself, and perhaps enjoys it less for this very reason. For an Englishwoman, it is a deliberate and important matter. A visit to Bath is very probably the result of six months of intrigue and consideration. The fair patient has had to feign illness, to win over the servants, to corrupt the doctor, to persuade an aunt, to deceive a husband, in a word to resort to all sorts of artifices to succeed. She naturally seeks compensation for all the trouble she has taken. Pleasure is the more attractive to Englishwomen, that it is unfamiliar to them, and that it costs them a good deal. The melancholy feel joy more intensely than those to whom it is habitual." (Ibid.)

11 "A maxim … universally prevails among the English people, namely, to overlook and wholly neglect on their return to the metropolis all the connections they may have chanced to acquire during their residence at any of the medical wells; and this social disposition is so scrupulously maintained, that two persons who lived in the most intimate correspondence at Bath or Tunbridge shall, in four and twenty hours, so totally forget their friendship as to meet in St James' Park without betraying the least token of recognition; so that one would imagine those mineral waters were so many streams issuing from the river Lethe, so famed of old for washing out all traces of memory and recollection." (Smollett, "Adventures of Ferdinand Count Fathom," chap. li. vol. ii. p 142. Cf on this point Prévost, "Pour et Contre," no. 38, p 175, note; the "Foreigner's Guide," p 210 ; Le Blanc, "Lettres d'un François," lxxxviii., vol. ii. pp 315–6.)

12 "St Ronan's Well," Introduction.

13 She returned shortly before her death (1786).

14 Goldsmith, "Life of Nash," p 542.

15 He refused at first, but yielding to Nash's solicitations, sent him the following inscription, desiring him not to reveal the author: "In memory of honour and benefit conferred on this city by His Royal Highness Frederick, Prince of Wales, and His Royal Spouse, in the year 1738, this Obelisk is erected by Richard Nash, Esq." As Goldsmith observes, "there was scarce a Common Councilman in the Corporation of Bath but could have done this as well." (See Goldsmith's "Life of Nash," p 543, where Pope's two letters are given).

16 Princess Mary, fourth daughter of George II, and Princess Caroline, daughter of the Prince of Wales (1740); the Duke of York, brother of George Ill (1761); the Duke of York, son of George III, and his Duchess (1795); the Prince of Wales, afterwards George IV (1796); the Duke of Gloucester, nephew of George III (1807), etc.

17 See Peach, "Historic Houses in Bath."

18 "As the next parliamentary campaign was likely to be an active one, a place of meeting was appointed by the anti-Ministerial party for mustering their forces, and settling their plan of operation. Bath was the spot fixed upon for that purpose, and a more convenient one could not have been chosen. This elegant town much resembles the Bajae of the luxurious Romans. Like that, it is distinguished by its waters, its magnificence and its pleasures. It is there that twice a year health, diversions, politics and play, attract what is called the best company" (Chesterfield, "Miscellaneous Writings," i. p 88, Memoir). This, it seems, was not the first time Bath had been the seat of political intrigue; or, at least, so the following passage in Pope's correspondence seems to indicate: "We expect better company here next week, and then a certain Earl [Oxford?] shall know what ladies drink his health every day since his disgrace, that you may be in the public pamphlets as well as your humble servant. They say here are cabals held, under pretence of drinking waters." (Letter of October 6, 1714, to Theresa and Martha Blount, "Works," ed. Elwin and Courthope, vol. iv. p 252).

19 An order enjoining persons who frequented the Prince Court to abstain from attendance at St. James' had been more rigorously enforced at the beginning of 1738 ("Memoir," loc. cit. note).

20 "Memoir," loc. cit.

21 See Chesterfield, "Miscellaneous Works," vol. i. and ii., and "Letters written by the Earl of Chesterfield to his Son." The obituary notices of Montesquieu and Fontenelle which he sent to the London Evening Post in 1755 and 1756 are also dated from Bath ("Miscellaneous Works," vol. i. p 273, note. The pagination of the volume is double).

22 Chesterfield, says a local poet, in a 1772:
Vouchsafes each night these brilliant scenes to grace,
Augments, and shares the pleasures of the place:
Admires the fair, enjoys the sprightly ball,
Deigns to be pleas'd, and therefore pleases all.
(Bath Chronicle, June 28, 1772.)

23 See below, chap. vi Lady Gertrude Hotham, Lord Chesterfield's sister, was a fervent Methodist.

24 In 1738. He was one of the first governors, and figures in this capacity, in an ordinance of 1741, between Allen and Nash (Wood, chap. vi p 299).

25 The author of the little work called "The Jests of Beau Nash" dedicates it to Chesterfield in these terms: "You, my Lord, was ever the Patron and Friend of Mr Nash, whose lively Sallies of Imagination are here offer'd to public Inspection. You have often been diverted by his wit; and have often excited that wit in him, which, like a Diamond in the mine, might have been hid in Obscurity, had not the sun of your genius, by enlightning the Object, called forth its Lustre.—Nash, therefore, though brilliant, was only the secondary Planet in the Sphere; and whatever you think of his Wit, you ought at least to approve of your own" (pp 2–3).

26 See above, pp 40. Chesterfield also patronised Nash's successor, Derrick (see the letters addressed by him to the latter on February 6 and March 17, 1767 ("Letters," Bradshaw ed., vol. iii. pp 1354–55 and 1358–59). He signs himself playfully: "Your faithful and loyal subject."

27 "While England and France are at war, and Mr Fox and Mr Pitt going to war, his lordship [Chesterfield] is coolly amusing himself at picquet at Bath with a Moravian Baron who would be in prison if his creditors did not occasionally release him to play with and cheat my Lord Chesterfield, as the only chance, they have for recovering their money" ("Letters of Horace Walpole," vol. ii. p 480, March 29, 1755). Lord Chesterfield was asked one day why he preferred playing with sharpers to gentlemen. "Why," says he, "if I play with sharpers and win, I am sure to be paid; but if I win of gentlemen, they frequently behave so genteelly, that I get nothing, but words and polite apologies for my money" (Fleming, " Life … of J. Ginnadrake," vol. iii. p 66).

28 "Je suis revenu des Bains tout aussi sourd que j'y suis allé; je n'ai plus d'espérance et me voice biffé pour toujours de la société." (" Miscellaneous Works," vol. ii. p 205, letter lxix., December 28, 1752. The pagination of the volume is double. As is well known, many of Chesterfield's letters are written in French.)

29 They were, at any rate, advised to do so by the author of the poetic eulogy quoted above (p 100, note 22), which concludes thus:
Hence, tho' unequal now the taste to hit,
Learn what was once politeness, ease and wit.
Cf the charming picture of Chesterfield at Tunbridge drawn by Thackeray in "The Virginians."

30 Walpole to G. Montagu, October 18, 1796, "Letters," vol. v. p 17.

31 "All crammed together, and surrounded with perpendicular hills that have no beauty. Oh! how unlike my lovely Thames!" (H. W. to H. S. Conway, October 2, 1766, ibid. p 13.)

32 "The elements certainly agree with me, but I shun the gnomes and salamanders, and have not once been to the Rooms … All my comfort is, that I lodge close to the Cross Bath, by which means I avoid the Pump Room and all its Works" (H. W. to G. Montagu, October 5, 1766, ibid. p 54). "I have not yet been at ball-rooms, or pump-rooms; I steal my glass at the Cross Bath" (H. W. to the Countess of Suffolk, October

6, 1766, ibid. p 15). "The public rooms and the loo, where we play in a circle like the hazard on 'Twelfth Night, are insupportable" (H. W. to H. S. Conway, October 18, 1766, ibid. p. 17).

33 H.W. to G. Montagu, October 6, 1766, ibid. pp 14–15.

34 H.W. to the Countess of Suffolk, October 6, 1766, ibid. p.15 … Lady Vane, the sorry heroine of the "Memoirs of a Lady of Quality," inserted in "Peregrine Pickle," was notorious for her unseemly conduct. Walpole mentions other visitors of note in another letter (to H. S. Conway, ibid. pp 13–14), among others, the Duke of Bedford, so fiercely attacked by Junius.

35 H.W. to G. Montagu, October 18, 1766, ibid. p 17.

36 Before his elevation to the peerage he was known as Robert Henley, and was a barrister by profession. His father, Anthony Henley, was the friend of Swift, Pope and Arbuthnot. See Lord Henley's "Life of the Earl of Northington," and Lord Campbell's "Lives of the Chancellors."

37 The Bear was one of the most fashionable inns at Bath. The works quoted in the note above relate that the youthful Robert Henley fell in love at Bath with young girl who had become lame after a long illness, and had come to the waters for her health. These worked wonders; the lady hung up her crutches as a votive offering in the baths, and the young couple became man and wife.

38 Also a barrister, Charles Pratt, before his elevation to the Peerage.

39 Many of his letters to his nephew, Thomas Pitt, afterwards Lord Camelford, are dated from Bath (October 12, 1751; January 12, 1754, etc.). He took the waters for the gout, to which he was a martyr (Letters … to … Lord Camelford, March 30, 1754).

40 See below, chap. ix.

41 The freedom of the city having been sent to him in a golden casket, Horace Walpole wrote the following somewhat commonplace quatrain on the subject:
To the NYMPH OF BATH.
Mistaken Nymph, thy gifts withhold,
Pitt's virtuous soul despises gold
Grant him thy boon peculiar, health
He'll guard, not covet, Britain's wealth.

42 Bath sent two members to Parliament. One of the two seats had become vacant by the appointment of Henley to the post of Keeper of the Seals.

43 The very limited electorate was composed of the Mayor, the Aldermen, and the Common Council; Ralph Allen's influence predominated.

44 For a detailed account of this difference see below, chap. ix.

45 In September, 1716 (letter of the Duchess of Marlborough to Lady Cowper in the journal of the latter, Appendix E, p 197).

46 In 1802 and 1805. It was during this second visit that he received the news of the Battle of Austerlitz, which, as is commonly known, overwhelmed him to a degree that probably hastened his death. It surprised him during a visit he was paying to Shockerwick, near Bath, at the house of Mr Wiltshire, the friend of Gainsborough. In 1860, Mr John Wiltshire, son of the above, who had witnessed the episode, gave the following account of it to the Rev. B. W. L. Davies: "A very remarkable incident

occurred to me once, when as a boy, and in the absence of my father, I was showing that picture [Gainsborough's portrait of Quin] to a gentleman, who, as I soon discovered, was no less a man than Mr Pitt, the distinguished statesman, and at that time Prime Minister of England. He was looking intently at the picture through the hollow of his two hands; when suddenly a sound caught his ear—it was that of a horse galloping furiously up the gravel road leading to the house. 'That must be a courier,' he said eagerly, 'with news for me!' and almost immediately a man, booted and spurred, and splashed from head to foot, entered the room and handed his despatches to the Minister, still standing before the picture. Tearing them open, he became intensely agitated, and exclaimed: 'Heavy news indeed! do get me some brandy!' On which I rushed out, and brought in the brandy myself; and can at this moment well remember the little water he added to the spirit, as he tossed off a tumblerful at a gulp; he then took another, and I believe if he had not done so, he would have fainted on the spot. The Battle of Austerlitz had been fought and won by Buonaparte … The disappointment overwhelmed him; it was more than he could bear, and in less than two months from that date he sank under the weight of it." (Peach, "Historic Houses," ii. p 13.) Mr Meehan's "Famous Houses of Bath," caricature of Pitt, by Mary Cruikshank, representing him ill and feeble, probably dates from this same period. Pitt died January 23, 1806, about seven weeks after the battle (December 2, 1805).

47 "Colonel Clive, the Nabob-Maker [is not that almost as great a title as the famous Earl of Warwick's?], lives at Westgate House with all the Clives about him … He lives in little pomp, moderate in his table, and still more so in equipage and retinue" (Mrs Scott to Mrs E. Montagu, 1762, in Doran's "Lady of the Last Century," chap. iv. pp 114–115).

48 "Letters have been sent to Mr Bickerstaff, relating to the present state of the town of Bath, wherein the people of that place have desired him to call home the physicians. All gentlemen therefore of that profession are hereby directed to return forthwith to their places of practice; and the stage-coaches are required to take them in before other passengers, till there shall be a certificate signed by the Mayor, or Mr Powell [the puppet showman], that there are but two doctors to one patient left in town" (Tatler, no 78, October 8). We see from this that during the season doctors were in the habit of leaving their usual residences to practise at Bath.

49 Guidott, "The Lives and Characters of the Physicians of Bath," the third part of A Discourse of the Bath."

50 Peirce, "Bath Memoirs," Preface, 14th page (they are not numbered), and chap. ii. p 24.

51 Ibid. book ii., chap. i. p 257. " … His Majesty and Queen Katherine, in 1663 (whose Court was then at my House, the Abby, in Bath)."

52 Guidott, p 199.

53 The Guardian, no. 174, September 30, 1713; cf also The Tatler, of October 6, 1709.

54 The degree of Doctor of Medicine was conferred on Smollett in 1750 by the Marischal College of Aberdeen.

55 "Peregrine," chap. lxx. Smollett is hardly better disposed towards his London brethren. He accuses them also of combining with apothecaries, nurses and

servants, and of dividing the profits of this association (see a long passage in "Ferdinand, Count Fathom," chap. lii.). Other satires on the physicians of Bath, less bitter in character, are to be found in "Diseases of Bath," p 58, and in Anstey, "New Bath Guide," letter ii.

56 He wrote an "Essay on the External Use of Water," dealing with the Bath waters. As to his intention of practising in the town, this is what his latest biographer says "That he ever did try to obtain a practice at Bath is hardly more than mere matter of guess work. He was certainly very fond of the town ; he introduces it into all three of his first novels, and went back to it in his last. The medical life of the place, and in particular its quackery, had an endless attraction for him, but his descriptions are enough to account for his failure as a doctor." (Hannay, "Life of Smollett," chap. i. p 112.)

57 See the numerous letters addressed to him and the terms in which he is mentioned ("Miscellaneous Works," passim).

58 His "Observations on Man, his Frame, his Duty, and his Expectations" (1743), was reprinted in 1775 (by Priestley), with certain omissions, and again in full in 1790. It was twice translated into French, by the Abbé Jurain (Rheims, 1775), and by Sicard (Paris, 1802). Hartley was the friend of Pope, Butler, Warburton, and Young. Later, Coleridge felt such reverence for his memory that he named his son after him. In one of his early poems, he ranks him with Milton, Newton, and Priestley ("Religious Musings," 11. 268–271).

59 Pope, "Works," ed. Elwin and Courthope, vol. x. pp 242–245.

60 "I am glad you found the benefit I promised myself you would from Dr Cheyne's care, to whom pray make my heartiest services. There lives not an honester man nor a truer philosopher" (Pope to Gerrard, May 17, 1740. "Works," ed. Elwin and Courthope vol. vii. p 342). "Dr. Cheyne … is yet so very a child in true simplicity of heart that I love him as he loves Don Quixote, for the most moral and reasoning madman in the world" (Pope to Lyttelton, December 12 [1736], ibid. vol. viii. p 172). Goldsmith merely speaks of him as "a man of some wit and breeding." ("Life of Nash," p 554 of the Globe edition; and for further details see "Dr. Cheyne's Account of himself and of his writings faithfully extracted from his various works.") He was no less famous for his whimsical humour than for his extreme corpulence. This he reduced by a vegetable diet, which furnished a confrère, Dr. Wynter, with a theme for some satirical verses, calling forth a retort from Cheyne. Both pieces are given in R. Warner, "Original Letters," in which Cheyne's correspondence with Richardson, the novelist, also appears.

61 See Murch, "The Bath Physicians of former Times," and Freeman, "Thermal Waters of Bath," for these doctors and several others.

62 See above, chap. i. p 20.

63 Their advent was duly announced: "Mr Nash talks of several gamesters that are coming this week" (Lady Bristol to her husband, August, 1721, "Hervey Letters," vol. ii. p 176). "Several of the deep gamesters arrived" (ibid. September 13 , p. 194). See also nos. 64, 65 and 68 of the Tatler (September 1709), as well as Smollett, in passages quoted below.

64 "Letters," p 72, December 27, 1740.

65 "The passion for gambling, which had been very prevalent since the Restoration, appears to have attained its climax under the first two Georges … It had long been inveterate among the upper classes, and it soon rose to an unprecedented height. The chief, or at least the most prominent centre, was White's Chocolate House … it was, however, only the most prominent among many similar establishments which sprang up around Charing Cross, Leicester Fields, and Golden Square … At Bath, which was then the centre of English fashion, it reigned supreme; and the physicians even recommended it to their patients as a form of distraction … Among fashionable ladies the passion was quite as strong as among men, and the professor of whist and quadrille became a regular attendant at their levées …" (Lecky, "History of England," vol. ii. chap. v. p 156). Cf ibid. vol. vii. chap. xxi. pp 194–195; also Thackeray, "The Four Georges" (George II), and Ashton, "History of Gambling in England," chap. iii. to vi.

66 See the letters of Lady Bristol, who was not herself very much addicted to play ("Hervey Letters," vol. ii., letters of August 12 and 16, and of September 13, 18 and 20, 1721); the Tatler of September 8, 1709 (no. 65); the Guardian of September 30, 1713 (no. 174); and, above all, a long article in the London Magazine, vol. vi. p 68 (December 1737): "Nothing is to be seen but Play, and the Preparations for it. Persons of all Characters and Denominations sit down to Cards from Morning to Night and Night to Morning," etc. The evidence of various contemporary spectators has been or will presently be quoted. Purely local literature would furnish additional testimony ad infinitum. The second edition of the "Tour thro' Great Britain" (1748) says, that gambling had obtained at Bath "to a scandalous degree," but that recent legislation had checked it to some extent (vol. ii. p 289). The spectacle, however, seems to have changed very little, judging from Anstey ("New Bath Guide," 1766, letter viii.), or still later writers ("Bath Anecdotes and Characters by the Genius Loci"), 1782; see pp 39–41. It is significant that in each of the two first plays in which the action takes place at Bath, there is a scene between players in a gaming-house. (Durfey, The Bath, act iv. scene i.; Odingsells, The Bath Unmasked, act i. scene ii.).

67 Guardian, no. 174, September 30, 1713.

68 Thicknesse, "A Prose Guide," p 82.

69 Goldsmith, "Life of Nash," p 26.

70 Nevertheless, suspicion was easily awakened. "A surprising run of luck in a gamester is often mistaken for somewhat else by persons who are not over zealous believers in the divinity of fortune. I have known a stranger at Bath, who hath happened fortunately (I might almost say unfortunately) to have four by honours in his hand almost every time he dealt for a whole evening, shunned universally by the whole company the next day" (Fielding, "Amelia," chap. v.; the author is speaking in his own person).

71 See, among other texts, those already referred to on p 97, note I, (Tatler, Sept. 8, 1709; Goldsmith's " Life of Nash," pp 526–530 and 560–565. Smollett, "Peregrine Pickle," chapters lxviii. lxix.; Anstey, "New Bath Guide," letter viii.)

72 The longest series of these is perhaps to be found in the "Bath Anecdotes and Characters by the Genius Loci," pp 35–45.

73 "Memoirs of the Life and Writings of Samuel Foote," p 49. The incident prompted one of Foote's witticisms. "The Baron [the detected cheat] meeting Foote some time after, was loudly complaining of this usage, and asked what he should do. "Do?" says the wit, "why it is a plain case; never play so high again as long as you live!"

74 "Bath Anecdotes and Characters," pp 42–43. The hero, or rather, the victim of the adventure (a certain Newman), committed suicide at Bath in 1789; there is a fairly long notice of him in the Gentleman's Magazine of that year (pp 1053–1054).

75 "Whenever ... Nash heard of a challenge given or accepted, he instantly had both parties arrested" (Goldsmith, "Life of Nash," p 523).

76 "A duel that has been fought lately, between one Jones, a gamester, and one Mr Price (a gentleman's son, but of the same profession too), has put us in great confusion. Price is kill'd and Jones has made his escape (Letter from Lord Orrery to Lady Kaye, "Historical MSS Commission," Eleventh Report, v. p 327). Goldsmith gives other instances ("Life of Nash," pp 523, 563, 566, the last from Nash's papers). A later encounter that made a great sensation was that in which a French adventurer, the Vicomte de Barré, was killed in 1778 by his accomplice, Rice, who had challenged him for some reason never explained (Bath Chronicle, November 26, 1778; cf also Bernard, "Retrospections," vol. i. chap. ii. pp 35–36).

77 See Nash's letters, as quoted by Goldsmith, "Life of Nash," pp 564, 566.

78 The name appears in the Gentleman's Magazine of September, 1731, and there can be no doubt as to the correctness of the identification.

79 Wood, "Description of Bath," chap. xii. pp 446–452; Goldsmith, "Life of Nash," pp 533–536. The accounts in the Gentleman's Magazine (September, 1732, the same month in which the suicide took place), and Modern Amours, pp 25–22 (1733), followed closely upon the event.

80 Guardian, no. 174, September 30, 1713. Cf a long passage of Anstey's written fifty years later ("New Bath Guide," letter viii. 47–96). Gambling was not confined to the Assembly Rooms: "The company is so complaisant to me that they play where I please," writes Lady Bristol ("Hervey Letters," vol. ii. p 200, September 8, 1721). In 1716, we find a Duchess playing publicly in the open air: "Her Grace of Shrewsbury is here ... She plays at Ombre upon the Walks that she may be sure to have Company enough." (Letter from the Duchess of Marlborough to Lady Cowper, September 3, quoted in the journal of the latter, Appendix E, p 597.)

81 An instance of such bargains is given in "Roderick Random": "If that be the case," said Banter, "perhaps you won't care to mortify your self a little in making your fortune another way. I have a relation who is to set out for Bath next week, with an only daughter, who, being sickly and decrepit, intends to drink the waters for the recovery of her health. Her father, who was a rich Turkey merchant, died about a year ago, and left her, with a fortune of £20,000, under the sole management of her mother, who is my kinswoman. I would have put in for the place myself, but there is a breach at present between the old woman and me ... As they are both utter strangers to life, it is a thousand to one that the girl will be picked up by some scoundrel or other at Bath, if I don't provide for her otherwise. You are a well looking, fellow, Random, and can behave as demurely as a Quaker. Now if you will give me an obligation

for £500, to be paid six months after your marriage, I will put you in a method of carrying her in spite of all opposition.'This proposal was too advantageous for me to be refused.The writing was immediately drawn up and executed, and Banter, giving me notice of the time when and the stage-coach in which they were to set out, I bespoke a place in the same conveyance" ("Roderick Random," chap. liii.).

82 "Peregrine Pickle," chap. lxviii.

83 "It is not, however, the games of cards, dice, billiards, etc., alone, by which mc may be ruined at Bath; we have here also some virtuous beings, who play one great game only, and that is to fix themselves upon some weak or unwary rich old man, to secure to themselves his whole fortune. By flattery or falsehood, they possess themselves of' his secrets by threats and knavery, of his estates when he dies. "If a young wife or an adopted child stands in the way, the very actions which youth and innocence naturally lead the honest, unsuspicious, often the best-hearted women into, are construed into vices of the deepest dye.The most wicked insinuations are thrown. out, under the specious appearance of friendship; and when the subject is prepared to receive the various matter, it is poured forth with such torrents, that the contagion spreads far and wide; the domestic happiness of whole families is disturbed, to give place, and fortune, to these hellish gamblers,, who by one infernal coup de main break through the bonds of all faith, honour and honesty" ("New Prose Guide," pp 83–84).

84 "Peregrine Pickle," loc. cit.

85 Mr Fitzpatrick ("Tom Jones," xi. Roderick Random, and Captain Cormorant ("New Bath Guide").

86 *Cf* in the "Bath, Bristol, Tunbridge and Epsom Miscellany," the piece entitled The Bath Fortune Hunter, or, The Biter Bit.

87 "New Prose Guide," introduction, pp. vi.-vii. Johnson writes in the same strain to Mrs Thrale "Bath is a good place for the initiation of a young Lady. She can neither become negligent for want of observers, as in the country; nor by the imagination that she is concealed in the crowd, as in London" ("Letters," ed. Birkbeck Hill, vol. ii. p 160). We may complete these suggestions by the testimony of foreigners "At all seasons we find here Beauties of all ages who come to display their charms, young Girls and Widows in search of Husbands." (Prévost, "Pour et Contre," no. 38.) "When a young Widow or an elderly Dowager desire to burn incense afresh on the altars of Hymen, it is here they come to sacrifice to the God" ("Lettres d'un François" vol. iii. p 312).

88 Less frequently, however, than might have been expected "Considering numbers, instances of marriages are very rare. Here people are so continually employed in trifles, that they hardly have a moment to spare on serious thought. Dissipation prevents real impressions of friendship or love" (Sutherland, "Attempts," part ii. p 124).

89 The Bath newspapers occasionally contain items of this sort: "The honourable Mrs, daughter of Lady Mrs, set off from her house near the city in a post-chaise and four with Mr L, a young gentleman, of good family and fortune in Dorsetshire" (Bath Chronicle, September 9, 1773). In extreme cases, violence was used, as we learn from the following strange apologies, taken from the same journal "Whereas we, the under-named, being Chairmen in the City of Bath, were unhappily engaged in a

violent and unlawful attempt to carry away Mrs Elizabeth Gibbon out of her own house about eleven on the night of the and of this instant March, against her will and consent: And whereas upon complaint made of the same to the Worshipful the Mayor and Justice of the City aforesaid, they have been pleased at the request of the said Mrs Gibbon to remit the punishment due to so great an offence, on condition of our making an acknowledgment and asking pardon for the same in the public papers of the said City, in order to deter and to prevent others from being concerned in such like violation of personal rights and the public peace, we therefore etc." ... The signatures follow (no. of May I 9, 1772). Cf the abduction of Miss Linley. by Sheridan, described in chap. v. below. In Sheridan's own play, The Rivals, his heroine Lydia is inconsolable at the idea of being married without a preliminary abduction. We know how frequently novelists turned adventures of this kind to account.

90 De B. (Moreau de Brazey), "Guide d'Angleterre," letter v. p 90. As late as 1845 Mrs Stone calls these watering-places "licensed and acknowledged marts for men and matrimony," and after having noted as one of the causes of their popularity the opportunities, real or supposed, that they offer for match-making, she adds: "To this day many a belle disappointed at the London season looks forward with renovated hope to the autumn one; many a hard-up lordling casts scrutinising glances over the lists of arrivals at the fashionable watering-places, etc' ("Chronicles of Fashion," vol. ii. pp 272–73).

91 Sir Leslie Stephen says in his article on Byron in the "Dictionary of National Biography" that the meeting took place at Bath. Moore only states that the marriage took place there, to the best of his belief ("Life of Byron," vol. i. p 8), and that it was purely a speculation on the part of the husband (ibid. p 7). This was not the only connection of Byron's family with Bath; in 1780 Miss Burney met there Mrs Byron, the wife of the admiral, and grandmother of the poet ("Diary," vol. i. p 169 of the Ward edition).

92 See Cominges' letter quoted above, p 20, note 3.

93 "OEuvres," letter 157, to Madame de Pélissor. Cf the rest of the letter, which bears no date, but was written between 1679 and 1694.

94 Epsom was no better. Cf the scandalous little story called "Merry News from Epsom Wells," which concludes thus: "He that loves his life, Let him keep his wife From drinking Epsom water."

95 Letter of the Comte de Cominges, August 1663, in Jusserand's "A French Ambassador," p 27. Cf "Mémoires de Grammont, xiii."

96 "Bath Intrigues," where the town is described as follows:
There is a Place adown a gloomy Vale
Where burden'd Nature lays her nasty Tail;
Ten thousand Pilgrims thither do resort
For Ease, Disease, for Lechery and Sport.—(ll. 39–42.)

97 The Bath, or the Western Lass. *Cf* below, chap. vii.

98 ("A Step to the Bath," pp 8–9). "In a word 'tis a Valley of Pleasure, yet a Sink of Iniquity; Nor is there any Intrigues or Debauch acted at London, but is Mimick'd there" (ibid. p 16).

99 *Ibid.* p 13 et seq. Cf "Bath Intrigues" (1725), a collection of similar anecdotes.

100 *Cf* Odingsells, The Bath Unmask'd, see following note, and "A Journey to Bath." We find a qualifying testimony, however, in 1722 "Common women are not to be met with here, so much as at Tunbridge and Epsom. Whether it's the Distance from London, or that the gentlemen fly at the highest game, I can't tell; besides everything that passes here is known in the Walks, and the Characters of Persons" ("A Journey Through England," letter xiii. p 132). But later on the establishment of such persons at Bath seems to have become proverbial. In "Tom Jones," Partridge, witnessing the arrival of Sophia Western and her maid at the inn at Upton, exclaims; "I warrant neither of them are a bit better than they should be, a couple of Bath trulls, I'll answer for them" ("Tom Jones," x. 5). Chantreau is still more explicit in 1788: "There are more loose women in the spring; there are in fact hardly any in London, except such as walk the streets, who have not been to Bath at least four or five times in their lives. There are some who go every year, etc." ("Voyage dans les trois Royaumes," vol. iii., chap. xi. p 229). Cf also these lines of De Quincey's, written about 1834, but referring to the end of the eighteenth century: "Never was there a baser insinuation … than that passage in some lampoon of Lord Byron's, where, by way of vengeance on Mr Southey … he described both him and Coleridge as having married 'two milliners from Bath.' Everybody knows what is meant to be conveyed in that expression, etc." (De Quincey, "S. T. Coleridge," vol. ii. of "Collected Writings," p 157).

101 "PANDER. As for Ladies—we have of all Degrees, as their several Interests draw 'em hither. Those of the first Rank—

"SPRIGHTLY. Who have too much Honour to keep an honourable Vow.

"PANDER. That's your own Comment—I say, who understand the Use of Nature better than to be confin'd to conjugal Constancy, improve their talents by private Intercourse; Coquettes enlarge their Conquests; Prudes indulge in a Corner, and are demure in Publick (though thanks to spreading Libertinism, that Class decreases daily); Profess'd Ladies of Pleasure find Cullies in Abundance," etc. (Odingsells, The Bath Unmask'd, i., sc. ii. p 6).

Cf these verses by a local poet:

Here roving Scandal has its regal Seat,
And Pride and Arrogance supports its State.
Curtzana here, that Spunge of filthy Lust,
Struts in a Sack, and thinks herself August.
Here that Wretch, who has Infamy outdone,
Who I view with Terror and with Caution shun,
So great's the power of Wealth, at Rooms and Ball
Gives Tea, makes Parties, and outbrazens all.
Judge then how low the Ebb of Wit and Sense,
How absent soft Politeness must be hence;
How Virtue blooms, and merit gains Applause,
How harmless Innncence supports its Cause.
Alas! Prophane's the Thought, to have it here
Here's none but thinks its Character severe.

Virtue's a Bubble, which only Husbands tool,
And who is Innocent, must be a Fool.
("Bath Miscellany," 1741, p 13.)

No one is likely to have demurred when, in 1766, the notorious Lady Vane opened the ball at the Assembly Rooms (Walpole to the Countess of Suffolk, October 6).

102 One of these is apostrophised by the author of "Drawings from Living Models taken at Bath," p 10 *et seq.* (1725). The author, who addresses her as Corinna, denounces her thus:

Sins not thy own, but caused by the;
Virgins of innocence despoiled,
By thy seductive arts beguiled;
Wives to adult couch convey'd,
At thy Circean feasts betray'd;
Victims unspotted e'en in thought
Till by thy impious maxims taught,
Till thou their passions didst inflame,
By means the Muse would blush to blame, etc.

103 "A Journey to Bath and Bristol," pp 19–21, in a tirade which fairly sums up this equivocal aspect of life at Bath.

104 The article is by Steele, who certainly had no very lofty idea of Bath morality. See also another article by him (*Guardian,* no. 174).

105 "Lettres d'un François," lxxxviii. vol. iii. p 312. The author adds: "He who has attracted much attention in the autumn at Bath will infallibly make a sensation in London the following winter. He excites the curiosity of Duchesses, and is the observed of all the women of the Court."

106 See the adventures of Peregrine and his companion at Bath, as set forth in chap. lxx. of the novel, and cf with chap. vii. below.

107 No doubt I may have overlooked some of these memoirs and letters, but the silence of the very large number I have examined seems to me remarkable.

108 It is true that some of this has disappeared, but in the portion that survives, the allusions to the reigning immorality are much rarer than might be expected, and by no means very definite. We cannot attach much importance to certain traditional pleasantries repeated to satiety, such as those inspired by the reputed virtues of the path waters against sterility ("A Step to the Bath," p 13; "A Journey through England," p 132; "A Song on the Multiplying Virtues of the Bath Waters," in the "Bath, Bristol, Tunbridge and Epsom Miscellany," p 11; "Lettres d'un François," lxxxviii. vol. iii. p 310; "A Journey to Bath and Bristol;" passage referred to above, p 94–95, *note* 103, etc.).

109 "A Lady of Fashion, on her leaving this place, is said to have looked back, uttering these words, 'Farewell, dear Bath, Nowhere so much Scandal, nowhere so little Sin'" (Sutherland, "Attempts to Revive Antient Medical Doctrines," and part, p 124).

110 *Cf* chap. vii. below.

111 For a further account of this local literature see below, chap. viii.

112 "We are allowed to accompany them [the men] to the booksellers' shops, which are charming places of resort, where we read novels, plays, pamphlets and newspapers

for so small a subscription as a crown a quarter; and in these offices of intelligence (as my brother calls them) all the reports of the day, and all the private transactions of the bath, are first entered and discussed" (Smollett, "Humphry Clinker," letter from Lydia Melford, April 26).

113 Lady Vane; inserted in "Peregrine Pickle."

114 Many of these works would be thought strange reading for a young girl in these days. On this subject see Lecky, "History of England," vol. ii. chap. v. pp 153 and 155.

115 "Our new books are read there, and, without flattery, I know of none that have been so much admired as yours. 'Tan Sai' has long been and long will be the delight of all Bath. This book has become one of those which form an item in the cure" ("Lettres d'un François," to Monsieur de Crébillon fils, vol. iii. p 312.)

116 See below, chap. ix.

117 See below, chap. viii.

118 Goldsmith, however, speaks of certain lectures that were given "People of fashion, when so disposed, attend lectures on the arts and sciences, which are frequently taught there in a pretty superficial manner, so as not to tease the understanding, while they afford the imagination some amusement" ("Life of Nash," p 525).

119 "Letters," vol. i. p 90; January, 1740.

120 See Fleming, "Life … of T. Ginnadrake," vol. iii. pp 126–128.

121 Dr. Johnson seems to have shown a certain appreciation both of his character and writings. Though he was a little severe upon these on one occasion (Boswell, "Life of Johnson," vol. i. p 361) he nevertheless maintained that if his letters had been written by some one of established reputation, they would have been very much admired (Boswell, ibid. and "Journal of a Tour to the Hebrides," p 90). He referred to the "Letters Written from Leverpoole, Chester, Cork, the Lake of Killarny, Dublin, Tunbridge Wells, and Bath," Johnson had sent him to collect documents relating to the life of Dryden. Derrick was also Boswell's Mentor and cicerone on his first visit to London (Boswell, loc. cit.). A collection of his witticisms was published after his death ("Derrick's Jests"). They are on the whole more remarkable for rudeness than for wit.

122 So, at least, says the anonymous author of the "Life of Quin." "Mr D … being at that time accidentally at Bath, and having lately complimented a certain noble lord in a poem, he, half in jest and half in earnest, said 'Suppose we make D. King of Bath?' This proposal was seconded by two or three ladies, who had been obliquely praised in the same piece, and they imagined it would be no small feather in their cap if they could say they had the Master of the Ceremonies for their panegyrist. Accordingly Mr D. was, by these ladies' interest, without opposition elected" ("Life of Quin," xiv. p 56).

123 "Life of Quin," ibid.

124 One of the characters in "Humphry Clinker" compares him to Tom Thumb (Letter from J. Melford, May 6).

125 Quin had often been suspected of intriguing to secure the post of Master of the Ceremonies for himself, but the accusation is repelled by his biographer at some length ("Life of Quin," xiii.).

126 Quin's biographer does not give the name of this Frenchman, but merely remarks that he failed to please, notwithstanding "the abject servility and outrée politesse, for which his countrymen are so celebrated" ("Life of Quin," xiv. p xiii.).

127 A detailed account of the whole affair and of the principal documents connected with it may be found in "The Bath Contest," 1769. Cf also Fleming, "Life ... of T. Ginnadrake," vol. iii. pp 131–136. A mock-heroic poem of some liveliness, "Rebellion in Bath" (by R. Warner), was based upon this incident, but contains allusions to persons and events of 1808.

128 He was a professional gambler, but offered to give up his calling "Should I be so fortunate as to have my attempt crowned with success, I most solemnly protest and declare that I will bid adieu to play." (Address quoted by Fleming, op. cit. vol. iii. pp 131–2.)

129 The collection fills a hundred pages in Fleming (vol. iii. pp 131–230). Garrick took part in the fray and composed a satirical piece (see "Bath Contest," pp 57, 59, 91).

130 "Among the gentlemen, scandalous epithets soon produced blows, and among the ladies (who began the fray), the spirit of opposition afforded work for the milliners, hairdressers, and mantua-makers. At last the Mayor appeared," etc. (Bath and Bristol Chronicle, April 13, 1769.)

131 "He was a nephew of Marshal Wade, the well-known suppressor of the Jacobite risings. Fleming tells us that he was presented with a gold medal as insignia of his office, bearing on one side a figure of Venus, with the words: Venus decens, and on the reverse a laurel branch, with the legend : Arbiter elegantiae, communi consensu" ("Life ... of T. Ginnadrake," vol. iii. p 230).

132 In 1771. Sheridan composed a satirical piece on the occasion, "A Panegyric to the Ridotto."

133 See "New Prose Guide to Bath," pp iii.-v; and cf Sheridan, The Rivals, I: FAG "At present we are like other great assemblies, divided into parties—High Roomians and Low Roomians. However, for my own part, I have resolved to stand neuter, and so I told Bob Brush at our last Committee." (This passage is omitted in many editions of Sheridan, but appears in his manuscript. Cf Rae's ed. introd. p. xv.)

V

Society in Bath: Sheridan's Marriage

The Sheridan family, as my readers know, is of Irish origin. Thomas Sheridan,[1] a Dublin schoolmaster, and the writer's grandfather, was one of Swift's few friends, and even one of his intimates.[2] Good-natured, lively and full of wayward intelligence, he was famous for his quaint and original wit, and also for his extraordinary carelessness, lack of foresight, and want of practical common sense. He it was who, having been appointed, thanks to Swift's influence, chaplain to the Lord Lieutenant, and desired to preach at Cork on August 1st, the anniversary of the accession, of George I, took it into his head to choose as his text the words: "Sufficient to the day is the evil thereof," a piece of thoughtlessness which cost him his chaplaincy, and ruined his future in the Church.[3]

His third son, also called Thomas, was a very different person.[4] While the father is chiefly remembered on account of the affection which bound him to Swift, the memory of the son is associated with that of Johnson. His figure is familiar to every reader of Boswell; he constantly appears in the celebrated Life of the Doctor, and we see him at one time enduring his terrible friend's scoldings, then quarrelling with him over some bitter phrase,[5] and utterly refusing to be reconciled. In Johnson's own opinion, he was, in spite of certain ridiculous faults, a worthy man,[6] not at all devoid of talent as an actor.[7] After having been applauded on the boards in Dublin and in London,[8] and managed a Dublin theatre, he settled in the capital as a teacher of elocution,[9] and there met with varying fortunes. Sometimes he was the fashionable teacher, much sought after, sometimes he was forced to live cheaply in France, and seek the benefit of a law for the relief of insolvent debtors.[10] Tired out, he betook himself to Bath, with his four children, in 1770.[11] The town was full of resources for a man who taught one of the superfluous arts; and might he not come across some important personage who would recommend certain projects—such as the foundation of an Academy of

Elocution, the head of which was ready to hand—to the Government? Failing such a patron, the professor of diction found pupils at all events, and forsook them occasionally to go back to the theatre; he also worked on a dictionary of the English language.[12] Charles, the elder of Thomas Sheridan's two sons, shared his father's labours; the second, Richard, who had just left Harrow, where he had been but a moderately successful scholar,[13] seems to have led a tolerably idle life, following his fancy, which led him, at this moment, in the direction of literature. In collaboration with a former school-friend, Halhed, he was composing a farce entitled *Jupiter*, in which some features of the Critic are already discoverable.[14] With this same Halhed he planned the, foundation of a periodical, and published a translation in verse of an obscure Greek writer, Aristaenetus;[15] he also made some fugitive attempts at poetry, certain of which are not devoid of merit.[16] It may be imagined that these first efforts of a brilliant and precocious genius by no means absorbed him altogether. The pleasures of Bath; amusement of every kind, the novel spectacle of society, and such a special form of society, these things chiefly occupied the twenty-year old author.[17] Witty, pleasing, good-looking, full of gaiety and spirit,[18] Sheridan possessed every quality likely to attract society. He delighted in it in any case, and while carried away by its gay whirl, he was unconsciously collecting precious data. His future comedies were played before him in real life. Lady Sneerwell and Mrs Candour vied with each other in mangling reputations. Bob Acres learnt fine manners, Lucy, the chambermaid, carried more than one secret correspondence to Lydia Languish, or to Mrs Malaprop. Better still, he himself, to some extent at least, was to enact own Captain Absolute and Faulkland. Cares other than literary suddenly filled his mind and heart. He fell in love with Eliza Linley, daughter of the director of the Bath Concerts, young, lovely, and. already famous, and to win her hand embarked on a series of romantic adventures.

The family to which Miss Linley belonged holds a peculiar and unique position in the history of English music. Not a of it but was more or less remarkable for his or her natural gift for this art.[19] Thomas Linley, the head of the family, having studied both in England and in Italy, had settled at Bath as a teacher of music and singing, and Was considered above all his rivals in England in this line. He was also an excel lent performer on the harpsichord, and a composer of merit.[20] He it was who brought Handel's music back into favour, and at Bath and even in London introduced a perfection of execution unknown or forgotten into concerted performances.[21] From childhood almost his three daughters ranked among the first singers of their time. His eldest son Thomas, a violinist, and the friend of Mozart, gave great musical promise, but perished in a boating accident at the age of twenty-two.[22] Samuel, another son, who performed on the hautboy, also inspired hopes, the realisation of which was prevented by his premature death.

At this time Thomas Linley's eldest daughter, Eliza, was sixteen years of age, and had already been singing for several years at her father's concerts and oratorios at Bath, Oxford, and London. She was gifted with a wonderful voice, and her

Richard Brinsley Sheridan
After the portrait by Gainsborough

beauty, her modest grace, and her intelligence equalled her gifts as a singer and a musician.[23] Wherever she went she exercised a sort of fascination and evoked universal enthusiasm. Of her personal attractions we can still judge by the pictures. Gainsborough[24] and Sir Joshua Reynolds[25] have left us. Of those of her heart and mind, by her letters to Sheridan and by some fugitive pieces written by her.[26] Burney, the historian of English music, and a competent judge, praises her voice, her expression, her method of singing, as much as her conversation and her face.[27]

The Sheridans and the Linleys, who had become acquainted during a previous stay of Thomas Sheridan's at Bath,[28] soon grew intimate, and the two brothers,

Charles and Richard, both fell in love with Eliza Linley. The elder soon avowed his passion. But Richard, whose feelings, were probably of slower growth, seems to have held his peace for a considerable time. A strange chance made him the rival, not only of his own brother, but of his friend and collaborator Halhed, then a student at Oxford, who had seen and heath Miss Linley at a concert in that city, and had straightway become enamoured of her. Halhed had confided the state of his affections to Sheridan, and all his extant letters to him are full of the subject.[29] Sheridan was desired to bear his friend's compliments[30] and messages to "St Cecilia."[31]

Neither suitor stood long in his way. Charles Sheridan, thoroughly discouraged by Miss Linley, wrote to relinquish his pretensions, and even left Bath. A little later,[32] Halhed, to his great despair, found himself obliged to go to India.[33] But there were many other suitors for the young girl's heart and hand.[34] During this very year her parents almost forced her into accepting one of these, of the name of Long,[35] who was sixty years of age, but very rich. Everything was made ready for the marriage, the jewels given, the settlement drawn up, while talk raged in the city, and public opinion blamed the greedy parents as much as the sexagenarian lover.

The general disapproval and indignation were finally expressed after a singularly striking and public fashion.[36] Foote, the actor and author, who was then at Bath, pounced on the ill-assorted match, and made it the subject of a play which he instantly wrote. It was produced at the Haymarket Theatre in London on June 26, 1771, with a prologue by Garrick and an epilogue by Cumberland.

A strange piece of audacity, surely, thus to put a private matter, affecting well-known living persons, on the boards! Stranger still, perhaps, was the impunity the author of the play enjoyed. To prevent any mistake as to the originals of his characters, he had entitled his piece *The Maid of Bath*, a name frequently applied to Miss Linley, and she herself figures under the scarcely altered appellation of "Miss Linnet." The first act passes at the Bear Inn, one of the most frequented in the watering-place. Here a certain Major Rackett, just returned after an absence from Bath, learns from his friend Sir Christopher Cripple that Miss Linnet, his petite rossignole (sic), is going to be married to "an old fusty, shabby, shuffling, money-loving, water-drinking, milk-marring, amorous old hunks, Mr Solomon Flint."[37] This Flint is painted in very unattractive colours. When he makes his appearance he does not belie his portrait. Rackett is not much better. He represents a certain Major Mathews, of whom we shall hear later on, and entertains anything but honourable views on the heroine. With honest Sir Christopher, though for very different reasons, he will endeavour to stop the marriage. In the next act we see the young lady enduring reproaches from her mother, who cannot understand her objection to such a fine match, with an income of ten thousand a year. Would she "refuse an estate because it happened to be a little encumbered?" She "must consider the man in this case, as a kind of mortgage," and, thanks to the disproportion of years, "encumbrance will be sooner removed."[38] The poor girl does her best to stand out against this weighty reasoning, but her mother and other folks continue to lecture her, and she ends by saying yes, unwillingly enough. This suits neither Sir Christopher nor Rackett, who both open their batteries on Flint. In a good scene (act iii.) they contrive to frighten him about his approaching marriage. The connection is beneath him, h health will be destroyed, and think of the expenses he will have to face! Flint wavers, changes his mind; he will try to possess Miss Linley on easier terms—and makes her an insulting proposal, which she angrily and scornfully rejects. In the midst of their conversation he is fallen upon by his adversaries, who have been in hiding, overwhelmed with reproaches, threatened with a scandal. All idea of marriage is over. Flint consoles himself with his beloved money; and the "Maid of Bath," having declined to marry Rackett, likewise declares, "I beg to remain in the station I am in my little talents have hitherto received the public protection, nor, whilst I continue to deserve, am I the least afraid of losing my patrons" (act iii. in fine).[39]

The man from whom the heroine thus escapes is a fool, a knave, and a miser. But it must be said that the real suitor, to judge him by his behaviour, of all events, was a far more honourable man. Sheridan's sister, Mrs Lefanu, tells us, indeed, that a few days before that fixed for her wedding, Miss Linley, in her despair, ventured to write in secret to Mr Long, telling him she had bestowed her heart elsewhere, and beseeching him, so greatly did she dread her parents' wrath, to take the initiative in breaking off the marriage; Mr Long, careless of the fresh blame he brought on his own head by this apparent insult to his betrothed, obeyed her wish. When Mr Linley threatened him with a law suit, he settled £3000 on Eliza Linley of his own free will, and also gave her the valuable jewels which had been his wedding presents. That Sheridan, certainly a good judge, held this conduct to be a proof of sincere and disinterested attachment is proved by the respect and affection he always showed Mr Long, who lived to a very advanced age.[40]

A much more faithful portrait is drawn in another character, Rackett, the original of'which, a certain Major Mathews, was well known at Bath, where, though a married man, he led an irregular and dissipated life.[41]

This Mathews, who was acquainted with the Linley family, had known Eliza from a child, and now took advantage of this long-standing intimacy to harass the young girl with secret and objectionable attentions, soon followed by disgraceful proposals. When she rejected these indignantly, he threatened to kill himself if she were not more tractable, and he also threatened to blast her reputation,[42] always an easy matter at Bath, and easier still with all the appearances with which a man of his character would be able to endow the calumny. The poor girl he thus persecuted did not dare to inform her parents of the conduct of their so-called friend; she was probably afraid of bringing about a duel between her father and Mathews. At last she confided her distress to her friends, Alicia and Eliza Sheridan. Their brother Richard happened to be on good terms with Mathews. He willingly put himself into communication with him, and, without exciting his suspicions, induced him to cease his insulting attempts. Miss Linley was left in peace for a time.[43]

But not completely, and for this there were reasons. There was nothing to prove that her present condition of tranquillity was to endure. Even supposing that Mathews had honestly relinquished his shameful design, how was she to prevent its being taken up by some other of the casual Don Juans whose presence, whose compliments and vows, the nature of her profession forced her to suffer and hear. And, indeed, she hated her profession, the exhibition she was obliged make of herself, the contacts to which it exposed her, and she hated it all without any hope that her father would permit her to leave it; he loved money, and his daughter's talent brought him in a good income. Thus a plan sprang up in Eliza's brain, and took firm root there,—a plan to leave her paternal roof and take refuge in a French convent. There she would stay till she came of age, and then the gift bestowed on her by Mr Long would enable her to indemnify her father for the pecuniary loss caused by her flight, and to wait for what the future might bring her. She secretly consulted Sheridan and his sister. They both approved her plan, and set about ensuring its success—the one hoping to deliver her friend from a painful position, while the other was overjoyed to seize the unexpected chance of ingratiating himself with the woman he loved. Miss Sheridan gave Miss Linley letters of introduction to friends of her own at St. Quentin;[44] Sheridan, on his side, offered to protect the fugitive, and escort her until she had found a refuge in France. He put himself forward as the chivalrous friend, who had no personal views at all; and to silence the evil tongues, so greatly to be dreaded, he engaged the services of a female companion. The heroine of the journey gratefully accepted his offer, as a disinterested service; neither she nor Sheridan's sister dreamt for a moment that the adventure was to end in a marriage.[45] When everything had thus been settled and arranged, a day was fixed. One evening, when Mr Linley and Miss Mary Linley were busy at a concert, Eliza excused herself on the score of illness, and slipped out of a sedan chair brought her by Sheridan into the post-chaise, standing ready with her lady travelling companion already seated in it.[46] Early next morning all three were in London. Sheridan took Miss Linley to the house of a middle-aged man, a friend and relation of his own, and passed her off as a rich heiress whom he had carried off, and intended to marry in France. A ship was just sailing for Dunkirk, and the fugitives embarked, armed with fresh letters recommending them to persons in that town, who were to recommend them in their turn to others at Lille.[47] Then only it was that Sheridan revealed the passion he had conceived for her to his companion, and pressed her to consent to marry him. Expediency pleaded for him as well as the fervour of his own feelings. Must not ill-natured tongues be wagging in England? Was there not a risk, in spite of all their precautions, that the young girl's reputation might be compromised? If they returned as husband and wife, they could put a stop to all scandal, if necessary. Miss Linley, "who already preferred Sheridan to every other man," allowed herself to be convinced without much difficulty, and the young people were married in a village tear Calais, by a priest "accustomed to such unions".[48]

They agreed to keep this clandestine marriage, of which nobody was informed, absolutely secret, unless some evident necessity for declaring it should arise.

In their own eyes, indeed, it was no more than a present reaction, and a future engagement.[49] This did not induce Miss Linley to abandon her retreat in France, where she intended merely to wait till Sheridan had attained his majority or secured some means of subsistence. As soon as the ceremony was over, he conducted the fugitive, with the same respect as before, to Lille. Here, not without some difficulty, she found shelter in a convent,[50] and afterwards, having fallen ill, in the family of an English doctor who had settled in the town. Here her father, who had received a letter apprising him of her place of residence, joined her. He had a conversation with Sheridan, and hearing at last of Mathews' past machinations[51] (which Mathews himself was, in his fury, loudly proclaiming[52]), perceiving, too, that the expedition had been strictly honourable, he accepted his explanations. All he asked was that his daughter should return with him to England, and there fulfil her previous engagements. She agreed and went back to Bath with her father. Public indignation had driven Mathews out of the town.[53] Sheridan travelled with them.

A fresh series of adventures awaited him. Amidst the universal surprise aroused by the fair singer's flight, two men were more astounded than their fellows, and their anger far exceeded their astonishment. These were Mathews and Charles Sheridan. Mathews, robbed of the quarry he had been stalking, was convinced Miss Linley's officious advocate had fooled him for his own advantage. Charles, a former suitor for Eliza's hand, and disheartened by her treatment of him, had been unaware, like all the world, of his brother's love for the young girl, and now accused them both alike of treachery. He had left Bath after his failure, and the unexpected news broke suddenly on his retirement. In his fury, he hurried back, met Mathews, in a fury likewise, outside his house, and spoke fierce words against his brother in his presence—words which Mathews remembered, and of which he made use at a later date.

The days dragged on. There was no sign of the fugitives, no explanation. Three weeks after Miss Linley's disappearance, Mathews, having written Sheridan several letters, full of threats and insults,[54] had the following notice inserted in the Bath Chronicle of April 8th: "Mr Richard S, having attempted, in a letter left behind him for that purpose, to account for his scandalous method of running away from this place, by insinuations derogating from my character, and that of a young lady, innocent as far as relates to me, or my knowledge; since which he has neither taken any notice of letter or even informed his own family of the place where he has hid himself; I can no longer think he deserves the treatment of a gentleman, and therefore shall trouble myself no further about him than, in this public method, to post him as a L … and a treacherous S" Then comes a challenge, worded in an equally violent way, to anybody maintaining or continuing to spread what he styles an infamous falsehood. "The world," he adds, "will be candid enough to judge properly (I make no doubt) of any private abuse on this subject for the future; as nobody can defend himself from an accusation he is ignorant of." The world, it appears, took a different view, and in face of the general reprobation,[55] Mathews beat a retreat, and betook himself to London.

It was while he was in France that Sheridan received Mathew's letters, and heard of the notice published in the Gazette. He swore he would not sleep a night on English soil till he had chastised his enemy, and wrote to inform him of his decision, and that he was starting to find him.[56] This happened just when Sheridan was about to set forth with Mr Linley and his daughter. His adversary replied, begging him not to deprive himself of so much sleep, adding that he might call on him, in any case, at any hour, and without ceremony.[57] Sheridan only hurried the more. At Canterbury, on his way, he spent the night on foot,[58] so as not to break his oath. Reaching London at last, he discovered that Mathews was in town. He hurried to his lodgings, with his pistols in his pocket. It was midnight; the door was only opened after many difficulties and after a two hours' delay; then Mathews,—most unexpected change!—received him with a very frightened air, called him his dear friend, made him sit down, kept him till the morning, assured him the notice in the Bath Chronicle was quite different from the report of it he had been given; and finally, recollecting the violent words Charles Sheridan had let fall, laid the whole business on him and on a third person.[59]

On this assurance Sheridan, without further delay, started off post haste to Bath. Arriving there, he procured a copy of the newspaper; saw he had been fooled, had an explanation with his brother, who was still very angry with him, but easily exculpated himself as to the part he had been accused of playing. And instantly, in the middle of the night, without warning their terrified family and friends,[60] the two brothers leapt into a post-chaise, to go together to Mathews. This time they were resolved on the duel. A message was despatched to Mathews, and towards six o'clock in the evening the two principals and their seconds were searching Hyde Park for a convenient place of meeting.[61] They found none, for the park was still a wilderness. Matthews, who did not seem at all resolute, suggested putting every thing off till next day, but this Sheridan refused to do. So they went to fight it out by candlelight, in a tavern room.[62] Sheridan's account of the duel, the exactness of which he declared himself ready to affirm on oath,[63] is curious reading nowadays, for it shows the somewhat strange fashion after which affairs of the kind were occasionally arranged at that time.

"Almost immediately on our entering the room we engaged. I struck Mr Mathews' point so much out of the line that I stepped up and caught hold of his wrist, or the hilt of his sword, while the point of mine was at his breast.[64] You ran in,[65] and caught hold of my arm, exclaiming, 'Don't kill him.' I struggled to disengage my arm, and said his sword was in my power. Mr Mathews called out twice or thrice, 'I beg my life!'—We were parted. You immediately said, 'There, he has begged his life, and now there is an end of it;' and, on Mr Ewart's saying that, when his sword was in my power, as I attempted no more you should not have interfered, you replied that you were wrong, but that you had done it hastily and to prevent mischief—or words to that effect. Mr Mathews then hinted that. I was rather obliged to your interposition for the advantage; you declared that 'before you did so both the swords were in Mr Sheridan's power.'

Mr Mathews still seemed resolved to give it another turn, and observed that he had never quitted his sword. Provoked at this, I then swore (with too much heat, perhaps) that he should either give up his sword and I would break it, or go to his guard again. He refused—but, on my persisting, either gave it into my hand, or flung it on the table, or on the ground (which, I will not absolutely affirm). I broke it and flung the hilt to the other end of the room. He exclaimed at this. I took a mourning sword from Mr Ewart, and presenting him with mine, gave him my honour that what had passed should never be mentioned by me, and that he might now right himself again. He replied that he 'would never draw a sword against the man who had given him his life'—but, on his still exclaiming against the indignity of breaking his sword (which he had brought upon himself), Mr Ewart offered him the pistols, and some altercation passed between them. Mr Mathews said that he could never show his face, if it were known how his sword was broke—that such a thing had never been done—that it cancelled all obligations, etc etc. You seemed to think it was wrong, and we both proposed that if he never misrepresented the affair, it should not be mentioned by us. This was settled. I then asked Mr Mathews whether (as he had expressed himself sensible of and shocked at the injustice and indignity he had done me in his advertisement) it did not occur to him that he owed me another satisfaction; and that, as it was now in his power to do it without discredit, I supposed he would not hesitate. This he absolutely refused, unless conditionally; I insisted on it, and said I would not leave the room until it was settled. After much. altercation, and with much ill-grace, he gave the apology, which afterwards appeared. We parted, and I returned immediately to Bath."[66]

The note handed to Sheridan ran as follows: "Being convinced that the expressions I made use of to Mr Sheridan's disadvantage were the effects of passion and misrepresentation, I retract what I have said to that gentleman's disadvantage, and particularly beg his pardon for my advertisement in the Bath Chronicle. (Signed) Thomas Mathews."[67]

It appeared in the same paper on May 7, 1772,[68] and Mathews, feeling uncomfortable on the scene of his former exploits, retired to Wales.[69] From that quarter Sheridan and the lady still known as Miss Linley had nothing more to fear, but the embarrassment of a false and difficult position still continued. Their marriage, it will be remembered, was unknown to anybody, even to their own families,[70] and the events which had brought them together now necessitated their appearing almost strangers to each other. They had become objects of public attention and curiosity abroad, they were watched by their own relations at home, and the free intercourse of former days was at an end. It was only in secret, and amidst a thousand difficulties, that they could meet or correspond, and the impatience with which they endured this constant discomfort and enforced separation may be readily imagined.[71] At all events—and the fact does honour to the society, frivolous and ill-natured though it was, in which they moved—universal, or a universal, esteem was still theirs. No one in their own homes doubted the perfectly honourable behaviour of the two young people

The Misses Linley
From the portrait by Gainsborough

during their French journey,[72] and general opinion had treated them with equal justice.[73] The romantic adventure in which Miss Linley had engaged had left her reputation unsullied; it had brought her commiseration, but no suspicion, much less any condemnation.[74] As for Sheridan, there was not a soul who did not praise his behaviour, and applaud it.

Mathews, meanwhile, was making ready for a reappearance. His reception, even in Wales, had been tolerably chilly, and he let a friend persuade him that his only chance of recovering the consideration he had lost was by fighting another duel. He went back to Bath, and there told the story after his own fashion, in other worth, much to Sheridan's detriment. Sheridan, who had hitherto kept silence as to the details, considered himself absolved from any bond of secrecy.[75] He then received a challenge from Mathews, and at dawn on the following day (July 2) the adversaries went out again. The spot chosen for this meeting was Kingsdown, a hill close to Bath.

We have several detailed accounts of this second duel, all differing a little from each other, according to the side which gives them.[76] If we compare these, and only retain the principal incidents, admitted by both parties, we find things happened as follows: Almost at the very beginning of the fight, Sheridan fell fiercely upon Mathews and tried, as on the first occasion, to lay hold of his sword.[77] The ground was uneven, and he fell, dragging his opponent with him.[78] In their fall both swords were broken, and the struggle went on between the two men lying clinging to each other on the ground. Mathews, the older and stronger of the two, contrived to get on top of Sheridan and keep him down. He was still holding the stump of his sword, or had been able to recover possession of it.[79] He called on his adversary to sue for mercy, and when he refused,[80] he picked up the other piece of his sword, and began striking and stabbing him in the neck, the face, and all over the body.[81] This unequal struggle went on for some time without any interference from the seconds. At last they separated the opponents.[82] Mathews got into a post-chaise which was waiting for him, and Sheridan, in a very bad way, was carried to the nearest inn, where surgeons dressed his wounds.

The lady who had been the involuntary cause of all these events, and of the final catastrophe, knew nothing of them for several days. Miss Linley was at Oxford, where she was to sing at a concert, and her father had carefully kept the newspapers which would have informed her of the duel, and Sheridan's danger, out of her sight. She appeared before an audience deeply moved, on her account by the blow which had fallen on her champion, of which she alone evidently had no suspicion.[83] It was not till she was on her way home, and within a short distance of Bath, that a clergyman, a friend of the family, led her apart, and, with many precautions, told her all that had happened. Greatly agitated, she cried out that she must see Sheridan, that she was his wife,[84] and had a right to nurse him. It was the first time she had avowed her marriage; but such were her confusion and distress that but small importance was ascribed to her words. The two fathers, indeed, seemed as little disposed to recognise such a union, even if it had taken place, as to authorise it if it had not, and the young people themselves, when pressed on the subject, both denied it.

Mr Sheridan, in fact, who had been away for some time, returned to Bath just after his son's fresh adventure had taken place.[85] In his rage, he refused to see Richard, though he was ill from his wounds, and ordered his daughters to break off all intercourse with the Linleys, an order which they did not completely carry out. But very soon, persuaded by his elder daughter,[86] he softened down, saw his son, who was recovering,[87] was reconciled to him, and would have gone to law with Mathews, a course which Sheridan opposed. But he still looked with an unfavourable eye on Richard's passion for Miss Linley, thinking, perhaps, she had been too much talked about, or perhaps dreaming of a better marriage for him.[88] To reassure him, Sheridan promised to break off all intercourse with her; he even bound himself, by "an oath equivocal,"[89] never to marry her. Did he mean to keep his word? He certainly broke his first promise very quickly. He had already written to Miss Linley, whom her father had carried off to Wells; he had received letters from her,[90] and, on her return, there were several secret meetings between them. Not so secret, however, but that Mr Sheridan got wind of them, and packed the young man off to Waltham Abbey in Essex, where he remained with friends from the end of August 1772, till the following spring.[91] He himself, having accepted an engagement at the Theatre Royal, Dublin, left Bath for Ireland, and took his family with him.

The two lovers being thus removed from Bath, the continuation and happy conclusion of their romance lies a little beyond our special limits. A rapid summary of them will suffice our purpose, and we will begin by a glance at Sheridan's letters to his friend, Thomas Grenville,[92] to obtain some idea of the feelings their writer had carried away into his retirement. They are filled with the most ardent passion, exasperated by despair.

"I hope you have seen her, I hope you *have* talked to her, if you have, and should again, I am sure your own feelings will suggest to you what I would say. Tell me she is happy: if she is otherwise, tell her to be so. Oh, upon my soul, it were the part of an angel to come down from Heaven, to watch over her, and reconcile her mind to peace. I wish dying could assure me of the power to come from Heaven to her with that happiness which I fear she will never know here. It is impious to say it, but I believe I should exchange a Robe of Glory for her livery."[93]

And in another letter: "Believe me, when I am most melancholy, when I am poring over Nature's large volume of affliction, I turn to the page of love (though a blotted one) for consolation. I find there, it is true, much cause for vexation, but were it a blank to me, I should be ten times more miserable. I am sick and without society; my love is almost the only feeling I have alive. Amo, ergo sum is the confirmation of my existence … But what shall I say of this attachment? To hope for happiness from it, I must agree with you, is and must be impossible!"[94]

When Miss Linley wrote to him, she placed him in a most cruel difficulty, for he had renewed his promise to his father to break off all correspondence with her, and, this time, the promise was sincere.[95]

"I have received," he says, "a letter from her, since I wrote to you, (contraband!) filled with the violence of affection, and concluded with prayers, commands, and entreaties that I should write to her. I did not expect such a desire, as she had acquiesced in my determination of not corresponding. Indeed, as we had always other subjects to employ us when together, she hesitated less in agreeing to a distant mortification, and I by that had less necessity to explain properly to her the necessity of it. I cannot now do it, for to tell her why I am right is to plunge into the wrong. To tell her why I did resolve is to break my resolution; yet to deny her, and not excuse my denial, is a hard mortification. I am determined not to write, from the conviction of the necessity of such a determination, but I cannot break a solemn promise. How strange is my situation!"[96]

To make it yet stranger and more perplexing, the only thing lacking was the reappearance of that perpetual intruder, Mathews. This is just what occurred. Returning to Bath, and finding his own behaviour in the second duel universally blamed, [97] the major was inspired to have an account of the meeting, which of course presented matters to his advantage, drawn up by his former second.[98] This account was submitted to Sheridan's second, Paumier, who, with certain reservations, agreed to sign it. Then Sheridan, not unreasonably, as it would seem, grew angry, declared the document was full of vile lies, and accused his friend of treachery or cowardice.[99] He would have fought a third duel with Mathews, and it was all his friends could do to restrain him. We may add that after this disagreeable episode Mathews never crossed his path again.[100]

The lovers may have seen each other again at this juncture,[101] for Miss Linley was singing at Covent Garden, and Waltham Abbey is within easy reach of London. But a violent quarrel took place between them at this time, followed by a temporary estrangement. To judge by two letters of the young girl's,[102] full at once of grief, reproaches, and affection, some inconstancy, real or imaginary, on the part of Sheridan was the cause. However this may have been, Miss Linley's indignation was such that she vowed she would never marry Sheridan of her own free will.[103]

Here we have another vow in an affair which caused the utterance of so many, and this was no more strictly kept than the rest. A common friend brought about a reconciliation without much difficulty, and by an unexpected stroke a happy dénoument followed on this last development. For reasons which have never been clearly explained,[104] Mr Linley, who had so strenuously opposed the marriage, declaring that he would rather see his daughter in her grave than married to Sheridan, and who had so lately caused her solemnly to renounce any intention of the sort, suddenly changed his mind, and consented to the union of the young couple.[105]

On April 13, 1773, they were married in London, braving the wrath of Mr Sheridan, who remained inflexible.[106] Sheridan was twenty-two years old, and had just entered at the Middle Temple as a law-student; his young wife was in her twentieth year.

London became thenceforth Sheridan's domicile, and the theatre of his strange and brilliant career. We must leave him here, on the very threshold of his precocious fame, but we shall note elsewhere[107] how his impressions of Bath, of the originals he met there, and the adventures in which he had been concerned, manifest themselves in his dramatic works. The first sketch for the *School for Scandal, The Slanderers*, bears as sub-title *A Pump-Room Scene.*[108] In that Pump Room the author had often seen scandalmongers and backbiters busily engaged; he himself and the young girl he loved had furnished them with material in plenty.[109] But it is in his first play, The Rivals, that we find his impression of Bath at its freshest, and the scene is laid in the town itself, amidst the joyous movement and the shifting variety of the passing throng. It is, no doubt, idle to seek in the comedy a sort of autobiography of the author, to see in the intrigue the story of his own marriage somewhat modified, and in the characters, portraits of his family, his adversary, his wife and himself.[110] Everything tends to controvert this theory both the purely imaginary imbroglio, and the characters, who are for the most part traditional types of the drama and the novel.[111]

But allowing all this, it cannot be denied that Bath gave the play its distinctive colour, so to speak, and that Bath was the place in all England which was the natural home of Bob Acres and Lydia Languish, of Captain Absolute and Mrs Malaprop. All these personages, the rustic lout and the romantic ingénue, the handsome young officer, and the pretentious old woman, had passed daily before the dramatist upon the Parades. The gay and frivolous agitation in which they move so vivaciously was that in which he himself had found so much amusement. The adventures into which he throws them, secret engagements, duels, abductions, were the daily routine of the place, in which he himself had played so prominent a part. A hundred little touches give local colour, from the "circulating library," that "evergreen tree of diabolical knowledge," to the "snug lying in the Abbey" that so alarmed Bob Acres. Here re reasons enough and to spare for the special interest and appreciation with which the piece was received at Bath.[112]

Bath was the first town after London in which he had it acted, and this was but giving the Western city her due. Where but there had he beheld the types, the absurdities, the man of a little society that faithfully summed up a larger world? Where but there did he acquire the precocious experience that enabled him at twenty-three to produce a masterpiece? What a store of rapidly accumulated observations, of precious material for future comedies, he had garnered here! The school had been good, just as the scholar had been unique.

1 See Swift's "Letters," Lord Orrery's "Remarks," and the "Life of Swift" by Thomas Sheridan the younger.

2 He attended the celebrated Stella on her deathbed.

3 "Swift's Works," edited by Thos. Sheridan, vol. i. p 372 ("Life of Swift").

4 See, besides Moore and Boswell, Miss Lefanu's "Memoirs … of Mrs F. Sheridan," and Rae's "Sheridan," vol. i. pp 17–57 *passim*.

5 Hearing Lord Bute had just given Sheridan a pension of £200 a year, to encourage him to write his dictionary, Johnson exclaimed: "What! have they given *him*

a pension? Then it's time for me to give up mine!" But, after a pause, he added: "However, I am glad that Mr Sheridan has a pension, for he is a very good man" (Boswell, vol. i. pp 306 and 308). Some officious person carried the satirical outburst to Sheridan, who never forgave it.

6 "GARRICK. Sheridan has too much vanity to be a good man." "JOHNSON. No, Sir, there is, to be sure, in Sheridan, something to reprehend and everything to laugh at; but, Sir, he is a good man. No, Sir, were mankind to be divided into good and bad, he would stand considerably within the ranks of good" (Boswell's "Life Johnson," vol. ii. p 92).

7 "And, Sir, it must be allowed that Sheridan excels in plain declamation, though he can exhibit no character" (Boswell, *ibid.*). Compare Johnson's judgment of his performance in Cats and in Richard Ill. (Letter to Bennet Langton, quoted by Boswell, vol. i. p 283).

8 See Taylor, "Records of my Life," vol. ii. p 26.

9 And of rhetoric likewise, for he was fond of combining these two branches of the art of oratory. His dream was to reform the whole of the educational system in England, and to make it first and foremost an apprenticeship in eloquence.

10 Boswell, vol. iii. p 370. The index of the Napier edition gives this experience to Richard Brinsley, the son of Thomas Sheridan, but the context and dates are sufficient proof that this is a mistake.

11 Mrs Frances Sheridan, a very accomplished woman and an authoress of merit, had died four years previously.

12 "Pronouncing Dictionary of the English Language," not published till 1780. He also wrote a life of Swift (1784). Johnson believed the Master of the Ceremonies, Derrick, was not favourable to Sheridan. "Sheridan will not succeed at Bath with his oratory. Ridicule has gone down before him, and, I doubt, Derrick is his enemy" (Boswell, vol. i. p 313). I have not discovered anything to confirm or contradict this suspicion.

13 See in Moore the celebrated letter from his old master, Dr Parr ("Memoirs of … Sheridan," vol. i., chap. i. pp 6–10).

14 Long quotation in Moore, ditto, pp 18–22. The rest is lost, or at all events the only thing left is Halhed's autograph manuscript of the farce as he wrote it, and before Sheridan touched it up. It was then called *Ixion*. The subject was taken up again by Disraeli (*Ixion in Heav'en*, in "Tales and Sketches") and by Mr Burnand (*Ixion, or the Man at the Wheel*).

15 "The Love Epistles of Aristaenetus, translated from the Greek into English Metre" (1771).

16 As, for instance, "Clio's Protest" (reply to "The Bath Picture," by M. P. Andrews), one passage of which "Marked you her cheek of rosy hue?" etc., is still popular, and "The Ridotto of Bath," an imitation of Anstey, which first appeared in the *Bath Chronicle*, Oct. to, 1771, was issued twice over in a separate form (advertised, in the same paper on October 13 and November 8, 1771), and finally inserted in the "New Foundling Hospital. for Wit," vol. i. pp 133, etc. Most of Sheridan's other fugitive poems belong to this period.

17 "[He] … was apparently entirely engaged in the amusements of the place" (Miss Lefanu, "Memoirs," chap. v. p 162).

18 Letter from Sheridan's eldest sister, Mrs Lefanu, with reference to a time very shortly before this: "He was handsome, not merely in the eyes of a partial sister, but generally allowed to be so. His cheeks had the glow of health, his eyes—the finest in the world—the brilliancy of genius, as soft and tender as an affectionate heart could render them: the same playful fancy, the same sterling and innoxious wit that was shown afterwards in his writings, cheered and delighted the family circle" (Moore, vol. i. chap. i. p 14). Miss Burney, less likely to be partial, writes, a few years later (1779): "Mr Sheridan has a fine figure, and a good, though I don't think a handsome, face. He is tall and very upright, and his appearance and address are at once manly and fashionable, without the smallest tincture of foppery or modish graces" ("Diary,". vol. i. p 123). Sheridan's features have been preserved to us by various painters, and notably by Sir J. Reynolds, but at a later date.

19 See, as to each, Parke, "Musical Memoirs," vol. i. p 204. Consult also Mr Sharp's and Miss Middleton's articles in the "Dictionary of National Biography," and the authors to whom they refer their readers.

20 Parke, "Musical Memoirs," vol. i. pp 203, 204. Burney, "History of Music," vol. iv. p 675. Fétis, "Biographie Universelle des Musiciens," vol. v. p 311. Grove, "Dictionary of Music," vol. ii. p 143, and vol. iv. p 701. Here is Grove's conclusion (vol. ii.): "As an English composer, Linley takes high rank," and that of Fétis: "Linley's airs have generally a tender grace and melancholy, which place them in the first rank among English compositions of the kind."

21 "[Linley] ... might with great truth be considered as having restored the music of Handel, and the performance of it, to the notice and patronage of the public, as Garrick restored the playing of Shakespeare. Through his taste and ability as a manager, assisted greatly by the exquisite singing of his two eldest daughters, afterwards Mrs Sheridan and Mrs Tickell, music was cultivated generally at Bath and its vicinity, and concerts were successfully performed not only there, but in the Metropolis, beyond all former precedents since the death of the illustrious Handel himself" ("Dictionary of Musicians," article on Linley).

22 " ... [Mozart] conversed with me a good deal about Thomas Linley, the first Mrs Sheridan's brother, with whom he was intimate at Florence, and spoke of him with great affection. He said that Linley was a true genius; and he felt that, had he lived, he would have been one of the greatest ornaments of the musical world" (Kelly, "Reminiscences," vol. i. pp 225, 226).

23 Here are a few amongst many other contemporary testimonies "The eldest [Miss Linley] I think still superior to all the handsome things I have heard of her. She does not seem in the least spoiled by the idle talk of our sex, and is the most modest, pleasing, delicate flower I have seen for a great while" (Wilkes, "Correspondence," vol. iv. p 97). "Miss Linley's beauty is in the superlative degree. The King admires her and ogles her as much as I dares to do in so holy a place as an oratorio" (Walpole, letter to the Countess of Ossory, March 26, 1773). A few years later (1779) Mme. d'Arblay says of her, in her "Diary": "I was absolutely charmed at the sight of her. I think her quite as beautiful as ever and even more captivating; for she has now a look of ease and happiness that animates her whole face ... The elegance of Mrs

Sheridan's beauty is unequalled by any that I ever saw, except Mrs Crewe. I was pleased with her in all respects. She is much more lively, and agreeable than I had any idea of finding her; she was very gay, and very unaffected, and totally free from airs of any kind" ("Diary," vol. i. p 183). See also Moore: "Mrs Sheridan was something quite divine: the Bishop [of Meath]'s phrase about her had always been that she formed the connecting link between angel and woman" ("Memoirs, Journal and Correspondence," vol. ii. p 298).

24 Full-length portrait of Mrs Sheridan and her sister, Mrs Tickell, in the Dulwich Gallery, of Mrs Sheridan (Miss Linley) with her brother at Knole, of Mrs Sheridan alone, in Lord Rothschild's collection, etc.

25 Famous portrait of Mrs Sheridan as St Cecilia, exhibited in 1775, now. in Lord Lansdowne's collection at Bowood. Other less famous artists also painted portraits of Mrs Sheridan.

26 See Mr Rae's numerous and lengthy quotations from these letters, "Sheridan", vol. i. chaps v. and vi. etc.), and also extracts from her poetical compositions (ditto, chap. v. p 195, note, and vol. ii. chap. iv. p 116). Also Moore ("Memoirs of Sheridan," vol. i. chap. iv. p 203, and vol. ii. chap. xii. p 9).

27 "The beauty, talent, and mental endowments of this 'Sancta Caecilia Rediviva' will be remembered to the last hour of all who heard, or even saw and conversed with her. The tone of her voice and expression, her manner of singing, were as enchanting as her countenance and conversation. In her singing, with mellifluous-toned voice, a perfect stroke and intonation, she was possessed of the double power of delighting an audience equally in pathetic strains and songs of brilliant execution, which is allowed to very few singers" ("Rees' Cyclopaedia," vol. xxi. Linley. The article is by Burney, so Moore tells us, "Memoirs of ... Sheridan," 1st edition, vol. i. p 33 note). See also Moore's panegyric of her beauty, talents, virtue, and domestic qualities ("Memoirs of Sheridan," vol. ii. chap. xv. pp 141, 142).

28 Mr Linley had then given singing lessons to Mrs Sheridan (Miss Lefanu, "Memoirs of F. Sheridan," chap. vii. p. 246). For everything that follows, our chief authority is the account drawn up for Moore by Mrs Lefanu, Sheridan's eldest sister, an eye—witness of almost every thing she tells, and in a position to obtain information first hand as to the rest. This account, which was consulted and occasionally quoted by Moore, has been published almost in its entirety by Mr Rae ("Sheridan," chaps. v. and vi.); we have followed it closely, with some abridgments, where no other authority is mentioned.

29 See extracts from these letters in Rae's "Sheridan," chap. v. Sheridan's letters have been lost.

30 "Pray don't forget my compliments you know where; for a comparison with the London ladies turns out, I think, much in favour of the Venus de Baiis" (Halhed to Sheridan [1771?] in Rae, as above, chap. v. p 150). Halhed knew the Linleys. On this point Moore accuses Sheridan of having played a double game, and hidden the fact of his being a favoured rival from his friend ("Memoirs of Sheridan," vol. i. p 46). Halhed would seem to have discovered the treachery and complained of it in the last letters he wrote before going to India (*ibid.* p 49), and a passage in the translation of

Aristaenetus, it is supposed to express his feelings at that time (*ibid.* p 41). But we have no proof that Sheridan had already fallen in love with Miss Linley when he became the recipient of Halhed's confidences, nor, more especially, that he had revealed his passion to her. Miss Lefanu says he seemed completely absorbed in the gaieties of Bath (passage previously quoted, p 127, note 17), and the thing is possible, at all events. Miss Linley, in a letter shortly to be quoted, would seem to assert that until the journey to France she looked on Sheridan merely as a friend, and in no wise as a suitor. Halhed's letters, published by Mr Rae ("Sheridan," chap. v. pp 151–157), though not always quite clear to us, do no appear to justify Moore's conclusions. As to the passage from Aristaenetus, it is a mere commonplace of amatory literature.

31 A sobriquet frequently applied to Miss Linley in this correspondence and elsewhere. Sheridan wrote to Thomas Grenville in 1772: "You will observe that I have omitted to say anything *de amore aut de Caecilia mea (utinam quidem mea esset)!*" (Rae, "Sheridan," vol. i. p 235.) Compare above, p 129, *note* 27.

32 In December 1771.

33 He returned to England in 1785, sat in Parliament, and ultimately became Secretary to the East India Company.

34 See Halhed's letters (Rae, *ibid.* pp 148–9).

35 According to Moore ("Memoirs of Sheridan," chap. i. p 43), he was a landowner in Wiltshire. Mrs Lefanu does not give this fact.

36 The following lines by Graves echo these feelings:

ON AN OLD GENTLEMAN MARRYING A FINE SINGING GIRL

Famed for the music of her rains,
A warbling linnet o'er the lains
And thro' the neighb'ring groves was known.
The Squire, as late he trudged along,
Was ravished with this linnet's song,
And wished to make the bird his own.
With curious art the snare was set,
He caught her in his silken net.
(Ye swains, the public loss deplore),
She flutters round her gilded cage;
Looks pretty, but I dare engage
Will charm him with her songs no more.
("Euphrosyne," vol. i. pp 84, 85.)

37 I Act i. sc. i.

38 Act ii. sc. 1.

39 See as to this piece, chap. vii. of this work. Miss Linley's adventure has also lately (1900) been the subject of a somewhat slight novel, "A Nest of Linnets," by Mr F. Frankfort Moore.

40 Moore, "Memoirs of Sheridan," vol. i. chap. i. p 44

41 In P. P. Pallet's (Warner) "Bath Characters" he is introduced under the name of Rattle, and, grown a little elderly, thus recounts his past existence: "Surfeited with fiddling and cassino, meagre petit soupees and stupid family dinners, with Monday's lies, and

everybody's scandal ... I turned my horse's head one morning, about three years ago, towards a mountain of Wales" (p 2). "There *was* a time, indeed, when I made a figure with the sex, and could select from my list of conquests a fair specimen of every degree of rank, from the duchess to the spouse of the Squire. But—*fuimus*—Jack! all my credit for successful gallantry has been extinguished, and my ardour in the chase has been gradually evaporating, since that very unseasonable *phlebotomical operation* which was performed upon me by Dick Merryman some years ago. A little Linnet, you know, was the subject of our dispute. We went out to settle it; he pricked my doublet as full of holes as a schoolgirl's sampler, and completed my obligations to him by carrying off the bird to his own nest. But, d—n it, don't make me melancholy by recalling past grievances to my recollection."

42 A threat which was put into partial execution: "Mathews had the baseness, out of vanity, to encourage the spirit of defamation as a compliment paid to his gallantry ... The old ladies, indeed, condemned the conduct of Captain Mathews in very affecting language and the young ones wondered at the levity of Miss Linley in walking about with a married man, whose courtesy to her redoubled in proportion as the world would make it the subject of conversation" (Watkins, "Memoirs of Sheridan," vol. i. p 127).

43 It was towards this time that Sheridan confided his love for Miss Linley to his eldest sister (Mrs Lefanu, in Rae, *op. cit.* vol. i. p 164), but this avowal, made soon after his brother's retirement, was not, as will be seen, very seriously received (comp. *note* 45). For all this and what follows our authority is still Mrs Lefanu. Certain of Sheridan's biographers, such as Mrs Oliphant ("Sheridan," pp 20, 21), found a somewhat different account on a letter said to be from Miss Linley to her friend, Miss Saunders, which was published in the *Gentleman's Magazine* for October 1823. But even in 1827 Moore had declared this letter to be a fabrication ("Memoirs of Sheridan," preface to the 5th edition). Sheridan's granddaughter, Mrs Norton, pronounces the same judgment on it (*Macmillan's Magazine*, January 1861). Mr Rae, who examined the manuscript of this letter, has recently demonstrated its lack of authenticity in the most convincing fashion (*Athenaeum*, January 26, 1893). Besides the fact that the handwriting bears no resemblance to that of Miss Linley, the document is full of false dates and gross mistakes (Mr Rae enumerates eighteen). It will suffice us if we quote two: the letter, describing events which happened in 1772, is dated 1770, and it speaks of Mrs Sheridan, Richard's mother, who died in France in 1776, as being mixed up in the affair.

44 It will be remembered that Thomas Sheridan and his family (except young Richard) had spent several years in France. Even after their father's return, the children remained on at St. Quentin for two years (Mrs Lefanu, in Rae, already quoted, vol. i. p 74), and did not go back to England till 1769.

45 "His sister had no idea that the projected excursion was to lead to an immediate marriage" (Mrs Lefanu, as above, p 166). As for Miss. Linley wrote to Sheridan as follows, just before their marriage;" are sensible, when I left Bath, I had not an idea of you but as a friend." And she adds, very much to his honour, "It was not your person that gained my affection. No, Sn, it was that delicacy, that tender com passion,

that interest which you seemed to take in my welfare, that were the motives which induced me to love you" (Rae, as above, vol. i. p 255).

46 Sheridan's biographers do not give the date of this flight, but the *London Chronicle* of March 24, 1772, contains the following piece of news: "Bath, March 23, Wednesday, the eldest Miss Linley, of this cityr justly celebrated for her musical abilities, set off with Mr Sheridan, junior, on a matrimonial expedition to Scotland." The 23rd of March, 1772, was a Monday, and the date is thus fixed as the 18th. I find no account nor advertisement in the Bath Chronicle of either this or the following week, of the concert; it was probably one of the ordinary performances. Nor is the elopement mentioned.

47 In the "Essays of Elia," Lamb mentions, as Elia's godfather, a certain F., a Holborn oil merchant, and a friend of Palmer, the actor. He adds: "He [F.] was also known to and visited by Sheridan. It was to his house in Holborn that young Brinsley [Sheridan's second Christian name] brought his first wife on her elopement with him from a boarding-school *(sic)* at Bath—the beautiful Maria (*sic*) Linley. My parents were present (over a quadrille-table) when he arrived in the evening with his harmonious charge." ("My First Play.") Mr Fitzgerald remarks, on this subject: "This seems like one of Elia's pleasant mystifications, but he was enwrapping the truth in a quaint disguise of invented names, etc., as. in the case of Barbara S." ("Lives of the Sheridans," vol. i. p 92.) But is this "mystification," though possible, even probable, really a fact? Moore does indeed call the friend who received Sheridan, Ewart, and ascribes another profession to him, but it is worth noting that he attributes the part Mrs Lefanu gives to two persons, to one only,—there may have been some confusion here. This is what Moore says: "On their arrival in London he introduced her to an old friend of his family (Mr Ewart, a respectable brandy merchant in the City) as a rich heiress who had consented to elope with him to the Continent;—in consequence of which the old gentleman, with many commendations of his wisdom for having given up the imprudent pursuit of Miss Linley, not only accommodated the fugitives with a passage on board a ship which he had ready to sail from the Port of London to Dunkirk, but gave them letters of recommendation to his correspondents in that place) who with the same zeal and despatch facilitated their journey to Lille" ("Memoirs of Sheridan," vol. i. p 66). Let us now hear Mrs Lefanu: "They reached London early the next day, when Sheridan introduced Miss Linley to a friend and relation [Mr Ewart], then in Town, as an Heiress who had consented to be united to him in France. Another friend, the son of a respectable brandy merchant in the City, suggested the idea of their sailing from the Port of London to Dunkirk, to which place his father had a vessel ready to sail immediately. This plan, as making a pursuit more difficult, was immediately adopted; and the old gentleman, not being entirely let into the secret, accompanied the young couple on board his ship, recommending them to the care of the captain as if they had been his own children. He gave them letters of introduction to his correspondent at Dunkirk, and they were from thence given recommendations to several persons at Lille" ("Rae," vol. i. chap. v. p 166).

48 Watkins relates that "there was an obstacle in the way of this marriage, which was not celebrated" ("Memoirs of … Sheridan," chap. ii. p 135). But there is no reason

for doubting Mrs Lefanu's account. Watkins is always a dubious authority: when his book came out, Mrs Lefanu wrote to her niece: "That book of Dr. Watkins', which he chooses to denominate a life of your Uncle, is a farrago of nonsense and a tissue of falsehoods," etc. (letter quoted by Rae, chap. ii., note to p. 6 Comp. *Macmillan's Magazine*, January 1861, p. 175, article by Sheridan's granddaughter, Mrs Norton.

49 A later letter from Miss Linley clearly shows that neither she nor Sheridan looked on the Calais marriage as a real one, nor considered themselves irrevocably bound by it. She asks him to return her letters after some quarrel, and we here give some significant passages: "You say you will not give them up till I declare I love another man. Do not distress me so much as to continue in that resolution. Believe me, I am incapable of loving any man ... There are insurmountable obstacles to prevent our ever being united, even supposing I could be induced again to believe you ... Know then, that before I left Bath," [not for her flight to France, but on another journey] "after I had refused Sir T. C. and other gentlemen of fortune, on your account, who I found had given up all thought of me, in the anguish of my soul, which was torn with all the agonies of remorse and rage, I vowed in the most solemn manner, upon my knees, before my parents, that I never would be yours by my own consent, let what would be the consqeuence. My father took advantage of my distress, and, by upbraidings mixed with persuasions, prevailed on me to promise that I would marry the first man (whose character was unexceptionable) that offered. I repented that I had made this promise afterwards; for though I resolved never to be yours, I had not the least intention to be another's." She then refers to a suitor her father is trying to force her to accept. "When I found my father so resolute, I resolved to acquaint the gentleman with every circumstance of my life. I did, and instead of inducing him to give me up, he is now more earnest than ever. I have declared it is not possible for me to love him, but he says he will depend on my generosity short, there is nothing I have not done to persuade him to leave me, but in vain" (quoted by Mr Rae, "Sheridan," vol. i. chap. vi. p 257). Can she, amidst these "circumstances of her life," have held her peace as to the Calais marriage, an acknowledgment of which had escaped once already, at all events? (*Cf* below, p 123.)

50 "Miss Linley is now fixing in a convent, where she has been entered some time. This has been a much more difficult point than you could have imagined" (Letter from Sheridan to his brother, Rae, chap. v. p 170).

51 Sheridan probably left a letter intended to enlighten him on this subject. This at least may be inferred from the opening words of the abusive paragraph inserted by Mathews in the *Bath Chronicle* of April 9, 1772, which will be quoted further on. "Mr Richard S ... ... having attempted, in a letter left behind him for that purpose, to account for his scandalous method of running away from this place, by insinuations derogating from my character," etc.

52 "He was outrageous at having been induced by R. B. S. to give up his pursuit of Miss L ... ... , and though he had been married many years made no scruple of avowing his passion and his hopes of success but for the intervention of her young friend" (Mrs Lefanu, in Rae's "Sheridan," vol. 1. chap. v., p 173). Comp. a letter to Sheridan

from W. B. (William Brereton?) lately published by Rae (*ibid.* p 172). "The morning after you left Bath, Mathews came to me, and has repeated his visits several times. It is impossible to give an account of his conversation. It consisted of many dreadful oaths and curses upon himself and his past life, but in my opinion they were little to the purpose. I am afraid his present situation and feelings are not to be envied. But bad as he is, the town has so little charity for him, that they make [worse, perhaps, than he deserves. I carried two messages from him to Mr Linley, but he would not hearken to a word about him. He said he had been deceived once and he never would trust him more; since that he has heard so many reports to his prejudice that their meeting may be of bad consequence, and I shall endeavour by ail means to prevent it."

53 Mr Linley seems to have waited till he was gone before he fetched his daughter. "In my last conversation with Mr Mathews I ventured to affirm that he had nothing now to do but to settle his affairs and leave Bath, with a resolution never to return again. This scheme (if anything he says can be depended upon) he solemnly promised should be immediately put into execution. After which, I know Mr Linley's plan is to get his daughter to return to Bath, in order to put an end to the many wicked suggestions which the malice of his enemies have (*sic*) propagated, and Betsy may expect soon to be persuaded to take this step by. letter, or, perhaps, by Mr Linley in person" (Letter from W. B., Rae, p 172).

54 "He wrote several abusive threats to Mr S. (Sheridan) then in France" (Sheridan's account, quoted by Moore, vol. i. chap. ii. p 73). Sheridan, in a letter to his brother, tells him he has written himself to Mathews, no doubt to explain his conduct with regard to him. "I wrote to M above a week ago, which I think was necessary and right. I hope he has acted the one proper part which was left him; and to speak from my feelings, I cannot but say that I shall be very happy to find no further disagreeable consequence; for, as Brutus says of Caesar, etc.—If I delay one moment longer I lose the post" (*ibid.* p 63). Was this the passage of Shakespeare of which Sheridan was thinking?

" ... For my part
I know no personal cause to spurn at him
But for the general."
(Julius Caesar, ii. i. 11–13.)

This letter is dated Lille, 15th April. That sent to Mathews by Sheridan was a week older (above a week ago), and Mathews had his notice inserted in the newspaper on the 8th. Probably, with the slow posts of those days, the letter had not yet reached him.

55 W. B.'s letter, already quoted, p 133, *note* 52.

56 "Mr S. (Sheridan) answered him from France (hurried and surprised), that he would never sleep in England till he had thanked him as he deserved" (account drawn up by Sheridan himself before his second duel, and quoted by Moore, vol. i. chap. ii. p 73).

57 Same account, *ibid.* p 74.

58 Same account, *ibid.* p 73.

59 All these details are drawn from the same account, which also contains the following lines: "Mr S. declares that on Mr M.'s perceiving that he came to answer *then* to his challenge, he does not remember to have seen *a man* behave so dastardly" (*ibid.* pp 74, 75) Mrs Lefanu also says: "That gentleman (Mathews) appeared most surprised at seeing him, and not a little alarmed at the prospect of his visit, the more so as one of the pistols peeped out of his pocket" (Rae, vol. i. chap. v. p 173). This surprise and alarm strike Mr Rae, as very improbable. Yet Sheridan is very precise, and calumny does not appear to have been at all characteristic of him.

60 This unforeseen disappearance, following on a quarrel, excited a fear of nothing less than a duel between the two brothers. Miss Linley and Miss Sheridan both fell ill from the fright. Priestley, the famous chemist, then an inmate of Mr Linley's house, was an eye-witness of their alarm (Mrs Lefanu, in Rae, p 177).

61 Sheridan's account (Moor; vol. i. chap. ii. p 79, etc.).

62 The Castle Tavern, Henrietta Street.

63 Mathews had written and put into circulation a very different account. Sheridan, in reply, composed a detailed history, which he submitted, with what success we do not know, to Mathews' second, Captain Knight.

64 Sheridan was no novice in the art of fencing. "My father, in return for the elder Sheridan's kindness as an occasional preceptor to me, instructed his on R. B. in the use of the small sword; and it was in consequence of the skill which he acquired under this tuition that he acquitted himself with so much address when opposed to the Captain, whose reputation was well known in circles of fashion as an experienced swordsman" (Angelo, "Reminiscences," vol. i. p 85). The elder Angelo was a celebrated fencing-master.

65 He is writing to Captain Knight.

66 Sheridan's account, quoted by Moore, vol. i. chap. 2, pp 80–2. Mr Rae, has not reproduced it in his book, and only gives another, also by Sheridan, which, though less detailed, agrees in every point with this one ("Sheridan," vol. i. chap. v. p 181).

67 See a facsimile of this note in Rae, chap. v., facing p 178.

68 The same issue contains the following paragraph: "We can with authority contradict the account in the *London Evening Post* of last night, of a duel between Mr M-t-w-s and Mr S-r-n, as to the time and event of their meeting, Mr S. having been at this place on Saturday, and both these gentlemen being here at present." I have not been able to examine this issue of the *London Evening Post.*

69 After a short stay at Bath, as the preceding paragraph from the *Bath Chronicle* would seem to indicate.

70 Many persons certainly expected. to see them united, being unaware that a marriage had already taken place. Miss Linley writes to Sheridan one day: "My Mother and me called on Miss Roscoe this evening, when we talked a great deal about you. Miss R. said she was sure you and I would make a match of it. Nay, she said the whole world was of the opinion that we should be married in less than a month" (letter quoted by Rae, vol. i. chap. v. p 193). Other persons thought Sheridan was in love with Miss Linley, but that she discouraged him (see the lines quoted on pp 136–137, *note* 74).

71 See Miss Linley's charming letters to Sheridan (Rae, chap. v. p 189, etc.), especially the second. Mr Rae also ascribes to this period, and with much probability, Sheridan's well-known lines beginning:

"Uncouth is this moss-covered grotto of stone ..."

72 We have previously (p 119) shown how Mr Linley received Sheridan's explanations at Lille. His own father seems to have been equally satisfied by them. "The elder Mr Sheridan ... though not altogether satisfied with some occurrences that had taken place during his absence, yet on the whole did not show much displeasure, considering his youngest son's flight under the light he chose to represent it ..." (Mrs Lefanu's account, Rae, chap. v. p 182). Yet, in a note, three pages further on, Mr Rae mentions, but does not quote, a less indulgent letter from Thomas Sheridan. Sheridan's elder brother, in spite of his indignation, gave the following verdict on his younger brother's conduct, in a letter to his uncle, Mr Chamberlain: "My dear uncle,—I wrote to you some time ago by Mrs Lynn, and mentioned my brother's romantic expedition: he had acquitted himself in the most honourable manner, and the whole of his conduct, however imprudent it might have at first appeared, has, from the motives which influenced his undertaking, acquired him the greatest credit" (Letter dated May 1772, quoted by Rae, chap. v. pp 182–183).

73 "I am surprised that in this age, when the world does not abound in Josephs, most people are (notwithstanding the general tendency in mankind to judge unfavourably) inclined to think he acted with the strictest honour in his late expedition with Miss L., when the circumstances might allow of their being very dubious on this head without incurring the reputation of being censorious" (letter of May 18, 1772, Rae, p 183).

74 The only trace of a contrary opinion I have discovered is in a long piece of poetry which appeared in the *Bath Chronicle* of June 11, 1772, under the heading: "Written after hearing a nominal friend join in condemning a celebrated Young Lady at Bath." The author, or authoress rather (she signs herself Cecilia), takes lip the cudgels for the young girl. Here are a few extracts:

With pain I hear my sex exclaim
Against a Maid the Sport of Fame,
Whose deep unhappiness alone
Might sure the greatest fault atone;
But even they who blame her most
Can only call her nearly lost.

★ ★ ★ ★ ★

But if resolved to censure, blame
The wretch who has betray'd her fame
But for his cool, his barb'rous art,
Some blameless youth had gain'd her heart;
Her heart was but his second view:
Perhaps he was not anxious who
Had that obtain'd—to blast her fame,
And boast his prowess was his aim;

Without desire or warmth to move,
The slave of vanity, not love—
Marked by contempt, long may he pine,
Scorned by his own sex, loath'd by mine ...

The lines close with this apostrophe to Sheridan:

For Thee, who nobly durst protect
E'en her who did thy vows reject,
Who when aspers'd didst clear thy fame,
And brand with infamy the name
Of him, who uniformly mean,
By slandering thee himself would screen—
To fame, to virtue, still aspire,
(Thy gen'rous conduct all admire,)
Still dare t' assert the virtuous cause,
And taste the sweets of self-applause.
What I could wish might far remove
The tortures of unhappy love,
The lenient hand of time may heal
The pangs thy bosom must now feel:
A maid as lovely, and more kind,
May then reward thy gen'rous mind,
Ma view thy worth with partial eyes,
And Happiness be Virtue's prize.

75 "I there [at Bath], to Colonel Gould, Captain Wade [Master of the Ceremonies], and others, mentioned the affair to Mr Mathews' credit—said that chance had given me the advantage, Mr Mathews had consented to that apology, and mentioned nothing of the sword. Mr Mathews came down, and in two days I found the whole affair had been stated in a different light, and insinuations given out to the same purpose as in the paper which has occasioned this trouble ... I then thought I no longer owed Mr Mathews the compliment to conceal any circumstance, and I related the affair to several gentlemen exactly as above" (Sheridan's account, quoted by Moore, vol. i. chap. ii. pp 82, 83). The *Bath Chronicle* of July 9 adds this item, which does not appear elsewhere: "The last affair between Mr Mathews and Mr Sheridan, we are-now assured, was occasioned by Mr S.'s refusal to sign a paper testifying the *spirit and propriety* of Mr M.'s behaviour in their former rencounter. This refusal induced Mr M. to send him a challenge," etc.

76 Besides the reports in the *Bath Chronicle* of July 2 and 9, we have (1) Mrs Lefanu's account, quoted by Rae, chap. vi. pp 598, 599; (2) a letter from Sheridan's father to his brother-in-law, Mr Chamberlain, written a week after the occurrence (Rae, chap. vi. pp 203, 204); this, no doubt, exactly reproduces the account of the incidents just furnished by the hero himself (it begins, "I did not choose to make any inquiries about the affair from my son *till this morning*," etc.); (the report of Matthews' second, Mr Barnett, handed to Captain Wade, the Master of the Ceremonies at Bath (Moore, vol. i. chap.

ii. pp 88, 89). This report was submitted to Captain Paumier, Sheridan's second, who approved it, saying he only differed from its author upon some unimportant points. It may therefore be taken to be fairly impartial. It does not, however, altogether agree with the letter referred to above, and Sheridan declared it to be false, and accused his second of having allowed himself to be frightened; he even drafted a letter on the subject, which was never finished, to Mr Barnett; it is quoted by Moore (*ibid.* pp 93–98).

77 "Endeavouring to get hold of Mr Mathews' sword" (Mr Barnett's report) "with a view of disarming him" (Mrs Lefanu's account).

78 According to Mr Barnett, Mathews broke his sword against Sheridan's ribs in this first engagement. He then seized his adversary's arm and tripped him up. But Barnett does not seem perfectly sure of his two facts, and Sheridan denies that Mathews' sword was broken at that moment, and also denies that he himself was wounded at that time and in that way.

79 The guard and a few inches of the blade, according to Barnett and Mrs Lefanu. The point, according to Sheridan.

80 Perhaps even before he did so. Mrs Lefanu reports, indeed, that he struck him as he lay defenceless on the ground, without calling on him to acknowledge he was beaten But Sheridan only mentions threats, at that moment. Barnett and the *Bath Chronicle* are both silent as to the incident.

81 According to Sheridan himself, he struck at him no less than twenty or thirty times. Sheridan only received four or five wounds, having been able to ward off the others with his hands.

82 According to Sheridan and Mrs Lefanu, Mathews then exclaimed, with an oath, "I've done for him!" Sheridan also asserts that during the whole course of their hand-to-hand struggle he never ceased swearing in the most hideous manner; but Barnett, on the contrary, says: "Mr Mathews discovered as much genuine, cool, and intrepid resolution as a man could do."

83 "Some persons, who were witnesses of the performance that day, still talk of the touching effect her beauty and her singing produced upon all present,—aware, as they were, that a heavy calamity had befallen her, pf which she herself was perhaps the only one in the assembly ignorant" (Moore, vol. i. chap. ii. pp 98, 99). Perhaps Moore is only enlarging on Mrs Lefanu's text here. "I perfectly remember his (Mr T. Grenville's) saying that Miss Linley's appearance on *that* day inspired the greatest interest in the company present, as her ignorance of the duel and its consequences were known to every person, and her beauty, joined to the effect of her truly enchanting powers, could not fail of exciting a degree of sympathy in youthful and susceptible minds, when they thought of the heavy calamity that hung over her" (quoted by Rae, "Sheridan," vol. vi. pp 200, 201).

84 " … She insisted on being permitted to see him, declaring she was his wife, and as such entitled to attend on him" (Mrs Lefanu, Rae, p. 201). Moore has somewhat dramatised the story: "… In the distress of the moment, she let the secret of her heart escape, and passionately exclaimed, 'My husband! my husband!' demanding to see him, and insisting upon her right as his wife to be near him and watch over him day and night" ("Memoirs of Sheridan," vol. i. chap. ii. pp 99).

85 Sheridan's elder brother Charles blamed him likewise. He had hardly made sure he was out of danger when he wrote to him: "We neither of us could approve of the cause for which you suffer. All your friends have condemned you. You risked everything, where you had nothing to gain, to give your antagonist the thing he wished, a chance for recovering his reputation. Your courage was past dispute: he wanted to get rid of the contemptible opinion he was held in, and you were good-natured enough to let him do it at your expense. It is not now a time to scold, but all your friends were of opinion you could, with the greatest propriety, have refused to meet him. For my part, I shall suspend my judgement till better informed, etc." (letter dated July 3, 1772, and quoted by Moore, vol. i. chap. ii. pp 100, 101).

86 "My father's displeasure threatened to involve me in the denunciations against him, for committing what he considered as a crime. Yet I risked everything, and in the event was made happy by obtaining forgiveness for my brother" (Letter from Mrs Lefanu to her brother's second wife, written in 1816 or 1817, Moore, vol. i. chap. i. p 15).

87 "It is with great pleasure we inform, our readers that Mr Sheridan is declared by his surgeon to be out of danger" (*Bath Chronicle* of July 9, a week after the duel).

88 "Old Mr Sheridan, who had naturally planned romantic schemes for the advancement of his highly-gifted son, disapproved of his marriage with a public singer …" (Angelo, "Reminiscences," vol. i. p 86).

89 Mrs Lefanu, in Rae, chap. vi. p 206.

90 See the remains of this correspondence (Rae, pp 206–9). It contains some very touching passages.

91 His first letter to his father (Rae, p 212), written two days after his arrival, is dated August 27. In a letter dated March 16, 1773 (Rae, p 258), Mr Sheridan says again to his son Charles, "Your brother is at present at Waltham Abbey, but preparing to set out for Yorkshire upon a proposal of his own." It was in April that he entered himself at the Middle Temple, and married.

92 Afterwards Marquis of Buckingham, and a political personage (1755–1846). Moore had these letters in his hands, but was not given leave to publish them ("Memoirs of Sheridan," chap. ii. p 106; "Diary," vol. ii. p 189, May 13, 1818); Mr Rae rediscovered them, and has given us the text of many of them ("Sheridan," vol. i. chap. vi. pp 217–251).

93 Quoted by Rae, vol. i. p 220.

94 Rae, vol. i. pp 226–7. It is noteworthy that even to this close friend, Sheridan does not breathe one word of his marriage.

95 Here is a passage from his first, letter from Waltham Abbey to his father: "I left you, Sir, at a time when from appearances you had reason to believe I had not been dealing ingenuously with you. I certainly had in some degree deserved the suspicion; however, some accidental occurrences served greatly to strengthen it. There were circumstances attending that connexion, which you so much wished me to break off, which made it almost impossible to deal with proper candour on both sides; and I can only reassure you that what might strongly seem to be a departing from my word, and your injunctions, was, sincerely, and to the best of my judgement, enter'd

on with a view to secure to myself the power of adhering effectually to both for the future. The merit or demerit of my having so involved myself is not now a question; but I can now have no motive in solemnly declaring to you that I have extricated myself, and that on this subject you shall never again have the smallest uneasiness" (quoted by Rae. chap. vi. pp 212–3).

96 Rae, p 227.

97 Here is what Mr Sheridan, whose impartiality may perhaps lie under some suspicion, writes to his brother-in-law: "Never was more concern shewn on any occasion than was here to be seen in all classes of people on my son's account; for he bears an excellent character and is much beloved. And never were more execrations poured upon any head than that of the vile assassin. Never was a man so universally detested; and I do verily believe, were he to appear in the streets of Bath by day, he would be stoned to death by the populace. If ever he should show his head here again, he will be shunned as one infected by the plague" (Letter dated July 9, 1772, Rae, p 203).

98 See *ante*, p x, *note* 2.

99 "Mathews has come to Bath, and bullying *Paumier* by attempting to call him out, has made him sign some infamous falsehoods, which, I am told, are credited ..." (Letter to T. Grenville, December 8, 1772, Rae, p 242; see also pp 244, 245).

100 Mathews returned to Bath at a later date (see *ante*, p 126, *note* 2). In his "Diary," Moore tells us the following story, on the authority of Lord Thanet "Lord John Townshend and Hare (I think) went down to Bath, to make Mathews' acquaintance and question him about his affairs with Sheridan. Mathews described the duel as a mere farce, declared Sheridan was drunk when he came on the ground, and that he, Mathews, could easily have killed him if he had chosen." As to which Moore cannot help exclaiming, "A precious fellow this Mathews was!" ("Memoirs," vol. iii. p 233.)

101 Moore relates that among other stratagems resorted to by Sheridan in order to exchange a few words with Miss Linley, he disguised himself several times as a cabman and drove her home when she left the theatre ("Memoirs of Sheridan," chap. ii. p 110). The anecdote may perhaps have been taken from Mrs Lefanu's narrative, which was in Moore's hands; the part relating to this period is lost. In any case, the story is given in "Sheridan and his Times, by an Octogenarian" (vol. i. chap. iv. pp 84–85). But it hardly agrees with this passage in a letter of Sheridan's to Grenville: "Eliza is within an hour's ride of me. and must have been for some time, yet, upon my honour I have and do industriously avoid knowing the particular place that is blest with her inhabiting. I was obliged to go to London the other day, and I protest to you, no country-girl passing alone through a churchyard at midnight ever dreaded more the appearance of a ghost than I did to encounter this (for once I'll say) terrestrial being. But I cannot say anything on this subject on paper" (quoted by Rae, chap. vi. p 251).

102 Rae, pp 252–7.

103 "Before I left Bath ... I vowed in the most solemn manner upon my knees before my parents that I would never be yours by my own consent, let what would be the consequence" (*Ibid.* p 256).

104 Moore only says: "At length, after a series of stratagems and scenes which convinced Mr Linley that it was impossible much longer to keep them asunder, he consented to their union ..." (chap. ii. p 111). Mr Rae concludes from various indications that Sheridan offered to give up a portion of the £3000 settled on Miss Linley by Long, thus conciliating Mr Linley, who was fond of money.

105 "He declared he would sooner follow me to the grave than see me married to you, as you would ruin me and yourself in a short time by your extravagance" (Letter from Miss Linley, quoted by Rae, vol. i. p 208).

106 He refused for several years to see his son.

107 See below, chap. vii.

108 Moore, "Memoirs ... of Sheridan," vol. i. chap. v. p 210.

109 *Cf* Miss Lefanu, "Memoirs ... of Mrs F. Sheridan," xii.: "I will briefly give the history of *The School for Scandal* upon the authority of the author's only surviving sister ... At Bath ... [his] duels and adventures [were] magnified and represented in a thousand different ways. When he was recovering of his wounds, it was one of his amusements to read the daily accounts of himself in the papers of the day. 'Let me see what they report of me to-day; I wish to know whether I am dead or alive ...'" (pp 405 and 406). Other inventions galled him more, and suggested a first idea for a play (*ibid.*)."

110 "In the piece, as we have said, are to be found the incidents of the recent escapade—the romantic Lydia, the 'Maid of Bath'; the elopement planned, though not carried out; the rivals and the duel. Sir Anthony was his own dictatorial father; Acres, Mathews; Sir Lucius, Captain Paumier, and Mrs Malaprop probably some vulgarian of the place. The jealous and desponding Faulkland is founded on himself, and long afterwards he used to tease his wife with the same morbid suspicions and imaginings. These, however, only supplied outlines and hints to be treated *secundum artem*. For a while he drew hints from his own temper for Faulkland, he also presented himself to the Bath public as the gay and gallant Absolute, though it was scarcely loyal to represent the character he intended for Mathews as a coward" (Fitzgerald, "Lives of the Sheridans," vol. i. chap. vi. pp 117–8). Others have tried to identify Sir Lucius O'Trigger with Barnett, Mathews' second, and Julia with Mrs Sheridan (Hartmann, "Ueber die Vorlagen zu Sheridan's *Rivals*," p 55); the disagreement is instructive. Without pointing out how forced and arbitrary such parallels are, we may note with Mr Brander Mathews (Sheridan's "Plays," p 75), how improbable it is that Sheridan should have put his wife upon the stage, when, as we know, he guarded her so jealously from publicity that even when destitute he would not allow her to turn her talents as a singer to account. Neither is there any real analogy between the plot of the play and the story of the lovers. If we have the preliminaries of a duel and the vague project of an abduction in the former, it must be admitted that these were very ancient dramatic devices, and sufficiently usual to be employed without necessarily reproducing personal experiences.

111 See on this point Hartmann's dissertation quoted above, and that of Weiss, *Sheridan als Lustspieldichter.* The conclusions of these two writers, especially the second, are altogether exaggerated, and inadmissible. 'Sheridan could not have consciously plagiarised

from so many works (the majority of them must, in fact, have been unknown to him), but it is quite true—and this is a totally different matter—that in the invention of his plots and characters he adhered to an ancient theatrical tradition.

112 See Mary Linley's letter to Mrs Sheridan, dated March 9, 1775 (Moore, "Memoirs ... of Sheridan," chap. iii. pp 139–40): "In my life I never saw anything go off with such uncommon applause ... I suppose the poor creatures never acted with such shouts of applause in their lives ... They lost many of Malaprop's good sayings by the applause; in short I never saw or heard anything like it;—before the actors spoke, they began their clapping." *Cf Bath Chronicle* of the same date: "Mr Sheridan's comedy of *The Rivals* was performed for the first time at our theatre last night; we have the pleasure to say that it was received every mark of approbation and applause from a numerous and polite audience."

VI

Society in Bath: the Methodists

A complete picture in little of English society, an abstract, as it were, of all its elements, the shifting population of Bath could not but abound in contrasts from its very genesis. At one point in the century certain novel and striking antitheses were developed, generated by that great religious and moral upheaval which transformed the English conscience in the eighteenth century: the Methodist movement. A band of apostles suddenly appeared among this assemblage of idlers, fribbles and libertines; above the din of this Vanity Fair rise voices, fervent and austere; Wesley elbows Nash on the Parades; and in the public streets, before a mocking or a hostile crowd, unbidden preachers speak of salvation and judgment, of the world that passeth away and of life everlasting.

For it was at this time that a handful of Oxford students, moral, enthusiastic and fearless, strove to rouse England from her religious lethargy, and, assisted by a few disciples, ardent and devoted as themselves, set forth to carry "the Word" to the four corners of the kingdom. Addressing themselves to all indiscriminately, they forced all to listen, sneering and sceptical aristocrats and rude Cornish miners, the drowsy flocks of the Anglican Church, and the masses of the populace, brutalised by over-work, degraded by poverty and drunkenness, which the growth of national commerce was drawing into the larger towns.[1] Though few in number, their extraordinary zeal and their utter indifference to danger carried them at once to every point of the kingdom. John Wesley appeared at Bath in 1739,[2] the year following his first preachings in London.

One may well be amazed to see him and afterwards his brother[3] and other missionaries directing their steps thus early towards a field that promised so little fruit.[4] What chance was there of a hearing from these people of fashion, frivolous if not corrupt, sceptical for the most part, in any case impervious to all mysticism, and hostile to any unfamiliar manifestation of religion? It was, indeed, as Charles

Wesley said, "attacking Satan at his headquarters,"[5] a remark which shows how important and urgent that attack was in their opinion. No community in the world stood more desperately in need of admonition and conversion; the attempt, desperate as it was, had to be made, and if, after all, the worldlings obstinately closed their ears, there was still some chance of finding the stationary population, the citizens, trades people, and artisans, less stiff-necked.

John Wesley accordingly appeared on the scene in 1739, and preached twice. On the first occasion curiosity drew as many as four thousand hearers,[6] on the second one thousand,[7] vast audiences, with a sprinkling of persons of quality.[8] But on the announcement of a third sermon the rumour suddenly spread abroad that the Master of the Ceremonies was going to interfere, and the curious assembled in crowds. Nash did indeed attend, and asked the new apostle by what authority he did these things.[9] "I replied, 'By the authority of Jesus Christ, conveyed to me by the (now) Archbishop of Canterbury, when he laid his hands upon me, and said: 'Take thou authority to preach the Gospel.' He said: 'This is contrary to Act of Parliament. This is a Conventicle.' I answered: 'Sir, the Conventicles mentioned in the Act (as the Preamble shows) are seditious meetings. But this is not such. Here is no shadow of sedition. Therefore it is not contrary to the Act.' He replied: 'I say it is. But, besides, your preaching frightens people out of their wits.' 'Sir, did you ever hear me preach?' 'No.' 'How then can you judge of what you never heard?' 'Sir, by common report.' 'Common report is not enough. Give me leave, sir, to ask, is not your name Nash?' 'My name is Nash.' 'Sir, I dare. not judge of you by common report. I believe it is not enough to judge by.' Here he paused a while, and having recovered himself, asked: 'I desire to know what these people come here for?' On which one replied: 'Sir, leave him to me. Let an old woman answer him. You, Mr Nash, take care of your body. We take care of our souls, and for the food of our souls we come here.'"[10] The discomfited Beau made no reply but walked away, while the crowd remained some time a prey to conflicting emotions.[11]

More at ease on the Parade—his true domain—Nash planned other annoyances for the Methodists, such as interrupting their open services by his orchestra, reinforced for the occasion by French horns and kettle-drums. He made it play "God save the King," well assured, that no one would dare protest against the National Anthem.[12] For had not these reformers the audacity to preach openly against gambling, and dancing, and even the frequenting of Assembly Rooms?[13] What would become, of the Master of the Ceremonies, or indeed of the ceremonies themselves, if he allowed such subversive doctrines free play?

There came a day, however, when Nash found himself in a dilemma. This was when he saw Methodism openly professed, championed, and propagated in Bath by a great lady, the Countess of Huntingdon.[14] A sect which could boast such a recruit, beside a few others equally patrician, was doubtless worthy of respect, or at least of some consideration, especially as with these persons of breeding there was less danger of eccentric or embarrassing manifestations. The Master of the Ceremonies accordingly unbent so far as to discuss religious questions with Lady Huntingdon; he even consented to hear Whitefield in her house. But the news having got about, his usual associates overwhelmed the supposed neophyte with mock congratulations, satirical verses were posted up in the Pump Room and the Assembly Rooms, and printed broadsheets were circulated announcing the conversion and resignation of the Master of the Ceremonies, and promising his first sermon on the morrow. Nash, greatly annoyed, never set foot, in the Countess's house again.[15]

He would, however, have found himself in good or, at any rate, in noble company. Throughout the long biography of Lady Huntingdon by a relative,[16] we read perpetually of the persons of quality whom she attracted to hear the Methodist preachers in London or elsewhere; the anonymous biographer never forgets to note the lineage of each illustrious convert, and the list of auditors at each sermon reads like a page of the Peerage. The Duchess of Marlborough,[17] Lord Chesterfield,[18] Lord Bolingbroke,[19] Lady Suffolk (the favourite of George II),[20] Horace Walpole,[21] Lord Chatham,[22] are but a few among the host of personages equally distinguished by birth, if not by fame,[23] whom, either at Bath or in London, in her own house, or at the chapels she patronised, she persuaded to hear Wesley or Whitefield.[24]

Several among them were proselytes, others merely curious, but the lady appears to have exercised a singular influence over them all. Who would have expected a Bolingbroke, for instance, to offer her his pen in defence of her opinions on grace and predestination,[25] or have imagined that a Chesterfield, though with certain reservations and a request for anonymity, should present her with twenty pounds towards the building of a new "tabernacle"?[26]

Lady Huntingdon was unquestionably a most remarkable personality. Of an original, enthusiastic and excitable temperament,[27] she devoted herself entirely, soon after her marriage, to a ceaseless crusade in the circle to which she belonged, consecrating to it her strength, her fortune, her whole life and—thanks to the evident sincerity and fervour of her religious zeal—gaining or retaining the admiration of many and the respect of almost all with whom she came in contact. Not that it was her desire, any more than Wesley's, to make innovations, or pose as the foundress of a sect. The aim she pursued so passionately was to awaken the dormant faith of the aristocratic society in which she moved, to revive its moral and religious life. All her conversation was to this end; and never did she make the smallest concession in doctrine, or soften the severity of her tenets. The sternest Calvinism breathed from all her utterances.[28] With her there was no respect of persons. One day when she was present in the Pump Room, a Quakeress suddenly thought fit to lift up her voice against the follies and vanities of this world; the assembled company gave noisy expression to their impatience, whereupon Lady Huntingdon, rising from her seat, went to the preacher, praised aloud her courage and zeal (although she differed widely from her in her own religious opinions), then, taking her by the hand, accompanied her to the door, and quietly returned to her seat.[29] On another occasion in Bath, in the open street, she publicly accosted the actor Shuter, with whom she had no acquaintance, but who had been noticed at Whitefield's services, and invited him to her house in the hope of inducing him to renounce his profession.[30] "There was a publicity in her

Selina, Countess of Huntingdon
From an engraving of the original picture by T. Russel

religion," says the biographer, "that no one else, Dissenter, Puritan, or Anglican, had admitted, at least since the Reformation."[31]

Other characteristics added to this religious fervour and sincerity give a marked originality to the person of this great lady. Her goodness of heart and charm of mind and manner were doubtless the two chief factors in her influence over persons so numerous and diverse, but she was endowed besides with extraordinary activity and energy;[32] one divines in her the temperament of a born organiser and leader of men. Her letters to the Methodist ministers, for instance, are a curious mixture of Christian humility and an unconscious tendency to domineer. The prevailing tone, whatever the subject, is mildly imperious; more than one of them might be a bishop's mandamus.[33] Her correspondents, on their side, always write to her with respectful deference, soliciting her advice and, in general, following it submissively. Whitefield, who became her chaplain in 1748, never addressed her but as "Honoured Madam" and obviously trembled before her.[34] She was in the eyes of the Methodists a model of saintliness,[35] but also a spiritual power, almost a Head of the Church. They called her "a mother in Israel";[36] she was chosen as fourth member of a directing Council, the other three being the brothers Wesley, and Whitefield;[37] at Trevecca in Wales she founded and directed a sort of seminary, from which she dismissed any teacher whose theology differed in the least particular from her own;[38] she dissociated herself vehemently from Wesley the moment his doctrines appeared to her to savour of Arminianism,[39] and the Declaration of Faith of the Calvinistic Methodists expressly mentions her patronage.[40]

This rupture did not take place till 1770, though it had been threatening for some time. During the past ten or twelve years Wesley had frequently preached at Bath, either in the Countess's house or, after 1766, in the chapel built by her.[41] In 1766 he gave a course of sermons there, and on one occasion had Horace Walpole among his auditors. Walpole in one of his letters gives an ironical sketch of what he calls "Mr Wesley's opera." The wit declares himself still unconverted,, which we readily believe. Wesley struck him as "eloquent in parts," but "as evidently an actor as Garrick," and "acting a very ugly enthusiasm." However; he does not regret hearing the sermon. He has heard some pretty voices; he has observed with amusement the luxurious appointments of the chapel—the Gothic windows and the mahogany furniture, the scarlet armchairs reserved for the officiating clergy, and the galleries for the elect ladies.[42] Can we wonder that the earnestness and sincerity of this religious manifestation should have escaped a sceptic of Walpole's pattern? He had eyes only for the ridiculous aspect, which doubtless was not wanting in a place of worship so like a drawing-room, to which one was admitted by ticket,[43] and where a curtained space like an opera-box was provided for persons desirous of hearing without being seen.[44]

The doctrines and morals preached there were, however, rigid and austere in the extreme, so much so as to offend the ears of some of the fine ladies. The Countess of Suffolk, persuaded by Lady Huntingdon to come and hear Whitefield in London, took such umbrage at certain shafts which she thought were aimed at her, that she quarrelled irrevocably with her friend. The Duchess of Buckingham told Lady Huntingdon point blank that she considered the Methodist doctrines were "most repulsive, and strongly tinctured with impertinence and disrespect towards their superiors, in perpetually endeavouring to level all ranks and do away with all distinctions. It is monstrous to be told that you have a heart as sinful as the common wretches that crawl the earth. This .is highly offensive and insulting, and I cannot but wonder that your Ladyship should relish any sentiments so much at variance with high rank and good breeding."[45]

However, we must not be guided by Walpole or the Duchess of Buckingham in judging of the congregations who went to hear the Methodist preachers, or of the effect of their discourses. In Bath, as everywhere else, the religious impression was profound and widespread. The number of converts and semi-converts in Bath must have been considerable, for on certain days the chapel could not contain the crowd who thronged to its doors—a crowd both respectful and devout.[46] But their number and their fervour are still better attested by the local authors and scribblers, who made these religious manifestations the butt of their facile wit,[47] not to mention the writers of articles and occasional poems who are not sparing of their sallies against the Methodists, etc.[48] Anstey, in his "New Bath Guide," devotes the whole of a very gross letter to them, recounting the gulling of a credulous servant wench by a hypocritical and dissolute minister;[49] and not content with this at tack, he returns several times to the charge in his poem.[50] Graves, the Anglican rector of Claverton, near Bath, the friend of Ralph Allen, of Warburton and Pope, went still further: he attacked the new sect in "The Spiritual

Lady Huntingdon's chapel at Bath

Quixote," a novel not without merit, long scenes of which took place in Bath. As soon as the heroes of the book, Wildgoose and Tugwell, two travelling preachers, come within sight of the city, they liken it to Jerusalem, similarly "closed about" with hills,[51] and the surrounding country to Canaan.[52] They hasten to an inn and inquire of the host if there are many Methodists in Bath. "Are there?" says mine host. "Yes, I believe there are; enough to turn the heads of all the 'prentices and journeymen in the nation. I am sure I cannot keep a chambermaid or a tapster, but the toads must be singing psalms, preaching to my customers, and be pox'd to 'em, from morning to night."[53] Discovering, however, with whom he has to deal, the innkeeper changes his tone, and the travellers are consoled by hearing the tabernacle described by a chambermaid "Ah, sir! we have such soul-searching teachers! Such ravishing ministers! They come so close to the point, and does so grapple with the sinner! They probe his sins to the very quick, and pour in such comfortable balsam! And (as Mr Twangdillo told us last night) though it may pain, yet, like physic in the bowels, it pains us for some purpose; and, to be sure, as he said, conversion follows conviction, as naturally as thread does the needle."[54] Thus encouraged, Wildgoose repairs to the Parade with intent to preach, but is prevented in the manner already described (p 144). He has better luck in the evening, and succeeds in pronouncing his discourse against the follies of the place (p 150, note 12), and afterwards accompanies Tugwell to the tabernacle, where they hear a sermon from a chandler.[55] But, little edified by their co-religionists, the two friends presently leave Bath and resume their peregrinations, from which they return home sadly disillusioned.[56]

But opposition and satire were alike futile, as futile indeed as were all the adversaries ranged against Methodism throughout England. They could not but prove powerless against a sect which, though small, was so fervid, so single-minded and so absolutely convinced. Moreover, powerful or insignificant, ridiculous or admirable, the sect, as such, whether in Bath or elsewhere, was the least important fruit of the Methodist movement. Not by its immediate creations, its organised societies, but by its indirect and far—reaching effects did the new faith transform England. It sent a shock through the souls of the people, a shock that ran from one to the other, and startled the nation out of its moral and religious apathy; even at Bath, that centre of frivolity, its influence was felt; here, too, it revived a forgotten ideal. Side by side with the equivocal or light-minded society of that city, we shall henceforth see a company of austere, clean-living and clean-thinking men and women, who reacted unconsciously, slowly but surely on the rest, and increased at its expense.[57] The dissipated, gambling, dissolute Bath will settle down by degrees and come in line with other English cities, reformed characters like herself, though their crop of wild oats had been less abundant. From the beginning of the nineteenth century this uniformity was almost complete, so complete, in fact, as doubtless to be one of the reasons why Bath was then deserted by a certain—not the most regrettable—section of the birds of passage she was wont to attract. Birds of prey or airy songsters, they demand an atmosphere less clear and less calm, and, finding it no longer in England, they hie them swift-winged to the Continent.

1 For details of the Methodist movement, see *i.a.* Lecky, "History of England," vol. iii. chap. viii., and Chevrillon, "Sydney Smith," chap. iv. section v.

2 The Tuesday before April 23 ("Wesley's Journal," under this date).

3 Also in 1739, but he met with a bad reception and only succeeded in preaching once or twice ("Life and Times of Selina, Countess of Huntingdon, by a Member of the Houses of Shirley and Hastings," vol. i. p 445).

4 The reader need hardly be reminded that religious unbelief was extremely prevalent in the upper and literary classes. "There is no religion in England," writes Montesquieu in 1730 in his "Notes" on that country ("Works," Laboulaye edition, vol. vii. p 195); Voltaire makes the same statement again and again. See also Green, "A Short History of the English People," chap. x.; Lecky, op. cit. chap. ii. and viii. passim; Rémusat, "L'Angleterre au XVIIIe Siecle," vol. i. chap. xxiv.

5 Quoted by Southey, "Life of Wesley," vol. ii. chap. xiv. p 28. Some years later his brother writes in the same strain: "I know not when I have seen a more serious, a more deeply attentive congregation. Is it possible? Can the Gospel have place where Satan's throne is?" ("Life and Times," vol. i. p 478, note.)

6 "Journal of Wesley," April 23, 1739.

7 *Ibid.* May 22, 1739.

8 "There were several fine gay things among them, to whom specially I called, 'Awake, thou that sleepest, and arise from the dead, and Christ shall put thee right" (*Ibid.*).

9 "There was great expectation at Bath of what a noted man was to do with me there: and I was much intreated 'not to preach, because no one knew what might happen.' By this report I also gained a much larger audience, among whom were many of the rich and great. I told them plainly, 'The Scripture had concluded them all under sin,' high and low, rich and poor, one with another. Many of them seemed to be

not a little surprised, and were sinking apace into seriousness, when the champion appeared, and coming close to me asked, 'By what authority I did these things'" ("Journal of Wesley," June 5, 1739).

10 "Journal of Wesley," June 5, 1739.

11 "As I returned, the street was full of people hurrying to and fro and speaking great words. But when any of them asked 'Which is he?' and I replied, 'I am he,' they were immediately silent. Several ladies following me into Mr Marchant's house, the servant told me 'There were some wanted to speak with me.' I went to them and said: 'I believe, ladies, the maid mistook; you only wanted to look at me.' I added, 'I do not expect that the rich and great should want either to speak with me or hear me, for I speak the plain truth: a thing you little hear of and do not desire to hear.' A few more words passed between us and I returned." (*Ibid.*)

12 "But Mr Nash, though he himself had greatly reformed and regulated the manners and behaviour of his subjects in the public room; yet, being orthodox in his tenets and very well content with the present state of religion amongst them, he did not desire any reformation in that article. Having notice, therefore, of this intended preachment, he got ready his band of music, with the addition of two or three French horns and kettledrums. And as soon as the Orator had exhibited his person on the Parade, stretched forth his hand, and (like Paul in the Cartoon) was in act to speak, Nash gave the signal for the grand chorus of 'God Save the King'; the music struck 'up; and playing so loyal a piece of music no one had the hardiness to interrupt them. Nay, a majority of the company were probably pleased with Nash's humour; and it being now, breakfast time, the mob was easily dispersed" (Graves, "Spiritual Quixote," book v. chap. v. pp 277–78). This incident is introduced as an anecdote in the novel but it may well have 'been founded on fact; 'there is nothing, however, to indicate which of the Methodist preachers was thus reduced to silence.

13 In Graves's story the preacher succeeds in delivering his harangue in the evening: " … [He] inveighed with great severity against luxury in dress, cards, dancing, and all the fashionable diversions of the place; and even against frequenting the rooms with the most innocent intentions of recreation and amusement." Certain Methodists maintained that "no recreation, considered as such, could be innocent" they especially condemned dancing (see the authorities quoted by Lecky, op. cit. vol. iii. chap. viii. pp 87–89).

14 She came to Bath in 1739 with her husband, a friend of Ralph Allen, with whom, at that period, Pope and Warburton were staying. Warburton naturally had hot religious discussions with the Countess, and having one day attacked the doctrines of Whitefield, and Allen and the rest siding with Lady Huntingdon, he was so incensed that he left the room ("Life and Times of Selina, Countess of Huntingdon," vol. i. pp 444 and 450–51). Widowed in 1746, Lady Huntingdon returned to Bath in 1747 (*ibid.*); and from that year till her death in 1791 she made frequent long visits to the city (*ibid. passim*); in 1765 she built her famous chapel (*ibid.* p 466).

15 *Ibid.* p 445, note.

16 "Life," etc. By a member of the Houses of Shirley and Hastings. See in the British Critic, v. xxviii. pp 263–295 (October 1840), an article by Newman on this work, reprinted in his "Essays Critical and Historical," vol. i.

17 "Life and Times," vol. i. pp 24, 25.

18 *Ibid.* p 463.

19 Lord Bolingbroke was very intimate with Lady Huntingdon, and had frequent discussions with her on the subject of religion. He often went to hear Whitefield, whom he praises in the following terms in a letter: "He is the most extraordinary man in our times. He has the most commanding eloquence I ever heard in any parson—his abilities are very considerable—his zeal unquenchable, and his piety and eloquence genuine, unquestionable ..." (quoted in "Life and Times," vol. i. p 179).

20 *Ibid.* pp 98, 99.

21 *Ibid.* p 477.

22 *Ibid.* pp 109 and 478.

23 Mention may also be made of George Selwyn (ibid. p 108), Lord Lyttelton. (ibid. p 228), Lord Camden, the Lord Chancellor, Lord Northington., the Duke of Bedford, Lord Rockingham (ibid. p 478), etc.

24 Southey, "Life of Wesley," vol. ii. chap. xxv. p 366. More particularly Whitefield who began preaching in Bath in 1752, in which year he preached for three weeks in succession "before a great number of the nobility" ("Life and Times," vol. i. p 453). He often returned. The biographer of Lady Huntingdon mentions Wesley preaching in 1759, 1766, 1769 (vol. i. pp 395, 474; vol. ii. p 26). Bath had also frequent visits from Venn, Romaine, Shirley, Fletcher, etc. (*ibid. passim*).

25 "The impression made upon him by Mr Whitefield's preaching may be judged by his saying to the Countess: 'You may command my pen when you will: it shall be drawn in your service. For, admitting the Bible to be true, I shall have little apprehension of maintaining the doctrines of predestination and grace against all your revilers'" ("Life and Times," vol. i. p 98).

26 "Your Ladyship is a powerful auxiliary to the Methodist Cabinet, and I confess, notwithstanding my own private feeling and sentiments, I am infinitely pleased at your zeal in so good a cause. You must have twenty pounds for this new tabernacle, whenever you think proper, but I must beg my name not to appear in any way" *(ibid.* vol. ii. p 379, a letter dated June 18, 1749, but not given either in the "Miscellaneous Works" or the editions of the correspondence published by Lord Mahon and by Bradshaw). Lady Chesterfield had been converted by Whitefield through the Countess of Huntingdon, who long hoped for similar results with Lord Chesterfield and Mr Stanhope ("Life and Times," vol. i. pp 462, 463; see also her sorrowful letter on the death of Chesterfield, p. 464). Lady Gertrude Hotham, Chesterfield's sister, and his sister-in-law, the Countess Delitz, were ardent Methodists.

27 Southey, who disliked her, and, one cannot but think, did her injustice; declares there was insanity in her family ("Life of Wesley," vol. ii. chap. xxv. p 358). This fact is denied by her anonymous biographer ("Life and Times," p 18).

28 "Wherever she went, she invariably produced an extraordinary degree of attention to religious subjects ..." Wherever she was, and in whatever company, her conversation was on religion, in which there was this peculiarity, that she spoke of the sins and errors of her former life, her conversion to God, the alteration in her heart and

conduct, and she plainly said to all it was absolutely necessary that the same change should take place in them, if they would have any hope in death" ("Life and Times," vol. i. p 443).

29 Mary Ann Schimmelpenninck, "Life," vol. i. pp 89–90.

30 "Life and Times," vol. i. p 208.

31 *Ibid.* p 443.

32 "The following amusing. anecdote shows how Lady Huntingdon sometimes worked off this superfluity of energy before her conversion. She was much interested in politics—she was of Walpole's party—and one day in 1738, on the occasion of an important debate, the Lords thought fit to forbid admission to all but actual members of the House to the galleries. Lady Huntingdon and a dozen or so of her lady friends refused to be thus excluded. They proceeded to lay siege to the door of the gallery and battered on it till the orators within could not hear one another speak. The ladies remained without food till five in the afternoon, and finally entered the forbidden precincts by a stratagem" (Lady Mary Wortley Montagu, "Letters and Works," vol. ii. pp 222–4; letter to Lady Pomfret, 1738).

33 As, for instance, a letter to Venn, in which she reproves him for certain theological opinions, and ends up thus: "And now, my dear friend, no longer let false doctrine disgrace your pulpit," etc. ("Life and Times," vol. i. p 225). Referring to this passage Newman remarks very justly and wittily: " … She speaks ex cathedra,—Selina Episcopa dilecto filio Henrico Venn" ("Essays Critical and Historical," vol. i. p 413). Fletcher writes to her: "I am greatly indebted to your Ladyship for what light I have into the nature of the foundation of Christianity; and, although I have great reason to be ashamed of the little use I have made of it, I hope it will work its way, by the power of Christ's Spirit, through the thick darkness of my self-righteous, unbelieving heart, and then to be a closer follower of you, as you are of Christ" ("Life and Times," vol. i. p 234).

34 Passages of this kind occur in his letters: "Ever since the reading of your Ladyship's condescending letter, etc … On Monday morning, from nine to near eleven, I will be at your Ladyship's, and wait to know your order concerning Tuesday. I am ashamed to think you will admit me under your roof," etc. (*ibid.* p 90).

35 Here is an extract from one of Venn's letters: "In Lady Huntingdon I see a star of the first magnitude in the firmament of the Church … When I compare my life and spirit with hers, I could not believe the same heaven will contain us both" (ibid. vol. ii. p 31). "I think I never saw so much of the image of God in any woman upon earth" (letter of Dr Doddridge, ibid. vol. i. p 154).

36 Whitefield, in a letter ("Life and Times," p 162)

37 *Ibid.* p 475.

38 Southey, "Life of Wesley," chap. xxv.; "Life and Times," vol. ii. chap. xxxix. The students were also completely under her control: "I wrote to the Cheltenham student to order him to France, as having a more able one to employ while the company was there. But he sent him back, and said he would not go. I then repeated my orders to both to change … The wicked and most shameful confusion they have made in Wales must not be continued …" (See the whole of this long and extremely

characteristic letter in "Life and Times," vol. ii. pp 434–437). Wesley, just before their rupture, remarked that Lady Huntingdon always speaks of 'my college, my masters, my students; I mixes with everything." (Letter quoted ibid. vol. ii. p 225; compare in the letter quoted in part above: "My own ministers must have the lead through all the work," *ibid.* p 436.)

39 The rupture was for theological reasons, but the Countess seems never to have been as intimate with Wesley as with the other Methodist preachers: "Wesley, who neither wanted nor would have admitted patron or patroness to be temporal head of the societies which he had formed … seems never to have been cordially liked by her, and gradually grew into disfavour" (Southey, "Life of Wesley," vol. ii. chap. xxv. p 362).

40 "We have therefore found it expedient, for the welfare and unity of the various congregations wherewith we are connected under the patronage of the Countess of Huntingdon," etc. ("Life and Times," vol. ii. p 440). In 1780 she sends round a sort of pastoral letter "To my well-beloved friends of the Congregation of my Chapel, Bath" (ibid. vol. ii. p 486). One branch of the Methodists call themselves to this day Methodists of the Countess of Huntingdon's Connexion.

41 *Cf* above p150, *note* 14.

42 "My health advances faster than my amusement. However, I have been at one opera, Mr Wesley's. They have boys and girls with charming that sing hymns, in parts, to Scotch ballad tunes; but indeed so long that one would think they were already in eternity, and knew how much time they had before them. The chapel is very neat, with true Gothic windows (yet I am not converted); but I was glad to see that luxury is creeping in upon them before persecution; they have very neat mahogany for branches, and brackets of the same in taste. At the upper end is a broad hautpas of four steps, advancing in the middle: at each end of the broadest part are two of my eagles [a gift by Walpole to Lady Huntingdon?] with red cushions for the parson and clerk. Behind them rise three more steps, in the midst of which is a third eagle for pulpit. Scarlet armchairs to all three. On either hand, a balcony for elect ladies. The rest of the congregation sit on forms. Behind the pulpit, in a dark niche, is a plain table within rails; so you see the throne is for the apostle. Wesley is a lean elderly man, fresh-coloured, his hair smoothly combed, but with a soupçon of curls at the end. Wondrous clean, but as evidently an actor as Garrick. He spoke his sermon, but so fast and with so little accent that I am sure he has often uttered it, for it was like a lesson. There were parts of eloquence in it; but towards the end he exalted his voice and acted very ugly enthusiasm; decried learning and told stories, like Latimer, of the fool of his college who said, 'I thanks God for everything.' Except a few from curiosity and some honourable women, the congregation was mean. There was a Scotch Countess of Buchan, who is carrying a pure rosy vulgar fate to heaven, and who asked Miss Rich if that was the author of the poets. I believe she meant me and the Noble Authors" (letter of October 10, 1766, addressed to John Chute, vol. v. of the Correspondence).

43 This detail occurs in the account of a German traveller: "The Methodists meet together in the Countess of Huntingdon's chapel, which is simply a little church

with benches and slightly raised places for the clergy and the singers. The sexes sit apart from each other. On Sunday I attended one of their meetings, to which one is admitted by a ticket, and listened awhile to their psalm-singing, but did not stay long. As far as I could judge the service is monotonous, though there is a good deal of ranting too" ("Bemerkungen eines Reisenden," by J. J. C. Grimm, vol. iii. 66th letter, p 88).

44 This retreat was known, as "Nicodemus' Corner," in allusion to that person in the Gospel. Bishops, it appears, occasionally occupied it ("Life and Times," vol. i. p 477).

45 Letter quoted in "Life and Times," vol. i. p 27.

46 "The congregation was not only large, but serious" ("Journal of Wesley," August 2, 1766). "The congregation was very large and very attentive. Let us despair of nothing" (ibid. March, 1769). "The chapel doors were set open, and people stood in the court as far as the houses" (letter of Venn, 1769, in "Life and Times," vol. ii. p 31). There are many similar evidences in that work; *cf* also above, p 149, *notes* 6, 7, and p 151, *note* 24.

47 It is needless to remark that in this they only echoed the majority of the writers of the time, Pope, Johnson, Fielding, Smollett, Sterne, etc. (see on this point Swallow, "Methodism in the Light of English Literature of the last Century").

48 See, for instance, "The Register of Folly," vol. ii. p 26, and vol. iii. p 40.

49 Letter xiv.

50 Letter vii. (postscript); Letter xv. (epilogue), the. letter following the epilogue. In the two first passages he has a hit in passing at the Moravian preachers. Thicknesse, in his "New Prose Guide," p 34, mentions in 1778 a Meeting House for the Moravians; they cannot have been very numerous.

51 "As mighty mountains, huge and large, Jerusalem about do close … I should compare it to Jerusalem in another respect, 'Jerusalem is built as a city that is at unity with itself.'" ("Spiritual Quixote," book v. chap. i. pp 264, 265.)

52 "Spiritual Quixote," book v. chap. i. p 265.

53 *Ibid.* chap. ii. p 270.

54 *Ibid.* p 273.

55 *Ibid.* chap. xv.

56 Tugwell remarks that "There was nothing but card-playing, gaming, and swearing from morning to night amongst the servants and apprentices that reformed thither" (*Ibid.* p 330).

57 Anstey notes the contrast, and describes "this adorable Scene":

Where Gaming and graces
Each other embraces,
Dissipation and Piety meet;—
May all who've a Notion
Of Cards or Devotion
Make Bath their delightful retreat.
("New Bath Guide," xv.)

VII

Authors at Bath: Bath in Plays and Novels; Sheridan, Smollet, Jane Austen, and Dickens

No English town, with the exception, as I have already said, of London, was so quoted, praised, criticised, and described by eighteenth-century writers as Bath. "The genius of Anstey and Smollett, Frances Burney and Miss Austen," has, as Macaulay declared, "made it classic ground."[1] But how many other names he might have added to this illustrious quartet, from Goldsmith to Dickens, to go no further! The list would become interminable, if, to the writers who have made Bath the subject of their pictures, we should add those who visited the city, either to mend their shattered health, or to divert themselves with the spectacle of her society. At the dawn of her prosperity, we have noted the presence within her gates of Rochester, who there wrote his pastoral dialogue, Alexis and Strephon."[2] Wycherley made several appearances there at a later date,[3] and also Congreve.[4] Defoe visited the town in 1711, and drew an elaborate picture of it in his "Tour Thro' Great Britain,"[5] which was re-edited and issued afresh many times afterwards. Addison took the waters the same year, accompanied by the poet Philips.[6] Two years later, Steele found material at Bath for certain satirical descriptions.[7] In 1714 Pope greatly enjoyed a visit there; he pronounced the Promenades the finest in the world, passed from the Assembly Rooms to the Chocolate Houses, from the Pump to the theatre, and tried, as he laughingly says, to make himself agreeable by imitating sometimes the civility, sometimes the impudence, and sometimes the folly of various acquaintances.[8] He went through all the round of amusements,[9] becoming, he says, so dissipated and perverse that he is ashamed to be seen in company of Dr Parnell (the author of "The Hermit"), and asks people "who that parson is?"[10] All his life Pope continued to be an habitué of Bath, an habitué, we shall find later, together with Fielding, Warburton, and Graves, under the hospitable roof of Ralph Allen.[11] After him, or at the same time with him, certain of his friends visited Bath: Bolingbroke,[12] Arbuthnot,[13]

Gay,[14] who was present at the performance of his "Beggar's Opera"; other poets, such as Shenstone, who came to visit his old friend Graves,[15] the author of the "Spiritual Don Quixote," Cowper, who in 1748 there composed the verses on a shoe with which the collection of his early poems opens. Lady Mary Wortley Montagu wrote a rhymed farewell to the town, in which she recalls the many balls she had led in the Assembly Rooms.[16] Two graver personages, Butler and Berkeley, came to the baths in quest, not of pleasure, but of health; a bootless quest, for they both died there within a year one of another.[17] Smollett probably thought of settling there to practise medicine, and wrote a treatise on the Bath waters;[18] though he abandoned the project, he at least carried away with him reminiscences of the town, with which he filled "Roderick Random" and "Peregrine Pickle," reminiscences he came back to renew before beginning "Humphry Clinker." Young, the author of the "Night Thoughts," restored his health at Bath in 1757.[19] Mrs Catherine Macauley wrote a great part of her once famous "History of England" there, receiving extraordinary ovations from enthusiastic admirers,[20] though the visit of a historian of a very different calibre, Hume, passed unnoticed.[21] Goldsmith went to Bath in 1762, and his biography of Nash was the outcome of this visit. It was during a second visit, in 1771, that the well-known adventure befell him while he was the guest of Lord Nugent. One day, instead of returning to his host's house, he entered the adjoining one in a fit of abstraction, and taking the Duke and Duchess of Northumberland, to whom it belonged, for visitors, he entertained them as such. Much amused, they put off the moment of enlightenment as long as possible, endeavouring to spare their heedless visitor a natural confusion, and finally invited him to dinner.[22] Sterne came to Bath in 1765,[23] and it was here that Gainsborough painted his portrait. In 1769, the Swiss Bonstetten made the acquaintance at Bath of Thomas Pitt (brother to the Minister) and of a friend of Gray's called Nicholls, connections that were to introduce him to the English Court and into political and literary circles.[24] In November 1775, Scott, then a child of four years old, paid his first visit to a theatre at Bath, an experience that made an indelible impression on his young mind;[25] a like pleasure, almost as keenly enjoyed, was to be the portion of the youthful Southey in the same theatre three years later.[26]

In 1776 Johnson accompanied the Thrale family to the waters, and the faithful Boswell followed; he had never seen this fine city, and wished to seize the opportunity of doing so while Johnson was there.[27] He stayed several days, and recorded, in his usual manner, all things grave or gay that fell from the lips of the great man during this period. With the Thrales again, Miss Burney, in all the glory of her recent success with "Evelina,"[28] spent the season of 1780 there, in an atmosphere of homage and compliments.[29] Gibbon wrote to a friend that Bath was the place of all others in England where he should prefer to live if he ever left his dear Lausanne.[30] Two distinguished foreigners, Pindemonte[31] and Madame de Genlis[32] passed through the city in the early days of the French Revolution. Hannah Moore, in the height of the great cataclysm, was amazed to see the same careless frivolity on every side as heretofore; "Bath, happy Bath, is as gay as if there

Frances Burney
From the portrait by Edward Burney

were no war, nor sin, nor misery in the world! We run about all the morning, lamenting the calamities of the times, anticipating our ruin, reprobating the taxes, and regretting the general dissipation, and every night we are running into every excess, to a degree unknown in calmer times. Yet it is the fashion to affect to be religious, and to show it by inveighing against the wickedness of France! I really know many who believe they are pious on no other ground."[33] She herself was not so easily satisfied, and set about the composition of little pamphlets, designed to check the revolutionary propaganda among the lower orders.[34] At about the same time, the famous scholar Porson cut a very singular figure in the Assembly Rooms, scandalising the Master of the Ceremonies by his disordered hair, his loose neck-cloth, and wrinkled stockings.[35] In 1796, Coleridge preached twice on a Sunday in the Unitarian Chapel. Did many devout persons, like the enthusiastic Hazlitt at a later date, walk ten miles to hear him,[36] and listen enthralled to the voice that "rose like a steam of rich distilled perfumes," the accents that seemed "to echo from the bottom of the human heart, and float in solemn silence through the universe?" Did they, like him, feel that they were listening to another "St John … crying in the wilderness, who had his loins girt about, and whose food was locusts and wild honey?" and declare themselves "as much delighted as if they had heard the music of the spheres?"[37] By no means. The congregation, which was meagre enough on the first occasion, dwindled to seventeen persons on the second; and the preacher, oddly dressed in a blue coat and white waistcoat, and discussing the Corn Laws and the tax on powder, astonished, but failed to edify or delight, his few hearers.[38]

Another and greater orator came on three occasions to the Bath waters at this period. This was Burke,[39] who visited the city in quest of health, first for his wife, and finally for himself. Unwearying in his political activity, he wrote his "Heads for Consideration in the Present State of Affairs" during his first stay, and during his second some fragments of his third "Letter on the Regicide Peace." To another visit, of no political significance, the long sojourn of Miss Austen at Bath (from 1801 to 1805) we owe several of the best chapters of "Northanger Abbey" and "Persuasion." The first was ready for publication in 1803, but the timidity of a local publisher deferred the novelist's appearance and her literary glory for eight years.[40] From September to December, 1816, Shelley was living at Bath with the Godwin family; it was the period of his life which was so darkly coloured by two suicides, that of Fanny Godwin, and that of Harriet Westbrook, his first wife.[41] No mere visitor, but a veritable citizen of Bath, was Beckford, the author of "Vathek," and the luxurious master of Fonthill Abbey, close to the gates of the city. The same may be said of Landor, who, in the midst of his wanderings, in 1808 chose for his headquarters the city of England that he thought most like Florence,[42] and architecturally, one of the most admirable in the world.[43] He attracted general attention there by his wit, his good looks, his wealth, his peculiarities, his gallantry a constant visitor at the Assembly Rooms.[44] "Here, in the spring of 1811, he met a young lady at a ball, and as soon as he had set eyes on her, exclaimed, in the true Landorian manner: 'By heaven, that's the nicest girl in the room, and I'll marry her!' And marry her he did …"[45] After an interval spent on his estate, and in Italy, he settled at Bath in his old age, enjoying the companionship of Napier, Carlyle, Forster, Dickens, and the friendship of the future Napoleon III. But here I am led beyond the limits I have fixed for this study. I will merely add, as I have mentioned Dickens, that several chapters of the "Pickwick Papers" are devoted to a satirical description of Bath, and that the very flame, Pickwick was borrowed from that of the postmaster of the town.[46] The great novelist draws a picture of Bath in its decline, prim, narrow, and languid, just as another great novelist, three-quarters of a century earlier, had painted it in its turbulent and scandalous vigour, and as several others had sketched its most curious aspects in passing. The authors we must read with more attention than the rest in this connection are those who, in the spectacle of a curious Society, found not merely amusement, but a subject for study. Let us see what impression the Bath of various periods made upon them, and how they translated this impression in their works.[47]

As was only natural, the comic writers were the first to present Bath and her visitors to the public. They began early; in 1701, at the very dawn of the new period, Durfey gave Drury Lane a comedy called The Bath, or the Western Lass, which was acted again the following year, and seems to have had some success.[48] Recollections of Epsom Wells, a fairly good comedy by Shadwell (1673), and Tunbridge Wells, or a Day's Courtship, by an anonymous writer[49] (in 1678), no doubt encouraged the author to choose a similar scene and subject, providing them, as he claims in his dedication, with "a pretty plot, and at least four new characters."[50] He expected a certain amount of applause for these creations, but he certainly exaggerates their merit; the only character of any originality in his piece is a country wench, as bold in words as in action, who speaks a broad Somersetshire dialect. It is by no means interesting: all the other personages belong to the current repertory of the day; they are the male and female rakes of contemporary English comedy. The manners and speech also belong to this comedy; we cannot therefore draw conclusions very adverse to Bath therefrom. As to the plot, this is the incident Durfey probably prides himself upon having invented: one of the characters is to find another's room in the dark by means of a small piece of furniture in front of the door; this is displaced by accident, and all sorts of mistakes follow. This is not very striking, and the play, not a very moral one, has nothing to recommend it but a certain vivacity. It does not attempt, save in a very general fashion, to paint the motley society which was already gathering round the wells, and the life they led there. The only picture of Bath is that with which the play opens; it is true that this, gives us some idea of the coarseness and brutality that still obtained there, and it is probable that these are by no means exaggerated. The scene is the King's Bath, or a room adjoining it, where a certain Colonel Philip asks the superintendent the meaning of the clamour and screaming that has been going on ever since five in the morning. It is all, replies the other, the fault of a certain Hairbrain, who, not content with regularly making his entry in naturalibus, thinks it a great joke to spring upon the backs of the other bathers, even the women, and beat a tattoo upon their bodies. The colonel laughs heartily at the description of these pleasantries; and, that the spectators may share his amusement, the author makes Hairbrain appear in a pair of drawers (this is a concession), and pursue a lady, blowing a horn the while. Was this really the state of things that obtained before the accession of King Nash? It is very probable, and Goldsmith was indulgent enough when he said merely that "the amusements of the place were neither elegant nor conducted with delicacy."[51]

Nothing, however, of the elegance and delicacy introduced by Nash seems to have been reflected in a comedy written some twenty-four years later, The Bath Unmasked, by Odingsells.[52] It is true that this mediocre play reveals no great power of observation or of description. The characters, feebly drawn and colourless, work out a trivial and uninteresting plot. But it is significant that it is still the same disreputable society, and the same lax manners that are. depicted. An heiress, whose tone and conduct, if not her heart, have been corrupted by her surroundings, is ensnared by a French swindler; her mother, a confirmed gambler, forwards the plans of the adventurer, in return for promises of money that are never kept, and, further, allows herself to be robbed by sharpers with whom she plays.[53] A despicable individual bearing the sinister name of Pander, carries off a young girl. If two virtuous lovers are contrasted with their neighbours, the picture, pale and lifeless as it is on the whole, suggests a frivolous and equivocal community.[54] This was evidently the idea London spectators had of Bath society, and not altogether without reason.

It appears, however, in a more favourable light in the unfinished play left us by Mrs Sheridan, the mother of the distinguished writer. Reading this, we feel that forty years have gone by, that Bath has expanded, and has become orderly and law-abiding. The picture, a more flattering one, is also more varied. It gives us something more than a mob of sharpers.[55] In the gardens, the Assembly Rooms, and the various places to which the author conducts us, types sufficiently varied are brought together. Most of these have ridiculous traits. A certain Mrs Tryfort apes the manners of the great, and makes comical essays in fine language.[56] Lady Bel Air Castle lives in terror of compromising her patrician dignity in inferior company; a Sir Jeremy Bull, a ruined gentleman, looks down upon the richest City merchants; one Champignon, a rich West Indian planter, wholly uneducated, is able to buy respect, social advantages, and titles with his money; all are creatures of average character, who have their faults, large and small, calculate, intrigue, etc., but are honest folks in the main. Even the two adventurers, Lord Stewkly[57] and Lady Filmot, are of a higher grade than their forerunners in the earlier comedies. Each on the look-out for a rich parti,[58] and operating in concert, they are nevertheless above the level of the vulgar swindler; they have good manners, and speak the language of educated people. Disappointed in their plans, they no doubt made up a match together, and lived fairly happily. But this dénouement is merely conjectural, for Mrs Sheridan only finished the first three acts. It is a pity she carried it no farther. Her play is amusing, if slightly thin and superficial, and we know that Sheridan did not disdain to borrow several features from it, as well as one whole character.[59]

Mrs Sheridan's invented plot and imaginary types were succeeded almost immediately[60] by the representation of real incidents, the picture or the caricature of living persons. In his Maid of Bath of 1771, Foote placed the romance of Miss Linley, and the various persons concerned in it on the boards. We have already seen[61] how audaciously he set, not only the fair heroine, but Mrs Linley, Mr Long, and Major Mathews in the glare of the footlights, how he did not hesitate to make the three latter play odious or ridiculous parts, and how careful he was to make their identity unmistakable. His audacity was successful with the public, and this success cannot be attributed solely to the love of scandal. The play, though merely a sketchily treated improvisation, is lively, well constructed, and amusing;[62] it occupies an honourable place among Foote's perhaps unduly neglected dramas, not much below the Mayor of Garratt.

Sheridan's Rivals, however, claims a very different rank in the history of the drama and of English literature. To how many comedies, since those of Shakespeare, have the favour of the public and the commendation of critics remained so faithful? Two only, we may reply—the School for Scandal and She Stoops to Conquer. The young Irishman's maiden enterprise— "the first heir of his invention"—is one in that glorious trinity of works that sheds lustre on the modern English stage. Conceived, no doubt, at Bath,[63] or at any rate when recollections of the city and its inmates were fresh in the author's mind, it is as a mirror wherein we see the changing and multi coloured images of that Vanity Fair, so frivolous, so reckless, but so gay, so varied, and so animated. It reveals no very profound or searching observation, nor ought we to demand any such; it would have crushed a subject that required the lightest handling. The characters are not particularly striking or original; but the psychology of these cheerful worldlings was neither singular nor complex. Nor does a comic writer of twenty-three sit down to analyse souls and societies, surprise the secrets of the human heart, and create new and immortal types. He does not undertake to give a faithful and uncoloured reproduction of events and persons. His young imagination paints life in vivid colours; it makes up for his necessary lack of study and experience; it revels in its own inventions. Moreover, in an author's first work there will always be reminiscences, perhaps unconscious, of older models; he imitates them more or less closely. If he is a dramatic writer, the general character of his piece, the springs of action, the types he introduces, will recall those of his predecessors. Thus, in The Rivals, Sheridan has taken some of the elements, and above all the tone and spirit, of the Restoration comedies; and his play is a masterpiece of the genus Lamb called, by way of definition and in no admonitory sense, Artificial Comedy. His characters are those of theatrical tradition. He rejuvenated, remodelled, and readjusted, but he made no radical changes in them. The audience expected them, and recognised them with pleasure. We have the hero, young, handsome and gallant; the heroine, tender and romantic; they trick a choleric father and an absurd duenna, who forgive them without much ado, for they are good souls at bottom. The minor figures are a cowardly boor, who plays the fop and bravo; a pugnacious Irishman, with his hand for ever on his sword; a crafty soubrette, who serves and betrays them all in turn, but always to her own advantage. Add to these the inevitable supernumeraries of an English play of this period, a pair of dolefully sentimental lovers. All these dramatis personae are set in motion by a very lively and nimble intrigue, but one which disdains none of the classic incidents of comedy, the disguise of the lover, intercepted letters, unforeseen meetings. It is the dexterity shown by the author in so combining these ancient motives as to make them produce unexpected effects, rather than any novelty of invention, which makes this plot original. The imbroglio is no newer than the characters; but a master craftsman has laid hold of the common bronze to work it after his own fashion, to polish it, to make of it a masterpiece. If he has melted down some ancient medals, to recast them, and stamp the with his own image, this in no sense detracts from his glory. It is the right and the habit of genius, and it would not be worth while to insist upon it, if a certain question did riot arise from the special point of view from which we are considering The Rivals. Setting aside the stage indications of the scene, what is the special connection of Bath with a work which contains an ancient theatrical tradition, and is inspired rather by imagination and unconscious reminiscences, than by direct observation? Is this comedy, a work so general in interest, and one which is not primarily concerned with the portrayal of a particular society, a local creation to some extent, or is the setting in which the author has placed his characters more or less fortuitous, and could it be exchanged for some other milieu without much damage to the general effect?

We may say at once that by certain touches deliberately applied to his picture here and there, the author has succeeded in suggesting the scene he has chosen for his action, and transporting his audience to one particular corner of England, to the exclusion of all others. He does not merely indicate in the stage directions that the scene is laid now on the North and now on the South Parade, now in King's Mead Fields.[64] He conjures up the whole town behind these painted canvases; a word, a phrase, a careless allusion, bring it before us with its daily life, its amusements, its walks, its stately dances, its gaming-tables,[65] its lodging-houses[66] its circulating libraries, those "evergreen trees of diabolical knowledge," its coffee-houses,[67] its rival Assembly Rooms,[68] its print-shops, where the "Devon monkerony" is to be seen (act iii. sc. iv), its Abbey, where there is such "snug lying" (act v. sc. iii.). The young captain is supposed to be on recruiting duty. He finds no candidates, but a few disbanded chairmen, minority waiters, and billiard-markers, all fit denizens of the place (act ii. sc. i.). He has an affair of honour. He hides his sword carefully under his coat (act v. sc. ii.), for he knows Nash's regulations, with which his antagonist, Sir Lucius, is also familiar (act iii. sc. iv.). And these persons, who are so well posted in the etiquettes and humours of their summer resort, have all assimilated what we might call the genius of the place. How admirably they typify its gay animation, its careless irresponsibility, its airy gallantry In such a place the traditional adventures which provide the comic intrigue in so many plays are no mere conventional incidents. Unexpected meetings surprise no one in this general rendezvous of society. Secret correspondence, hidden rivals, elopements and duels, all were episodes of Sheridan's own life in this place two years before. In no other spot would the action appear so natural, in none would the chief characters seem so perfectly at home. The very artificiality of the characters brings them into harmony with the essentially artificial society they represent. If sometimes they seem to reflect the brilliance of the footlights rather than that of the sun, to be playing a part rather than living, this does not make them false and unreal. For the candles of the Assembly Rooms were a good deal like footlights, and the actual Bath was a stage on which a perpetual comedy was enacted.

Tobias Smollett
From an original portrait, painted in Italy about 1770

To transfer it to the boards, Sheridan had no need to falsify it; he simply sketched the outline, and filled in the colours of his original.[69]

This original is portrayed, of course, even more faith fully and minutely by the novelists, to whom a fashionable watering-place offered such a rich and fertile field. Three famous writers of fiction treated it at different periods Smollett in his three principal works, Miss Austen in "Northanger Abbey" and "Persuasion," and Dickens in the "Pickwick Papers."

Smollett, who was able to write an essay on the properties of the Bath waters in 1752,[70] must, it would seem, have spent some considerable time in the city prior to this date. It is not known whether this sojourn preceded or followed the publication of his earlier novels, which appeared a year or two before the essay,[71] but it is certain that the novelist was familiar de visu with the scenes to which he introduces Roderick Random and Peregrine Pickle, scenes, indeed, in which these picaresque heroes necessarily figure. What theatre could have been more suitable, what field of action more appropriate to- such? This nest of sharpers and adventurers, this centre of vice and intrigue, was waiting to receive them; they frolic freely among the rogues and dupes of this microcosm, giving the rein to their rough good humour, and finding endless opportunities for stratagems somewhat unscrupulous, and exploits not over-refined. If in "Roderick Random" the rapid succession of incidents leaves little space for descriptions of the scenes among which they take place, the sketch, though summary, is none the less exact. In the first place, the cause of Random's visit to Bath is very characteristic. He comes with the intention of marrying a fortune. His friend Bantam has told him of a certain Miss Snapper, deformed and insolent, but rich, who is going to the springs. Some scoundrel is certain to "pick the girl up";[72] if Random will agree to pay £500 sterling six months after his marriage, his friend will undertake to forward his suit. The bargain is promptly concluded, "the proposal being too advantageous to be refused." Random gets into the stage coach in which Miss Snapper sets out, wins her admiration by the courage he shows in an encounter with highwaymen, becomes her cavaliere servente, and in this capacity takes her to the Assembly Rooms. Here a curious mortification awaits him. Miss Snapper, as we have seen, was deformed. According to Smollett, the fashionable world treated her affliction in the following manner: "... We no sooner entered than the eyes of everybody present were turned on us: and when we had suffered the martyrdom of their looks for some time, a whisper circulated at our expense, which was accompanied with many contemptuous smiles and tittering observations, to my utter shame and confusion. I did not so much conduct as follow my charge to a place where she seated her mother and herself with astonishing composure, notwithstanding the unmannerly behaviour of the whole company, which seemed to be assumed merely to put her out of countenance."[73]

But this was not the sum of the affronts offered to the victim. Nash, the Master of the Ceremonies, the arbiter of good manners, saw the incident and intervened. Was it to make the company blush for their cruelty and ill-breeding? Not at all; he came to crown the general malignity and impertinence; he approached Miss Snapper with bows and grimaces, and in a loud voice asked her an insolent question, which has been recorded elsewhere.[74]

Happily, he had met his match; a stinging repartee sent him off in confusion; and the laughing auditors, to their credit be it said, ranged themselves on the side of their quondam victim, and became as politely assiduous as they had been rude and ill-bred. Was this little incident an imaginary one, invented by Smollett?

Apparently not, since Goldsmith accepts it as historic, completes it by another anecdote, and tells us that the novelist took it from life.[75]

But even if it had been an invention, the fact that it was accepted as probable by Goldsmith and other readers of Smollett is another evidence, among many, of the coarseness and rusticity which still obtained in English society in the eighteenth century, even in the fashionable circles. No doubt they did not reign alone; high breeding, polished manners, and elegance were also to be found; but these were qualities Smollett did not discover at Bath, for his eye was generally fixed on the base, the brutal, and the cowardly aspects of humanity. Still, coarseness and rusticity existed, and long continued to exist. If they gradually diminished, and finally disappeared, Bath, and other social centres of the same class, had a good deal to do with the improvement. It was here that an example of politeness was given by that limited section of society which had been polished by familiarity with courts, by foreign travel, or by an instinctive sense of refinement; here only, thanks to facilities of intercourse that existed nowhere else, such examples were imitated with more or less success and completeness, by the other classes of the nation. It was in the Assembly Rooms that the some what rough and boorish Englishman and Englishwoman of the eighteenth century became the modern lady and gentleman.

This consummation was still a distant one, according to Smollett; and why should we reject his testimony à priori, if we allow the novelist's other pictures to be not unfaithful, though generally incomplete and extravagant? Let us follow and observe his hero, when, after various trivial adventures, he brings him back to the Assembly Rooms. A woman Random had formerly offended, has circulated unfavourable reports about him; a violent altercation takes place in consequence directly he crosses the threshold of the Assembly Rooms. "I was met at the door by a servant, who presented a billet to me without a subscription, importing that my presence was disagreeable to the company, and desiring I would take the hint without further disturbance, and bestow myself elsewhere for the future. This peremptory message filled me with indignation. I followed the fellow who delivered it, and, seizing him by the collar in presence of all the company, threatened to put him instantly to death if he did not discover the scoundrel who had charged him with such an impudent commission, that I might punish him as he deserved. The messenger, affrighted at my menaces and furious looks, fell on his knees, and told me that the gentleman who ordered him to deliver the letter was no other than Narcissa's brother, who, at that time, stood at the other end of the room, talking to Melinda. I went up to him immediately, and, in the hearing of his inamorata, accosted him in these words: 'Lookee, squire, were it not for one consideration that protects you from my resentment, I would cane you where you stand, for having had the presumption to send me this scurrilous intimation,' which I tore to pieces and threw in his face at the same time, darting an angry regard at his mistress, I told her I was sorry she had put it out of my power to compliment her on her invention, but at the expense of her good nature and veracity. Her admirer, whose courage never rose but in proportion to the wine he had swallowed, instead of resenting my address in what is called an honourable way, threatened to prosecute me for an assault, and took witnesses accordingly; while she, piqued at his pusillanimous behaviour, and enraged at the sarcasm I had uttered against her, endeavoured to make her quarrel a public cause, and wept aloud with spite and vexation.

"The tears of a lady could not fail of attracting the notice and concern of the spectators, to whom she complained of my rudeness with great bitterness, saying, if she were a man I durst not use her so. The greatest part of the gentlemen, already prejudiced against me, were offended at the liberty I had taken, as appeared from their looks, though none of them signified their disgust any other way, except my Lord Quiverwit, who ventured to say, with a sneer, that I was in the right to establish my own character, of which he had now no longer any doubt. Nettled at this severe equivoque, which raised a laugh at my expense, I replied with some wrath, 'I am proud of having in that particular got the start of your lordship.' He made no answer to my repartee, but with a contemptuous smile walked off; leaving me in a very disagreeable situation."[76]

This disagreeable situation culminates in a duel between Random and Lord Quiverwit, an eccentric duel, the final developments of which are not unlike those of the actual encounter that took place later between Sheridan and Mathews.[77] After a long engagement without any result, Random is touched under the arm, and fancies himself seriously wounded: "Therefore, determined not to die unrevenged, I seized his shell, which was close to my breast, before he could disentangle his point, and keeping it fast with my left hand, shortened my own sword with my right, intending to run him through the heart … Disappointed in this expectation, and afraid still that death would frustrate my revenge, I grappled with him, and, being much the stronger, threw him on the ground, where I wrested his sword out of his hand; and so great was my confusion, instead of turning the point on him, struck out three of his fore teeth with the hilt."[78] All this, it appears, was perfectly legitimate, and even magnanimous, for later on we find the wounded nobleman sending for his opponent to thank him for having shown such moderation in using the advantage fortune had given him.[79] This incident at once re-established Random's damaged reputation; thenceforth he was received and sought after by the best company, and it was only the departure of his beloved Narcissa that induced him to leave Bath.

Like Roderick Random, Peregrine Pickle, the hero of Smollett's second novel, goes to Bath, but for a less mercenary reason. He was "panting with the desire of distinguishing himself at that resort of the fashionable world." Immediately after his arrival he succeeded in making himself and his friend, Godfrey Gauntlet, as notorious as he wished. This was effected by means of a plan, carried out partly by stratagem, partly by skill in play, which resulted in the spoliation of a gang of sharpers. The battle was fought round a billiard-table. Gauntlet, a first-rate player, feigned awkwardness and inexperience, until his adversary and dupe risked a high stake, which was soon increased by the bets of the other swindlers. The account of this duel between the professional gamester and the sham novice is very entertaining; each draws on the other, trying to take his measure, alternately allowing him to win, and beating him. But Gauntlet is a clever actor; his rage with the very billiard-balls, which he throws out of the window, and the cues, which he breaks in pieces, allays suspicion, and induces the most distrustful to risk a stake. Just before his success, he reviews the gang with triumphant irony: "The visages of these professors had adopted different shades of complexion at every hazard he had taken: from their natural colour they had shifted into a sallow hue; from thence into pale; from pale into yellow, which degenerated into a mahogany tint; and now they saw seventeen hundred pounds of their stock depending upon a single stroke, they stood like so many swarthy Moors, jaundiced with terror and vexation. The fire which naturally glowed in the cheeks and nose of the player seemed utterly extinct, and his carbuncles exhibited a livid appearance, as if a gangrene had already made some progress in his face; his hand began to shake, and his whole frame was seized with such trepidation that he was fain to swallow a bumper of brandy in order to re-establish the tranquillity of his nerves. This expedient, however, did not produce the desired effect, for he aimed the ball at the lead with such discomposure that it struck on the wrong side, and came off at an angle which directed it full in the middle hole. This fatal accident was attended with a universal groan, as if the whole universe had gone to wreck; and notwithstanding that tranquillity for which adventurers are so remarkable, this loss made such an impression upon them all that each in particular manifested his chagrin by the most violent emotions. One turned up his eyes to heaven, and bit his nether lip; another gnawed his fingers while he stalked across the room; a third blasphemed with horrible imprecations; and he who played the party sneaked off, grinding his teeth together, with a look that baffles all description, and as he crossed the threshold exclaiming: 'Add bite, by G— !"[80]

The circumstance, of course, made a great sensation; the fame of it was on every tongue, and the two friends found themselves the objects of universal curiosity. The best of the business was that, having now acquired the reputation of "consummate artists in all the different species of finesse, which they would not fail to practise with the first opportunity," so far from being disqualified for the best society, "this opinion of their character proved no obstacle to their reception into, the fashionable parties of the place; but, on the contrary, such a recommendation (as I have already hinted) never fails to operate for the advantage of the possessor."[81] Every one expected to see them repeating their first exploit; but, disappointing the general expectation, they suddenly shifted their ground, neglected the tables, and devoted themselves to gallantry, in which their successes were equally conspicuous. The good-looking, intelligent Peregrine, in particular, who is soon discovered to be well-born and heir to a considerable property, becomes irresistible. lie multiplies his facile conquests, flutters from one love to another, excites and maintains jealousy among a host of devotees. Before he has been at Bath a fortnight, he has sown dissension among all the women, and furnished food for all the hundred tongues of calumny. Leaving to his friend the seduction of married women, "Peregrine set up his throne among those who laboured under the disease of celibacy, from the pert miss of fifteen, who; with a fluttering heart, tosses her head, bridles up, and giggles involuntarily at the sight of a hand some young man, to the staid maiden of twenty-eight, who, with demure aspect, moralises on the vanity of beauty, the folly of youth, the simplicity of woman, and expatiates on friendship, benevolence and good sense, in the style of a Platonic philosopher."[82] A thousand rivals contended for the young hero's heart; terrible animosities broke out among them; a veritable contest began, and opposing factions were formed. "The younger class took all opportunities of mortifying their seniors in public, by treating them with that indignity which, contrary to the general privilege of age, is, by the consent and connivance of mankind, levelled against those who have the misfortune to come under the denomination of old maids: and these last retorted their hostilities in the private machinations of slander, supported by experience and subtlety of invention. Not one day passed in which some new story did not circulate to the prejudice of one or other of those rivals."[83] Smollett gives us a sample of these stories, which certainly presages the *School for Scandal*; Sheridan may well have had it in his mind when writing some of the most famous scenes in his comedy.[84] He does not, however, describe any particular intrigue or adventure, but restricts himself to general traits, which give the most unfavourable idea of the women and girls of Bath society. Was this calumny? No, for many, no doubt, were persons of easy virtue; and yes, for he ascribed to all the frailties of some. His pictures, in general, emphasise the disagreeable or odious aspects of reality; noble and endearing qualities are left in shadow; the painter seems incapable of seeing them even. Smollett surrounds his hero with infamous scoundrels and abandoned women; Peregrine fights the first with their own weapons, and amuses himself without scruple among the second. To complete the rascally horde, Smollett introduces the doctors, those doctors for whom he had all a rival's hatred, portraying them every where in general, and here in particular, as grotesque and dishonest charlatans.[85] Peregrine declares war against the whole confraternity; he plans a mystification which makes them ridiculous, he dupes them, and has them soundly thrashed. Smollett was content thenceforth; he had unmasked, exposed, and pilloried all he thought detestable at Bath. Having no further reason to detain his readers on this scene, he transports his personages elsewhere to pursue their fantastic course.[86]

Twenty years passed. In 1771, just before his death, Smollett finished his masterpiece, "Humphry Clinker." Strange to say, although neither in subject nor characters are we reminded of his earlier novels, the author again took as his stage, in part at least of his work, that city of Bath which he had already sketched twice, and in which he had stayed again before his departure for Italy.[87] He takes even greater pleasure in describing it than before, devoting long passages to the place on its own account, and not merely as a stage for the exploits of his heroes. He makes it not merely a frame, but the background of his picture, which he ingeniously illumines with a variety of changing lights. "Humphry Clinker" is a novel told in letters, wherein correspondents of very different minds and temperaments impart their observations, impressions, and reflections to us in turn.[88] The spectacle before them affects each of them so differently that their opinions offer an amusing contrast, while at the same time they complete and correct each other. Whereas Matthew Bramble, the irritable valetudinarian,[89] looks upon Bath as a vast lunatic asylum, his young niece, Lydia Melford, just escaped from school, thinks it an "earthly Paradise," and Lydia's brother, the Oxonian, though less enthusiastic, does not hesitate to compare it with London for interest and enjoyment, besides seeing in it special merits of its own.[90] What to one is "noise, tumult, and hurry," is to the others "gaiety, good-humour and diversion"; the young folks spend their time laughing, the old man in lamenting and inveighing with more or less sincerity.

One of the causes, and not the least, of Matthew Bramble's ill-humour is the growth of the city within the past thirty years, the invasion of a heterogeneous crowd, the amalgamation of all classes and conditions in their common eagerness to enter the temple of pleasure and fashion.[91] Bath, too small to accommodate the invaders, has climbed the circle of hills that enclosed her. The architects had finished the grandiose buildings of Queen's Square (1728–1735), had built the Circus,[92] and were about to begin the Crescent.[93] "Houses are starting up in every outlet and every corner of Bath" ... and "what sort of monster it will become in a few years with those excrescences may be easily conceived."[94]

These additions were necessary, for the town had to lodge a very large population, at least during certain months of the year. The growth of trade and industry, the wealth acquired in the colonies throughout this quarter of a century, had given rise to an important class of rich merchants and citizens, eager to share the pleasures of the aristocracy, and, above all, to be brought into contact with its members.

"Every upstart of fortune, harnessed in the trappings of the mode, presents himself at Bath, as in the very focus of observation. Clerks and factors from the East Indies, loaded with the spoil of plundered provinces; planters, negro-drivers, and hucksters from our American plantations, enriched they know not how; agents, commissaries and contractors, who have fattened in two successive wars on the blood of the nation; usurers, brokers, and jobbers of every kind; men of low birth, and no breeding, have found themselves suddenly translated into a state of affluence, unknown to former ages; and no wonder that their brains should be intoxicated with pride, vanity and presumption. Knowing no other criterion of greatness but the ostentation of wealth, they discharge their affluence, without taste or conduct, through every channel of the most absurd extravagance; and all of them hurry to Bath, because here without any farther qualification they can mingle with the princes and nobles of the land."[95]

The movement was not confined to these; it carried away not only these parvenus, but spreading from one to the other, gradually swept along the whole nation.

"Even the wives and daughters of low tradesmen, who, like shovel-nosed sharks, prey on the blubber of those uncouth whales of fortune, are infected with the same rage of displaying their importance; and the slightest indisposition serves them for a pretext to insist on being conveyed to Bath, where they may hobble country dances and cotillons among lordlings, squires, counsellors and clergy."[96]

This invasion had utterly transformed society, to its great disadvantage. "A very inconsiderable proportion of genteel people are lost in a mob of impudent plebeians, who have neither understanding nor judgment, nor the least idea of propriety and decorum; and seem to enjoy nothing so much as an opportunity of insulting their betters."[97]

This is obviously a depressing view to take of men and things. Fortunately, there are others, as Jeremy Melford, Bramble's own nephew, shows us. He, on the other hand, rejoices in the daily opportunities he has "of seeing the most remarkable characters of the community . . . in their natural attitudes and true colours, descended from their pedestals, and divested from their formal draperies, undisguised by art, and affectation."[98]

As to the chaos of ranks and conditions, far from being moved to indignation thereby, he considers it one of the greatest diversions of the place. The spectacle he describes in the following passage excites his laughter, and not his spleen: "I was extremely diverted, last ball night, to see the Master of the Ceremonies leading, with great solemnity, to the upper end of the room, an antiquated Abigail, dressed in her lady's cast clothes, whom he, I suppose, mistook for some countess just arrived at the Bath. The ball was opened by a Scotch lord, with a mulatto heiress from Saint Christopher's; and the gay Colonel Tinsel danced all the evening with the daughter of an eminent tin-man from the borough of Southwark. Yesterday morning at the pump-room, I saw a broken-winded Wapping landlady squeeze through a circle of peers to salute her brandy-merchant, who stood by the window, propped on crutches; and a paralytic attorney of Shoe Lane, in shuffling up to the bar, kicked the shins of the Chancellor of England, while his lordship in a cut bob drank a glass of water at the pump."[99]

No such comic and unexpected episodes are to be seen elsewhere. Moreover, he looks for good results from this confusion; he maintains very justly "that those plebeians who discovered such eagerness to imitate the dress and equipage of their superiors, would likewise, in time, adopt their maxims and their manners, be polished by their conversation and refined by their example." Already, in his opinion, the assemblies at Bath are no whit behind those of London or anywhere else in elegance, and "on the whole, the individuals that composed them would not be found deficient in good manners and decorum." Anxious to convince his uncle, and Quin, the actor,[100] less indulgent observers, that they are prejudiced and unjust, he persuades them to come and see for themselves what gentility prevails in this motley society! An opportunity occurs at once: a tea-party, given by some nouveau riche, at the conclusion of which, at a given signal, the ladies are invited to help themselves to the bouquets and sweetmeats prepared for them. Alas, young Melford reckons without his host! What a scene met their eyes as they looked down from the gallery which did duty as observatory for the trio! "There was nothing but jostling, scrambling, pulling, snatching, struggling, scolding and screaming. The nosegays were torn from one another's hands and bosoms; the glasses and china went to wreck; the tables and floors were strewed with comfits. Some cried, some swore, and the tropes and figures of Billingsgate were used without reserve in all their native zest and flavour, nor were those flowers of rhetoric unattended with significant gesticulation. Some snapped their fingers, some forked them out, some clapped their hands, and some their backsides; at length they fairly proceeded to pulling caps, and everything seemed to presage a general battle."[101] When peace was at last restored, they learned that "the two amazons who singularised themselves most in action did not come from the purlieus of Puddledock,[102] but from the courtly neighbourhood of St. James' Palace. One was a baroness, and the other a wealthy knight's dowager."

James Quin
From the portrait by Hogarth

Uncle Bramble was right, too right indeed! We shall have no further illusions as to the society of Bath. Vicious and silly to the core, it has not even the merit of showing an outward semblance of politeness, good- breeding, even decency!

Must Smollett be accused of exaggeration? He would, no doubt, have replied that he only copied nature, transcribing actual events. The episode of the public tea seems to have been taken from life; was it not merely a description of the uproar and fighting that took place in the Assembly Rooms at the election of Derrick's successor, transported with very little modification to the novel? The scandal was of recent occurrence; it took place in 1769, two years before the publication of "Humphry Clinker."[103]

But, as was his wont, the pessimistic and misanthropic novelist at once fastened upon exceptional and isolated disturbances, of which there are no other instances in the local annals, and put them forward as typical. He took pleasure in insisting on the coarseness, nay, brutality, which lurked beneath a habitual, but thin, veneer of elegance, barely concealed by this veneer, and ready to break forth at any moment. This was what struck him, whereas he scarcely mentions the general politeness and real refinement; he seems hardly to have noticed it. His Bath, like the rest of the world he paints, is peopled almost exclusively by rogues, debauchees, fools, and boors. There were such, no doubt, in the city, but it seems to have escaped him that they were not alone; and this is why his picture, being incomplete, is false.

We might further ask if there were so many as he supposed, and if even these were all so villainous, so depraved, so inane and so loutish as he made them. We may reasonably doubt it, taking into account the peculiar temperament of the author, his special outlook upon the world, his desire to excite "that generous indignation which ought to animate the reader against the sordid and vicious disposition of the world."[104]

It is hardly credible that this society should so have mended its manners in the space of a generation, that the keen eye of a Jane Austen should have discerned not a single one of Smollett's coarse and odious person ages, and that the Bath of "Northanger Abbey" and "Persuasion,"[105] sketched with a touch so light and yet so sure, should reveal only the amused curiosity of the writer, a trifle contemptuous, perhaps, but betraying neither disgust, repulsion, nor indignation. Are the Assembly Rooms in which Catherine Morland and Anne Elliot, those pure and charming heroines, display their innocent coquetry, their artless motions, their girlish dreams, the same which Random and Pickle astounded with their swaggering insolence, which Matthew Bramble quitted more incensed than ever against humanity? They are, it is true, just as noisy, just as crowded, perhaps more so; the throng is as motley as ever; the ultra fashionable still affect to hold themselves aloof from the throng; but how different place and people appear in Smollett's violent lithographs and Jane Austen's delicate pastels. In the latter we find no trace of the coarseness, the brutality, the vice that flaunted so brazenly under the eyes of the Scotch doctor; not a word, not a touch that alludes, even covertly, to equivocal proceedings below the surface, not a hint of the shady reputation of Bath in former days, nor of facts that might still justify it.[106]

The daughter of the pastor of Steventon saw nothing worse around her than a good deal of frivolity, a little dissipation, and a touch of vulgarity. This was all, and we are bound to accept the evidence of an observer so sincere, acute and conscientious, familiar from childhood with the society she describes. Jane Austen had every opportunity of studying Bath and its guests, at first during her visits to relatives in the city,[107] and afterwards during her own residence there for several years.[108]

If, then, Smollett did not unduly thicken the lines and harden the contours of his pictures of Bath, we must believe that Bath had reformed considerably during the last quarter of the eighteenth century, and that Nash himself, especially the Nash of his earlier period, would have been quite at sea there.

In nineteen out of the thirty chapters of "Northanger Abbey," and nine out of the twenty-four of "Persuasion," Bath is the scene of action. Descriptions of the town and its amusements, which had already been written a hundred times, occupy but a small space; the author cared little for these. Her chosen task was the minute and exact delineation of character; her purpose was not to give us the picture of a society, but to analyse minds and hearts. The chosen environment is not unimportant; it affords her a thousand circumstances which give rise in her characters to fugitive or durable impressions, and sentiments, declared, intimate or avowed, volatile or quietly profound, which interest her, and which she makes intensely interesting to us in our turn. Her Catherine Morland[109] brings to Bath all the charming inexperience of her seventeen years, the ingenuous and somewhat timorous joy of a first appearance in society, the amiable gaucherie of a guileless soul. When an agreeable partner is presented to this young girl at the Assembly Rooms by the Master of the Ceremonies, and shows himself courteous, attentive and intelligent, the first impulses of a vague and hesitating inclination stir in this virgin heart, hidden under the simple desire to meet such a pleasant cavalier again some day. Henry Tilney's temporary absence on the morrow causes her some regret, but she would soon have forgotten him, had not the ordinary conditions of life at Bath, the meetings every day in the same places, the familiar relations that spring up immediately after an introduction, developed the imperceptible germ of unconscious affection. All the little incidents proper to such surroundings tend to foster it—a dance imprudently promised to another partner, a vexatious misunderstanding about a walk, the consequent coldness, and the explanation that makes amends for all, an expedition enjoyed together—these are so many causes of sweet and incessant agitation to a young and tender heart, so many bonds that entangle her without her own knowledge in a true and serious attachment. All these motives and bonds of union are multiplied, brought together, and reinforced by the chances and opportunities that succeed each other in a special society, the mode of life and habits of this society. In a few days the intimacy has made more progress than it would have done in months or years under different conditions.[110] The transformation of the young girl, the awakening of her mind and heart, the blossoming of her young affections, would certainly have been a slower and tardier process in her native village of Fullerton. Had she even met a Henry Tilney in her home, the obscure growth of her feelings would have been lengthier an less decisive they would not have revealed themselves so swiftly to her; her love, less definite and decisive, would have followed a very different course.[111]

The same may be said of the young man. In his case also, external circumstances stirred, solicited, and hastened his wandering sensibility; if they did not exactly determine his choice, they precipitated it. The little country girl from Wiltshire, whose acquaintance he makes by chance at Bath (he would hardly have made it elsewhere), may very well have seemed agreeable but insignificant to him at first. He barely noticed her, and had no recollection of their first brief conversation. But thanks to circumstances and local custom, an immediate intimacy springs, up, the result of repeated, almost daily meetings. The little incidents that move the young girl so much have far less effect upon Henry Tilney, with his riper and colder temperament. But his curiosity is aroused, then his sympathy and his interest; and, finally, a warmer feeling. He is clear-sighted; he discerns in this transparent soul, as yet unconscious, that which it does not as yet recognise itself, the first impulses of dawning love touched by this artless and spontaneous passion, won by this grace, simplicity and charm, he too loves.[112] What remains to be done? Only that Bath, which brought the two young people together, and arranged everything for their union, should at first forward that union, then prevent it, and finally bring it about. Such are the developments and the conclusion of the novel, furnished in a very natural fashion, and without recourse to any other springs of action, by the effects of one of those baseless rumours, those idle inventions which pass. from tongue to tongue in watering-places. A gossip gives Henry Tilney's father an exaggerated idea of Catherine's fortune, and this father, a violent and avaricious man, at once does all in his power to hasten the regular and peaceful progress of a mutual affection. Eager to secure a rich wife for his son, he takes every means to increase the intimacy of the two young people, and make them think more and more of each other. Undeceived a few weeks later, he endeavours to frustrate the project he had so strongly supported by a very brutal course of conduct; the son hereupon declares himself, and braves the wrath of his father, who finally gives way. In the construction of the plot, as well as in the psychological development of the characters, the novel owes a good deal to Bath, and it was not without reason and not without profit that the novelist laid the scene of her drama here, and studied the action of her characters under its light.

"Persuasion" differs from "Northanger Abbey" in many of these particulars. Bath is not the principal scene of action here, and the heroine, does not, in fact, make her appearance upon this stage till rather late in the day, when her future fate is already clearly marked out. The visit is, indeed, of small importance; surroundings could have but little effect upon the sentiments and actions of Anne Elliot and Captain Wentworth. Firm and thoughtful characters, matured not only by age, but by a painful experience, they are unmoved by fortuitous accidents and external circumstances; their griefs and joys and intimate resolutions demand more powerful motives and occasions. But if the leading characters of the drama are highly individual types, who owe little to their environment, the writer allows these to dominate the inferior personages, the brainless and heartless supernumeraries, who find ample satisfaction and a congenial sphere in the capital of worldly vanities. In "Northanger Abbey" we have already met an Isabella Thorpe, false and frivolous, eager to attract attention, bent on the conquest of a wealthy suitor, and finding a favourable field for her manoeuvres in the Pump Room and the Assembly Rooms. Here we have a baronet, inordinately proud of his rank, a narrow-minded Adonis, and his daughter, the worthy inheritor of her father's defects, who are consoled for the loss of their ancestral home, when they find that "they can be important at Bath at comparatively little expense,"[113] that their acquaintance is sought for on every side, that they enjoy opportunities of being as haughty as they please, of granting or refusing the honour of an introduction,[114] and finally (supreme triumph!) that in a comparatively small city like Bath, they are able to publish to all the world the fact that they are related to the wife and daughter of a lord! These were perennial sources of delight, not to be had either in the country, with its restricted society, nor in the immensity of London, with its court and aristocracy. Admirable indeed was the town where Sir Walter Elliot, of Kellynch Hall, was a personage from the moment of his arrival, where Elizabeth, when she bowed to a Captain Wentworth, felt all the satisfaction of condescension, and where even more sensible folks, such as Lady Russell and William Elliot, attached a certain value to such honours, and shared to some extent the sentiments of their friends and kinsfolk![115]

In the Bath of Miss Austen's time, differences of rank were observed and insisted upon much more jealously than before. Throughout the eighteenth century, community of pleasures and habits had temporarily effaced, or at least attenuated, the line of demarcation between persons of various classes; at the close of the century, and the beginning of a new one, the barriers were set up again. There had been a society at Bath; "Persuasion," on the other hand, shows us the birth of rival coteries, a change which was a natural consequence of the excessive prosperity of the English watering-places, and marks at once its culmination and its decline.

Miss Austen's two novels, indeed, show us Bath at its zenith, a more universal centre of attraction than it had ever been before. Not one of the causes that had drawn people to Bladud's springs for over a hundred years had ceased to operate; all, in fact, had become more potent, or, at any rate, tended to influence an ever-increasing part of the nation; the very wars of the French Revolution and of the Empire sent travellers to whom the continent was closed, to the English city. Matthew Bramble would have had fresh reason to complain of the monstrous development of Bath![116] Disgusted in 1771, what could he have thought of the "Londonised … over-built and over-sized" city after thirty years of steady growth?[117] What a tumult pervaded those once quiet streets![118] What a crowd of horsemen, carriages, sedan-chairs and vehicles of every sort! What a throng in the Assembly Rooms, where the ladies squeeze in with great difficulty, and seek

Jane Austen as a girl
From "Jane Austen, her Homes and her Friends," by Constance Hill, published by John Lane

anxiously for some place to sit down![119] True, this crowd and this turmoil are attractions to many of the visitors.

Good company, nevertheless, continued to pay its periodical visits to this enlarged and invaded Bath. The various characters in "Northanger Abbey," nobles, country gentlemen, divines, officers, and students, arrive from all quarters of the kingdom, and meet without surprise, such meetings being expected and looked upon as one of the pleasures of the place. "We are always meeting with some old friend or the other; the streets full of them every morning," says Admiral Croft.[120] To some, the place of resort became a place of residence. Sir Walter Elliot, giving up his country house, and seeking another home, hesitates only between two cities, London and Bath, and soon decides in favour of the latter; residents of this kind, could not fail to increase the aristocratic prestige of the place. Yet, though the upper classes had remained faithful to Bath, they had long ceased to have the city to themselves. They were, in fact, submerged in the crowd; every Sunday they discovered that there was not a genteel face to be seen in the Pump Room,[121] congratulated themselves when they remarked a visitor with an air of breeding,[122] and declared that six weeks was the utmost limit of time they could spend in the city without growing weary of its amusements.[123] From those public entertainments, which were so long the distinguishing characteristic and chief attraction of the English watering-places, they gradually seceded, inaugurating private receptions, and forming an exclusive society.[124] The theatre, for instance, and the Assembly Rooms, are not sufficiently "genteel " for the Elliots; their "evening amusements were solely in the elegant stupidity of private parties." The special character of Bath under Nash had been that it offered a sort of public salon to the aristocracy, the gentry, and the upper middle class; reduced to a minority, they formed into separate clans. Bath continued to be a city of pleasures, but these pleasures began to be enjoyed in the same manner as in other places. Twenty or thirty years later, it was nothing but a little English town, similar, but for its memories, to any other pleasant provincial capital, and differing from these only by virtue of its thermal waters, and the presence of the invalids attracted by them.

These changes came about slowly, of course, and their effects were not felt for some time. The Bath to which Dickens introduced Mr Pickwick, his friends, and the faithful Sam Weller in 1827,[125] was still a very animated place, "with a great deal of conversation, and liveliness, and pleasantry."[126] This time, the writer, unlike Smollett and Miss Austen, seems to have had no opportunity of himself observing the scenes through which he makes his characters pass;[127] but if he described it from hearsay, he could not have diverged much from realities familiar to so many. Even his caricatures do but exaggerate features well known to all; and if the contemporary Master of the Ceremonies becomes a grotesque figure in his hands, it was that his functions, and perhaps his manner of exercising them, offered a fair occasion for ridicule. If we find no more than a reflection of current opinion about Bath in Dickens, even the opinion of persons who had never visited the city, it is interesting to see what this was.

The very title of the chapter in which Mr Pickwick is transported to the roof of his namesake at the White Hart arrests our attention;[128] nothing could be simpler: Chapter xxxv. In which Mr Pickwick thinks he had better go to Bath, and goes accordingly." But the reader of 1837 no doubt interpreted these three words, "go to Bath," both literally and metaphorically. For some little time past they had formed a familiar locution,[129] meaning to disappear, to retire. "Go to Bath" has long been the advice offered to persons who, for one reason or another, need change or distraction; but it has also been for some years past the advice tendered, more or less politely, to those who have some good reason for leaving their homes, or whom others may wish to get rid of.[130] Not, indeed, that the worthy Mr Pickwick belonged to this category; still, it was not, perhaps, quite an accident that he should at once have thought of this destination after the disastrous conclusion of his lawsuit;[131] the author indicates it as suitable to the condition of his hero, by the title of his chapter. The rendezvous of rank and fashion had become a universal rendezvous; it was in a fair way to become a convenient retreat, almost a refuge. It must be allowed that its glory was departing.

The exterior aspect, however, is that of the old days. The statue of Nash continues to adorn the large room, where the visitors swallow the yellow water with edifying gravity and perseverance; the orchestra plays to congratulate the non-bathers on the purification of the bathers.[132] The visitors meet in the morning at the Pump Room; they meet again, in full dress, on the Parades; they go home, and come out again, on foot, in carriages, in bath chairs, to meet again. The men go to the reading rooms, rejoining friends they have just quitted. In the evening they meet again at the theatre or the Assembly Rooms. And it was all very pleasant, save for a touch of monotony.[133]

In the Assembly Rooms the young folks, daintily dressed, brilliant and joyful, waited impatiently for the first chords that gave the signal for dancing to begin. "In the tea-rooms, and hovering round the card-tables, were a vast number of queer old ladies and decrepit old gentlemen, discussing all the small talk and scandal of the day, with an evident relish and gusto which sufficiently bespoke the intensity of the pleasure they derived from the occupation. Mingled with these groups were three or four match-making mammas, appearing wholly absorbed by the conversation in which they were taking part, but failing not from time to time to cast an anxious sidelong glance upon their daughters, who, remembering the maternal injunction to make the best use of their time, had already commenced incipient flirtations in the mislaying scarfs, putting on gloves, setting down cups, and so forth; slight matters apparently, but which may be turned to surprisingly good account by expert practitioners."[134] Here, again, we find certain ridiculous figures: "lounging near the doors, and in remote corners were various knots of silly young men, displaying every variety of puppyism and stupidity, amusing all sensible people near them, with their folly and conceit, and happily thinking themselves the object of general admiration—a wise and merciful dispensation which no good man will quarrel with. And, lastly, seated on some of the back benches, where they had already taken up their positions for the evening, were divers unmarried ladies past their grand climaterics, who, not dancing because there were no partners for them, and not playing cards lest they should be set down as irretrievably single, were in the favourable Situation of being able to abuse everybody without reflecting on themselves."[135] There was no lack of material for this pastime: " In short, they could abuse everybody, because everybody was there. It was a scene of gaiety, glitter, and show; of richly dressed people, handsome mirrors, chalked floors, girandoles, and wax candles; and in all parts of the scene, gliding from spot to spot in silent softness, bowing obsequiously to this party, nodding familiarly to that, and smiling complacently on all, was the sprucely attired person of Angelo Cyrus Bantam, Esquire, the Master of the Ceremonies."[136]

For there was still a Master of the Ceremonies, arbiter of elegance and organiser of pleasure. Nash had survived in an uninterrupted line of successors, who continued his work, and did their best to imitate him. Was it the contemporary holder of the office, a certain Lieutenant-Colonel Jervoise, whom Dickens caricatured?[137] Or did his humour, kindling at the very name and nature of such functions, create a type that was imaginary in nearly every point? The second hypothesis seems the more probable for various reasons.[138] But, in any case, the caricature is amusing, and the personage, real or imaginary, is well worth seeing and hearing.

He was, says the novelist, a "charming young man of not much more than fifty, dressed in a very bright blue coat with resplendent buttons, black trousers, and the thinnest possible pair of highly polished boots. A gold eye-glass was suspended from his neck by a short, broad black ribbon; a gold snuff-box was lightly clasped in his left hand; gold rings innumerable glittered on his fingers, and a large diamond pin set in gold glistened in his shirt frill. He had a gold watch and a gold curb chain with large gold seals; and he carried a pliant ebony cane with a heavy gold top. His linen was of the very whitest, finest, and stiffest; his wig of the glossiest, blackest, and curliest. His snuff was prince's mixture; his scent, bouquet du roi. His features were contracted into a perpetual smile; and his teeth were in such perfect order that it was difficult at a small distance to tell the real ones from the false."[139] Such was the outward aspect of Nash's worthy successor, and such his costume in the early morning. His conversation and manners are in perfect keeping with these. "'Mr Pickwick,' said Dowler, 'my friend, Angelo Cyrus Bantam, Esquire, MC. Bantam, Mr Pickwick. Know each other. Welcome to Ba-ath, sir. This is indeed an acquisition. Most welcome to Ba-ath, sir. It is long, very long, Mr Pickwick, since you drank the waters. It appears an age, Mr Pickwick. Re-markable!' Such were the expressions with which Angelo Cyrus Bantam, Esquire, MC, took Mr Pickwick's hand; retaining' it in his meantime, and shrugging up his shoulders with a 'constant succession of bows, as if he really could not make up his mind to the trial of letting it go again. 'It is a very long time since I drank the waters, certainly,' replied Mr Pickwick, 'for, to the best of my knowledge, I was never here before.' 'Never in Ba-ath., Mr Pickwick!' exclaimed the Grand Master, letting the hand fall in astonishment. 'Never in Ba-ath! He! he! Mr Pickwick, you are a wag. Not bad; not bad. Good, good. He! he! he! Remarkable.' 'To my shame, I must say that I am perfectly serious,' rejoined Mr Pickwick; 'I really never was here before ...' 'Bantam,' said Mr Dowler, 'Mr Pickwick and his friends are strangers. They must put their names down. Where's the book?' 'The register of the distinguished visitors in Ba-ath will be in the Pump Room this morning at two o'clock,' replied the MC. 'Will you guide our friends to that splendid building, and enable me to procure their autographs?' 'I will,' rejoined Dowler. 'This is a long call. It's time to go; I shall be here again in an hour. Come.' 'This is a ball night,' said the MC, again taking Mr Pickwick's hand as he rose to go. 'The ball nights in Ba-ath are moments snatched from Paradise, rendered bewitching by music, beauty, elegance, fashion, etiquette, and—and—above all by the absence of tradespeople, who are quite inconsistent with Paradise, and who have an amalgamation of them selves at the Guildhall every fortnight, which is, to say the least, re-markable.[140] Good-bye, good-bye!' and protesting all the way downstairs that he was most satisfied, and most delighted, and most overpowered, and most flattered, Angelo Cyrus Bantam, Esquire, MC, stepped into a very elegant chariot that waited at the door, and rattled off."[141] He reappears in the evening in the same splendour at the Assembly Rooms: "The only observable alterations in his appearance were, that he wore a brighter blue coat, with a white silk lining, black tights, black silk stockings, and pumps, and a white waistcoat, and was, if possible, just a thought more scented."[142] Mr Pickwick is further indebted to him for the privilege of seeing the richest lord in Bath, and of hearing him say to Mr Bantam that it is very warm; and, again, thanks to his exertions, Mr

Pickwick is set down to a whist-table, with a dowager and a colonel's wife. And here we take a final leave of this grotesque puppet.

Such, in its main lines, is the amusing, if somewhat overcharged satire in which Dickens displays some of the ridiculous aspects of Bath.[143] There is no cruelty in it, nothing but good temper throughout, no trace of the aversion and contempt which a very similar spectacle excited in his predecessor and model, Smollett. The sympathetic, indulgent and optimistic observer, the gay and cordial companion, delights, on the contrary, in the sight of innocent pleasure and youthful gaiety, frank and healthy, that meets his eye. What a different spirit breathes from the following passage, to that which inspired Smollett! "In the ball-room, the long card-room, the octagonal card-room, the staircases, and the passages, the hum of many voices, and the sound of many feet, were perfectly bewildering. Dresses rustled, feathers waved, lights shone, and jewels sparkled. There was the music—not of the quadrille band, for it had not yet commenced; but the music of soft tiny footsteps, with flow and then a clear merry laugh—low and gentle, but very pleasant to hear in a female voice, whether in Bath or elsewhere. Brilliant eyes, lighted up with pleasurable expectation, gleamed from every side; and look where you would, some exquisite form glided gracefully through the throng, and was no sooner lost than it was replaced by another, as dainty, and bewitching."[144]

This pleasant picture, and the comic scenes that accompany it, give us the last reflection of Bath in English letters. So long original and curious, the city was about to lose this character, and losing it, she ceased to be described, or became an object of arch reconstruction. A few novelists of unequal merit, none of them eminent, occasionally attempt to resuscitate her, more or less successfully,[145] but these retrospective descriptions, of no special distinction, lie outside the scope of this work, in which we are concerned solely with the impression directly received from Bath by contemporaries, and the fashion in which they translated it; in a word, the trace left by Bath in their works. My readers will perhaps agree that at least among the dramatists and novelists this trace is not unimportant, and that the various traits recorded here and there in their works make up an animated and piquant picture of a special microcosm. Unity is not lacking in this picture ; if each image bears the mark of the artist, and reveals his own point of view, no sooner do we bring them together than, far from contradicting each other, they harmonise completely. By merely observing their chronological order, we can follow from its birth, through its full development to its final decline, that little social institution, the English watering-place of the eighteenth century; as in so many more important cases, literature will suffice to illuminate this chapter, or sub-section, of the history of English manners.

1 "History of England," chap. iii.

2 "Written at the Bath in the year 1674" ("Works," ed. of 1714). The play called *Bath Intrigues* (see above, chap. iv. p 106) may have been written on the spot.

3 On March 2, 1705–1706, Wycherley writes to Pope that he intends to go to Bath (Pope, "Works," ed. Elwin and Courthope, vol. vi. p 27). We find him there in 1711 (letter from Cromwell to Pope, *ibid.* p 125) and in 1714 (letter from Pope to Caryll, *ibid.* p 219).

4 Letter from Miss Bradshaw to Mrs Howard, September 19, 1721, in the "Letters to and from Henrietta, Countess of Suffolk," vol. i. p 77. Lord Hervey, sending Lady Mary Wortley Montagu, at her request, "a list of the sojourners and inmates of this place" [writes to her on October 8, 1728, as follows: "The Duchess of Marlborough, Congreve, and Lady Rich are the only people whose faces I know, whose names I ever heard, or who, I believe, have any names belonging to them" (Lady M. Wortley Montagu, "Letters and Works," vol. i. p xlvii; *cf* the letter from Gay to Swift, March 26, 1728; Swift, "Works," Bohn ed. vol. ii. p 616). It was on returning from this last journey that Congreve, already ill and blind, had the carriage accident that hastened his end.

5 "A Tour Thro' the Whole Island of Great Britain," by a Gentleman (published in 1719).

6 "No, Mr Addison does not go to Ireland this year: he pretended he would; he is gone to Bath with pastoral Philips, for his eyes" (Swift, "Journal to Stella," August II, 1711, p 229).

7 See above, chap. iv. pp 91–92.

8 Letter of October 6 (1754) to Theresa and Martha Blount ("Works," Elwin and Courthope's edition, vol. ix. pp 251–252): "Madam,—If I may ever be allowed to tell you the thoughts I have so oft of you in your absence it is at this time, when I neglect the company of a great number of ladies to write this letter. From the window where I am seated I command the prospect of twenty or thirty in one of the finest promenades in the world, every moment that I take my eye off from the paper. If variety of diversions and new objects be capable of driving our friends out of our minds, I have the best excuse imaginable for forgetting you; for I have slid, I can't tell how, into all the amusements of the place. My whole day is shared by the Pump assemblies, the walks, the chocolate-houses, raffling-shops, medleys, etc ... I endeavour (like all awkward fellows) to become agreeable by imitation: and, observing who are most in favour with the fair, I sometimes copy the civil air of Gascoin,. sometimes the impudent one of Nash, and sometimes for vanity, the silly one of a neighbour of yours, who has lost to the gamesters here that money of which the ladies only deserve to rob a man of his age."

9 "I have in one week run through whatever they call diverting here, and I should be ashamed to pass two just in the same track" (*ibid.* p 252).

10 "I am so much a rake as to be ashamed of being seen with Dr Parnell. I ask people abroad who that parson is?" (*ibid.*)

11 See below, chap. ix.

12 Letter from Gay to Swift, March 16, 1728 (Swift, "Works," Bohn's ed., 1864, vol. ii. p 616).

13 Letter from Gay to Mrs Howard, 1724 ("Countess of Suffolk's Correspondence," pp 176–77).

14 Letter from Mrs Bradshaw to Mrs Howard, *ibid.* p. 78 (1721); letter from Pope to Gay, September ii, 1722 (Pope, "Works," Elwin and Courthope ed., vol. vii. p 422); letter from Gay to Swift, Mar 16, 1728 (Swift, "Works," Bohn's ed. 1864, vol. ii. p 616).

15 Their friendship began at Oxford (*cf* Graves, "Recollections of some Particulars of the Life of Mr Shenstone").

16 To all you ladies now at Bath,
And eke, ye beaus, to you,
With aking heart and wat'ry eyes
I bid my last adieu.
*   *   *
Lindsey's and Hayes's, both farewell,
Where in the spacious hail
With bounding steps and sprightly air
I've led up many a ball.
Poor Nash, farewell! may fortune smile,
Thy drooping soul revive,
My heart is full, I can no more,
John bid the coachman drive.
("Farewell to Bath," in "Water Poetry," pp 26–28).

17 1752 and 1753.

18 "Essay on the External Use of Water, with Particular Remarks on the Mineral Waters of Bath," London, 1752.

19 Thomas, "Le Poète Edward Young," p 195.

20 Thicknesse states that her birthday was publicly celebrated every year ("New Prose Bath Guide," p 6 His statements are not always to be received without reserve; but an extract he quotes from the *Monthly Review* shows us the historian receiving a tribute of six odes, which were afterwards published, and a gold medal, in the presence of a select and brilliant company, on April 2, 1777, the anniversary of her birth.

21 "Letters to Strahan," May 10, 1776, p 323.

22 This anecdote, told by Percy, who said he had it from the Duchess herself, is accepted by Mr Austin Dobson as authentic ("Life of Goldsmith," p 260).

23 Fitzgerald, "Life of Lawrences Sterne," vol. ii. p 250.

24 Steinlen, "C.V. de Bonstetten," pp 70, 71.

25 See Lockhart, "Memoirs of the Life of Sir Walter Scott," chap. ii. The piece was *As You Like It.*

26 Southey, "Life and Correspondence," vol. i. letter vii. pp 41–3. He was four years old at the time (1778). In this and the preceding letter there are other childish reminiscences of Bath.

27 Boswell, "Life of Johnson," vol. iii. (pp 90–5, Bell's ed.). Mr and Mrs Thrale often went to Bath (see Johnson's letters to Boswell, April 8 and August 21, 1780, pp 407, 408, and 419 of the same work). On the death of Mr Thrale in 1781, his widow settled at Bath, and there, three years later, she made that second marriage with the musician Piozzi which estranged Johnson, and drew down so much censure upon her.

28 It was published in 1778.

29 See her Journal for this year (vol. i. pp 565–95, Ward's ed.). We know nothing, of an earlier visit, paid some three or four years before, but there are reminiscences of it in "Evelina" (letter lxxxiii.). Miss Burney came back in August 1791 (*cf* Journal, under this date, vol. ii. pp 423–9 of the same ed.), and after her marriage with M. d'Arblay settled there from the end of 1815 to the middle of 1818 (*ibid.* vol. iii. pp 385–398). In November, 1816, she wrote: "I wish to live at Bath, wish it devoutly, for at Bath we shall live, or nowhere in England. Bath is … in England, the only place for us, since here, all the year round, there is always the town at command, and always the country for prospect, exercise, and delight" (*ibid.* p. 394). It was at Bath she died, in 1840.

30 "… I am still deeply rooted in this country [Switzerland] … Yet in England, when the present clouds are dispelled, I could form a very comfortable establishment in London, or rather at Bath" (letter to Lord Sheffield, July 25, 1789, vol. ii. pp 200–201, Prothero ed.). His stepmother lived there, and he went to see her in 1793 (see his letters of October 4, 9, 13, *ibid.* pp 389–90).

31 Pindemonte, "Lettters," October 4, 1789.

32 Letter from Miss Weston to Dr Whalley, November 28, 1791 (Whalley, "Journal," vol. ii. p 6)

33 Roberts, "Memoirs of Hannah More," vol. ii. p. 312, letter of January 1, 1792. She returns to the subject six years later, almost in the same terms (letter to Mrs Boscawen, December 27, 1797, *ibid.* vol. iii. pp 27–8), adding: "Every place of diversion is overflowing, with a fullness unknown in former seasons, and as a proof that everybody is too rich to need to stay at home, there is not a lodging to be had in this whole quarter for love or money." In an undated letter of the same year (*ibid.* p 12) she says further: "Grave as the times are, Bath never was so gay. Princes and kings that will be, and princes and kings that have been, pop upon yon at every cornet; the Stadtholder and Prince of Wales only on a flying visit; but their Highnesses of York are become almost inhabitants, and very sober and proper their behaviour."

34 Thus initiating the "Cheap Repository Tracts."

35 "Once … I had the pleasure of conversing with the illustrious Porson; and, strange to say, it was at a Ball in the Lower Rooms, on an unusually crowded night. A very ingenious friend of mine, Dr Davis of Bath, who was this same learned Theban's chaperon on the occasion, did me the favour of introducing me to him. The Professor appeared to be quite at sea, and neither to understand nor to relish the scene before him. On separating from him, Mr King, the Master of the Ceremonies, addressed me: 'Pray, Mr W., who is the *man* you have been speaking to? I can't say I much like his appearance.' And to own the truth, Porson, with lank, uncombed locks, a loose neck-cloth, and wrinkled stockings, exhibited a striking contrast to the gay and gorgeous crowd around.—'Who is that gentleman, Mr King?' replied I, 'The greatest man that has visited your rooms since their first creation. It is the celebrated Porson, the most profound scholar in Europe, who has more Greek under that mop of hair than can be found in all the heads in the room; ay, if we even include those of the orchestra.' 'Indeed!' said the monarch—and ordered a new dance" (Warner, "Literary Recollections," vol. ii. chap. xiii. p 5).

36 "It was in January 1798 that I rose one morning before daylight, to walk ten miles in the mud to hear this celebrated person preach" (H. C. Haalitt, "Memoirs of William Hazlitt," vol. i. chap. iii. p 41).

37 "Memoirs-of William Hazlitt," vol. i. p 42.

38 Cottle, "Reminiscences of ... Coleridge," pp 94, 95.

39 September to November 1792 (Macknight, "History of the Life and Times of Edmund Burke," vol. iii. pp 483–9. *Cf* Burke, "Correspondence," vol. iii. p 533). September, 1796 (*ibid.* pp 667–70). January to the end of May, 1797 (*ibid.* pp 694–706). He died in the following July. During the last visit, when exhausted by illness, he had Wilberforce constantly with him, and Windham and Lawrence very frequently. "The whole scene is now before me: Burke was lying on a sofa, much emaciated; and Windham, Lawrence, and some other friends were around him. The attention shown to Burke by that party was just like the treatment of Ahitophel of old. It was as if one went to inquire of the oracle of the Lord'" (Wilberforce, quoted by Macknight, p 703).

40 "It ["Northanger Abbey"] was sold in 1803, to a publisher in Bath, for ten pounds, but it found so little favour in his eyes that he chose to abide by his first loss rather than risk further expense by publishing such a work. It seems to have lain for many years unnoticed in his drawers, somewhat as the first chapters of 'Waverley' lurked forgotten amongst the old fishing-tackle in Scott's cabinet. Tilneys, Thorpes and Morlands consigned apparently to eternal oblivion! But when four novels of steadily increasing success had given the writer some confidence in herself, she wished to recover the copyright of this early work. One of her brothers undertook the negotiation. He found the purchaser very willing to receive back his money, and to resign all claim to the copyright. When the bargain was concluded, and the money paid, but not till then, the negotiator had the satisfaction of informing him that the work which been so lightly esteemed was by the author of 'Pride and Prejudice'" (Leigh, "A Memoir of Jane Austen," chap. viii. pp 129–30). As is well known, "Northanger Abbey" was not published till 1818, after the author's death. Mr Leigh thinks it was written in 1798 (*ibid.* chap. iii. p 7), but it is very probable that the descriptions of Bath in it owe something to earlier visits of the author to the town.

41 Dowden, "Life of Shelley," vol. ii. chap. ii. Mary Godwin, his second wife, wrote a part of her novel, "Frankenstein," at Bath (*ibid.* p 59).

42 "Lander, who knew and loved both cities well, compared it [the situation of Bath] to that of Florence, and from more than one point on Bathwick and its neighbour hills, the prospect may not unworthily challenge comparison with the view from Fiesole or San Miniato." (Traill, "Two Centuries of Bath," in the *English Illustrated Magazine* of June 1884). *Cf.* Swinburne, "A Ballad of Bath," 11. 7–9:

"Our fairest, whose charms no rival wears,
Hailed as England's Florence of one whose praise gives grace,
Landor, once thy lover, a name that love reveres ..."
("Poems and Ballads," third series.)

43 See this note in "Imaginary Conversations": "In London, with St Paul's and St Stephen's before us, in Bath with Queen's Square, the Crescent, and the Circus

(which last nothing in Rome or in the world is equal to), we build cottages like castles and palaces like cottages." ("Pericles and Sophocles," vol. ii p 141 of the second edition.)

44 He danced badly, however, to his great mortification: "How grievously has my heart ached when others were in the full enjoyment of that recreation which I had no right even to partake of" (letter written at a later date to Lady Blessington, and quoted by Mr Colvin, "Landor," chap. iii. p 43. See this work for Landor at Bath.

45 *Ibid.* p 8.

46 See below, chap. vii.

47 It will, of course, be understood that the foregoing enumeration does not pretend to give a complete list even of the more distinguished writers who visited Bath in the eighteenth century, nor of all the occasions on which they came to the city. The names I have mentioned suffice to show that to men of letters, as to all other classes of Society, Bath had become a habitual holiday resort. See also below, chap. ix.

48 Genest, "Some Account of the English Stage," vol. ii. p 235.

49 This piece is generally attributed to Thomas Rawlins. I may also mention *Tunbridge Wells, or the Yeoman of Kent*, by Thomas Baker, written somewhat later, 1703.

50 *The Bath*, dedication.

51 "Life of Nash," p 520 of the "Globe" edition.

52 First given at Lincoln's Inn Fields on February 27, 1725, and acted about seven times (*cf* Genest, "Some Account of the English Stage," vol. iii., p 167).

53 The first scene is in a "Gaming Room, Lady Ambsace rising from the Table in a Fury, while several sharpers divide her money."

The dialogue opens thus:

FIRST SHARPER. "I profess we would not refuse your Ladyship a few pieces, but cash runs low at this time—and this is such an Iron Age that a Gentleman has a villainous Time of it to live upon Credit. Your Ladyship cannot want money. Whenever you are prepared we will give you your Revenge."

LADY AMBSACE. "Get you gone for insatiable Bloodhounds! Quite stript! Yet here are my Deities [takes up the Dice], though I have no sacrifice to offer them. Fame and Fortune ye have had already; my hourly Prayer ye have, tho' ye requite me ill. Yet such is the power of your charms that rather than want Offerings for you, I'll keep a set of Bravos in pay who shall cut Throats and rob Altars to adorn your Shrine."

In Durfey's *Bath* there is also a scene at a gaming-fable (act iv. scene i.). One of the characters, Crab, discovers some professional cheats, whom he fights with their own weapons, and finally unmasks.

54 We may quote the following sketch, which is rather more lively than the rest:

SPRIGHTLY. "Prithee, how stand Affairs? Come, let's have a little Scandal."

PANDER. "Much after the old Sort. People a come to the Bath with the same happy Disposition for Idleness and Pleasure. Men of large Fortunes come to spend 'em; those of small ones expect some lucky cast of Chance to raise them; the Wise and Witty are content to play the Fool, and Fools pass for Wits ; Politicians turn Gamesters, and Gamesters top the Politique upon them; Intrigues of the Council-Board are turn'd into Intrigues of the Chamber; Lords and Pickpockets consort very amicably together; and a profound Statesman shall sit as well diverted at a Puppet-show, or a Match ofWhistling, as if he was projecting a Scheme to cheat the Nation or buy himself a Title."—(Act i. scene ii.).

55 The play is unfinished in the MS preserved in the British Museum, and published by Mr Fraser Rae in 1902 in his edition of Sheridan's works. It is called *A Journey to Bath*, and not, as sometimes asserted, *A Trip to Bath*. Mrs Sheridan wrote it at Blois in 1763, and gave it to Garrick, who found a good deal of fault with it, condemning it as empty and inconsequent (see letter from Mrs Sheridan to Madame Victor, November 16, 1763, in Garrick's "Correspondence, vol. i. pp 17–18).

56 Mrs Tryfort, as is well known, was the prototype of the famous Mrs Malaprop of The Rivals. Sheridan conveyed some of her "derangements of epitaphs" textually to his play.

57 Not *Hewkly*, as Mr Sanders writes it in his "Life of Sheridan," (pp 30–1), having no doubt misread the manuscript.

58 LADY FILMOT (to Lord Stewkly): "Your business is to marry a fortune—so is mine" (p 5 of the manuscript). They thereupon enter into an agreement to help each other.

See Sanders, "Life of Sheridan," chap. ii. pp 30–3, for a detailed comparison of *A Journey to Bath* and *The Rivals*.

59 See Sanders, "Life of Sheridan," chap. ii. pp 30–3, for a detailed comparison of *A Journey to Bath* and *The Rivals*.

60 Between *A Journey to Bath* and the *Maid of Bath*, a comedy acted at Drury Lane in 1767, *The Widow'd Wife* (by W. Kenrick), calls for no special notice, though the watering-place is the scene of the action.. In this poor play, both incidents and characters are too conventional to have any real local interest.

61 See above, chap. v. pp 116–117.

62 It had a certain measure of success. Genest speaks of the twelfth representation (vol. v. p 312); it was revived in 1772, and again in 1775. This was not the only dramatic version of Miss Linley's adventures. Lord Dufferin mentions having seen a very curious performance in Italy last century: "I remember having had the satisfaction of admiring in a play, at Bologna, a remarkable achievement of Sheridan himself, who rescued Miss Linley, the beautiful Maid of Bath, from the clutches of her persecutor by bringing a gondola under the windows of her house in Bond Street" ("Sheridan's Plays," Fraser Rae ed., introd. p x).

63 "According to a local tradition, *The Rivals* was written in the house of the bookseller, Leake, in a room which still exists and is used as a solicitor's office" (Peach, "Life and Times of Ralph Allen," p 7 *note* I).

64 Act ii. Sc., ii.; act iii. sc. i.; act iv. Sc. iii.; act v. Sc. Iii.

65 See the description by Fag (act i. Sc. i.).

66 In all cases but two, the indoor scenes are described in the stage directions as taking place in lodgings. "Good apartments, Jack," says Acres, praising Captain Absolute's quarters (act Sc. i.).

67 SIR LUCIUS: "I was only taking a nap at the Parade Coffee House" (act ii. sc. ii.).

68 See above, last *note* of chap. iv.

69 In 1834, Douglas Jerrold, as I have mentioned (*cf* chap. ii. p 55, *note* 71) made Bath the scene of a lively comedy called *Beau Nash*. But he did not attempt to give a picture of eighteenth-century society. He contented himself with taking a few traits from Goldsmith.

70 "Essay on the External Use of Water, with particular Remarks on the Mineral Waters of Bath."

71 "Roderick Random," 1748; "Peregrine Pickle," 1751.

72 "It is a thousand to one that the girl will be picked up by some scoundrel or other at Bath, if I don't provide for her otherwise" ("Roderick Random," liii.).

73 *Ibid.* chap. lv.

74 See chap. ii. p. 53, *note* 61.

75 "Life of Nash," p 550, Globe ed. It is also recorded, with slight variations, in the "Jests of Beau Nash" (pp 67–8) "A young Lady, who was just come out of the Country, and affected to dress in a very plain Manner, was sitting on a Bench at Bath, as Nash and some of his Companions were passing by; upon which, turning to one of them, he said: 'There's a smart Country Girl, I will have some discourse with her.' Then, going up to the Lady, 'So, Child,' says he, 'you are just come to Bath, I see.' 'Yes, Sir,' answered the Lady. 'And you have been a good Girl in the Country, and learned to read your Book, I hope.' 'Yes, Sir.' 'Pray now,' says he, 'let me examine you. I know you have read your Bible and the story of Tobit and his Dog. Now can you tell me,'" etc.

76 "Roderick Random," chap. lix.

77 See above, chap. v. p 123.

78 "Roderick Random," chap. lix.

79 "When we were left by ourselves, he thanked me in very polite terms for having used the advantage fortune had given me over him with such moderation … " (*ibid.* chap. lx.).

80 "Peregrine Pickle," chap. lxix

81 *Ibid.* chap. lxx.

82 *Ibid.*

83 "Peregrine Pickle," chap. lxx.

84 *Cf* the following passage with act i. scene i., and act v. scene ii., of Sheridan's piece: "On the other hand, when Peregrine, in consequence of having danced with one of the minors overnight, visited her in the morning [this was a recognised and customary attention], the Platonists immediately laid hold on the occasion, tasked 'their imaginations, associated ideas, and with sage insinuations retailed a thousand circum stances of the interview, which never had any foundation in truth. They observed, that if girls are determined to behave with such indiscretion, they must lay their accounts with incurring the censure of the world; that she in question was old enough to act more circumspectly: and wondered that her mother would permit any young fellow to approach the chamber while her daughter was naked in bed. As for the servants peeping through the keyhole, to be sure it was an unlucky accident; but people ought to be upon their guard against such curiosity, and give their domestics no cause to employ their penetration. These, and other such

reflections, were occasionally whispered as secrets among those who were known to be communicative; so that, in a few hours, it became the general topic of discourse; and, as it had been divulged under injunctions of secrecy, it was almost impossible to trace the scandal to its origin; because every person concerned must have promulgated her own breach of trust, in discovering her author of the report" *(ibid.)*.

85 See above, chap. iv., for the description he gives of them.

86 Bath is mentioned again several times in the course of the novel, in the long interlude which Lady Vane had inserted under the name of "Memoirs of a Lady of Quality."

87 It will be remembered that he left England in 1768, and settled at Leghorn, where he died three years later. In the "Adventures of Ferdinand, Count Fathom," published in 1753, the scene of several chapters is laid, if not at Bath, in the adjoining town of Bristol. The society of watering-places reappears persistently in Smollett's works.

88 Sixteen of the letters are dated from Bath. The characters are supposed to spend about a month in the city, arriving on April 2 ("Three days ago we came hither from the Hot Well," J. Melford's letter of April 24), and leaving on May 20 ("I shall to-morrow set out for London," M. Bramble's letter of May 19).

89 This brief description by no means sums up the complex character of Matthew Bramble, at once sympathetic and humorous. It merely indicates that aspect of it with which we are here concerned.

90 "London itself can hardly exhibit one species of diversion to which we have not something analogous at Bath, over and above those singular advantages that are peculiar to the place" (*Ibid.* J. Melford to Sir Watkin Phillips, April 30). Eight years later Mrs Montagu, making the same comparison, judges differently: "In point of society and amusement, it comes next (but after a long interval) to London ... The society and mode of life are infinitely preferable to what one can find in any other country town, but much less agreeable than London. I believe if I was to act the part of Minos in this world, I should use it as a kind of purgatory, to which I should send those who had not the taste or qualifications which deserved to be put into the capital city, nor were yet so disagreeably unsociable as to merit suffering the terrors and horrors of a long winter in the country" (letter quoted in Doran, "A Lady of the Last Century," pp 248 and 250).

91 See the letter of April 23 (M. Bramble to Dr Lewis).

92 Finished in 1765 by the younger Wood. See an elaborate and somewhat unjust criticism of all these buildings in the letter of April 23.

93 Mr Peach ("Historic Houses," vol. i. p 239) notes the inaccuracy by which Smollett ascribed the Circus and the Crescent to the same architect. Though the younger Wood finished the former, it was designed, and begun by his father. By another inadvertence, also noted by Peach, after speaking of the Crescent as merely projected, he introduces Derrick as Master of the Ceremonies (Lydia Melford, April 26; J. Melford, May 6). Derrick did not obtain the post till 1763, after the Crescent was built.

94 Letter of M. Bramble, April 23. Lydia Melford also speaks of "new buildings, such as Prince's Row, Harlequin's Row, Bladud's Row, and twenty other Rows" (April 26).

95 M. Bramble, April 23.

96 *Ibid.*

97 *Ibid*

98 Letter from Jeremy Melford, April 30.

99 Letter from Jeremy Melford, April 30.

100 Quin, when he left the stage, retired to Bath, where he spent the last sixteen years of his life (1751–1766). His reputation, his wit, certain eccentricities (such as his pretended gluttony), made him one of the most remarkable persons of the little city. He is mentioned several times in "Humphry Clinker" (see more especially Jeremy Melford's letters of April 30 and May 6, and *cf* "Life of Quin," chap. xii.-xiv.).

101 "Humphry Clinker," Jeremy Melford, April 30.

102 Puddlledock was at the end of Thames Street.

103 See above, chap. iv. p 114. Derrick is introduced as the Master of the Ceremonies' in "Humphry Clinker" (letter from Jeremy Melford, May 6, and passim). But Smollett may very well have made use of an adventure that took place just after his death, for the purposes of his novel, modifying it a little.

104 Preface to "Roderick Random."

105 These two novels were not published till 1818, after the writer's death. But the first was finished as early as 1798 (Austen Leigh, "Memoir of Jane Austen," chap. iii. p 47), and sold to a publisher (who did not publish it) in 1803 (ibid. chap. viii. p 129), that is to say, twenty-seven and thirty-two years respectively after the publication of "Humphry Clinker" (1771). The interval between them and "Roderick Random" (1748), or "Peregrine Pickle " (1751) is greater, it is true.

106 We are told, it is true, at the beginning of the second chapter of "Northanger Abbey," that Catherine Morland was about to be "launched into all the difficulties and dangers of a six weeks' residence in Bath;" but this expression must not be taken very seriously. Here, as throughout the novel, the writer satirises the tendency of contemporary authors to write of the simplest and most ordinary actions as if they were perilous and complicated adventures. The close of the following passage may be more significant, but even this is slight enough: "Prettier musings of high-wrought love and eternal constancy could never have passed along the streets of Bath than Anne was sporting with from Camden Place to Westgate Buildings. It was almost enough to spread purification and perfume all the way" ("Persuasion," vol. ii. chap. ix.).

107 "The [Austen] family lived in close intimacy with two cousins, Edward a Jane Cooper …" I believe that Cassandra and Jane sometimes visited them there, and that Jane thus acquired the intimate knowledge of the topography and customs of Bath, which enabled her to write 'Northanger Abbey' long before she resided there herself" (Austen Leigh," Memoir of Jane Austen," chap. ii. p 23). In one of her letters, dated April 8, 1805, she recalls a visit made seven years and four months before (*ibid.* p 71). Four others, written in 1799, are dated from Bath ("Letters of Jane Austen," edited by Lord Brabourne, vol. i. p 205), but she was then twenty-three and a half. Lord Brabourne mentions several relative's she had in the city (*ibid.* pp 205 and 277).

108 From 1801 to 1805; her father had retired to Bath, a fact confirmed by a remark Mr Austen Leigh makes in reference to another person, that Bath was at this time a

favourite place of residence for retired clergymen ("Memoir," p 23). The observation is of interest, as showing the change that had taken place in the ordinary society of the town, and its new character of respectability.

109 "Northanger Abbey."

110 It is curious to note how rapidly the action of the novel is developed. It is well advanced before the heroine has been a week at Bath "Monday, Tuesday, Wednesday, Thursday, Friday and Saturday have now passed in review before the reader; the events of each day, its hopes and fears, mortifications and pleasures, have been separately stated, and the pangs of Sunday only now remain to be described, and close the week" (vol. i. beginning of chap. xiii.).

111 In this connection, compare Catherine Morland with Miss Austen's other heroines.

112 See vol. ii. chap. xv.: "Though Henry was now sincerely attached to her—though he felt and delighted in all the excellences of her character, and truly loved her society—I must confess that his affection originated in nothing better than gratitude."

113 "This was one of their principal reasons for establishing themselves at Bath: Sir Walter had at first thought of London; but Mr Shepherd felt that he could not be trusted in London, and had been skilful enough to dissuade him from it, and make Bath preferred. It was a much safer place for a gentleman in his predicament: he might there be important at comparatively little expense. Sir Walter and Elizabeth were induced to believe that they should lose neither consequence nor enjoyment by settling there" (vol. i. chap. ii. p 221).

114 "They had the pleasure of assuring her that Bath more than answered their expectations in every respect ... Their acquaintance was exceedingly sought after. Everybody was wanting to visit them. They had drawn back from many introductions, and were still perpetually having cards left by people of whom they knew nothing" (vol. ii. chap. iii. pp 326, 327).

115 *Ibid.* chap. iv. "How to have this anxious business set to rights, and be admitted as cousins again, was the question; and it was a question, which in a more rational manner, neither Lady Russell nor Mr Elliot thought unimportant ..." (p 337). "Lady Russell confessed that she had expected something better; but yet 'it was an acquaintance worth having'" (p 338). "In London, perhaps [says Mr Elliot further on] in your present quiet style of living, it might be as you say; but, in Bath, Sir Walter Elliot and his family will always be worth knowing, always acceptable as acquaintance ... Here you are in Bath, and the object is to be established here with all the credit and dignity which ought to belong to Sir Walter Elliot" (p 339).

116 See above, pp 169–170.

117 "O Bath, how fair wert thou to view,
When last I said, 'Dear Bath, adieu!'

Such wert thou, when I saw thee last,
Some twenty fleeting summers past,
But now, so mighty art thou grown,
Thy head so large, thy trunk so swol'n,
Thy legs and arms so long and wide,

And such an air of City pride,
Thy sides so blacken'd by the smoke,
Thy streets so cramm'd, thy views so broke;

In short, thou art so Londoniz'd,
So over-built and over-siz'd,
That my old friend I scarcely knew
Since last I said,'Dear Bath, adieu

(Pratt, two pictures of Old and New Bath, 1801, in "Harvest Home," vol. iii. pp 338–440).

118 "Everybody has their tastes in noises as well as in other matters, and sounds are quite innoxious or most distressing, by their sort rather than by their quality. When Lady Russell, not long afterwards, was entering Bath on a wet afternoon, and driving through the long course of streets from the Old Bridge to Camden Place, amidst the dash of other carriages and heavy rumble of carts and drays, the bawling of newsmen, muffin-men and milkmen, and the ceaseless clink of pattens, she made no complaint. No, these were noises which belonged to the winter pleasures, &ç." ("Persuasion," vol. ii. chap. ii. p 325). See also "Northanger Abbey," vol. i. beginning of chap. vii.

119 "The season was full, the room was crowded, and the two ladies squeezed in as well as they could … Mrs Allen made her way through the throng of men by the door … ; Catherine … linked her arm too firmly within her friend's to be torn asunder by any common effort of a struggling assembly. But, to her utter amazement, she found that to proceed along the room was by no means the way to disengage themselves from the crowd; it seemed to rather increase as they went on," etc. ("Northanger Abbey," vol. i. chap. xi. pp 7, 8.)

120 "Persuasion," vol. ii. chap. vi. p 356.

121 After staying long enough in the Pump Room to discover that the crowd was insupportable, and that there was not a genteel face to be seen, which everybody discovers every Sunday throughout the season, they hastened away to the Crescent, to breathe the fresh air of better company" ("Northanger Abbey," vol. i. chap. v. pp 19–20). 122 "A very fine young man, indeed!" said Lady Dalrymple. "More air than one often sees in Bath ". ("Persuasion," vol. ii. chap. viii. p 372).

123 "'Do you find Bath as agreeable as when I had the honour of making the inquiry before?' 'Yes, quite—more so, indeed.' 'More so!—Take care, or you will forget to be tired of it at the proper time. You ought to be tired at the end of six weeks.' 'I do not think I should be tired, if I were to stay here six months.' 'Bath, compared with London, has little variety, and so everybody finds out every year.' 'For six weeks, I allow Bath is pleasant enough, but beyond that, it is the most tiresome place in the world.' 'You would be told so by people of all descriptions, who come regularly every winter, lengthen their six weeks into ten or twelve, and go away at last because they can afford to stay no longer.'" ("Northanger Abbey," t. i. chap. x. pp 58–9).

124 As early as 1780, we find Miss Burney, who spent the whole season at Bath, holding aloof from the public entertainments, which she barely mentions ("Diary," vol. i. pp

165–97 of the Ward edition); she only goes to one of the balls (*ibid.* pp 184–88), and speaks contemptuously of the "showy, tonish people, who are only to be seen by going to the Rooms, which we never do" (*ibid.* pp 176–77).

125 "Pickwick Papers," chapters xxxv.-x]. Two other novels, written in the interval that divides Miss Austen from Dickens, deal with the same scenes. They are "A Winter in Bath," by an anonymous writer (1807), and "Bath," by Thomas Brown (2nd edit. 1818). Both are unimportant

126 "There is an immensity of promenading, on crutches and off, with sticks and without, and a great deal of conversation and liveliness and pleasantry" ("Pickwick," chap. Xxxvi.). *Cf* with this passage and others quoted further on the following lines written by Dickens in 1852 "Lapsing then out of date … she [Volumnia Deadlock] retired to Bath … She has an extensive acquaintance at Bath among appalling gentlemen with thin legs and nankeen trousers, and is of high standing in that dreary city" ("Bleak House," chap. xxviii.). In chap. lvi. of the same novel we read of "that grass-grown city of the ancients, Bath …" 'The description in "Pickwick" marks the extreme limit of its fashionable vogue; indeed, this was, even then, a trifle retrospective (*cf* the various texts of earlier or contemporary date quoted below, chap. xi.).

127 Forster, in his "Life of Dickens," does not mention any visit made by the novelist to Bath before this date, though he does not overlook one of his journeys to Brighton, Broadstairs, etc. But Dickens pilots his characters through the streets and squares of Bath and the neighbouring town of Bristol with remarkable ease; touches like the following seem to transmit personal impressions and recollections: "Having taken a short walk through the city and arrived at the unanimous conclusion that Park Street was very much like the perpendicular streets a man sees in a dream …" (chap. xxxv.). "Away he walked up one street and down another, only it's all up hill at Clifton" (chap. xxxix.), etc. Later in life Dickens was a frequent visitor to the city, one of its attractions to him being the presence of Landor. It was here, as we know from the latter, that he conceived the character of Little Nell (Forster, "Life of Dickens," xii. p 177).

128 It seems probable that this coincidence was by no means accidental. Dickens, it has been declared, had never seen the White Hart, or heard of its worthy landlord till the publication of his book in periodical numbers was far advanced. (Peach, "Historic Houses in Bath," vol. ii. p 14.) But this is unimportant. The landlord furnished the coaching service between London and Bath, and his name was painted on the carriages, as Sam Weller discovered. ("Pickwick Papers," chap. xxxv.) Dickens no doubt noticed it, and was pleased by its grotesqueness.

129 Since when I have been unable to discover. For my own part, I have found no earlier instance of their use in this sense. If it had been of more ancient origin, would it not have been mentioned in one of the many works on Bath read or consulted by the present writer?

130 The locution is going out of fashion; but is still heard occasionally Mr Plumptre indicates another use of the phrase, but of this I have found no example: 'I may note, by the way, that the Bath waters were in high repute for cases of brain and nervous diseases. Their fame survives in the familiar formula for suggesting madness in one

from whom we differ: "Go to Bath and get your head shaved" ("Contemporary Review," April, 1889, p 589 *note*).

131 "'And now,' continued Mr Pickwick, looking round on his friends with a good-humoured smile, and a sparkle in the eye which no spectacles could dim or conceal, 'the only question is, where shall we go to next?' Mr Tupman and Mr Snodgrass were too much affected by their friend's heroism to offer any reply. Mr Winkle had not yet sufficiently recovered the recollection of his evidence at the trial to make any observation on any subject, so Mr Pickwick paused in vain. 'Well,' said that gentleman, 'if you leave me to suggest our destination, I say Bath. I think none of us has ever been there'" ("Pickwick Papers," chap. xxxv).

132 "The great Pump-Room is a spacious saloon, ornamented with Corinthian pillars, and a music gallery, and a Tompion clock, and a statue of Nash ... There is a large bar with a marble vase, out of which the pumper gets the water, and a number of yellow-looking tumblers, out of which the company get it; and it is a most edifying and satisfactory, sight to behold the perseverance and gravity with which they swallow it. There are baths near at hand in which a part of the company wash themselves, and a band plays afterwards to congratulate the remainder on their having done so" ("Pickwick Papers," chap. xxxvi.).

133 "Every morning the regular water-drinkers, Mr Pickwick among the number, met each other in the Pump-Room, took their quarter of a pint, and walked constitutionally. At the afternoon's promenade Lord Mutanhed, and the Honourable Mr Crushton, the Dowager Lady Snuphanuph, Mrs Colonel Wugsby, and all the great people, and all the morning water-drinkers, met in great assemblage. After this, they walked out, or drove out, or were pushed out in bath chairs, and met one another again. After this the gentlemen went to the reading-rooms and met divisions of the mass. After this, they went home. If it were theatre night, perhaps they met at the theatre; if it were assembly night, they met at the rooms; and if it were neither, they met the next day—a very pleasant routine, with perhaps a slight tinge of sameness" (*ibid.*).

134 "Pickwick Papers," chap. xxxv.

135 *Ibid.*

136 *Ibid.*

137 Mr Wright ("Historic Guide to Bath," p 304) writes the name thus. We also find it spelt Jervois. This officer filled the post from 1825 to 1849, apparently to the general satisfaction: "During fourteen [twenty-four?] years, and whilst his military promotion was unaffected, and the colonel had become major-general, his discipline of the ball-room was a subject of admiration; but on the 22nd July, 1849, he tendered his resignation, having been appointed military governor of Hong Kong" (Wright, *op. cit.* pp. 304–5).

138 Referring to the appointment at Hong Kong, Mr Fitzgerald justly observes: "We could scarcely fancy Mr Bantam filling such an office," and he adds: "Mr Peach, of Bath, who recalls Colonel Jervois, writes that he cannot perceive the slightest resemblance or verisimilitude to Jervois" ("History of Pickwick," p 182). I am surprised, therefore, to find that he retracted his opinion later; and in an article

called "Pickwickian Bath" (*Gentleman's Magazine*, May 1898), stated that "Bantam was drawn from life, from an eccentric functionary named Jervois." The few lines by Mr Wright quoted above, seem to me, on the other hand, to confirm Mr Peach's testimony. It is indeed hardly probable that so absurd a picture should have been given as a portrait even a satirical one ; its very excess suggests fancy.

139 "Pickwick Papers," chap. xxxv.

140 Cf "Rebellion in Bath," p 4 (1808):
Stately the monarch stept the lively floor,
Eyeing with smile benign the open door,
Through which pour'd in his subjects, young and old,
The parson sleek, fair maid, and captain bold.
The speculating youth of Irish blood,
Brawny and brazen from his native wood,
Proud peer, fat dowager, with head of puff,
All, save Bath tradesmen, and such common stuff,
Who, banish'd from the fashionable ball,
Cut vulgar capers in the vile Town Hall.

141 Pickwick Papers," chap. xxxv.

142 *Ibid.*

143 See also the comical scenes in which Sam Weller diverts himself at the expense of the Bath servants, and the manner in which they mimic their masters.

144 "Pickwick Papers," chap. xxxv.

145 Bulwer Lytton, in some of the chapters of his "Paul Clifford" (the description is rather vague); Ainsworth, in his "Beau Nash," a work of little merit. Among the more modern works we may mention "The King of Bath," by Mrs Hibbert Ware (1879), an insipid paraphrase of Goldsmith's "Life of Nash," and several more entertaining stories, such as "Her Season in Bath," by Emma Marshall (1890), "Mr Zinzan of Bath" by Mary Deane (1891), "The Bath Comedy," by Agnes and Egerton Castle (1900), "Monsieur Beaucaire," by Booth Torkington (1901). This author and Mr G. E. Sutherland dramatised this last work; the play was acted in London in 1902 and 1903. Mr F. Frankfort Moore's "Nest of Linnets," a novel founded on the story of Miss Linley, has already been mentioned. (*Cf* above, chap. v. p 130, *note* 39.) In his "Virginians," Thackeray has admirably described the analogous though smaller society of Tunbridge Wells, as it was about the year 1756; and Messrs Besant and Rice laid the scene of the second part of their "Chaplain of the Fleet" at Epsom, a little earlier.

VIII

Authors at Bath: the "Water Poets"; the Bath Easton Parnassus; Anstey

Described in prose by a Smollett, a Goldsmith, a Sheridan, a Dickens, Bath never inspired an English poet of the first or even of the second rank.[1] Anstey alone, among the throng of those who have extolled or satirised her in verse, had any real gifts, and has preserved a legitimate reputation. He is, and justly, the sole survivor of that host of versifiers who, for over a century, chose Bath as their temporary residence, and there poured forth a stream of descriptive pieces and madrigals, of panegyrics and satires, conundrums and acrostics—all those fugitive pieces, in short, which were evoked by certain evergreen themes: the charms and diversions of the place, the beauty of the fair visitors, the merits of their respective cavaliers, the pangs of love, the absurdities of this or that individual, diversified by the petty scandals and local events of the town. The number of visitors stung by the poetic tarantula swells to such dimensions that in 1713 Steele describes them as a special genus, and dubs them the "Water Poets,"[2] presenting them to us as "an innocent tribe" worthy of all encouragement. "It would be barbarous," he adds, "to treat those authors with bitterness, who never write out of the season, and whose works are useful with the waters ... There are a hundred general topics put into metre every year, viz., 'The lover is inflamed in the water;' or, 'he finds his death when he sought his cure;' or, 'the nymph feels her own pain, with out regarding her lover's torment.' These being for ever repeated have at present very good effect; and a physician assures me, that laudanum is almost out of doors at the Bath."[3] Some of the happy results here described by Steele must assuredly have been the work of "A Dream: or the Force of Fancy," the oldest local poem we have yet discovered (1710).[4] It is a series of short poems, each an eulogy of one of the ladies then taking the Waters. It is without a trace of style, wit, or charm—a mere piece of Battery of the most fulsome and insipid kind.[5] However, it started an interminable series. Portraits, real or imaginary, in the same style and of the same order of merit, follow after this at short intervals, now published separately, now alternating with epigrams and madrigals in one or other of the miscellanies or keepsakes of the period. Collections were nevertheless made of all the little verses perpetrated by visitors to Bath, Tunbridge Wells, or Epsom;[6] and the editor of one of these hopes thereby "to oblige the Publick, by showing these specimens of conceal'd Genius's, and to convince Pope and Swift that there are more Poets in England than themselves."[7] Alas! neither Pope[8] nor Swift had any cause to tremble for his laurels. This farrago of stale compliments, of silly and pretentious gallantries, of pointless epigrams, acrostics and bouts-rimés is the dullest reading in the world. Ingenuity, facility and charm, if not entirely wanting, are even rarer than in the French Almanachs des Muses—dreary as these are! Some of these jeux d'esprit, the improvisations of a moment, may have been diverting for an hour to a particular society on a particular occasion They might fitly have passed away with the moment that suggested them.

That they were, nevertheless, taken very seriously is proved by the fact that in 1769 we find weekly or bi-monthly poetic contests instituted in Bath, which continued for a period of about twelve years. They were accompanied by a peculiar ceremonial, and a great part of the aristocratic and lettered society of the place competed for the prizes. These competitions were initiated by a certain John (later Sir John) Miller, a retired officer, and his wife, the owners of a villa standing in a picturesque garden,[9] at Batheaston) two miles from Bath, where they were fond of entertaining good company,[10] but had long been quite content to show themselves amiable folks without any literary pretensions,[11] when suddenly Mrs Miller returned from a tour on the Continent transformed into "a beauty, a genius, a Sappho, a tenth muse, as romantic as Mlle Scuderi and as sophisticated as Mrs Vesey."[12] At least, so Horace Walpole tells us, and he continues thus: "The captain's fingers are loaded with cameos, his tongue runs over with virtue; and that both may contribute to the improvement of their country, they have introduced bouts-rimés as a new discovery. They hold a Parnassus fair every Thursday,[13] give out rhymes and themes, and all the flux of quality at Bath contend for the prizes A Roman vase, distressed with pink ribands and myrtles, receives the poetry, which is drawn out every festival, six judges of these Olympic games retire and select the brightest compositions, which the respective successful acknowledge, kneel to Mrs Calliope, kiss her fair hand, and are crowned by it. with myrtle—with I don't know what. You may think this a fiction, or exaggeration. Be dumb, unbelievers! The collection is printed, published—yes, on my faith! there are bouts-rimés on a buttered muffin by her Grace the Duchess of Northumberland, receipts to make them by Corydon the venerable, alias [George Pitt]; others very pretty by Lord P[almerston], some by Lord C[armarthen], many by Mrs M[iller] herself, that have no fault but wanting metre; and immortality promised to her with out end or measure. In short, since folly, which never ripens to madness but in this climate, ran distracted, there never was anything so entertaining, or so dull—for you cannot read so long as I have been telling."[14]

Christopher Anstey
From an engraving

Walpole may well repudiate the charge of exaggeration or invention. The truth of his statements is borne out by a detailed account of the ceremonial, given by a constant visitor to the house, one of those who more than once competed for the wreath of myrtle. "Lady Miller,"[15] we are informed by the Rev. Richard Graves, "once a fortnight, gave out a subject for poetical composition; on which, when the company was assembled, those whom the Muses, or perhaps vanity, or the love of fame; had influenced, produced their performances, and put them into an elegant antique marble vase brought from Rome, and placed on a pedestal in the bow window: when the company were seated, some young nymph put in her delicate arm, and took out a single poem, which the author, or some one who either had, or fancied he had, an agreeable elocution, read to the assembly. When, in this manner, the whole collection was gone through, the gentlemen retired into a contiguous apartment; where amidst a profusion of jellies, sweetmeats, ice-creams, and the like, they decided on the merits of the several performances; from which they selected three, which were deemed the best; and of course entitled to prizes, which her ladyship distributed to the respective authors; a pompous bouquet of flowers to the first, a myrtle wreath to the second, and a sprig of myrtle to the third. These were then usually presented by the successful candidate to some lady, who wore them in her hair or her bosom the next evening to the publick rooms."[16]

Not every one was free to enter these poetic lists. Just as at the mediaeval tournament competitors had to produce proofs of their nobility, so for the entrée at Batheaston, rank, or a certain degree of fame, were almost indispensable, and in any case, an unblemished reputation.[17] The lady of the house weeded out her visitors with extreme care, and very probably desire to be admitted to an exclusive circle contributed quite as much as the affectation of culture to establish and maintain the success of these extraordinary gatherings. Nothing was more elegant in the fashionable world than to appear either as candidate,[18] judge, or spectator at Batheaston. Fifty carriages were some times to be seen at the gates of the villa, and duchesses galore within,[19] so enamoured of poetry, or so delighted with the company provided by their hostess, that they overlooked her anything but aristocratic appearance and manners. Lady Miller, indeed, can scarcely have had the air and breeding of St James'; she must even have figured very strangely as Sappho or Calliope, to quote Walpole's malicious designations. Mme D'Arblay describes her thus:—fourteen years later, it is true—"Lady Miller is a round, plump, coarse-looking dame of about forty, and while all her aim is to appear an elegant woman of fashion, all her success is to seem an ordinary woman in very common life, with fine clothes on. Her movements are bustling, her air is mock-important, and her manners inelegant."[20] Let us hasten to add that she gives her credit for much civility and a kind heart.[21] And we may take her word for it; moreover, passages in Lady Miller's "Letters from Italy" (1776), a superficial but entertaining work, show that the Bath Muse was not a simpleton. Though her literary gatherings were rather absurd, it is possible that in instituting them, and thus following an example set in London,[22] she was influenced by a laudable wish to banish cards and vapid gossip from her entertainments. One may, in that case, give her the benefit of good intentions, while acknowledging that literature was not greatly the gainer thereby,[23] and that the bouquet of "artificial flowers"[24] gathered at Batheaston deserved both Johnson's contempt[25] and Walpole's ridicule.[26] When the entire edition of the "Poetical Amusements" was bought up in ten days[27] the public gave evidence either of singular indulgence or un commonly bad taste. In all this mass of laboured trivialities[28] there are but two or three agreeable pieces,[29] and even these do not rise above mediocrity.

Four pieces by Garrick,[30] three by Graves,[31] one by Anstey,[32] several by Pratt,[33] by Miss Seward,[34] by a Frenchman, M du Tems, or Dutens (in French), have no particular merit. As for the rest, including the numerous—far too numerous—productions of Captain Miller and his wife, one must criticise them with the indulgence craved in the preface: "The candid reader will please to recollect, whilst he turns over these pages, that they were frequently the production of a few days, most of them of a few hours:—That they originated amidst the hurry of plays, balls, public breakfasts and concerts, in all the dissipation of a full Bath Season, alike unfriendly to contemplation and the Muses:—That the authors did not foresee their appearance under their present form, and had for the most part little leisure to improve or to correct them."[35]

This indulgence is not required, nor are excuses necessary for another collection of society verses which appeared three years before the institution of the Batheaston contests, Anstey's "New Bath Guide," the success of which was immediate, widespread, and enduring in it we have a masterpiece of society verse, and of verse wholly inspired by Bath, a work of art which is far more than a mere local curiosity. A perfectly new and original departure, Anstey's poem has left its mark on English letters; it exercised a notable influence on Goldsmith's[36] later works in verse; it set a fashion in style which was destined in the nineteenth century to achieve great success in the hands of Moore, Hood, Praed and Barham in England, and of Oliver Wendell Holmes in America.

The new poet was a country squire, who divided his time between the House of Commons, of which he was a somewhat obscure member, his seat at Trumpington,[37] and Bath.[38] Educated at Eton and Cambridge, where he took a prize for English poetry, he afterwards with a collaborator, translated Gray's "Elegy" into Latin verse. But the "New Bath Guide" was his first real entry into the world of letters, a somewhat late one, since he was forty-two when he wrote it (1766).[39] The poem was published anonymously, far from Bath and London, at Cambridge, and under an ambiguous and somewhat misleading title; but it made its way rapidly and brilliantly nevertheless. Let us hear what that witty gossip and fastidious critic, Horace Walpole, has to say about it. Writing to his friend, George Montagu, he announces the appearance of the new poem thus:

"What pleasure have you to come! there is a new thing published … called the 'New Bath Guide.' It stole into the world, and for a fortnight no soul looked into it, concluding its name was its true name. No such thing. It is a set of letters in verses, in all kinds of verses, describing the life of Bath, and incidentally every thing else; but so much wit, so much humour, fun and poetry, so much originality, never met together before. Then the man has a better ear than Dryden or Handel. Apropos to Dryden, he has burlesqued his St Caecilia, that you will never read it again without laughing. There is a description of a milliner's box in all the terms of landscape, painted lawns and chequered shades, a Moravian ode, and a Methodist ditty, that are incomparable, and the best names that ever were composed. I can say it by heart, though a quarto; and, if I had time, would write it you down, for it is not yet reprinted, and not one to be had."[40]

Gray, more briefly, recognises "a new and original kind of humour" in the poem, and adds," it is the only thing in fashion."[41] Gibbon (or his collaborator Deveyrdun) translated whole passages of it into his "Mémoires littéraires de la Grande-Bretagne" accompanied by an eulogistic notice.[42] Smollett, in his "Humphry Clinker," pays Anstey the compliment of frankly borrowing certain characteristic traits; indeed, he may have been still more deeply indebted to him.[43] Ten successive editions in as many years[44] bear witness to a vogue which was not exhausted by half a century of popularity.[45]

The scheme of the poem is that which—either by accident or design—Smollett adopted a few years later in his "Humphry Clinker." A family, visiting Bath to take the waters, describes in a series of letters the impressions, adventures, experiences and amusements offered by the place; but in Anstey's case, encouraged and inspired by the example of the local poets, they express themselves in verse. There is another point of divergence, too: the characters of the poem, at least those who write, are far less numerous, less varied in type, and above all, less realistic, than those of the novel; in so slight a work the author has not troubled himself much to be profound or analytical. Simkin Blunderhead, the chief character, who is responsible for eleven out of the fifteen letters, is distinguished by a sly and sarcastic turn of mind, a quaint mixture of inexperience and common sense; a good fellow at heart, he is an ironical observer, with a humour that becomes at, times somewhat crude and brutal.[46] His cousin Jenny, writer of three of the letters, a sentimental and romantic soul, adopts a more lyric vein. She is fond of invoking Apollo and the Muses, and is easily gulled by the pressing attentions of a soi-disant captain, who talks to her of Milton and Shakespeare.[47] The party is completed by his sister, a simpleton, who only appears to describe the unedifying fashion in which she falls a prey to a canting Methodist preacher. It is needless to analyse these characters more closely—in so doing one would be apt to regard them as more complex and more definite than the author intended them to be.

In the letters he attributes to them, the scenes we know so well, the scenes which have enlivened the pages of so many writers, are once more painted in a satirical vein, and the usual procession of comic actors defiles across the stage. The bells of the Abbey ring a full peal to welcome Simkin Blunderhead,[48] the town band serenades him at his lodging as though he were "a broker, a statesman, a gamester or a Peer, a naturalised Jew, a Bishop or a retired cheesemonger."[49] However, this merely costs him two guineas, and a dispute with a gouty neighbour who objects to the noise. The morning after his arrival the doctors take charge of his health,[50] looking "very thoughtful and grave, to be sure,"[51] and talking at length "of the Peritoneum and Colon, of Phlegmatic Humours oppressing the Women, from Foeculent Matter that swells the Abdomen,"[52] or, under the pretext of a consultation, assembling in his rooms, and discussing at their ease, and with all the jargon of their profession the news of the day:

This *Stamp Art*, no doubt, might be good for the Crown,
But I fear' tis a Pill that will never go down—
What can *Portugal* mean?—is She going to stir up
Convulsions and Heats in the Bowels of *Europe*?
'Twill be fatal if *England* relapses again,
From the ill Blood and Humours of *Bourbon* and Spain.[53]

The invalid waxes impatient; fortunately he is not seriously ill, he can go to the baths, where he is much amused

to behold the Fair Sex
All wading with Gentlemen up to their Necks,
And view them so prettily tumble and sprawl
In a great smoking Kettle as big as our Hall.[54]

Seeing that so many persons of quality and fortune consent to be "boiled" under order of the Faculty—

It pleas'd me to see how they all were inclin'd
To lengthen their Lives for the Good of Mankind;
For I ne'er would believe that a Bishop or Judge
Can fancy old Satan may owe him a Grudge,
Tho' some think the Lawyer may choose to *Demur*,
And the Priest till another Occasion *Defer*,
And both to be better prepar'd for herea'ter,
Take a Smack of the Brimstone contained in the Water.[55]

What surprises him is that—

Since the Day that King Bladud first found out the Bogs,
And thought them so good for himself and his Hogs,
Not one of the Faculty ever has try'd
These excellent Waters to cure his own Hide … [56]
Thus *Chiron* advis'd Madame Thetis to take
And dip her poor child in the Stygian Lake,
But the worthy old Doctor was not such an Elf
As ever to venture his Carcase himself;
So *Jason's* good Wife us'd to set on a pot
And put in at once all the Patients she got,
But thought it sufficient to give her Direction,
Without being coddled to mend her complexion.[57]

The card-rooms offer a no less diverting spectacle to the young man. Here he sees the virtuous woman spoken of by Solomon:

She will do a Man good all the days of her Life;
She deals like a Merchant, she sitteth up late;
And you'll find it is written in verse Twenty-eight.
Her husband is sure to be known at the Gate.
He never hath Need or Occasion for Spoil,
When his Wife is much better employ'd all the while;
She seeketh fine Wool and fine Linen she buys,
And is clothed in Purple and Scarlet likewise.[58]

Such women

to their Husbands more Profit can yield,
And are much like a Lilly that grows in the Field;
They toil not indeed, nor indeed do they spin—
Yet they never are idle when once they begin,
But are very intent on encreasing their Store,
And always keep shuffling and cutting for more.[59]

In the Assembly Rooms he is dazzled by the bevy of beauties he encounters, and invokes the nymphs of Helicon that he may sing their praises worthily. He is delighted with the order and decorum that prevail. The gods, it seems, have sent Hermes, in the person of Nash, to preside over the pleasures of Bath! He extols Beau Nash in appropriate terms, and pays a solemn tribute to his memory:

Him mourn'd all the Dryads on Claverton's[60] Mount,
Him Avon deplor'd, Him the Nymph of the Fount
The Crystalline Streams.
Then perish his Picture, his Statue decay,
A Tribute more lasting the Muses shall pay.
If true what Philosophers all will assure us,
Who dissent from the Doctrine of great *Epicurus*,
That the Spirit's immortal: as Poets allow,
If Life's occupations are follow'd below:
In reward of his Labours, his Virtue and Pains,
He is footing it now in th' Elysian Plains,
Indulg'd, as a token of Proserpine's Favour,
To preside at her Balls in a Cream-colour'd Beaver ...[61]

A public breakfast affords Simkin Blunderhead an opportunity of seeing a lord making himself agreeable to the reigning toast "by playing the part of a Host at an Inn,"[62] and he is more and more charmed with Bath, till suddenly his bills, added to his losses at play, oblige him to depart, somewhat crestfallen, with an empty purse. His companions, equally delighted at first, end their visit in equal or worse confusion. The lively and romantic Jenny, beguiled by the insinuating captain (who has rooked Simkin at lansquenet), has the mortification of discovering him to be a mere chevalier d'industrie. A worse fate still has befallen Prudence and her maid Tabby, who have been deceived, the one by a hypocritical Methodist, the other by a Moravian preacher. Accordingly they all pack up and return home, bearing, however, no grudge against the joyous city.

Of course there is nothing very Pew in all this; the poem does not aspire to be anything but a piece of raillery;[63] its merit lies in its apt and sprightly style and in the irresistible swing of the metre. The author's wit—though perhaps not of the most refined, descending, indeed, on occasion to sheer indecency—is rich, at any rate, in original and unexpected sallies; it is at its best in quiet sarcasm and again in parody. Walpole particularly enjoyed a burlesque on one of Dryden's poems;[64] other travesties, such as those on the "Allegro" and the "Penseroso" of Milton, are not less amusing.[65] The versification is particularly noteworthy; very varied, for the author uses different metres for each of his epistles, it shows throughout an extraordinary briskness and vivacity. The anapaestic metre, more especially, which presents almost insuperable difficulties to the generality of poets, is the one in which Anstey excels and seems perfectly at home. Nothing could be smoother, more haunting than this rhythm with its four swinging beats, which seems to carry the reader along with it. A contemporary felicitously compared it to the rapid, even pace of a cantering horse.[66] If, as is possible, it was from Prior Anstey borrowed this metre—hitherto much neglected[67]—he made it his own by right of having manipulated it with the utmost dexterity, of having made it the instrument best adapted to his particular theme. By the rhyme, too, delightfully easy and full of quaint and un expected turns, Anstey is able to produce the most comic effects. For instance, he constantly uses the dissyllabic or feminine ending, so fruitful of curious echoes, or he suddenly introduces a proper name at the end of the line to make the rhyme,[68] little tricks of style which he, of course, was not the first to employ (we need only recall the rhymes in Butler's "Hudibras"), but which have seldom been used with more felicitous effect. It is, I think, very evident that Goldsmith was particularly delighted both with the rhyme and the metre, for he certainly imitated them quite frankly in his three last poems:
"The Haunch of Venison," "Retaliation," and the "Letter in Prose and Verse to Mrs Bunbury,"[69] the least among the tributes paid to them. And what shall we say of other disciples, less famous, no doubt, but still more enthusiastic—that great army of "Water Poets" who acclaim the singer of Bath and follow panting in his steps. One of these compares him unhesitatingly to Tibullus and Gray, finds in him Sterne and Swift combined, and places him above Chaucer;[70] another, who has difficulty in finding a poet in all Europe to set beside him,[71] addresses a whole collection of laudatory epistles to him, wherein he scarcely ventures to hint a few timid criticisms on his somewhat free and irreverent pleasantries. Nor did they stop at panegyric; imitation began at once in Bath and continued throughout fifty years. "Poetical Epistles" (1767), "'Water Poetry"[72] (1771), Sheridan's "Ridotto" (1771), "The Register of Folly"[73] (1773), are among the first echoes of the "New Bath Guide"; then, after an interval, comes a fresh batch still impregnated with Anstey, and at

Oliver Goldsmith
From the portrait by a pupil of Sir Joshua Reynolds

times almost as racy as the model;[74] "Postscript to the New Bath Guide"[75] (1790), a "Bagatelle" (2nd ed. 1792), "Rebellion in Bath"[76] (1808), "The Wonders of a Week at Bath"[77] (1811), "The Cross-Bath Guide"[78] (1815), "An Intercepted Epistle from a Person in Bath" (2nd ed. 1815), "Epistles from Bath"[79] "The Bath Pump Room"[80] ("Rough Sketches of Bath"[81] (5th ed., 1820), "A Summer in Bath" (1822). Among these trifles we have only mentioned those in which Anstey's influence is most direct and obvious, and as such works are of their very nature perishable, or, at least, extremely difficult to find nowadays, no doubt this list is anything but complete.

Sixty years after the publication of Anstey's poem, its title was still commonly used to describe a certain style of light society verse.[82]

It was fitting that this particular genre should take its rise in Bath, and in the following century the delightful fooling of Moore, of Hood, of Praed, Barham and Oliver Wendell Holmes still retained—perhaps unconsciously to the writers—some echo of the good-natured satire, the lively, swinging numbers which so delighted the gay world of the watering-places at which it was aimed. There have been numberless repetitions, growing fainter with distance; the rhythm has become so familiar to our ears that we forget where it was first employed. More over, it is long since it died away altogether. For when a poet, and so great a poet as Swinburne,[83] evokes in accents of profound emotion: "The lovely city whose grace no grief deflowers," the city "girt about with beauty by days and nights that creep, soft as breathless ripples that softly shorewards creep," the city, "lulled asleep by the chime of passing years," over which "Time lies lighter than music on men's ears," who would recognise in this dim and melancholy spot, where "Peace has found a harbourage mild as very sleep," the merry, noisy, perhaps somewhat vulgar casino of the. past? How remote indeed, is this from the poet's thought! How utterly it has passed away! What a different music hovers in the air for "him who dreams and hears"! What novel "phantoms ... pass with smiles and tears"! Bath has become a "queen enchanted that may not laugh nor weep, Glad at heart and guarded from change and care like ours ... Age and gray forgetfulness, time that shifts and veers" touch her not; "dawn and noon and sunset are one before [her] face." This takes us into regions remote indeed from the very mundane Elysium where we have been wandering, regions loftier, serener, and vaguer, where Anstey's jingling bells would sound strangely indeed! The Bath of the past must surely be dead and gone, if the Bath of the nineteenth century can awaken these solemn harmonies, and appear to the poet a venerable, antique, and sacred city, slumbering in a haze of dreams and memories! Dead indeed, she is, and with her all her little literature, with the exception of a single poem.

1 A contemporary poet, Swinburne, has sung its praises admirably in his "Ballad of Bath" ("Poems and Ballads," Third Series); but, as will be seen further on, p 240, he is affected chiefly, if not solely, by the natural beauty of the place and by the memory of Landor and his friends. The modish Bath of the eighteenth century has, as may be supposed, no part in this lyric gem.

2 The nickname seems in no way to have displeased them, as we find one of their collections bearing the title, "Water Poetry, a Collection of Verses written at several Public Places."

3 Guardian, no. 174, September 30, 1713.

4 At any rate in print, for the publications of the "Commission on Historical Manuscripts" (12th Report, Appendix, part iii. p 188) contains an eulogy in verse on the ladies present in Bath in 1699, from the pen of Thomas Coke, afterwards Vice-Chamberlain of the King's Household. It is hardly likely that "A Dream" should

have been the first poem of its kind to appear in print, but works of this category, of purely ephemeral and local interest and issued in small numbers, are for the most part altogether lost, or surviving copies are exceedingly difficult to meet with. This is notably the case with the majority of the pasquinades or lampoons cited by Pope (Guardian, no. 11, May 24, 1713), and Gay (letter to Parnell of March 8, 1715, Pope "Works," ed. Elwin and Courthope, vol. vii. p 455), as being so much in vogue at Bath. Frequently too, effusions of this kind would appear at Bath, in London or elsewhere, in the form of leaflets, or in some periodical, and were never collected or published separately (see, for instance, in the Gentleman's Magazine, 1731, p 170, a poem on the beauties then present in Bath; and 1743, pp 13, 96, another on Nash's beaver). Others again—and these were legion—never got beyond the manuscript stage, as the following curious passage relative to Tunbridge Wells shows: "A few minutes are spent by some in making verses, as the waters, or genius of the place, or as love and leisure inspire. These verses, *jeu des esprits*, are various and occasional, but chiefly complimentary to the ladies in general, or to some particular fair one. A copy of them is usually left at the bookseller's shop, and entered into a book there for the inspection and entertainment of the company. This poetical pastime, when confined within the bounds of decorum and politeness, is very pleasing and agreeable, and is always supposed to be exempt from the severity of criticism" ("A General Account of Tunbridge Wells," p 11).

5 One or two extracts will serve as samples of the whole. Here is a portrait of the Duchess of Norfolk:

Julia Good humoured, yet Majestic too,
In her full Bloom met my Fancied View;
The Noble Dame, for highest Honours born,
The well-placed Coronet do's so well adorn,
That when with Girding Gold her Brow it binds
With double Lustre it unenvi'd shines.—(p 4.)

This is one of the longest; the rest are about the length of the following on a certain Mrs Noel:

You noble **Zetzea** next in Grandeur shine,
Well-made and stately as a Lofty Pine,
Which o'er the forest rears its tow'ring head,
Adorned with Silver Leaves, and widely spread.—(p. 5.)

6 For the titles of some, see Bibliography.

7 "Bath Miscellany" (preface).

8 Pope, by the way, does not forget the Water Poets in his "Dunciad." In the vision in the third canto the shade of Settle points out to Cibber:

Each cygnet sweet of Bath and Tunbridge race
Whose tuneful whistling makes the waters pass.
(ll. 155–56)

Which lines may be a reminiscence of these by Young:

Is there a man of an eternal vein
Who lulls the town in winter with his strain;

At Bath, in summer, who chants the reigning lass,
And sweetly whistles as the waters pass ? etc,
("Love of Fame," satire i., 11. 277–80)

9 Horace Walpole thus describes it in a letter: "They have a small new-built house, with a bow window, directly opposite to which the Avon falls in a wide cascade, a church behind it in a vale, into which two mountains descend, leaving an opening into the distant country. A large village, with houses for gentry, is on one of the hills to the left. Their garden is little, but pretty, and watered with several small rivulets among the bushes. Meadows fall down to the road; and above, the garden is terminated by another view of the river, the city and the mountains. 'Tis a very diminutive principality with large pretensions." ("Letters," vol. v. p 20. To George Montagu, October 22, 1766.) Later he writes in a more ironical strain: "You must know, that near Bath is erected a new Parnassus, composed of three laurels, a myrtle tree, a weeping willow, and a view of the Avon, which has now been christened Helicon" *(ibid.* vol. vi. p 170. To the Hon. H. S. Conway and Lady Aylesbury, January 15, 1775). This description is confirmed by an anonymous satire:

Bless us!—what toil, what cost has been bestowed,
To give that prospect—of the London road!
Our admiration knows not where to fix—
Here a cascade, and there a coach and six, etc.
("Bath, its Beauties and Amusements," 1. 15, et seq.)

10 Horace Walpole dined with them in 1766 (letter of October 22 quoted above).

11 "An agreeable family ... " ("Letters.") " ... Her daughter [of a Mrs Riggs, who was by way of being a wit], who passed for nothing, married to a Captain full of good-natured officiousness. These good folks ... caught a little of what was then called taste, built and planted, etc (*ibid.* vol. vi. p 170).

12 Ibid. Mrs Vesey, a cultivated and witty woman, had a famous salon in London; with Mrs Montagu, she was one of the first "blue stockings."

13 Once a fortnight, according to Graves (see p 226).

14 "Letters," vol. vi. pp 170–72.

15 Her husband was made a baronet in 1778.

16 Graves, "The Triflers," pp 11, 12.

17 "Do you know, that notwithstanding Bath Easton is so much laughed at in London, nothing here is more tonish than to visit Lady Miller, who is extremely curious in her company, admitting few people who are not of rank or fame, and excluding all of those who are not of character very unblemished" (Madame D'Arblay, "Diary and Letters," 1780, vol. 1. p 175, ed. Ward).

18 As witness the great personages Walpole cites among the successful competitors (see above, p 196), and these were not the only ones. It was an unpremeditated supplement to his "Catalogue of Royal and Noble Authors."

19 "I counted one morning above fifty carriages drawn up in a line from Bath Easton, towards Lambridge; and was at one time present at it, with four duchesses, the duchess of Cumberland, Northumberland, Ancaster and Beaufort" (Graves, "The Triflers," p 13).

20 "Diary and Letters," 1780, loc. cit. The writer, however, is by no means prejudiced against Mrs Miller; she speaks of civilities received from her, and while presenting the above unflattering portrait, excuses herself as follows: "After all this, it is hardly fair to tell you what I think of her. However, the truth is, I always, to the best of my intentions, speak honestly what I think of the folks I see, without being biased either by their civilities or neglect; and that, you will allow, is being a very faithful historian" (*ibid.*).

21 "So much for the lady of Bath-Easton; who, however, seems extremely good-natured, and who is, I am sure, extremely civil" ("Diary and Letters").

22 About the middle of the century a few ladies—Montagu among the first—had started this movement, endeavouring in their receptions to replace cards by conversation, giving literary breakfasts, establishing the "Blue Stocking" Club, etc. See on this subject Doran, "A Lady of the Last Century," chap xi.

23 The contests at Batheaston revealed to Miss Seward her poetic vocation (see her "Poem to the Memory of Lady Miller"). But this was perhaps a result which Poetry could have dispensed with.

24 Term used by Walpole (letter to the Countess of Ossory, January 12, 1775, vol. vi. p 69 of his "Letters").

25 "Lady Miller's collections of verses by fashionable people, which were put into her vase at Bath-Easton villa, near Bath, in competitions for honorary prizes, being mentioned, he held them very cheap: 'Boats rimés,' said he, 'is a mere conceit, and an old conceit now; I wonder how people were persuaded to write in that manner for this lady.' I named a gentleman of his acquaintance who wrote for the Vase.

"JOHNSON. 'He was a blockhead for his pains.'

"BOSWELL. 'The Duchess of Northumberland wrote.'

"JOHNSON. 'Sir, the Duchess of Northumberland may do as she pleases: nobody will say anything to a lady of her high rank. But I should be apt to throw... ... 's verses in his face'" (Boswell, "Life of Johnson," 1775, vol. ii. pp 308, 309, "Napier" ed.). Johnson's acquaintance alluded to here was probably the Rev Richard Graves, who for some years was chaplain to Mr William Fitzherbert, a friend of the doctor's.

26 See the letter already quoted, as also several others (to the Countess of Ossory, January 21, 1775; the Hon H. S. Conway, January 9, 1779, vol. vi. p 178, and vol. vii. p 168 of the correspondence). He was not alone in ridiculing this absurd Parnassus, as witness a long poem on the vase of Batheaston in the Gentleman's Magazine, August, 1780 (pp 387, 388). Madame d'Arblay remarks, as we have already seen (p 227), that "Batheaston is ... much laughed at in London;" and Sheridan, having to thank some one for a present, writes thus to his father-in-law: "I believe I shall try a little jingle on the occasion; at least a few such stanzas as might gain a cup of tea from the urn at Bath-Easton" (letter quoted by Rae, "Sheridan," vol. i. chap. iii. p 95). Compare, too, "The Sentence of Momus on the Poetical Amusements at a Villa near Bath," and satirical passages in "Bath, its Beauties and Amusements," p 69, and in "Bath, a Simile," etc. At Bath itself, there appeared in 1777 "A Receipt to make a Bath Easton Poet and to obtain a Prize from the Vase."

27 "Poetical Amusements at a Villa near Bath," vol. ii. p v. At the first reprint a second volume was added (1776), a third in 1777, a fourth in 1781. They were all sold for the benefit of a charitable object. Of the same origin and very similar, though less extensive and less varied in style, are two other collections, "On Novelty" (1778), and "Hobby Horses " (1780).

28 It consists chiefly of *bouts-rimés*, poems on the various themes pro posed, as the Power of Love, of Music, Fashion, the Month of April, Beauty, Dancing, the Opening of the Vase at Batheaston, and so forth.

29 Such as the one by Lord Palmerston on "Beauty," praised (some what excessively) by Walpole. It is too long to be quoted here.

30 "Grace" and "Simplex Munditiis" (vol. ii.); the "Pleasures of May," and "On the Use and Abuse of Curiosity" (vol. iii.).

31 "On Beauty" (vol. ii.); "Dreams" (vol. iii.); "On the Transmigration of Souls" (vol. iv.).

32 "Winter Amusements" (vol. iv.). Anstey was one of the habitués of the house, and dedicated to Captain Miller a poem entitled "An Election Ball" first read at Batheaston.

33 "The System of Pythagoras"; "The Family of Time"; Tenderness" (vol. iv.).

34 "The Pythagorean System"; "Thalia"; "Ode on Ignorance" (*ibid.*).

35 "Poetical Amusements," preface, p 4.

36 See below, p 203.

37 The village of Trumpington, near Cambridge, is well-known as the scene of one of Chaucer's Canterbury Tales—the Miller's.

38 For Anstey's life, see the biographical notice by his son in his poetical works (1808), and the introduction by J. Britton to the new edition of the "New Bath Guide" (1852).

39 We need only glance at Anstey's other works. They consist of some small pieces written for the Batheaston gatherings (one, "An Election Ball," recalls the "New Bath Guide"), and the "Journey of Doctor Bongout and his Wife to Bath" (1778), a humorous poem in sixteen cantos. The last, a not very interesting narrative of the adventures of a gluttonous doctor and his avaricious wife, was not reprinted in the "Complete Works" published by his son (1808). There is a memorial tablet to Anstey in Poets' Corner, Westminster Abbey.

40 "Letters," vol. iv. p 50.

41 Letter to Wharton, August 26, 1766, vol. ii. p 476 of Mitford's first edition.

42 "These letters," he says, "sparkle with characteristic touches of what the English call Humour, play upon words, little allusions impossible to translate. The verse, which varies in metre according to the subject, is nearly always agreeable and often picturesque. The vices and follies of a fashionable watering-place are depicted with so much subtlety and warmth that one cannot regard the book merely as a pleasantry. It has had the most favourable reception, and has gone through several editions already" (pp 43–4).

43 Not to mention the name Tabitha, which figures in Anstey's work and reappears in Smollett, Melford's letter of April 24 reproduces a scene exactly similar to that

described, by Simkin Blunderhead in letter v. of the "New Bath Guide" (the episode of the musicians); compare, too, despite certain differences, the consultations of the doctors. ("New Bath Guide," letter iv.; "Humphry Clinker," J. Melford, April 18; or the reflections on the cleanliness of the waters ("New Bath Guide," letter vi. in fine; "Humphry Clinker," Matthew Bramble, April 24). Other analogies may be put down to. similarity of subject, but it was surely to the poet that the novelist owed the idea of describing Bath and other watering-places in a series of letters from correspondents differing widely in humour and intelligence. "Humphry Clinker" was written five years after the "New Bath Guide."

44 When the second appeared, Dodsley, a London publisher, purchased the rights from Anstey for two hundred pounds; at the tenth he restored them to the author gratuitously, declaring that no work had ever brought him in so much money in the same length of time (Anstey, "Poetical Works," ed. 1808, introduction, p 25).

45 Byron shows that it was still generally read in 1819. Referring to the outcry raised against his "Don Juan," he exclaims: "Pretty cant for people who read 'Tom Jones,' 'Roderick Random,' the 'Bath Guide,' Ariosto and Dryden, and Pope—to say anything of Little's poems" (letter of October 28 to Hoppner, in Moore's "Life of Lord Byron," vol. ix. p 250). Anstey's work figures in "Don Juan" as one of the volumes of verse the Duchess of Fitz-Fulke was found reading (canto xxi. v. 50, 1. 2).

46 As witness his portrait sketched by his cousin Jenny (letter i. v. 72–103). But the reader may not discern in him all the traits that she enumerates.

47 Letter ii. I. 81.

48 Letter v.

49 Letter v. II. 17–22

50 *Ibid.* ii. and iv.

51 *Ibid.* 11. 34–42.

52 *Ibid.* vi. II. 47–51.

53 *Ibid.* iv. 11. 19–24

54 *Ibid.* vi. ll. 47–51

55 *Ibid.* II. 57–64.

56 Letter vi. 11. 65–8.

57 *Ibid.* 11. 76–82.

58 *Ibid.* viii. 11. 59–67.

59 *Ibid.* 11, 83–8.

60 A hill near Bath.

61 Letter viii. 11. 85–97.

62 Now my Lord had the honour of coming down Post,
To pay his Respects to so famous a Toast;
In Hopes He her Ladyship's Favour might win,
By playing the Part of a Host at an Inn.
(Letter xiii. ll. 29–32.)

63 'Tis true, on Parnassus I never did dream,
Nor e'er did I taste of sweet Helicon's Stream.
(Epilogue, v. 44).

64 See the letter quoted above, p 235, note I. In the following two verses, he parodies a passage in "Alexander's Feast":
The Prince was in Pain,
And could not contain
While Thais was sitting beside him,
But before his Peers,
Was for shaking the Spheres
Such Goods the kind Gods did provide Him.
Grew bolder and bolder
And cocked up his Shoulder,
Like the Son of great Jupiter Ammon,
Till at length quite opprest
He sank on her Breast
And lay there as dead as a Salmon.
(Letter xiii.)

65 Letters iii. and ix.

66 Your Rhime is so noble, so nimble your Measure,
One cannot but read' em with infinite Pleasure.
Some Verses resemble a Newmarket Horse,
Now trotting, now galloping over the Course,
And some glide o'er the Tongue as smooth and as nice,
As scates a Dutchman o'er the polished Ice.
("Poetical Epistles to the Author of the 'New Bath Guide,'" ii. p 9),

67 Or at least used very sparingly, for one seldom meets it but in songs, ballads, or pieces designed to be set to music (Dryden); Prior employed it in satirical and light poetry.

68 For instance, plicae and spicy (letter iv.), rake-hell and Tabernacle (letter iv.). Very often we find proper names or scientific terms put thus at the end of the line, while the unaccented syllable of the corresponding rhyme is supplied by a pronoun or non-variable word (stir up, Europe, letter iv.; hair on, Aaron, letter xiv.; Flaccus, attack us, Epilogue; whole on, colon, letter ii.; decorum, before 'em (letter xiii.) The termination ing is made to rhyme with the final sound n, the verb is with the finals es or ies (hearken, embarking, letter xiv.; ashes, Nash is, letter xi.; ponies, alone is, letter v., etc.).

69 All three written between 1770 and 1774.

70 Not contented to rival Tibullus and Gray,
Say, whence this most charming diversify'd lay?
How came you by such an extraordinary gift,
Thus to blend in one poet Yorick and Swift?
Dan Chaucer, bred up at old Granta before ye,
Ne'er told with such humour his Trumpington story;
His Simkin and Allen no more can compare
With the heroes of Bath than the clown at a fair.
("Water Poetry," p 2.)

71 What poet in Europe like you can excel

In writing on many subjects so well, etc.

("Poetical Epistles to the Author of the 'New Bath Guide,'" p 18.)

72 This collection is not dated, but I find it advertised at the end of "A General Account of Tunbridge Wells," a little volume of 1771.

73 By "An Invalid."

74 Particularly the poems by Warner, by T. (?) and by J. Wolcot.

75 By Anthony Pasquin (John Williams).

76 By Peter Paul Pallet (Richard Warner).

77 By T. (?)

78 By Sir Joseph Cheakill.

79 By Q. in the Corner.

80 By Peter Pindar (Jo Wolcot).

81 By Thomas Bayly.

82 "(He) bepommelled it through three pages of Bath Guide verses" (Miss Mitford, "Our Village," 4th series, p 79). "Our Village" began to be issued in volume form in 1824.

83 "A Ballad of Bath" (Poems and Ballads, Third Series). See in the Appendix the text of this fine poem.

IX

Authors at Bath: Prior Park; its literary guests (Pope, Warburton, Fielding), and other famous visitors

The various poets and prose writers whom we have now considered used Bath more or less as the background of their pictures. Their work, therefore, associates them for all time with the city which was their temporary abode and the object of their sympathy or aversion. But these are not the only figures memory conjures up before us, as we pace the broad streets and spacious squares, all peopled with historic shades. Among the others, we find traces there of a few who form a small and brilliant group apart, the men who shared with princes and states men the sumptuous and cordial hospitality of a liberal- minded Mectnas, an enlightened friend of art and letters, Ralph Allen, Sheriff and sometime Mayor of Bath.[1] His house (at first one in the town, still standing a stone's throw from the North Parade and afterwards, from 1743, the fine mansion of Prior Park, on Widcombe Hill, a precursor on a small scale, of Holland House) was not only open to, but eager to receive every kind of talent passing through Bath. Among those who were more or less regular guests at Prior Park we may mention Pope, Warburton, Richardson, Garrick and the elder Pitt.

Ralph Allen, the host round whom so many eminent men gladly gathered, was himself not without some remarkable characteristics. His career deserves a brief sketch as that of one of those men so numerous in England, who, though of mean origin, are born with a genius for enterprise and, affairs, and who, after attaining to wealth and consideration by hard work and bold initiative, use both fortune and a legitimately achieved influence for the good, the relief of private distress, and the benefit of the deserving.[2]

He was the son of a small innkeeper in Cornwall, and his grandmother kept the Post-office at St Columb in that county. Here he attracted the attention of an inspector,[3] through whose influence, when he was eighteen, he entered the post-office at Bath. Some three years later, in 1715, he was able, it seems, to render

Marshal Wade
From the picture by Hogarth

the Government a service of considerable importance. He discovered, by what means we know not,[4] that a consignment of arms was being sent from the West in the interests of a projected Jacobite rising which was to support that in Scotland and the North. He warned General Wade, at that time quartered in Bath. Wade, in return, made him postmaster as soon as the place was vacant,[5] and shortly after gave him his natural daughter in marriage.

The young man, now the head of his department, and provided, no doubt, with an increase of income by his marriage, or at any rate with credit and with influential friends, conceived the notion of transforming the entire postal system of England, no less to the advantage of the general public than to his own.

At that time, the first quarter of the eighteenth century, the postal service in England was in a deplorable state. The roads being few and bad, and the staff, the horses, and vehicles[6] of the poorest quality, the trans mission of letters was necessarily slow and irregular, and besides all this, the general organisation was extremely defective. But bad as was the service on the high roads that ran from London to all points of the kingdom, these were about the only ones that had any service whatever. Except on these obligatory routes, postal facilities could hardly be said to exist at all, and letters despatched from one county to another, or even between neighbouring places, only reached their destination by long and circuitous routes, sometimes having first passed through London. Hence, of course, delay, useless expense, difficulties of every description, and finally the reduction to a minimum of postal matter. These were the inconveniences which Allen proposed to remedy by establishing cross country lines of communication, and a service that would bring all parts of the kingdom into direct contact one with another. By this means, he argued, not only would the lessening of distances diminish the expense, but the sphere of activity of the post office would be greatly enlarged, and its revenues proportionately increased, since such a reform could not fail to multiply correspondence. He laid his project before the, Government, soliciting powers to carry it out and finance it himself. His request was granted; and in 1720, being then twenty-six, he obtained a seven years' concession to work the postal service of England and Wales.[7]

In return, he was to pay the Government a yearly rental of two thousand pounds[8] sterling and to defray all expenses of working.

The speculation was a hazardous one, necessitating, as it did, heavy expenditure at the outset, and demanding an intricate organisation, indefatigable supervision, and the suppression of frauds widely practised and difficult to detect.[9] For three years Allen worked the undertaking at a loss,[10] but after that, by dint of energy and intelligence, the new system began to bear fruit and to develop, and the profits, in consequence, to increase rapidly. On the expiry of the contract, it was renewed at a double royalty, and successively for three and four times the original sum.[11]

The returns from this concession, which he retained till his death, would alone have sufficed to make him one of the wealthiest men in the kingdom[12] but not content with this abundant source of income, he opened up another for himself by exploiting the almost inexhaustible stone quarries at Combe Down, near Bath. Here, too, his ingenious and enterprising spirit was displayed: he invented a machine by which huge blocks of stone were conveyed with ease from the top of Combe Down to the Avon, where they were shipped for Bristol,[13] and thence conveyed by water to all parts of England.[14] First largely used on the spot, to rebuild the greater part of a transformed and rapidly growing Bath,[15] the stone soon found an extensive and ready market at Bristol, London, and numerous other points of the kingdom.[16]

Both these enterprises, while making Allen a rich man, had also been extremely profitable to the public. The one opened up a field of natural riches till then neglected, but never afterwards allowed to lie waste; the other effected so enormous an improvement in a great national service that it ranks in the history of the English post with the reforms of Palmer[17] and of Rowland Hill. Allen, however—and this is greatly to his credit—did not consider that this two-fold advantage bestowed upon his fellow citizens released him from further obligations to them, or gave him the right to devote his great fortune to his own enjoyment. He contributed generously to all public expenses, giving now a thousand pounds for a hospital and the stone for building it,[18] now building a bridge

Ralph Allen
From the drawing by William Hoare, of Bath

at his own expense,[19] or again, in the "'45" equipping and maintaining a corps of a hundred volunteers.[20] Private distress had an equal claim on his benevolence, and he was wont to search out and relieve hard cases secretly.[21] He came spontaneously to the aid of poverty-stricken merit. Thus it is said that he sent Fielding £200 before knowing him,[22] and that, having read the first volume of Pope's letters, he immediately offered to publish the second at his own expense.[23] The soul of modesty, affable, simple in dress[24] and manner, intelligent, a good judge of character and merit, he inspired the most distinguished men of his time with sympathy and respect. "In Mr Allen," Pitt wrote at his death, "mankind has lost such a benevolent and tender friend as, I fear, not all the example of his virtues will have power to raise up to the world again."[25] Warburton, twenty years before, writing to Dr Doddridge, says, "I verily believe Mr Allen to be the greatest private character that ever appeared in any age of the world. You see his munificence to the Bath Hospital; but this is but a small part of his charities, and charity but a small part of his virtues. I have studied his character, even maliciously, to find where his weakness lies; but have studied it in vain. In a word, I firmly believe him to have been sent by Providence into the world, to teach men what blessings they must expect from Heaven, would they study to deserve them."[26] As for Fielding, after having lauded him in "Tom Jones" in the fullest, the most glowing, and at the same time the most obviously sincere of panegyrics, he regards the person he has just described, though not named, as to admirable and so rare, that he denies to the novelist, bound as he is to keep within the limits of the probable, careful as he must needs be to find credence with his readers, the right to portray such a character.[27] Deducting from these eulogies and a hundred others that we might quote,[28] the exaggeration natural to friendship or gratitude, Allen still remains a most interesting, original, and sympathetic figure. His public career reveals him as a man of bold initiative and determination, capable of conceiving and carrying through vast enterprises; the use he made his wealth and of his activity attests his goodness of heart and his benevolence, and finally, that his company should have been so agreeable and he himself so dear to the men of intellect and genius (to say nothing of princes and great persons) whom he delighted to gather round him, proves him to have been richly endowed with intellect, with taste, with judgment and with tact.[29] In the frivolous Bath of Beau Nash he represents the solid qualities and the virtues of private life. He is also the great civic figure; it is he who presides over the material development of the city of his adoption, encourages architecture in the person of Wood, whose talent he discovered,[30] and, seconding the architect's vast plans and those of his son, assists in the amazing transformation of Bath. Though he never tried to get into Parliament, he directed more or less ostensibly, not only the municipal but the political[31] affairs of the city, and directed them well, as witness the part he played in the election of Pitt to the House of Commons by his fellow citizens. The public man, therefore, was not unworthy of the private citizen, and equally deserves not to be forgotten by posterity. For us, however, what keeps Allen's memory green, and especially recommends him to our attention, is his connection with the poets and men of letters of his time, particularly with Pope and Fielding.

We have already seen Pope in Bath in 1714;[32] he returned in 1715;[33] in 1728 he remained there six weeks for his health,[34] his friends Gay and Arbuthnot[35] with him at least part of the time. He may possibly have been there in the interval.[36] In 1734 there was another prolonged sojourn, in company with Bolingbroke.[37] We do not know exactly when he made Allen's acquaintance, but there seems to have been no intimacy between them till about 1732,[38] when Allen was suddenly filled with regard and admiration for the poet, made him the most gratifying advances, proposed spontaneously to render him a great service, and became his close friend. What was the cause of this strong and sudden sympathy? Strangely enough, an action with which we may justly reproach Pope, namely, the underhand publication of his letters in 1735. At the cost of what scheming this publication took place, by what surreptitious and far from delicate means it was prepared and carried out, we all know now;[39] and though less well than we are, and lacking the documents at our disposal,[40] a number of his contemporaries divined in some degree the equivocal part played by the poet. No Suspicions seem to have occurred to Allen. After reading the first volume of the letters he conceived a great affection for Pope;[41] like the greater part of the nation, he found these letters full of "candour, tenderness and benevolence, purity of purpose and fidelity in friendship."[42] In his admiration for the genius of the poet a certain repugnance to the asperity and the violence of his satire had mingled hitherto[43] the amiable qualities revealed by this correspondence touched and conquered him completely, and made him desire the friendship of a great man, who so thoroughly approved himself as good as he was great.

That the friendship was as eager and sincere on the one side as the other Pope's correspondence abundantly proves. Eleven of the letters addressed by the poet to Allen have been preserved,[44] as well as a certain number of fragments; they show us in one of the two men, solicitude, generosity, and tact, in the other, gratitude and dignity,[45] in both a mutual affection. Though Bath itself had lost all its charms in the eyes of the poet, though the flowery meads of Twickenham and the smiling banks of the Thames had, disgusted him with the rocks, the mud, and the fogs of Somersetshire, Allen's mere presence counterbalanced all these discomforts[46] Henceforth he went to Bath almost every year,[47] his stay frequently extending over several months.[48] "Were it not for a hankering ('tis a good expressive English word) after some friends," he "could live with honest Mr Allen all his life."[49] At any rate, whether at Hampton Manor, Allen's villa at Bathampton, or later on at Prior Park[50] he was a familiar and constant guest, ever expected, ever welcome, whom his host sometimes went a hundred miles to fetch.[51]

This correspondence, published by Curll to Pope's noisy indignation, but really as the result of his private machinations, furnished Allen at once with an opportunity of serving the poet. On the appearance of the second volume,[52] Pope had declared himself compelled to bring out an edition of his own, so that the letters might at least be correct and authentic, and this proposed edition he advertised.[53] He feigned, however, an extreme reluctance to keep his word, and, in opening the subscription, expressed the hope that it would fail, and that he would be relieved of the obligation of publishing.[54] He proved a better prophet than he had any desire to be, and there seemed every prospect that his forecast would be fulfilled,[55] a result he was really far from desiring, when Allen came forward most opportunely with his offer to defray all the expenses of the edition. Pope thanked him warmly, but made some difficulties at first, depreciating the value of his letters. There could be no great gain either to the public or his reputation in giving them to the world.[56]

In the end he allowed himself to be overruled He would willingly, he said, strike out certain idle passages which never, or at least no longer, expressed his real sentiments;[57] he also wished to gratify Allen without, however, imposing so great a burden on him alone.[58]

"That you may be convinced," he protests, "what weight your opinion and your desires have with me, I will do what I have not yet done: I will tell my friends I am as willing to publish this book as to let it alone. And, rather than suffer you to be taxed at your own rate, will publish in the news next winter the proposals for the subscription."[59] Finally, he accepts Allen's assistance, should need arise, to some moderate extent.[60] Five months later, when three-quarters of the book was printed, Pope once more beat up the laggard subscribers, in a last endeavour, he said, to save Allen's purse, declaring at the same time that nothing could lessen his obligation to him.[61] It is therefore reasonable to conclude that this "moderate" assistance represented in the end a considerable sum,[62] thanks to which the second volume of the "Letters" appeared in 1737.[63]

But it would be unfair to treat Pope's attachment to Allen merely as the outcome of self-interest. His letters—most dignified in tone, and very sober both in compliment and protestation[64] throughout both affection and a profound and unfeigned esteem. This esteem he was even anxious to make evident in his works, and he begged Allen's permission to mention his name incidentally in one of his poems.[65] He accordingly introduced it into his "One Thousand Seven Hundred and Thirty-Eight,"[66] using it as a symbol of unostentatious worth, and enlarging somewhat clumsily—at least in the first edition his friend's shining virtues as compared with his obscure birth.

Let low-born Allen, with an awkward shame,
Do good by stealth and blush to find it fame.[67]

The qualification is scarcely happy[68] any more than the company, very worthy, but not precisely exalted, among whom he places his hero.[69] Did Allen show a touch of resentment, or did the poet himself perceive his breach of good taste?[70] Be this as it may, in the second edition the unlucky epithet is watered down, and "*low-born* Allen" becomes "*humble* Allen," the alteration being explained to the person Concerned in a flattering letter.[71] So great was the intimacy between Pope and Allen that we find the hospitality of Prior Park unhesitatingly extended to the friends of the poet, who, for instance, invites Warburton[72] and Arbuthnot;[73] for, as he says himself, "Nothing in all my life has been so great a pleasure to my nature as to bring deserving and knowing men together. It is the greatest favour that can be done, either to great geniuses or useful men."[74] As regards Warburton, the service was even greater than Pope could have thought, for the relations thus established with Allen laid the foundation of both his ecclesiastical and worldly fortune.

Although known to the public by his first writings,[75] and the friend of Pope since he had defended his "Essay on Man" against the criticisms of Crousaz,

Warburton was merely incumbent of a small benefice in Nottinghamshire[76] and of another[77] in Lincolnshire. In November 1741 Pope presses him to join the party at Allen's, and the letter shows once again how pleasant he found the life at Prior Park, and how highly he valued his host.

"I am here," he says, "in more leisure than I can possibly ever enjoy in my own house, *vacare literis*. It is at this place that your exhortations may be most effectual to make me resume the studies I have almost laid aside, by perpetual avocations and dissipations. If it were practicable for you to pass a month or six weeks from home, it is here I could wish to be with you: and if you would attend to the continuation of your own noble work,[78] or unbend to the idle amusement of commenting[79] upon a poet who has no other merit than that of aiming by his moral strokes to merit some regard from such men as advance truth and virtue in a more effectual way; in either case, this place[80] and this house would be an inviolable asylum to you, from all you would desire to avoid in so public a place as Bath. The worthy man who is the master of it, invites you in the strongest terms; and is one who would treat you with love and veneration rather than what the world calls civility and regard. He is sincere and plainer than almost any man in this world, *antiquis moribus*[81] If the Waters of Bath may be service able to your complaints (as I believe from what you have told me of them), no opportunity can ever be better. We are told the Bishop of Salisbury[82] is expected here daily, who I know is your friend, at least, though a bishop, is too much a man of learning to be your enemy. You see I omit nothing to add to the weight in the balance, in which, however, I will not think myself light, since I have known your partiality. You will want no servant here. Your room will be next to mine, and one man will serve us. Here is a library and a gallery ninety feet long to walk in, and a coach whenever you would take the air with me … Is all this a dream? or can you make it a reality? can you give ear to me? 'Audistin'? an me *ludit amabilis insania*?'"[83]

Warburton gave ear to him; he joined his famous friend as requested, and their reunion was not without importance to the literary world, since they now definitely mapped out Book iv. of the "Dunciad."[84] Warburton himself was greatly attracted to his new acquaintances, and pleased them equally in return; for he was, or could be, just as urbane and agreeable in private as in his writings he was arrogant, passionate and vituperative.[85] He repeated the visit the following year.[86] In 1745 Allen gave him his niece in marriage, and Prior Park became his home. Later, in 1757, Allen's influence with Pitt procured him the deanery of Bristol, and in 1759[87] the bishopric of Gloucester. Finally, Allen, at his death, bequeathed to him and his wife the bulk of his fortune, with the estate of Prior Park, which Warburton occupied till 1769.[88]

Long before these events, even before Warburton's marriage, Pope had passed away (May, 1744), and some few months before his death, the close friendship which bound the poet to Allen had been suddenly and violently ruptured, to be but imperfectly patched up again. A quarrel, the precise cause and details of which are not quite clear, had broken out at Prior Park between Mrs Allen[89] and him[90] during a visit on which he was accompanied by his friend and constant

William Warburton
From the portrait by Charles Philips

companion, Martha Blount. This lady was, according to various accounts at any rate, the original cause of the quarrel, either, as Johnson[91] asserts, and also Ruffhead, who, as we know, was inspired by Warburton,[92] because she acted towards her hosts with "indecent arrogance," or because, as she told Spence, she herself had reason to complain of their insulting coldness.[93] It is difficult and indeed, immaterial to know the truth of the matter. Be it as it may, there was a violent scene, and the poet left the house incontinently, counting on being followed immediately by his friend.[94] She, delayed by some practical obstacle, complains in a letter over flowing with resentment, of fresh affronts,[95] to which Pope responds by the injunction "not to stay a moment at the only place in England (I am satisfied) where you can be so used; and where for your sake and for my own too, I never will set foot more. However well I might wish the man," he goes on, "the woman is a minx, and an impertinent one, and he will do what she will have him."[96] Warburton who, passively at any rate, had sided with the Allens, is now "a sneaking parson."[97] Allen, as has been seen, was not directly implicated, which left a loophole for reconciliation; this took place shortly. From the beginning of 1744,[98] the correspondence between them resumes its friendly tone. In March, Allen went to see Pope in order to extinguish the last smouldering differences by a frank explanation on both sides;[99] he vindicated himself and his wife against the reproach of wishing in any way to offend Pope or Martha Blount either, and put down everything to a misunderstanding between the two women.[100] Pope evidently received both visit and explanation with a certain affectation of haughty reserve, but the two old friends must have parted on. good terms, for Allen invited himself to return in a fortnight.[101] A few weeks later the poet died, leaving a will[102] in which some echo of the quarrel still lingered. "In case," runs the document, "Ralph Allen, above said, shall survive me, I order my executors to pay him the sum of one hundred and fifty pounds, being, to the best of my calculations, the account of what I have received from him, partly for my own, partly for charitable uses. If he refuses to take it himself, I desire him to employ it in a way I am persuaded he will not dislike, to the benefit of the Bath Hospital."[103] This posthumous restitution was very severely criticised by the public.[104] "Mr Pope," Allen observed simply, "was always a bad accomptant, and if, to £150 he had put a cipher more, he had come nearer to the truth!"[105] and he handed over the legacy to the Bath Hospital.

If Pope acquitted himself somewhat shabbily of the duties of gratitude towards his friend and benefactor, another great writer, very similarly situated, discharged them to the utmost. This was the novelist Fielding, several of whose works hand down to posterity the name and fame of Allen. His sister, Sarah Fielding, authoress of the "Adventures of David Simple," lived at Widcombe, near Bath [106] she was without private means, and it seems that Allen allowed her a pension of a hundred a year; she dined frequently at his table.[107] She may possibly have been the means of bringing together Allen and Fielding, the origin as well as the details of whose relations have remained somewhat obscure. In "Joseph Andrews" (1742) Allen is thus alluded to by the hero of the book: "Some gentlemen of our cloth report charitable actions done by their lords and masters; and I have heard Squire Pope, the great poet, at my lady's table, tell stories of a man that lived at a place called Ross,[108] and another at the Bath, one Al— Al— I forget his name, but it is in the book of verses."[109] If we may believe Derrick, no personal acquaintance existed between the two men when, at a date which he does not give, but at any rate before the publication of "Tom Jones," Allen, entirely on his own initiative, sent Fielding a present of two hundred pounds.[110] If this be true, all honour is due to Allen for having sought out, assisted, and afterwards treated with due consideration, an author who, unlike Pope, did not yet command the attention of the public either by his personal qualities or his genius;[111] a representative, it must be added, of a class of writing then looked down upon as inferior, scarcely even reckoned as literature.[112] Be this as it may, while "Tom Jones " was being written, Fielding, who had been living for some time[113] at Twerton, quite close to Bath,[114] was a daily guest at Allen's table at Prior Park,[115] and conceived that warm admiration for him, which he manifested openly throughout the course of his great novel, and later in the dedication of "Amelia."

"Tom Jones," indeed, is full of reminiscences of Allen. If it cannot be actually said, as many would have it,[116] that Prior Park served the novelist as the model for his description of Allworthy's estate,[117] Fielding certainly desired to unite in that personage, a paragon of all the virtues, the combined characteristics of Allen and Lyttelton. This he frankly proclaims in the opening lines: "If there be in this work," he says, "as some have been pleased to say, a stronger picture of a truly benevolent mind than is to be found in any other, who that knows you, and a particular acquaintance[118] of yours will doubt whence that benevolence hath been copied? The world will not, I believe, make me the compliment of thinking I took it from myself. I care not this they shall own, that the two persons from whom I have taken it, that is to say, two of the best and worthiest men in the world, are strongly and zealously my friends."[119]

Of these two persons the one most clearly represented, the most highly praised under the transparent veil of fiction, the one whose most characteristic traits[120] are reproduced in Allworthy, is undoubtedly Allen. He makes Allworthy a landed proprietor like Allen, living in the same county,[121] in a similar residence, surrounded by the same degree of luxury, the same evidences of wealth. He endows him with exactly those virtues and talents so admired in Allen benevolence, piety, justice, generosity, a solid understanding, and a keen intelligence, which more than supplied the deficiencies of a neglected education.[122] He extols his hospitality, and particularly the kind of protection he extended to men of genius and learning; favours in which there was no trace of domineering, no insulting condescension, which neither demanded nor desired any return, but respected the independence and proper pride of the recipient.[123]

Not content with this pointed description, he proceeds (in one of those charming prologues in which the novelist leaves his characters for a moment to converse with the reader), to drop the veil of fiction altogether, and introduce Allen in person, to hold him up as a character too noble to be credible, yet, nevertheless, true. "Should I tell my reader," he says, "that I had known a man whose penetrating genius had enabled him to raise a large fortune where no beginning was chalked out to him; that he had done this with the most perfect preservation of his integrity, and not only without the least injustice or injury to any one individual person, but with the highest advantage to trade, and a vast increase of the public revenue; and that he had expended one part of the income of this fortune in discovering a taste superior to most, by works where the highest dignity was united with the purest simplicity, and another part in displaying a

Henry Fielding
From Basire's engraving of the portrait by William Hogarth

degree of goodness superior to all men, by acts of charity to objects whose only recommendation were their merits or their wants; that he was most industrious in searching after merit in distress, most eager to relieve it, and then as careful (perhaps too careful) to conceal what he had done; that his house, his furniture, his gardens, his table, his private hospitality, and his public beneficence, all denoted the mind from which they flowed, and were all intrinsically rich and noble, without tinsel or external ostentation; that he filled every relation in life with the most adequate virtue; that he was most piously religious to his Creator, most zealously loyal to his sovereign; a most tender husband to his wife, a kind relation, a munificent patron, a warm and firm friend, a knowing and cheerful companion, indulgent to his servants, hospitable to his neighbours, charitable to the poor, and benevolent to all mankind. Should I add to these the epithets of wise, brave, elegant, and, indeed, every amiable epithet in our language, I might surely say:

> Quis credet? nemo Hercule! nemo
> Vel duo, vel nemo.

And yet I know a man who is all I have here described."[124]

Can a more complete panegyric be imagined? The eulogy is altogether magnificent and unreserved. Let us make some allowances, of course, for possible exaggeration, for a certain amount of embellishment, but let us deduct no more from it: Fielding's natural pride, his nobility of mind, forbid us to see in the foregoing passage merely the dithyrambic and self-interested flattery of the author. Rather we may believe that his heart, warm as those of his various glows with genuine enthusiasm, no less than with affectionate' gratitude, for the generous being it, is his good fortune to have encountered, for a character adorned with just those virtues he holds most dear: benevolence, kindness, charity. And these sentiments must find expression; he repeats them once more in the terse and manly dedication of his last novel, "Amelia." "The best man," he says, addressing himself to Allen, "is the properest patron of such an attempt. This, I believe, will be readily granted, nor will the public voice, I think, be more divided to whom they shall give that appellation. Should a letter, indeed, be thus inscribed, *Detur Optimo*, there are few persons who would think it wanted any other direction."[125] But he is determined not to make use of "the fulsome style of common dedicators," and since it is impossible to trace a true and faithful portrait of Allen "without incurring the suspicion of flattery in the bosoms of the malignant," he postpones this task till the day—should he be so unfortunate as to see it—of Allen's death. He did not live to see it, for he died[126] ten years before Allen, who contributed largely towards the education of his orphan children,[127] and left to each of them, as well as to their aunt, Sarah Fielding, the sum of one hundred pounds.[128] Thus did Allworthy pay his debt to his portrait-painter.

The author of the "Dunciad" and the author of "Tom Jones"—these are the two guests whose presence sheds an undying lustre on the splendid domain of Prior Park, whose memory lingers round all its stately rooms, its avenues, its terraced gardens; the two whom the imagination best loves to picture there in all their diversity of mind and person.[129] Standing in the long gallery, once the library. If the house, one can call up the frail, slightly deformed figure of Pope, his delicate and expressive face; he appears in his morning undress—a dark grey waistcoat and blue dressing gown[130] discusses the plan of the last Book of the Dunciad with Warburton. Or again, the centre of a chosen group, he retails some anecdote; less brilliant, however, in conversation than in his writings,[131] he falls readily into silence or abstraction, seldom going "beyond a particular easy smile,"[132] laughing very rarely, and "never … very heartily."[133]

Very different is Fielding—tall, broad-shouldered, robust, overflowing with life and spirits; chatting heartily and noisily with every one he comes across, his frank and wholesome fun keeping the rest of the company in good humour. Between these two, the serene figure of Allen, amiable, yet gravely dignified, or Warburton[134] with his massive head and the naturally imperious manner that softened for his intimates. Tripping gaily up to them comes the excellent Graves,[135] an agreeable writer, a still more agreeable talker, the familiar friend of Allen and Warburton. Turning from this group, we catch sight of Richardson,[136] then of Hurd, the friend and disciple of Warburton, a writer inferior to his master, but already well-known as a critic and theologian;[137] further, of Thomas Edwards, the future author of "Canons of Criticism,"[138] of whom we learn that he gave Warburton a lesson in Greek at Prior Park one day, and so started the long series of literary duels in which he measured swords with his great opponent.[139]

Here, too, is the great actor, Garrick,[140] and his ancient rival, Quin;[141] here the architects Wood,[142] father and son; there Hoare, the portrait painter;[143] finally, among a group of politicians of various persuasions,[144] the greatest statesman of his time, William Pitt, afterwards Earl of Chatham, whose relations with Allen call for special mention.

Allen, indeed, was privileged to call him friend,[145] and was able, moreover, to be of service to him in his career. Disposing, as he did, of considerable local influence and devoid of political ambition for himself, he placed all this influence at the command of the "Great Commoner." It was thanks in a great measure to him that Bath had the honour of returning Pitt to Parliament during the years (1757–1766) which preceded his elevation to the Peerage.[146] At the express invitation of the Corporation, entirely subservient to Allen, Pitt resigned his seat for Okehampton in order to stand for Bath, where a vacancy[147] had occurred; he was elected unanimous and at the General Election in 1761 re-elected under the same circumstances The letters he addressed on both occasions to Allen leave no doubt that he attributed the chief share in the election to him; and in addition to the sentiments of gratitude which he expressed to Allen personally, he sent him his open letters of thanks to the Mayor and Corporation, begging him to transmit them after having read them.[148]

When, in 1763, he suddenly finds himself gravely at variance with his constituents (Allen included) on the question of the Peace of Paris, a measure vigorously resisted by him, but lauded by them in a special con gratulatory address to the King,[149] it is once more Allen, to whom he explains the reasons which prevent him from presenting the address to George III, and whom he charges, in his turn, to lay them before the other members of the electoral committee.[150]

The correspondence between Pitt and Allen on this occasion does honour to both men. Differing on an important question, each maintains his own right of judgment with dignity, recognising the rectitude of the other, and showing no trace of personal resentment. Their friendship remained unbroken, and at his death a year later Allen confirmed his bequest of £1000 to Pitt, describing it in his will as a last token of his esteem and gratitude to the best of friends and the most upright and capable of Ministers. Pitt, on his side, wrote as follows to Allen's widow: "I will only say that, in Mr Allen, mankind has lost such a benevolent and tender friend as, I fear, not all the example of his virtues will have power to raise up to the world again. Admiring his life and regretting the shortness of it, I shall ever respectfully cherish his memory, and rank the continuation of the favourable opinion and friendship of a truly good man amongst the happiest advantages and the first honours which fortune may have bestowed upon my life."[151] At Bath he remained an unique personality, memorable not only for his virtues, but for the benefactions his philanthropy and public spirit led him to dispense. He was also the one Mecaenas of the city, and his patronage, unlike that of many of the genus, left no sting of humiliation, but inspired its recipients with gratitude and affection. Thanks to him, the most sumptuous home of the city became the hostel of art and letters, sheltering, among literary guests of varying merit, the greatest poet and the greatest novelist of eighteenth-century England.

1 He was actually so only once, in 1742; but his influence in the Town Council was always considerable, not to say predominant.

2 Allen's biography may be found in a number of works, most of which merely repeat one another, without Supplying any fresh information (the article on Allen in the "Dictionary of National Biography" mentions thirty). My account is taken chiefly from Graves, "Trifling Anecdotes of the late Ralph Allen" in "The Triflers" (Graves was for years his intimate friend), from Polwhele, "Biographical Sketches in Cornwall " (where the writer collected local traditions), and from Warner, "History of Bath." Some pages of Thicknesse in his "New Prose Bath Guide" bear the impress of his warped and habitually disparaging mind. To a conscientious and interesting study by Kilvert entitled "Ralph Allen and Prior Park" (in his "Remains in Prose and Verse") we owe several other sources of information which will be mentioned in due course. He also printed in his work (pp 175–7) a short manuscript notice full of very precise information, which apparently formed part of the journal of a certain Jones, Allen's head clerk. See also Peach, "Life and Times of Ralph Allen."

3 Thicknesse gives a slightly different version ("New Prose Bath Guide," pp 76, 77), but Graves and Polwhele were in a position to be better informed.

4 Possibly by watching the correspondence and opening the letters of suspected persons; but this supposition, though often advanced, is a pure surmise. Even if it were better founded we must not forget that, odious as is the practice in question, it was far from exciting the same reprobation in those days as at present; and, secondly, that the Government may have imposed this unpleasant duty on it agents (*cf* on this subject Lecky, "History of England," vol. ii. ch. iv. p 70, and vol. iv. ch. xi. p 148).

5 This, at any rate, is Graves' version ("The Triflers," p 63). Certain details may not be quite correct, but there seems no adequate reason for rejecting the story altogether, as Peach does in his "Life and Times of Ralph Allen" (pp 55, 56).

6 The first mail-coach was introduced in 1784. On the state of the English postal service at the period see Joyce, "History of the Post-Office," ch. x.

7 The concession embraced all letters which had, to travel over roads running transversely to the great main routes (*cross-road* or *cross-post* letters), and those exchanged between two intermediate towns on the Bath road (*bye-way* letters, also called *bye-letters* and *way-letters*). This interpretation of the term *bye-way letters* is taken from Joyce's "History of the Post-Office," chap. x. p 147; the "New English Dictionary" does not give it, and seems to make no distinction between *cross-road* and *bye-way* letters, save that they travelled on different kinds of roads.

8 This is the sum named in the manuscript already referred to p 227, end of *note* 2. We learn from the same source that Allen's father-in- law, General Wade, stood security for him. The sums, £4000 for the second term of seven years, £6000 for the third and £8000 for the rest, are also mentioned in the same place. Joyce (*op. cit.* p 147) raises the amount to £6000 from the beginning, and adds that this sum was already half as much again as the Exchequer had hitherto derived from this branch of the postal service. Kilvert ("Remains," p 145) gives the sum of £6000 for the first term of twenty-one years, and £20,000 for the rest, adding, however, that the original contracts no longer exist, in default of which, the manuscript—considering the probable source of the information it contains—would seem the more reliable authority.

9 For these frauds, and other difficulties which Allen had to surmount, see Joyce, *op. cit.* pp 145, 155, 157, 161–5.

10 *Ibid.* p. 149.

11 Jones' manuscript (*cf* above 227, *note*)

12 £10,000 clear profit per annum, according to a calculation found among Allen's papers at his death (Murch, "Biographical Sketches of Bath Celebrities," p 63). The manuscript already quoted gives a higher sum: "Jones saw a stated account, twenty-six years before Allen's death, which showed a clear gain of £16,000 a year" (Kilvert's "Remains," p 176). The revenues probably fluctuated, but were, in any case, evidently very high.

13 Defoe describes it in his "Tour thro' … the Whole Island of Great Britain" (ed. 1769, vol. ii. p 300), and Mrs Chandler, in her "Description of Bath," lauds:
… "the new-made road and wonderful machine,
Self-moving downward from the mountain height,
A Rock, its burden of a mountain's weight."—(p 16.)

14 "Tour Thro' … Great Britain," *ibid.*

15 See in the manuscript (Kilvert's "Remains," p 176) the list of the first buildings in Bath for which it was used. Allen himself, according to his architect, Wood, was mainly induced to build his sumptuous house at Prior Park by his desire to exhibit the excellence, of the material, which had been questioned (Wood, "Description of Bath," 4th part, ch. xi. p 227). It is of course due to the proximity and the exploitation of these quarries that Bath, unlike the majority of English towns, is built of stone instead of brick.

16 Thus the Bristol Exchange and St. Bartholomew Hospital in London were built of Bath stone ("Tour," etc., ed. 1769, vol. ii. p 300). Its employment there and elsewhere, the extent a the costliness of the workings (see the manuscript in Kilvert, before

alluded to) sufficiently refute the insinuation of certain contemporaries, who looked upon the Combe Down quarries as a cloak to hide from the public the true source of Allen's enormous fortune, namely, his profits as lessee of the postal service. This allegation is found in Thicknesse ("New Prose Guide," p 77), and Graves quotes it to refute it ("The Triflers," p 64).

17 Palmer, in 1784, introduced the mail-coach to replace the slow vehicles in use till then. The first ran between London, Bath, and Bristol. Palmer, who was born at Bath and lived there, was director of the Bath Theatre, as also of that of Bristol. It is certainly noteworthy that the two great reforms of the English postal service in the eighteenth century should have had their origin and their first application at Bath. This is not purely fortuitous, however, for nowhere would the need for rapid and reliable means of communication be more keenly felt than in a place flooded regularly by streams of visitors from every county in England.

18 The Bath Hospital. On this liberality and more of a like nature see Peach, "Life and Times of Ralph Allen," pp 118–20.

19 At Newton St Loe (*cf* the manuscript in Kilver "Remains," p 177).

20 Kilvert, "Remains," p 177.

21 … He had expended … another part [of his fortune] in displaying a degree of goodness superior to all men, by acts of charity to objects whose only recommendations were their merits or their wants; he was most industrious in searching after merit in distress, most eager to relieve it, and then as careful (perhaps too careful) to conceal what he had done …" (Fielding, "Tom Jones," viii. i, extract from a long passage in which the author, without naming him, clearly refers to Allen.)

22 See below, p 222.

23 See below, p 218 and following.

24 Thicknesse derides as an affectation "his plain Quaker-coloured suit of clothes, and shirt sleeves with only a chitterling up the slit" ("New Prose Bath Guide," p 77). *Cf* Derrick, "Letters," May 20, 1763.

25 Pitt, "Correspondence," vol. ii. pp 289–90, letter to Mrs Allen, June 4, 1764.

26 Warburton to Doddridge, February 1743, quoted in Pitt, "Correspondence," vol. ii. p 290, *note*).

27 See book viii. chap. i, the long passage beginning, "But now, on the other hand, should I tell my reader that I had known a man," etc. Quoted in full further on.

28 See, for instance, those collected by Kilvert ("Remains," Ralph Allen and Prior Park, *passim*). In the preparation of this work I have come across numbers of others, all concurring. The censorious Thicknesse alone accuses him of pride ill-concealed by an affected humility: "That he affected a simplicity of Manners and Dress, we can testify; but we can by no means allow that he was not a Man deeply charged with Pride, and without Address enough to conceal it" ("New Prose Guide," p 77).

29 For further details see the portrait drawn of him by Kilvert.

30 See below, chap. x.

31 His preponderance was in 1763 made the subject of a skit entitled "The Knights of Baythe, or the One Headed Corporation," which had, and still retains, a certain local fame, and may be found in Peach, "Life and Times of Ralph Allen," p 181.

32 See above, chap. vii. p 155.

33 Letter to Caryll, October 11, 1715 ("Works," Elwin and Courthope, vol. vi. p 233). Pope made part of the journey on horseback, accompanied by Arbuthnot, Jervas, and other friends (letter to Jervas, August 12, 1715, *ibid.* vol. viii. p 18).

34 Letter to Martha Blount, September 4, dated from Bath (*ibid.* vol. ix. p 310); the year suggested is only conjectural, but very probable; letter to Lord Oxford, September 14, 1728 (*ibid.* vol. viii. p 243); letter to Swift, November 12 (probably a copyist's error for October 12, see *note* in the Elwin and Courthope ed.), 1728: "I have passed six weeks in quest of health and found it not, etc." (*ibid.* vol. vii. p 138).

35 *Ibid.* vol. ix. p 312, letter to Martha Blount.

36 Mr Courthope, one of his latest biographers, after speaking of the journey in 1714, adds: "His health was restored by the waters and the change of scene, which proved altogether so agreeable to hint that for the rest of his life he rarely failed to pay a yearly visit to Bath" (*ibid.* vol. v. p 119). As regards the period 1715–1728, it is not clear on what this assertion is founded.

37 "Our friend [Pope] … who is setting out in three days with me for the Bath, where he will stay till towards the middle of October, etc." (Bolingbroke to Swift, October 16, 1734, *ibid.* vol. vii. p 325). *Cf* also a letter of Swift's to Pope, November 1, 1734 (*ibid.* p 327). A letter addressed to Fortescue in which Pope says he has arrived from Bath (*ibid.* vol. ix. p 113) is difficult to date precisely (1729 perhaps, as Pope mentions the illness of his mother).

38 *Cf* below, p 233, *note* 62.

39 See the careful examination and account of tile whole matter (painted perhaps rather blacker than is strictly necessary) by Elwin (Pope, "Works," vol. i., introduction, pp xxvi.-cxliii.). Sir Leslie Stephen comes to the same conclusion (Pope, chap. vii.).

40 Mr Duke was, as we know, the first to study the question closely and to elucidate many important points (*Athenaeum,* July 8, 1854, September 1, 8, and 15, 1860). *Cf* "Papers of a Critic," vol. 1., by the same writer (1875).

41 "As to any advantage they [the letters] may do to my own character, I ought to be content with what they have done already, I assure you; I do not think it the least of those advantages that they have occasioned me the good will (in so great a degree) of so worthy a man" (Pope to Allen, June 5, 1736; Elwin and Courthope, vol. ix. p 188). "Mr Allen's friendship with Mr Pope was contracted on the reading of his volume of letters, which gave the former the highest opinion of the other's general benevolence and goodness of heart" (note by Warburton on the above passage).

42 Johnson, "Lives of the Poets," Pope, p 400, Chandos ed.

43 "Though he had long been acquainted with our poet and *admired* him for the excellence of his genius, yet the asperity of his satirical pieces was so repugnant to the softness and suavity of that worthy man's disposition, that it in some degree estranged him from his intimacy. But no sooner had he read our author's letters, than he *loved* him for the goodness and virtues of his heart; and ever after entertained the most candid affection for him" (Ruffhead, "Life of Pope," p 406, note). Ruffhead no doubt learned these particulars from Warburton.

44 Nine were published by Warburton in 1751; the other two, with some fragments, appeared first in Ruffhead's "Life of Pope," and he most probably got them from Warburton. Our faith in the sentiments expressed in this correspondence may be increased by the following passage: "These letters will 'never come into our collection, therefore let us commend ourselves honestly, when we do or suffer anything in a' good cause" (Ruffhead, "Life of Pope," pp 469–70). It is true that the sincerity of Pope's declarations is sometimes open to doubt. None of Allen's letters to Pope have been preserved.

45 This quality is invariably shown by Pope in his dealings with the great, and with influential people in general. See on this point, Beljame, "Le Public et les Hommes de Lettres," chap. iv., sections iv. and v.

46 "But for [your] news of my quitting Twitnam for Bath, inquire into my years if they are past the bound of dotage? Ask my eyes if they can see, and my nostrils if they can smell? To prefer rocks and dirt to flowery meads and lovely Thames, and brimstone and fogs to roses and sunshine. When I arrive at these sensations I may settle at Bath, of which I never dreamt, further than to live just out of the sulphurous pit, and at the edge of the fogs at Mr Allen's for a month or so. I like the place so little, that health itself could not draw me thither, though friendship has twice or thrice" (letter to Richardson, November 21 "Works," Elwin and Courthope, vol. ix. p 508).

47 Pope's letters show him to have been in Bath in 1736 (*ibid.* vol. ix. p 171); 1737 (June 8, vol. ix. p 192; September 3, *ibid.* p 140); 1739 (November 22, vol. ix. p 483; December a, vol. x. p. 223; December 17, *ibid.* p 94); 173 208); '74° (about October 27, vol. ix. p 212; December, 29, vol. viii. p 471); 1741 (October 13, vol. v. p. 412; November 12, vol. ix. p 219; November 22, *ibid.* p 221; date uncertain, *ibid.* p 483); 1742 (April 23, vol. ix. p 224; November 27, *ibid.*); 1743 (July 11, vol. x. p 216; July 8, vol. ix. p 233; July 23, vol. vii. p 49; August 6, vol. v. p 418). It must be said, however, that the year in which some of these letters were written is not certain, also that the fact of his staying with Allen is expressly mentioned in only a few; once (June 8, 1737) he regrets having to be in Bath instead of joining Allen at Widcombe. Though not under the same roof, they certainly had interviews; on August 21, 1743, Pope begs the Duchess of Marlborough to let Allen know that having spent only half a day in Bath he was unable to go and see him (vol. x. p 245).

48 "I have been full three months about Bath and Bristol, endeavouring to amend a complaint which more or less has troubled me all my life … (letter to Warburton, January 17, 1739–1740, vol. ix. p 208). "I am going to Bath for near two months" (to the same, October 27, 1740, vol. ix. p 212).

49 Letter to Lyttelton, December 12 [1736], vol. ix. p 172.

50 The house was begun about 1736, but not finished till 1743.

51 "Both your Grace and Mr Allen have done for me more than I am worth; he has come a hundred miles to fetch me, and I think in gratitude I should stay with him for ever, had I not an equal obligation to come back to your Grace" (Pope to the Duchess of Marlborough (1742), vol. v. p 416). Graves, Allen's intimate friend, writes: "Mr Pope was almost a constant inmate in the family during the Bath season for many years" ("The Triflers," pp 66–7).

52 July, 1735. This was the volume which contained—or professed to contain, for it only gave three—the letters of Atterbury to Pope.

53 A note by Warburton, quoted in the Elwin and Courthope edition (vol. ix. p 188, *note*), says that Allen offered to have the letters printed at his expense.

54 "I hope the subscription will fail, so far at least as to excuse me from the thing I never liked, and have been over to do" (letter to Fortescue, April 1736, vol. ix. p 136). *Cf* another letter to the same of March z6, 1736, *ibid.* p 135, as also one to Allen, April 30, 1736: "I have heard little yet of the subscription ... After my return I will inquire what has been done; and I really believe what I told you will prove true, and I shall be honourably acquitted of a task I am not fond of" (*ibid.* p188).

55 "As I find, what I imagined, the slowness of subscribers," etc. (Pope to Allen, November 6, 1736, *ibid.* p 191). The subscription had been open seven months.

56 "But in a word I think your notion of the value of those things is greatly too high, as to any service they can do to the public; and as to any advantage they may do to my own character, I ought to be content with what they have done already. I assure you, I do not think it the least of those advantages that they have occasioned me the good will (in so great a degree) of so worthy a man" (Pope to Allen, June 5, 1736, *ibid.* p 188). A fragment of a letter to Allen preserved by Ruffhead ("Life of Pope," p 345, *note*) no doubt refers to the same part of the correspondence: "I am sure, if you thought that they would be of any service to virtue, or answer any one good purpose, whether (considered as writings they brought me any credit or not, they should be given to the world: and let them make me a worse writer, provided they could but make one better man."

57 "I do grant it would be some pleasure to me to expunge several idle passages, which will otherwise, if not go down to the next age, pass, at least in this, for mine; although many of them were not, and God knows, none of them are my present sentiments, but, on the contrary, wholly disapproved by me" (*ibid.* p 189). Had Allen perhaps suggested some of these curtailments? The passage immediately preceding this one would lead one to conclude so. Pope sets forth therein the reasons that prompt him to give to the public "all that even discretion would leave out," but declares (in 1737?) "I ... determine to leave out every syllable, to the best of my judgment, that can give the least ill-example to an age too apt to take it, or the least offence to any good or serious man" (fragment quoted by Ruffhead, "Life of Pope," p 465).

58 "And I do not flatter you when I say, that, pleasure would be in creased to *me* in knowing I should do what to please you. But I cannot persuade myself to let the whole burden, even though it were at public good, lie upon you, much less to serve my private fame entirely at another's expense" (*ibid.*).

59 *Ibid.* pp 189–90.

60 *Ibid.* p 189.

61 "As I find, what I imagined, the slowness of subscribers, I will do all I can to disappoint you in this particular, and intend to publish in January, when the town fills, an advertisement, that the book will be delivered by Lady Day, to oblige all that will subscribe, to do it. In the meantime, I have printed receipts, which put an end to any person's delaying upon pretence of doubt, by determining that time. I send you a few, that you

may see I am in earnest, endeavouring all I can to save your money, at the same time that nothing can lessen the obligation to me." (Pope to Allen, November 6, 1736, *ibid.* p 191.) Allen also collected, or pretended to collect, subscriptions among his friends (fragment of a letter of Pope's quoted by Ruffhead, "Life of Pope," p 499).

62 Pope seems, however, to have undertaken a certain liability in the matter, since he hopes "not to lose too much." "Provided I do not lose too much (for a man of more prudence than fortune), etc (fragment of a letter to Allen in Ruffhead, *op. cit.* p 465).

63 This volume of letters is not the only one on which Pope corresponded with Allen. Some years later (October 1740?), he discourses at length on his correspondence with Swift (*ibid.* pp 195–96). Needless to say, his various protestations on this subject must be accepted with great caution, designed as they obviously were to divert possible and only too justifiable suspicion (see on this point Elwin's introduction to his edition of Pope, pp lxxxiii.-cxviii; the passages that relate especially to the letters to Allen will be found chiefly in pp ciii.-cvi. and cviii.-cix.).

64 He says very properly: " … Moreover to be perpetually repeating assurances is both a needless and suspicious kind of treatment with such as are sincere; not to add the tautology one must be guilty of, who can make out so many idle words as to fill pages with saying one thing. For all is said in this word, *I am truly yours*." (November 6, 1736, *ibid.* vol. ix. p 190.)

65 "Pray, tell me if you have any objection to my putting your name into a poem of mine (incidentally not at all going out of the way for it), provided I say something of you, which most people will take ill, for example, that you are no man of high birth or quality? You must be perfectly free with rue on this, as on any, nay, on every other occasion" (April 28, 1738, *ibid.* p 194).

66 A title changed in 1740 to "Epilogue to the Satires."

67 "Epilogue to the Satires," Dialogue I, ll. 135–36. The distich is found in this form only, in the quarto of 1738 and the Dublin edition of the same year.

68 The letter quoted above (*note* 65, p 233) would imply that Allen had authorised some allusion of the kind; but the epithet presses heavily on a point which delicacy would have refrained from even touching.

69 The dissenting minister, Foster, and the Quakeress preacher, Mrs Drummond

70 Graves says Warburton suggested the correction ("The Triflers," p 62); but from the letter of Pope to Warburton November 1, 1741, quoted further on, pp 220–221, Warburton seems not to have known Allen at that date. *Cf* too the last sentence of the letter quoted below, *note* 71.

71 "I always profit myself of the opinion of the public to correct myself on such occasions (a new edition); and sometimes the merits of particular men, whose names I have made free with, for examples of either good or bad, determine me to alteration. I have found a virtue in you more than I certainly knew before, till I had made experiment of it, I mean humility I must therefore in justice to my own conscience of it bear testimony to it, and change the epithet I first gave you of *low-born* to *humble.* I shall take care to do you the justice to tell everybody this change was not made at yours, or at any friend's request for you, but my own knowledge you merited it," etc. (November 2 [1738], ed. Elwin and Courthope, vol. ix. pp 194, 195).

72 Pope to Warburton, November 12 and 22, 1741, *ibid.* pp. 219 and 221. Warburton had counted on finding Pope at Twickenham at a time when the latter happened to be at Bath. Learning this, Allen begged Pope to invite his friend to join him (Graves, "The Triflers," pp 68, 69).

73 Pope to Arbuthnot, June 23, 1743, ed. Elwin and Courthope, vol. vii. p 490.

74 Pope to Allen, January 20, [1744], *ibid.* vol. ix. p 197.

75 In particular by "The Alliance between Church and State" (1736), the first part of "The Divine Legation of Moses" (1738, n.s.), and by the "Commentary on Mr Pope's Essay on Man," in its two first forms (1738, 1739.)

76 Brant Broughton, near Newark.

77 Frisby.

78 Probably the "Divine Legation of Moses," vols. iv., v. and vi. of which appeared in that year (1741).

79 We know that even during Pope's lifetime Warburton was his authorised commentator. it was he who wrote the chief part of the notes on Book iv. of the "Dunciad." in 1743 he issued an edition of the complete poem; the preface, signed Ricardus Aristarchus, is also from his pen.

80 Widcombe, at the gates of Bath, where Allen's residence was situated.

81 He says again in the next letter: "You will owe me a real obligation by being made acquainted with the master of this house; and by sharing with me, what I think one of the chief satisfactions of my life, his friendship" (November 22, 1741, ed. Elwin and Courthope, vol. ix. p 221).

82 Sherlock, well known by various books, sermons, etc., and the part he took in the debates in the House of Lords.

83 Pope to Warburton, November 12, 1741, ed. Elwin and Courthope, vol. ix. pp 220, 221.

84 "Here accordingly they met; a great part of the new poem was read and highly approved; the rest was finished in the year 1742 … " (Warburton, "Works," preface by Hurd, vol. i. p 40). It was Warburton who suggested this continuation to Pope (*ibid. cf* Pope's letter to Warburton of November 22, 1741, and a note to it in Elwin and Courthope, vol. ix. pp 221, 222).

85 See, on this subject, various evidences in Watson's "Life of Warburton," chap. xxxiii. p 617, *et seq.* Here is another which touches on Warburton's stay at Bath: "At the first visit which I made at Prior Park, I met Dr. Warburton for the first time, whom I ventured to pronounce one of the politest men I had ever seen. Those who only know him as engaged in controversy may be surprised at this. But I found him so attentive to every one who spoke, particularly to myself, who am the worst of all possible speakers, setting everything that I said in the clearest light, and, in short, paying such deference to his inferiors, as most of the company were … that he had certainly a claim to the character of a polite man, if destitute of superficial gentle ness of manner" (Graves, "The Triflers," pp 70–1). Disraeli therefore seems justified in his opinion that "the arrogant and vituperative Warburton was only such in his assumed character; for, in still, domestic life, he was the creature of benevolence, touched by generous passions" ("Quarrels of Authors," vol. i. p 534).

86 Watson, "Life of Warburton," chap. xii. p 250. "A Critical and Philosophical Commentary on Mr Pope's 'Essay on Man," 1742, is dedicated to Allen. Warburton preached a sermon in the Abbey Church at Bath, which was printed (Sunday, October 24, 1742).

87 Watson, "Life of Warburton," chap. xxxii. p 495.

88 After this he lived in the Bishop's palace at Gloucester till his death.

89 Allen's second wife—the first, Marshal Wade's daughter, died young.

90 Between Mrs Allen and Martha Blount, says Courthope in his "Life of Pope": "A difference arose between her and Mrs Allen, of which the poet was in some way the cause" ("Pope's Works," vol. v. p 340). He probably founded the assertion on the following passage: "So strange a disappointment as I met with, the extreme sensibility which I know is in your nature, of such monstrous treatment, and the bitter reflection that I was wholly the unhappy cause of it, did really so distract me," etc. (*ibid.* vol. ix. p 333). But it is not entirely clear as to who has suffered the "monstrous treatment," and other passages seem to point to Pope as being the person actively concerned in the affair. "I was like a man stunned or stabbed, where I expected an embrace; and I was dejected to death, etc ... When you bid me first go to Lord B.'s from them and then hasten thither, I was sensible it was in resentment of their conduct to me, and to remove me from such treatment, though you stayed alone to suffer it yourself ... I dread their provoking you to any expression unworthy of you" (*ibid.*). From this last we may suppose that at least no violent discussion had taken place between Mrs Allen and Miss Blount. Pope refers the contention only to himself in a later letter: "I told him [Allen] what I thought of Mrs Allen's conduct to me before you came, and both hers and his after ... I told him I did not impute the unkindness shown me, in behaving so coldly, to him originally, but to Mrs Allen ... I told him he should not see my behaviour altered to Mrs Allen so much as hers had been to me ... " (letter to Martha Blount, March 23, 1744, *ibid.* pp 336, 337). *Cf* finally the remarks of Miss Blount quoted here, p 236, *note* 93. All of which, of course, does not prevent the root, if not the actual pretext of the quarrel having lain, as Allen explained to Pope, in a "mutual misunderstanding" between the two women (*ibid.* p 337).

91 Mrs Blount, as the known friend and favourite of Pope, had been invited to the house of Allen, where she comported herself with such indecent arrogance that she parted from Mrs Allen in a state of irreconcilable dislike, and the door was ever barred against her" (Johnson, "Lives of the Poets," Pope, p 412, Chandos Classics ed.). *Cf* "With a sister of Mr Allen, Mrs Elliot ... I was well acquainted; and I remember various stories with which the old lady used to entertain me, when a schoolboy, about ... Pope and Miss Blount, causing much uneasiness to Mr Allen in consequence of what Dr Johnson calls her 'indecent arrogance'" (Polwhele, "Biographical Sketches in Cornwall," vol. i. p 11).

92 "About a year before Mr Pope's death, this lady, at the desire of Mr Pope and Mr Allen, paid a visit to Prior Park, where she behaved herself in so arrogant and unbecoming a manner that it occasioned an irreconcilable breach between her and some part of Mr Allen's family" (Ruffhead, "Life of Pope," p 547). It is an open

secret that Ruffhead's "Life "was written under the inspiration of, if not in collaboration with, Warburton, who shows more than once that he was ill-disposed towards Martha Blount. Thus Pope dedicated his Epistle "Of the Characters of Women" "to a Lady," and everything points to Martha Blount as the anonymous recipient of the poem and the compliments it conveys. Yet Warburton, in his edition of Pope's "Works," issued after the poet's death, does his utmost to deprive her of that distinction, and to prove that the lady of the dedication was a purely imaginary person (see Elwin and Courthope, vol. iii. pp 10–11). For his share in the present quarrel, see below, p 237, *note* 97. As regards Martha Blount's character, contemporary authorities give very conflicting opinions (see some of these in Elwin and Courthope, vol. v. pp 339–40).

93 "They often invited me to their house, and I took an opportunity of paying them a visit. I soon observed a strangeness of behaviour in them. They used Mr Pope very rudely, and Mr Warburton with double complaisance, and me they used very oddly in a stiff, over-civil manner. I asked Mr Pope whether he had observed their usage of him he said he had not, and that the people had got some odd thing or other in their heads. This oddness continued as long as we staid" (Spence, "Anecdotes," pp 358–9). As to the immediate cause of the difference, Sir John Hawkins (*note* in his edition of Johnson, vol. iv. p 89) asserts that it arose out of a refusal by Allen to let Miss Blount have his carriage to take her to the Roman Catholic chapel. Another cause is given in a letter from Pope to Martha Blount quoted below, p 237, *note* 100, namely, that Mrs Allen had taken umbrage at certain proposals of Pope connected with Allen's villa at Bathampton, near Prior Park. Allen repudiates this (*ibid.*), but it must be admitted that some months before Pope had asked to install himself there with Arbuthnot and been refused (Pope to Arbuthnot, July 23, 1743, Elwin and Courthope, vol. vii. p 490). There may have been a fresh solicitation from him now which was taken amiss. The letter to Martha Blount already alluded to, gives a glimpse, however, of a much more serious motive, which, in spite of Allen's denial, is probably the true one. The poet writes to his friend: "I pressed then that she [Mrs Allen] must have had some very unjust or bad thing suggested to her against you … " which can only be referred to adverse comments aroused long ago by the intimacy between Pope and Martha Blount, comments at which Pope himself had taken alarm (letters to Caryll, December 25, 1725, and July 20, 1729, Elwin and Courthope, vol. vi. pp 287 and 316). Small wonder that Mrs Allen should have looked askance at this intimacy, carried on under her own roof? Hence these sentiments, which find expression first in coldness of manner, then, perhaps through some occurrence insignificant enough in itself, in a more or less violent outburst. This collision may well have been brought about either by Pope or Martha Blount, the one being none too considerate a guest (compare Johnson, "Lives of the Poets," Pope, p 413, Chandos Classics), and the other by all accounts (p 235, *note* 91) no less indiscreet. Added to all this, Pope's morbid self-consciousness led him frequently to make mountains of mole-hills; it is certainly curious that he should have failed to notice any change of front towards himself till Martha Blount pointed it out to him, and that Allen on another occasion repeatedly declares that he had never observed any thing of the kind (letter quoted here, p 237, *note* 100). The poet's imagination probably ran away with him.

94 Letter to Martha Blount [1743] Elwin and Courthope, vol. ix. p 333.

95 Mr and Mrs Allen never said a word, not so much as asked me how I went, where or when. In short, from every one of them much greater inhumanity than I could conceive anybody could show ... They talk to one another without putting me at all in the conversation ... I do really think these people would shove me out if I did not go soon" (Martha Blount to Pope [1743] *ibid.* pp 332, 333).

96 Pope to Martha Blount [1743] *ibid.* p 334.

97 "W. is a sneaking parson, and I told him he flattered" (*ibid.* p 335). This can only be Warburton. Martha Blount had said in the foregoing letter: "Mr Warburton took no notice of me—'tis most wonderful'" (*ibid.* p 332). Pope, however, bore him no grudge for it.

98 Pope to Allen, January 20 [1744] *ibid.* p 196.

99 To the announcement of his impending visit Pope replies: "I am sure we shall meet with the same hearts we ever met; and I could wish it were at Twickenham, though only to see you and Mrs Allen twice there instead of once." Further on he begs him to remain as long as possible (letter to Allen, March 6, *ibid.* p 197).

100 "I told him what I thought of Mrs Allen's conduct to me before you came, and both hers and his after. He did pretty much what you expected; utterly denied any unkindness or coolness, and protested his utmost desire, and answered for hers, to have pleased you; laid it all upon the *mutual dissatisfaction* between you and her, and hoped I would not be altered towards him by any *misrepresentation* you might make; not that he believed you would tell an untruth, but that you saw things in a mistaken light. I very strongly told him you never made any such; nor, if he considered, was it possible, since all that had passed I saw with my own eyes, and heard with my own ears. I told him I did not impute the unkindness shown me, in behaving so coldly, to him originally, but to Mrs Allen; and fairly told him I suspected it to have proceeded from some jealousy she had of some designs we had upon his house at Hampton, and confirmed it by the reports I had heard of it from several hands. But he denied this utterly too. I pressed then that she must have had some very unjust or bad thing suggested to her against you; but he assured me it all rested upon a mutual misunderstanding between you two, which appeared in two or thee days, and which he spoke to his wife about, but found he could not make her at all easy in, and that he never in his whole life was so sorry at any disappointment. I said much more, being opener than I intended at first; but finding him own nothing, but stick to this, I turned to make slighter of it, and told him he should not see my behaviour altered to Mrs Allen so much as hers had been to me (which he declared he did not see); and that I could answer for it, Mrs Blount was never likely to take any notice of the whole, so far from misrepresenting any particular" (Pope to Martha Blount [March 25, 1744], *ibid.* pp 336–7).

101 "I thought his behaviour a little shy; but in mine, I did my very best to show I was quite unconcerned what it was. He parted, inviting himself to come again on his return in about a fortnight" (*ibid.* p 337.)

102 Made in the previous December (Courthope's "Life of Pope," *ibid.* vol. v. p 34.

103 Ruffhead, "Life of Pope," p 546. He also bequeathed some books to Allen. Ruffhead, followed by Johnson, makes Martha Blount responsible for this will, declaring that

she would not accept the portion set aside for her but on condition that Pope should ostentatiously reimburse all he owed Allen. She herself, however, told Spence just the contrary: "I had never read his will, but he mentioned to me the part relating to Mr Allen, and I advised him to omit it, but could not prevail on him to do so. I have a letter of his by me on that subject" (Spence, "Anecdotes;" pp 357–358).

104 "He brought some reproach upon his own memory by the petulant and contemptuous mention made in his will of Mr Allen, and an affected repayment of his benefactions" (Johnson, "Lives of the Poets," Pope, p 412, Chandos Classics). *Cf.* a letter of Lord Orrery to Mallet, July 14, 1744: "I find people in general seem surprised at the last act of our late departed friend … It is reported that Mr A [llen]is extremely enraged at his share of money, not of books, or rather at the manner in which it is given, and which is indeed a perfect mystery to me" (Pope, "Works," Elwin and Courthope, vol. viii. p 523).

105 Johnson, *loc. cit.*

106 The village in which Prior Park is situated. The house she lived in still exists, but the question is, when did she settle there? A local historian, Mr Peach, while admitting that there is nothing to show definitely when she established herself in Bath, judges that there is "no doubt" it was about 1739 ("Historic Houses," ii. p 32). He does not state his reasons. If it is the year of the publication of "Joseph Andrews," 1742, which inclines him to this date, it would only be begging the question, because Allen may quite well have made Fielding's acquaintance before that of his sister. Sir Leslie Stephen, in the "Dictionary of National Biography," in the article Fielding (Sarah), concludes from letters exchanged between her, Miss Collier, and Richardson from 1748 to 1757 (Richardson's "Correspondence," vol. ii. pp 57–112), that she was then living in Ryde. However, in 1754 the mention of waters that have done her good would seem to refer to Bath (*ibid.* p 69). A passage in Graves (see following note) shows her to have been in Bath in 1758, or after that date. According to Peach (*loc. cit.*) she left Widcombe for Bathwick, another suburb of Bath, in 1757, and remained there till her death in 1768. She is buried in the Abbey, where her friend, the Rev. John Hoadley, erected a monument to her memory.

107 "After Mr Allen had purchased Claverton, in the year 1758, as I mentioned, he was so much pleased with the romantic situation and with the manor-house, that he brought most of his company to see it, and generally dined there once a week. I dined there more than once with Mrs Fielding, the author of 'David Simple,' 'The Cry,' and some other works … Mr Allen very kindly allowed her £100 a year" (Graves, "The Triflers," p 77).

108 This is, of course, John Kyrle, "the Man of Ross" (*cf* Pope, "Moral Essays," iii. 1. 250).

109 "Joseph Andrews," book iii. chap. vi.

110 "You cannot forget that 'Tom Jones' was dedicated to him by Fielding, to whom he was a great friend; and, before he personally knew him, sent him a present of two hundred pounds in consideration of his merit; nor had he any other solicitations to this act of kindness than his own heart" (Derrick, "Letters," vol. ii. letter 33, pp 57, 58). There is an error in this passage; "Amelia," not "Tom Jones," is dedicated to Allen. What seems to confirm the idea that their acquaintance was of somewhat

later date is that Allen's name is not among the four hundred odd subscribers to Fielding's "Miscellanies" (1743) "Joseph Andrews" appeared in 1742, "Tom Jones" in 1749. Tradition also says that the publication of "Tom Jones" was followed by a present of £500 (Warner, "A New Guide," p 149).

111 The meagre information that has come down to us regarding Fielding's life shows how long he remained in relative obscurity. For instance, even after the publication of his masterpieces, Horace Walpole speaks of him in a very supercilious tone (letter of May 18, 1749, to George Montagu); so too Hurd, afterwards Bishop of Worcester: "I dined with him (Allen) yesterday, when I met Mr Fielding, a poor, emaciated, worn-out rake, whose gout and infirmities have got the better even of his buffoonery" (letter to Balguy, March 19, 1751, quoted by Kilvert, "Memoirs of Hurd," p. 45).

112 See on this point the biographical essay by Sir Leslie Stephen ("Works of Fielding," 1882, vol. i. p v.).

113 Nothing is known of the duration or even of the exact date of this stay. Some verses of his apparently improvised in the Pump Room in Bath are dated 1742 ("Miscellanies and Poems, to Miss H—and," vol. vii. p 422 of the Leslie Stephen edition). On the other hand, a tradition, purely oral but seemingly not very far out, has it that after the death of his first wife (1743?) Fielding sought some distraction by going to Bath (*cf:* Peach, "Historic Houses," vol. ii. pp 37, 38). This tradition, but in an altered and improbable version, is also given by Hunter in a letter to Kilvert ("Remains," p 179).

114 The house he lived in is still shown and has retained the name of "Fielding's Lodge"; a coat-of-arms carved above the door passes (wrongly, according to Peach, "Historic Houses," vol. ii. pp 34, 35) for his. Local report, confirmed by Graves (see *note* following), avers that it was here he wrote "Tom Jones." At Widcombe House, near Prior Park, they show a room he is said to have occupied several times at the invitation of the Bennet family, which is also associated with the composition of that novel. These traditions and another, current, it seems, at Salisbury (Dobson, "Fielding," chap. v. p 118), are not irreconcilable; the author himself states in the preface that the work cost him several years of labour, and it was very likely carried on in different places. At Widcombe, too, there was a tavern, The Old Pack Horse, pulled down in 1824, which claimed the honour of having frequently entertained him (Tunstall, "Rambles about Bath," p 112).

115 "Mr Fielding also, who then lived at Twerton ... dined almost daily at Prior Park, while he was writing his novel of 'Tom Jones'; in return for which hospitality he complimented Mr Allen—in conjunction with his other patrons, John, Duke of Bedford, and George, Lord Lyttelton—in the, character of Allworthy, though disguised with many fictitious circumstances" (Graves, "The Triflers," p 67).

116 "Fielding—who, as we before observed, laid the scene of the early years of Tom Jones at this place—has also, in his work ... given a picture of the beautiful situation of Mr Allen's house, the Allworthy of his novel. Making allowances for the fancy of an author, in an imaginary river, sea, distant island, and ruined abbey, the description is tolerably correct; at least many of its most agreeable features are real" (Warner, "A New Guide," p 149). With these differences (and several others, such as the style

of architecture, which is Gothic in Fielding but classical in reality), the description agrees sufficiently well with the situation and aspect of Prior Park; there too we find the terrace in front of the mansion on which Allworthy, walking forth as the sun rose, presented 'that one object alone in this lower creation which could be more glorious … a human being replete with benevolence, meditating in what manner he might render himself most acceptable to his Creator by doing most good to His creatures.' But it must also be said that there is nothing unusual in all these features, which may be met with on a thousand estates. The identification of Widcombe House (see above, p 239, *note* 114) with the residence of Squire Western, of the churchyard at Claverton with the scene of the battle described in book iv. chap. viii. (Wright, "Historic Guide," p 381) seems even less well founded though equally current. It has even been asserted that Philip Bennet, the owner of Widcombe House and sometime member for Bath, was the prototype of Squire Western (see Peach, "Bath Old and New," pp 225–6). Some have gone further still, as witness the following: "It is singular, yet satisfactory, that no *personal* designation has been given by biographers; *local* is sufficient. But this may be asserted, 'A sporting Squire' 'of high degree,' and a neighbour of Ralph Allen's, had a daughter, 'the brightness of whose cheek would shame the stars,' and the fair lady *did* marry a foundling, and thus she became possessed of two adjoining estates" (Wright, "Historic Guide," p 382). Of all this, of course, not the slightest proof is offered.

117 "Tom Jones," book i. chap. iv.

118 He designates him clearly enough a little further on by quoting one of the lines by Pope referred to above. It is Lyttelton whom he addresses.

119 "Tom Jones," dedication.

120 Yet not all of these, for the energetic, active, practical side of Allen is not apparent in the rather weak and credulous kindness of Allworthy, and the figure—over simple, over conventional—suffers, from the literary point of view, in consequence.

121 "Tom Jones," book i. chap. ii.

122 For this trait, which was certainly inapplicable to Lyttelton, see the passage in the second paragraph of the following note.

123 The passage is worth quoting. It confirms and enlarges upon what we have already learnt from Pope (*vide supra*, pp 261–2). "Neither Mr Allworthy's house nor his heart were shut against any part of man kind; but they were both more particularly open to men of merit. To say the truth, this was the only house in the kingdom where you were sure to gain a dinner by deserving it.

"Above all others, men of genius and learning shared the principal place in his favour; and in these he had much discernment; for though he had missed the advantage of a learned education, yet, being blessed with vast natural abilities, he had so well profited by a vigorous, though late application to letters, and by much conversation with men of eminence in this way that he was himself a very competent judge in most kinds of literature.

"It is no wonder that, in an age when this kind of merit is so little in fashion and so slenderly provided for, persons possessed of it should very eagerly flock, to a place where they were sure of being received with great complaisance, indeed, where they might employ almost the same advantages of a liberal fortune as if they were entitled to it in their own right; for Mr Allworthy was not one of those generous persons who are ready most bountifully to bestow meat, drink, and lodging on men of wit and learning, for which they expect no other return but entertainment, instruction, and subserviency; in a word, that such persons should be enrolled in the number of domestics, without wearing their master's clothes or receiving wages.

"On the contrary, every person in this house was perfect master of his own time: and as he might at his pleasure satisfy all his appetites within the restrictions only of law, virtue and religion: so he might, if his health required, or his inclination prompted him to temperance, or even to abstinence, absent himself from any meals, or retire from them when ever he was so disposed, without even a solicitation to the contrary: for, indeed, such solicitations from superiors always savour very strongly of commands. Bu all here were free from such impertinence, not only those whose company is in all other places esteemed a favour from their equality of fortune, but even those whose indigent circumstances make such an eleemosynary abode convenient to them, and who are therefore less welcome to a great man's table because they stand in need of it." ("Tom Jones," book i. chap. x.)

124 *Ibid.* book viii. chap. i. And he adds: "But a single instance (and I really know not such another) is not sufficient to justify us, while we are writing to thousands who never heard of the person, nor of anything like him. Such *raroe aves* should be remitted to the epitaph writer, or to some poet who may condescend to hitch him in a distich, or to slide him into a rhyme with an air of carelessness and neglect, without giving any offence to the reader," Allen is actually named in book xiii. chap. i.: "And thou, almost the constant attendant on true genius, Humanity, bring all thy tender sensations. If thou, hast already disposed of them all between thy Allen and thy Lyttelton, steal them a little 'while from their bosoms."

125 "Amelia," Dedication.

126 October 1754.

127 Murphy, "Essay on the Life and Genius of Fielding," in the edition of the latter's Works published in 1762, vol. i. p 46.

128 Allen's Will in Peach, "Life and Times of Ralph Allen," p 236. The first edition of the complete works of Fielding (1762) was dedicated to Allen. It may here be mentioned that shortly before his death Fielding had intended visiting Bath to try the waters, but was deterred by various circumstances (see "Journal of a Voyage to Lisbon," Introduction, "Works," vol. vii. pp 13–25, ed. Leslie Stephen).

129 We have seen above, p 239, *note* 114, how tradition still associates the name of Fielding with Prior Park and neighbouring places. Nor has the memory of Pope faded: a rustic summer-house is still called Pope's Study, and the same name is sometimes given, though without any justification, to a monument raised by Warburton to the memory of Allen. A cottage at the foot of Beechen Cliff has become Pope's House (Kilvert, "Remains," p 124); finally, near Prior Park there is a Pope's Walk, though of later date than the poet's sojourn in that neighbourhood.

130 See his pastel portrait by Hoare in the National Portrait Gallery, London.

131 "In familiar or convivial conversation it does not appear that he excelled. He may be said to have resembled Dryden, as being not one that was distinguished by vivacity in company. It is remarkable that, so near his time, so much should be known of what he has written, and so little of what he has said … " (Johnson, "Lives of the Poets Pope," p 414, Chandos Classics).

132 Spence, "Anecdotes," section v. p 206.

133 Mrs Rackett, sister of Pope, in Spence, *ibid.* Others, however (*ibid.*, and p 357), describe him as high-spirited and animated in conversation, but this refers to his youth.

134 See his portrait by Hoare as the frontispiece of his complete works.

135 Author of the "Spiritual Quixote" (see above, chap. vi. pp 147, 148, and pp 197–198). Kilvert has devoted an interesting essay to him ("Remains, pp 91–116). He was the intimate friend of the poet Shenstone, of whom he wrote a volume of memoirs.

136 "About the year 1752, I met Mr Richardson in Mr Leak, the bookseller's parlour, who told me he was going to dine with Mr Allen at Prior Park. 'Twenty years ago,' said he, 'I was the most obscure man in Great Britain; and now I am admitted to the company of the first characters of the kingdom" (Graves, "The Triflers," p 68). The remark is very characteristic of Richardson.

137 *Ibid.* p 77. He was introduced at Prior Park by Warburton (*ibid.* p 69).

138 Published 1748.

139 A correspondent of the *Gentleman's Magazine* (1782, p 288), claims to have had the following anecdote from Edwards himself: "Having been some time in the army, it so happened that being at Bath, after Mr Warburton's marriage to Mr Allen's niece, he was introduced at Prior Park *en famille*. The conversation not unfrequently turning on literary subjects, Mr Warburton generally took the opportunity of showing his superiority in Greek, not having the least idea that an officer in the army understood anything of that language, or that Mr Edwards had been bred at Eton; till one day, being accidentally in the library, Mr Edwards took down a Greek author and explained a passage in it in a manner that Mr Warburton did not approve. This occasioned no small contest, and Mr E. (who had now discovered to Mr W. how he came by his knowledge) endeavoured to convince him that he did not understand the original language, but that his knowledge arose from French translations. Mr W. was highly irritated; an incurable breach took place; and this trifling altercation (after Mr E. had quitted the army and was entered at Lincoln's Inn) produced 'The Canons of Criticism.'" There are, however, in this story two definite misstatements which incline one to doubt the accuracy of the rest: Edwards was not educated at Eton, and at the period in question he had long been a lawyer, and was not in the army.

140 Garrick's correspondence shows an unbroken intercourse with Allen and Warburton. He begins by asking for information about a property he wished to purchase near Bath ("Private Correspondence," vol. i. p 63, letter to Warburton, March 2, 1756); he sends them his works (letter of April 28, 1762, *ibid.* p 141), etc.

141 Quin and Warburton were not on good terms, and some lively passages occurred between them, in which the actor, who was never at a loss for a repartee, usually had the best of it. Taylor ("Records of my Life," i. p 87) relates the following couple

of anecdotes: "Quin was in the habit of meeting Warburton at Mr Allen's, at Prior Park, near Bath ... Warburton was mortified at the superior powers of conversation which Quin possessed, but was afraid of encountering his talents for prompt repartee. On one occasion, after a conversation on the subject of the martyrdom of Charles I, for the justice of which Quin contended, Warburton asked him 'by what law the King was condemned.' Quin, with his usual energy, exclaimed: 'By all the law which he had left in the land!'—an answer which was more ingenious than founded on truth and reason, but which, however, at once put an end to the controversy. On another occasion, when Warburton with grave subtlety endeavoured to degrade Quin from the social and equal companion to the player, he professed his desire to hear Mr Quin recite something from the drama, as he had not an opportunity of hearing him on the stage. Quin delivered the speech from Otway's 'Pierre,' in which there is the following passage:

"Honest men
Are the soft, easy cushions on which knaves
Repose and fatten,

alternately looking at Allen and Warburton in so marked a manner that the reference was understood by all the company, and effectually prevented any subsequent attacks from the divine on the actor."

142 Wood's first work on settling in Bath was to rebuild Allen's town house (1727); he afterwards built Prior Park. Allen also employed him as technical adviser in the working of the quarries (Wood, "Description of Bath," part iv. ch. xi. p 433).

143 Graves, "The Triflers," p 67.

144 Among others, Marshal Wade, father of Allen's first wife and for a long time member for Bath; Charles Yorke, son of Lord Hardwicke, afterwards Attorney-General and Keeper of the Great Seal under George III; Thomas Potter, who plays a certain part in Parliament among Pitt's adherents, and became Vice-Treasurer of Ireland (see in Kilvert, "Remains," pp 155, 156, a letter from the one to Warburton, 1746, from the other to Pitt, 1756, in which Prior Park, and more particularly Allen, are mentioned in terms of praise). Derrick brought the French Ambassador, the Duke de Nivernois, to Prior Park ("Derrick's Letters," ii., letter p 57 May 10, 1763). The Princess Amelia, second daughter of George II, was received there in 1752 (Kilvert, *op. cit.* p 161). Many another guest more or less known to fame might be mentioned—for instance, Sir John Cope, commander of the royal troops at Preston Pans (Graves, "The Triflers," pp 67, 68); Lady Huntingdon ("Life and Times of Selina, Countess of Huntingdon," vol. i. p 4.55) Drs Oliver and Hartley, physicians of repute (*ibid.*), etc.

145 Their connection dated from 1754 at least, when Pitt happened to be ill in Bath, and Allen was associated with the Corporation in organising demonstrations in his honour. Besides, through his father-in-law, Marshal Wade, Allen had of course, ready access to all the politicians of the day.

146 See the letters exchanged between Thomas Potter (cf p 243, note 144), Collibee, Mayor of Bath, Pitt and Allen on the occasion of the election of 1757, collected in Peach, "Life and Times of R. Allen" pp 161–567). The letter from Pitt quoted

below (p 244, note 148) would even warrant our concluding that in 1760 Allen gave him some pecuniary help.

147 One of the two members for Bath, Robert Henley (afterwards Lord Northington) had just been nominated by Pitt Keeper of the Great Seal.

148 Letter of June 28, 1757. Shortly before the second election, December 16, 1760, Pitt again expressed his lively sense of obligation to Allen: "Dear Sir,—The very affecting token of esteem and affection which you put into my hands last night at parting has left impressions on my heart which I can neither express nor conceal. If the approbation of the good and wise be our wish, how must I feel the sanction of applause and friendship accompany'd with such an endearing act of kindness from the best of men, etc.?"

149 The address sent to the King by the Mayor, the Sheriffs and Corporation of Bath, expressed their joy at the conclusion of so "adequate" and advantageous a peace. The first of these adjectives must have been particularly galling to Pitt, seeing that in his famous speech of December 9, 1762, he had applied to the projected peace the exactly opposite term, "inadequate." Was the coincidence accidental or deliberate Pitt suspected Warburton of having in some way or other suggested both the idea of the address and the offending epithet (for the text of the address, as also the letters exchanged between Pitt and Allen, see Peach, "Life and Times of R. Allen," pp 175–9; see also the letters between Warburton and Pitt in the correspondence of the latter, vol. ii. pp 253–7). This difference between Pitt and his constituents suggested a skit entitled "The One-Headed Corporation," to which reference has already been made (p 229, *note* 31). In a second skit, (Peach, *op. cit.* p 183), Pitt exclaims: "Let who will represent such wretches, I won't." Allen shortly afterwards retired from the Corporation.

150 Pitt's letter to Allen (June 2, 1763) concludes with these words: "Give me leave, my dear good sir, … to confess that I perceive that I am but ill qualified to form pretensions to the future favour of gentlemen who are come to think so differently from me on matters of the highest importance to the national welfare" ("Correspondence," vol. ii. p 224–25). It was a definite rupture with his constituents, of which he gave further proof the same year by selling his house at Bath.

151 Pitt's "Correspondence," vol. ii., p 289, June 4, 1764.

X

Art and science: the Woods, Gainsborough, Lawrence, Herschel

Three at least of the friends Allen gathered round him at Prior Park represented the fine arts. These were the two excellent architects, the Woods, father and son, and a respectable painter, William Hoare, all inhabitants of Bath, whither they had come from various parts of England, to settle permanently. These names, and others we shall presently mention, prove that Bath attracted a certain number of artists, to whom the presence of a rich and fashionable society gave reasonable hopes of patronage. After the capital, there was, indeed, no place in which the portrait-painter, for instance, or the musician, had a better chance of finding employment;[1] none in which obscure talent could more easily make itself known, in which a success attracted more attention, in which a dawning reputation advanced more rapidly, especially in the circles it was most important to interest at the outset of a career. Gainsborough and Lawrence formed themselves and rose to fame at Bath, just as Henderson and Mrs Siddons had done in a different art. And if these two great men soon quitted the scene of their first successes to practise in London, others, less eminent, remained contentedly all their days on the spot where their first efforts had been rewarded, and by their presence kept alive, at least in a certain section of Bath society, some taste, knowledge and practice of the arts, especially those of music and painting.

The work of the architects, especially that of the elder Wood, was of great local importance, so much so indeed that he may be coupled with Nash as one of the founders of modern Bath. He did not leave traces of his art in two or three isolated buildings. As soon as society began to flock to the city, Wood undertook to provide it with an entirely new town on a homogeneous plan—squares, streets, avenues, public and private buildings. His projects were so vast that for all his untiring industry and the favourable circumstances under which he worked, he could only carry them out partially. His son continued his task, handing it on at his own death to his pupils. Wood's tradition so governed the ultimate development of the town, that nearly every remarkable building in Bath[2] owes its existence to the first Wood, or to the second, or to contemporaries and successors guided and more or less inspired by them.[3] Hence the unity of the impression made on the traveller as he passes through this charming city, at once graceful and grandiose, coquettish and precise.[4] It is large and varied; it took, as a fact, a considerable time to build; but, broadly speaking, it is the work of one man, or of two very similar men, who, confronted with an exceptional and difficult task, acquitted themselves of it with unerring taste and great fertility of talent.

Wood's first suggestions for the methodical extension and embellishment of Bath date from 1724.[5] The old mediaeval town, confined within its Roman wall,[6] no longer sufficed for the growing influx of visitors, in spite of the new streets by which it had lately been enlarged.[7]

Wood proposed to build certain new quarters: "After my return to London, I imparted my first Design to Mr Gay, an eminent Surgeon, in Hatton Garden, and Proprietor of the Land; and our first Conference was upon the last Day of December, 1725; the 31st of March following, I communicated my second Design to the Earl of Essex, to whom the Land on which it was proposed to be executed then belonged; And in each Design, I proposed to make a grand Place of Assembly, to be called the Royal Forum of Bath: another Place, no less magnificent, for the Exhibition of Sports, to be called the Grand Circus; and a third Place, of equal State with either of the former, for the Practice of medicinal Exercises, to be called the Imperial Gymnasium of the City, from a work of that Kind, taking its Rise at first in Bath, during the Time of the Roman Emperors."[8] It is unnecessary to say that these last words express a purely gratuitous conjecture of the writer's. We must not be astonished at these echoes from antiquity. Wood was a representative, and one of the most meritorious, of classic architecture. Like most of his contemporaries, he belonged to that school, called in England Palladian, which took as its exemplar Vitruvius, as interpreted by the Italians of the Renaissance. That he was an enthusiastic worshipper of Greece and Rome, not only in matters relating to art, is shown by the confused and absurdly credulous mass of ill-digested erudition that pervades the two volumes of his "Description Of Bath." After all, it was a Roman city he had to restore and resuscitate, the most Roman spot perhaps in all Great Britain, the ancient *Aquae Solis*, roused from her long slumber, and not too much surprised to find herself once more adorned with those pediments and colonnades, pilasters and capitals that decked her temples and basilica, her villas and *thermae,* centuries ago. This time, indeed, she was to be more stately and magnificent than of old, challenging admiration by a calm dignity, a symmetry that does not exclude variety, a grandeur that loses little by a touch of theatricality.

What these first plans of Wood's actually were, how they were modified, amended, or completed, what parts of them were carried out, and in what manner,[9] what new details were introduced, and how these fared, are technical and local questions which lie outside the scope of my study.[10]

I do not propose to follow Wood in the exercise of his indefatigable activity, and in the details of his work, nor should I be competent to criticise it. I must, how ever, remind my readers that, among many other works, we owe to him Queen's Square (1728–1735),[11] with its dignified and monumental façades, its garden and its obelisk; the design for the Circus,[12] a vast circular space, the uniform houses of which combine the three Greek orders with classic severity; and Prior Park, on Widcombe Hill, with its noble hexastyle portico, its pavilions and arcades.[13] The Circus excited Landor's enthusiasm to such a pitch that he declared "there was nothing in Rome or in the world to equal it."[14] The eulogium is, of course, extravagant; but this Circus, as well as Queen's Square and the neighbouring streets, would not be unworthy of more than one great capital.

The architect did not see it completed;[15] his son carried out his plans after his death. But this son was his worthy successor, his equal in talent as in activity and enterprise. The Royal Crescent, for which he was solely responsible, is perhaps the most striking and imposing feature of modern Bath. The long Ionic row of uniform buildings, ranged in elliptical form at the top of a hill, astonishes the spectator with its grave simplicity, its majesty, the beauty of its approaches, the harmonious manner in which the surrounding scenery is made to enframe it; often imitated, even at Bath itself, it has never been surpassed or even equalled.[16]

A graceful and commodious building, the New Assembly Rooms,[17] the scene of fashionable fetes and reunions from 1771 onwards, is the most remarkable of the younger Wood's works, after the Royal Crescent; but, like his father, he devoted his talents more especially to the design and construction of whole streets, squares and avenues. These are very numerous; between the beginning of the elder Wood's activity and his death (1726–1754), Bath, throwing down her walls, spreading out across the plain, and climbing the hills that encircle her, had doubled her superficial area.[18] When, after a career of the same length, the younger Wood died, the town had again increased so much that it was no longer recognisable to persons who had not seen it for thirty years.[19] Wood, supported by his son, had been the initiator, the principal artificer of this development, but above all, and this is what makes them interesting, they both directed it as men of taste, as artists. Speculators would always have been found, provided there was a profit to be made, to transform the old Bath, and arrange it to suit the requirements of its new population more or less, to extend its boundaries in proportion to the growing influx of visitors. The peculiar merit of the Woods, in proposing and accomplishing this task, was, that they were architects and not mere builders, that they had the beauty of the city they were transforming always before their eyes, that they conceived and carried out a vast and harmonious whole. Their ideal is no longer ours altogether; their academic style is far from having retained the universal favour, the exclusive respect it enjoyed about a century and a half ago. Rigorous criticism will find their regularity a little cold sometimes, their solemnity a little heavy, their decoration some what poor, their invention somewhat circumscribed. But granting all this, their conceptions remain original, dignified and happy enough, in Macaulay's opinion, "to charm even eyes familiar with the masterpieces of Bramante and Palladio."[20] Who that has once seen them can forget the grandiose effect of the Crescent, the imposing mass of Prior Park, the sumptuous houses and spacious roads, the many vistas adroitly opened out in a smiling and varied landscape? The Woods were partly the authors, partly the direct or distant inspirers, of these monuments and this urban arrangement; if Bath owed her social organisation to Nash, it was thanks to the elder Wood and by his means that the city became one of the most agreeable in Great Britain, and perhaps in Europe. One metamorphosis no doubt invited the other, and the dandy's work claims priority; but that of the architect has been more enduring, and now that the first has vanished, this still gives Bath a place apart among the towns of the United Kingdom.

The work of artists has naturally left fewer local traces; it is less closely bound up with the places where it is executed, and is easily removed. If Sir Thomas Lawrence's first essays and several of Gainsborough's masterpieces date from their sojourn at Bath, we must go elsewhere now to study or to admire them. Their canvases and sketches, even during their lifetime, much more after their death, were dispersed among a variety of public and private galleries. Two portraits only by Gainsborough, that of Captain Wade in the Assembly Rooms, and that of Anstey in the Victoria Art Gallery, remain in the city, while Lawrence is represented by a few drawings in private collections.[21] Yet these two great men figure prominently in the history of Bath society; not only were they among its ornaments, but it was neither chance nor caprice that led the one to transport, the other to open his studio there. The same reasons that brought Wood, to the city, invited and retained them; like him, they found there esteem, profit and reputation.

Gainsborough was by no means the first of his profession who had thought of establishing himself at Bath. Mrs Barber, the friend of Swift, writing in 1736, notes that the city has attracted many painters, each one of whom, however indifferent, finds more work than he can do.[22]

Leaving these obscure artists to oblivion, I may mention among Gainsborough's predecessors, William Hoare, whose pictures and pastels are still considered respectable.[23] He was one of the first members of the Royal Academy; he left London for Bath (at a date not recorded), and was so successful there that he remained in the city till his death. Among the persons he painted were: Pitt (twice),[24] Lord Camden, Anstey, Nash,[25] and Derrick.[26] It was, no doubt, at Bath that Lord Chesterfield, the Duke of Newcastle, the Duke of Grafton, and Pope sat to him.[27] Graves tells us that he was one of Allen's friends,[28] and notes in the same passage that he was long at the head of his profession at Bath, leaving us to infer that he had *confrères* of less repute in the city.[29] Be this as it may, his success was of good augury for Gainsborough, when, in 1758, the painter, aged thirty, and almost unknown, came to settle at Bath.

He had been induced to take this step, it seems, by one Philip Thicknesse, Governor of Landguard Fort, whose acquaintance he had made at Ipswich, and who soon discounted the obligation by his tactless and intolerable patronage.[30] Thicknesse, who prided himself on having discovered Gainsborough's talent,[31] undertook to advertise it, and ordered a portrait of himself to serve as a bait for the public. The intention was good, but superfluous; before the picture was finished, or even sketched in, Gainsborough had sitters enough to ensure his independence henceforth, and shortly afterwards to give him wealth and renown.[32]

In London it might have taken this unknown provincial year to attract public attention; at Bath he was famous in a day. The public fell in love at once with his free, yet spirited and unerring brush, his brilliant and harmonious palette, his grace, his sincerity, his freedom from conventionality.[33] Though they did not as yet, perhaps, fully appreciate those landscapes which the artist loved best to paint, works which posterity has adjudged one of his chief titles to fame,[34] the portrait-painter was already recognised as a master of the first rank; and great persons, leaders of fashion, and men of letters, came in rapid succession to sit to him in his studio in the Circus. During the sixteen years he spent in Bath, he painted a considerable section of the English aristocracy: Lady Spencer and her daughter (the future Duchess of Devonshire), Lady Grosvenor, the Duke of Argyll, Lady Molyneux, Lady Sussex, Lord and Lady Ligonier, Lord Camden, the Duke of Cumberland, and many others;[35] he also painted Garrick (several times), Henderson, Foote, Quin, Miss Linley,[36] Mrs Macauley and Graves,[37] a varied, and in parts distinguished company, which sufficiently proves how widely his talents were appreciated.[38] Of a social temper in company where he did not feel restraint, gay and companionable, he appears to have been on terms of friendship with many of his sitters. This is certain, at any rate, as regards Henderson, whom he encouraged on his first appearance,[39] Quin, who left him £50,[40] and Garrick, whom he admired enthusiastically, and whom he found "ever a sincere and generous friend."[41] From Bath his fame spread rapidly to the metropolis, where he sent his pictures for exhibition,[42] and in 1768 he was elected a member of the Royal Academy on the foundation of that famous body. Nothing, however, indicates that he had any idea of settling in London till 1774, when a quarrel that lasted for some time, and was marked by vexatious incidents of constant recurrence, broke out between himself and Thicknesse in connection with an unfinished portrait.[43] Gainsborough was quick-tempered and impatient; enraged by a letter he received one day from Thicknesse, he went off immediately to London, took a house there, and returned to Bath only to pack up his belongings, and announce his departure to his friend.[44] Hereupon, his persistent patron, if we are to believe him, could not refrain from recommending him in London; he even attributes the painter's rapid success in the capital to his own good offices.[45] If this service was really rendered, it was probably unknown to Gainsborough; he had indeed, small need of such a passport; his fame, which had spread from Bath throughout the United Kingdom, was already a national boast.[46]

When we remember that Thomas (afterwards Sir Thomas) Lawrence left Bath at the age of eighteen, it may seem over-bold to assert that he, too, started on his career, manifested his talent, and won his first laurels in the city, though after a somewhat different fashion. Such is nevertheless the case, for at this early age the young artist could already look back on a professional career. This precocious

Thomas Gainsborough
From the portrait by himself

Sir Thomas Lawrence
From an engraving by W. H. Worthington

son of an innkeeper at Devizes came to settle at Bath as a painter of portraits in pastel at the age of eleven.[47] Scarcely had he arrived, when his talent and his intelligence, his grace and beauty, attracted the admiration and favour of society.[48] Two of his portraits, one representing Mrs Siddons, the other Lord Barrington, were immediately engraved,[49] an honour that was rarely accorded at the time to any but famous pictures.[50] Patrons, advisers, and those who were merely curious, flocked round the youthful prodigy,[51] and in addition, such a crowd of sitters that he had great difficulty in executing all his commissions, though he finished three or four portraits a week,[52] and received four sitters regularly every day.[53] It was not till he had had six years of this eventful and laborious life that the youth, who had meantime won the medal of the Adelphi Society of Arts[54] and begun to paint in oil, went at last to London to present himself to Reynolds, and, preceded by a most flattering reputation, entered the Royal Academy schools as a student.[55]

Another precocious artist found similar encouragement and help at Bath. This was Thomas Barker, still commonly known as Barker of Bath.[56] Although very celebrated in his time, he was a painter of far less distinction, and it will be sufficient just to mention him here. Unlike his predecessors, he was mainly a painter of genre and landscape, and consequently appealed to a more restricted circle of amateurs. He nevertheless spent his whole life at Bath, with no thought of seeking wider opportunities in London or some larger provincial town, content with those he found in the watering-place, no doubt with good reason. Hoare, and after him Gainsborough, had long found these sufficient, and no doubt they had increased since their time.[57]

Favourable to painters, the environment of Bath was no less so to musicians, at least for executants and teachers of the art. Ever since Nash had installed his orchestra at the Pump Room (and this was the origin of his reign),[58] concerts of every kind had been one of the chief diversions of the place; in the regular programme of amusements they figured as largely as the balls, and more frequently than the theatre. When once the vogue of Bath was established, musicians of talent came to conduct them; we have seen what a brilliant reputation they acquired under the direction of Linley, supported by his remarkable family.[59] The Italian Rauzzini, who succeeded him, and directed them for forty years[60] in collaboration with the violinist Lamotte, kept them up to a very high level of excellence. In his youth, at the Opera House of Vienna, he had been honoured with the friendship of Metastasio,[61] and afterwards with that of Haydn, who visited him at Bath in 1794.[62] Like Linley, he was a composer and a singing-master,[63] as well as conductor of the orchestra, and music seems to have been greatly appreciated and widely studied in his time, probably owing in some measure to his influence.[64] To cull from the local journals the names of the various singers, instrumentalists, and *virtuosi* of all kinds who delighted the fastidious ears of the *dilettanti* of Bath at various seasons, would be an unprofitable task. These names, if we except that of Incledon,[65] and, more particularly, that of Braham,[66] are now more or less forgotten. There is but one we cannot pass over in silence, an unexpected name, for it does not owe its immortality to art. Herschel, the distinguished astronomer, worked at Bath for sixteen years as music-master, organist, and conductor of the orchestra at the Assembly Rooms.[67] He was still practising in this triple capacity when he discovered the planet Uranus, and only resigned in the following year at the command of George III. His sister, the indefatigable partner of all his labours, has given us the history of those years of incessant toil, when, engaged with his concerts, his lessons[68] and his musical compositions, he found time to study astronomy, to take observations, and, with infinite labour, to manufacture his own instruments on the pattern of a borrowed telescope.[69] Not content with seeing what others had already observed, he then undertook the construction of telescopes more powerful than any hitherto known, working on occasion for sixteen hours at a time at the burnishing of a mirror, his sister putting pieces of food into his mouth the while.[70] In 1781, on March 13, he discovered the planet which was called successively *Georgium Sidus* (the name he himself gave it), Herschel, and Uranus, and received the gold medal of the Royal Society. He was nevertheless preparing to conduct oratorios with Rauzzini[71] (working at the same time on a new telescope), when the King appointed him director of the Observatory at Datchet. In the whole history of science there is perhaps no more admirable record than that of this poor Hanoverian, without education or resources, originally a regimental bandsman, who, by his industry his energy, his perseverance, overcame a thousand difficulties that might well have seemed insurmountable, mastered all the knowledge of his age in an abstruse branch of science, contributed magnificently to the sum of that knowledge, and added a chapter to the ever unfinished book of human learning.

The history of this great man during his sojourn at Bath was too independent of his environment to make it an appropriate theme for detailed treatment here. But his name makes a glorious conclusion to that muster of famous and distinguished persons who passed across the stage of Bath from the beginning to the close of the eighteenth century. It may be said that the ties which linked them to the city were in many cases slight and fortuitous enough. This is true, but they belong to her nevertheless, in so far as she attracted them all; to her they flocked to her in serried ranks, some in quest of gain or health, but more impelled by curiosity or inclination, and they willingly allowed themselves to be carried along by the current that periodically bore fashionable society to the city. Bath was to nearly all of them, as to all the rest of England, a place of amusement and recreation. Some, like Wood and Gainsborough, found a field of action there; others, a centre of observation. It is because of these last, indeed, the writers, who claim the largest share of our attention, that the city and society of Bath have a perennial interest for all students of English letters. It is no exaggeration to say that English literature owes something of Smollett, Sheridan, and Jane Austen to this city and this society.

1 The same may be said of all professors of polite accomplishments. We have seen that Sheridan's father chose Bath as a favourable spot in which to give lessons in elocution, and what he supposed to be oratory (see chap. v. above).

2 I except, of course, the Roman ruins and the Abbey, which, with one or two churches, are almost the sole relics of a time prior to the eighteenth century.

3 Some of them were men of talent, notably Baldwin (1750–1820), the author of the imposing plan of Pulteney Street, Laura Place, and their approaches, of the New Pump Room and of the Town Hall. But their work, in spite of its originality, harmonises with and continues that of Wood. Among the architects contemporary with Wood, the best known was perhaps Richard Boyle, Earl of Burlington (see Meehan, "Famous Houses of Bath," opposite pp 2 and 12, which reproduce two houses he built at Bath).

4 A French traveller justly said in 1811: "All the streets are fine and new. It looks like a city that has been cast in a mould all at once, and turned out of it perfectly fresh and youthful" ("Voyage d'un François en Angleterre," vol. i. p 22).

5 Wood, "Description of Bath," vol. i. chap. xii. p 232.

6 There is very little difference between the plan given in Jones' "Bathes of Bathes Ayde" (1572) and that of Joseph Gilmore (1694). A local archaeologist could only find seventeen new houses on the second (Warner, "History of Bath," chap. v. p. 219; *cf* Wood, *op. cit.* second part, chapters x., xi., xii.). The wall, composed in part of Roman materials, was pulled down in the eighteenth century.

7 For details of these enlargements, see Wood, *ibid.* chap. xii. pp 225–8.

8 *Ibid.* p 232.

9 These vast works were for the most part speculations, but Wood never forgot his art for his interests.

10 All these points are discussed at great length by Wood (see more especially chap. xii. of part ii., chapters ii.-iv. and ix.-xii. of part iii., and chap. xi. of part iv.).

11 The most remarkable portion is the north side, the only one in which Wood was free to carry out his design completely.

12 Finished in 1765, eleven years after his death.

13 He it was, too, who built the famous Parades, the Lower Rooms, the Hospital, etc. Outside Bath, his most notable achievements were the Exchanges at Bristol and Liverpool.

14 "Imaginary Conversations," "Pericles and Sophocles," *note.* (This note is omitted in the complete edition of Landor's Works recently published by Mr Crump; *cf* p xxvii. of the introduction). Smollett, on the other hand, dismissed the Circus as "a pretty bauble, contrived for show … like Vespasian's amphitheatre turned outside in" ("Humphry Clinker," letter of April 23). It is true it is the splenetic Matthew Bramble who is speaking; he is better pleased with Queen's Square *(ibid.)*.

15 He died in 1754.

16 It has inspired at least one poem, the "Ode on an Evening View of the Crescent at Bath" (London, 1773).

17 There was a certain rivalry between the New or Upper Assembly Rooms, and the Lower Rooms (see "New Prose Guide to Bath," dedication, pp iii.-v.), but the former soon triumphed. They still exist. The Lower Rooms, built by the elder Wood in 1729, were burnt to the ground in 1820.

18 "Long before 1755, Bath outside the walls was larger and more important than Bath within the walls" (Peach, "Bath Old and New," pp 228, 229).

19 "The very extraordinary and rapid increase of the city of Bath during the last twenty years, both as to the number and quality of its inhabitants, as well as the extent of its buildings, has been so great that we question whether a person acquainted with this city thirty years ago would be able to find out more than one mark whereby he could ascertain its originality ..." ("New Prose Guide," introd. p iii.). In Smollett's "Humphry Clinker," published seven years before this, Matthew Bramble declares Bath to be "so altered that I can scarce believe it is the same place that I frequented about thirty years ago" (letter of April 23). This progress continued after their time: *cf* "Madame d'Arblay's Diary," 1791. On seeing the city again eleven years after a first visit, she writes: "Bath is extremely altered; its circumference is perhaps trebled," etc. (October 2, vol. ii. p 423).

20 "History of England," chap. iii. p 34 of the 1st edition.

21 This was so, at least, in Warner's time (see "Literary Recollections," vol. ii. p 256, *note*).

22 "My son [Rupert Barber, afterwards miniature painter and engraver], who is learning to paint, goes on well, and if he be in the least approved of, in all probability he may do well at Bath, for I never saw a painter that came hither fail of getting more business than he could do, let him be ever so indifferent" (letter dated from Bath, November 3, 1736, in "Works" of Swift, Bohn ed., 1864, vol. ii. p 780).

23 See, for this painter, Murch, "Biographical Sketches," chap. xviii. pp 188–90. "His portraits are solidly painted, natural, and full of character" (Mr O'Donoghue, in the "Dictionary of National Biography," article William Hoare).

24 The first time in 1754, for Pitt himself, who presented the portrait to Lord Temple with a strong encomium on the painter (Murch, "Biographical Sketches," p 189); the second time for the municipality of Bath, ten years later.

25 This is the portrait engraved in Goldsmith's "Life of Nash."

26 The portraits of Lord Chatham (Pitt), of Lord Camden, of Allen and of Derrick are still at Bath, the three first in the Town Hall, the last in the Assembly Rooms. The Hospital, St. Michael's Church, and the Octagon Chapel at Bath possess other canvases by Hoare.

27 National Portrait Gallery, London. These portraits are all pastels, except that of the Duke of Grafton.

28 "The Triflers," p 67.

29 Taverner, for instance, the earliest of the English water-colour painters, whom Smollett praises in "Humphry Clinker" (letter from Matthew Bramble, May 19); he, however, was a landscape painter. Hoare had a sculptor brother, who made a bust of Nash, and a son, Prince Hoare, who, after practising as a painter, became a dramatic writers and had a certain share of success.

30 This Thicknesse was the author of various books of travel, memoirs, libels, etc., which gained him a certain notoriety in his time, a notoriety increased by his noisy quarrels with several persons, notably his own son, Lord Audley. His writings, which have but little literary merit, do not give a very favourable idea of their author,

betraying as they do an irritable, vindictive, and sometimes malevolent spirit. It may be, how ever, that some of Gainsborough's biographers, such as Cunningham and Fulcher, have painted him somewhat over black. He seems to have taken a sincere, if indiscreet, interest in the painter. The respective faults of the two, in the quarrel that parted them, have never been clearly established. After the death of Gainsborough, he published notice of him ("A Sketch of the Life and Paintings of Thomas Gainsborough"), in which he lauds the artist, and speaks becomingly of the man (*cf* Sir Walter Armstrong on Thicknesse, "Gainsborough," chap. iv.)

31 "I was the first man who perceived, through clouds of bad colouring, what an accurate eye he possessed, and the truth of his drawings, and who dragged him from the obscurity of a country town at a time when all his neighbours were as ignorant of his great talent as himself" (*ibid.* pp 3–4).

32 "My head was to be held up as the decoy-duck, but the first sitting (not above fifteen minutes) is all that has ever been done to it ... business came in so fast ..." ("A Sketch of the Life and Paintings of Thomas Gainsborough," pp 16–7). "'Fortune,' said a wit of the day, 'seemed to take up her abode with him; his house became Gainsborough" (Fulcher, "Life of Gainsborough," chap. v. p 61).

33 "The notion that a 'Bath Gainsborough' is something inferior, that it holds a place in his *oeuvre* distinctly below the pictures painted in London between 1774 and his death, is quite a delusion. Many of his finest things date from his years at Bath" (Sir W. Armstrong, "Gainsborough," chap. vi. p 114). "I most of the portraits painted at Bath," continues the critic, "colour is used with a vigour and a success unsurpassed at any subsequent period, and in many, especially in the Linley group, and, of course, the *Blue Boy,* the brushing is almost as free and the paint at least as fat and as rich as in the best things from his later years." (*ibid.*)

34 Many of these represent places near Bath, as, for instance, the two sent by Lord Tweedmouth to the Paris Exhibition of 1900. Hampton Rocks, just outside Bath, was one of the spots where he was fond of sketching; and an elm tree near the road from Bath to London is known as Gainsborough's Elm (Murch, "Biographical Sketches," p 184).

35 Perhaps Lord Chesterfield and the Duke of Bedford among them. Sir W. Armstrong says the date of their portraits is uncertain.

36 Thicknesse tells the following anecdote about Gainsborough and Miss Linley: "After returning from the Concert at Bath near twenty years ago [writes Thicknesse in 1788] where we had been charmed by Miss Linley's voice, I went home to supper with my friend, who sent his servant for a bit of clay from the small beer barrel, with which he first modelled, and then coloured her head, and that too in a quarter of an hour, in such a manner that I protest it appeared to me even superior to his paintings! The next day I took a friend or two to his house to see it, but it was not to be seen; the servant had thrown it down from the mantelpiece and broke it" ("A Sketch of the Life," etc., p 40).

37 According to the late Cosmo Monkhouse ("Dictionary of National Biography"), the portraits of Richardson and Sterne were also painted at Bath. Sir W. Armstrong does not mention this.

38 See Fulcher, "Life of Gainsborough," chap. v.; Conway, "The Artistic Development of Reynolds and Gainsborough," pp 44–68; "Dictionary of National Biography," article "Gainsborough," by Monkhouse, and, above all, Sir Walter Armstrong, "Gainsborough," chaps. v. and vi., for fuller details. The lists of sitters do not always agree, in consequence of the uncertainty of many of the dates. Ours, an abridgment from the last-mentioned work, is intended merely to give an idea of the painter's reputation at Bath, and the acquaintances he made in the city; I have therefore restricted it to portraits of notable persons, or such as have been already mentioned in the course of my book, and have made no attempt to follow the chronological order, often very difficult to determine, nor to indicate the relative merits of the pictures. Many works I have omitted may greatly surpass others I have mentioned (for instance, this may be the case with the famous *Blue Boy*, if, as Sir Walter Armstrong supposes, it was painted at Bath), but such considerations would be foreign to my subject, nor do I pretend to such knowledge as would enable me to discriminate. For the same reason, I abstain from any attempt to trace the gradual development of the master (on this point, see the works by Sir Walter Armstrong and Sir Martin Conway quoted above). It is interesting to recall in passing that Mrs Delany, who saw several of these portraits at Bath, declared them to be poor likenesses: "This morning went with Lady Westmoreland to see Mr Gainsborough's pictures (the man that painted Mr Wise and Mr Lucy,), and they may well be called what Mr Webb unjustly says of Rubens—they are 'splendid impositions'" ("Autobiography," vol. iii. p 60 October 23, 1760).

39 He was present at it in 1772. "So pleased was he with the ability the young man displayed, that he invited him to his house, painted his portrait, and before the first season was over, became the firm friend and patron of John Henderson" (Fulcher, "Life of Gainsborough," chap. v. p 81).

40 Quin's will, given in "Life of Quin," p 63.

41 Letter to Henderson, June 27, £773, given at length in Fulcher; see also another of July 18, 1773, also in Fulcher, *op. cit.* pp 83–85.

42 Eighteen from 1761 to 1768 ("Dictionary of National Biography," article "Gainsborough "). The first he sent was a portrait of Mr Nugent (afterwards Lord Clare) in 1761, according to Fulcher.

43 Thicknesse gives the history of the quarrel in great detail ("Sketch," pp 17–31). According to him, Gainsborough had promised Mrs Thicknesse a portrait of her husband, in exchange for a valuable musical instrument she presented to the painter; but after many delays and importunities, he sent her a hasty sketch, which was returned to him with a few reproachful lines. Gainsborough's family gave a different version, declaring that the instrument had been paid for, and that the artist had made no such promise (Cunningham, "Lives of the Most Eminent Painters," vol. i. p 269).

44 Thicknesse, "Sketch," p 31.

45 "I was much alarmed lest with all his merit or genius he might be in London a long time before he was properly known to that class of people who could *essentially* serve him … I therefore wrote to Lord Bateman, who knew him, and who admired his talents, stating the above particulars, and urging him at the same time, for both

our sakes, to give him countenance and make him known. His Lordship, for me, or both our sakes, did so, and his remove from Bath to London proved as good a move as it was from Ipswich to Bath" (Thicknesse, "Sketch," p 32).

46 Gainsborough was then forty-seven.

47 In 1782.

48 Williams, "Life and Correspondence of Sir Thomas Lawrence," vol. i. chap. ii. pp 68–72.

49 *ibid.* p. 70. The author adds: "This was immediately after his arrival at Bath."

50 "This distinction is not to be overlooked, for engraving was at a low ebb in England, and it was not customary to engrave any paintings that were not very much admired" (Lawrence's biographer makes this remark in reference to a second portrait of Mrs Siddons, painted a little later, which was also engraved. *ibid.* p 78).

51 Among those mentioned by the biographer are the Duchess of Devonshire, the Marquis of Ely, Lord Barrington, Lord Cremorne, the Bishop of Durham, etc. (Williams, "Life and Correspondence of Sir Thomas Lawrence," vol. i. chap. ii. pp 71–2), all interesting names, for they denote a sort of adoption of young Lawrence by the aristocracy. Amateurs threw open their galleries and collections to him, to forward his education (*ibid.* p 70), but his principal Mentor and most devoted patron was a Bath physician, the learned and cultured Falconer (*ibid.* p 84).

52 *ibid.* p 73.

53 *Ibid.* p 76.

54 For a copy in pastel of *The Transfiguration*, in 1784.

55 In 1787 (*ibid.* chap. iii. pp 95–99).

56 See a somewhat detailed account of this artist in Murch, "Biographical Sketches," and *cf* Sir E. Harrington, "A Schizzo on the Genius of Man, in which, among various Subjects, the Merit of T. Barker, the Celebrated Young Painter of Bath, is particularly considered," 1793. He was born in 1768, and had a considerable reputation at a very early age. His *Woodcutter*, which he painted at the age of twenty-one, was made popular all over England by Bartolozzi's engraving. Two other *Woodcutters*, earlier by seven and five years respectively, had a great success. His brother Benjamin was also a respectable painter and his son one of Horace Vernet's best pupils.

57 After the painters, the caricaturists claim a few words. We must recall at least two who found subjects for their pencils at Bath, Bunbury (The Long Minuet as Danced at Bath), and Rowlandson (The Comforts of Bath, illustrating verses in the "New Prose Guide"). Cruikshank also illustrated an edition of Anstey's poem in 1832.

58 See above, chap. ii. pp 35–36.

59 See above, chap. v. p 114.

60 From 1780 to 1820.

61 Peach, "Historic Houses," vol. ii. p 72.

62 Grove, "Dictionary of Music," article "Rauzzini." On this occasion Haydn set the epitaph of a favourite dog of Rauzzini's to music (*ibid.*).

63 Among his pupils were Incledon, the famous tenor Braham, Storace, Madame Mara, Mrs Billington, etc.

64 Warner attests this in his "Literary Recollections," vol. ii. pp 8–9. See also Bernard, "Retrospections of the Stage," vol. ii. chap. ii., where there is a long account of the foundation of a musical society by Rauzzini and a local amateur and composer, Dr Harington.

65 See Penley, "The Bath Stage," chap. xii. pp 71–2. He stayed at Bath for five years (1765–1770), before getting an engagement at Covent Garden.

66 See Penley, *op. cit.,* chap. xvii. p 104, on Brahani at Bath. He received his first instruction in music from Rauzzini at Bath, for three years.

67 From 1766 to 1782. He was born in 1738.

68 The actor Bernard, to whom he gave music-lessons, tells how, one January evening, in the middle of a lesson, the sky, which had been cloudy, began to clear. "There it is at last!" cried Herschel, to the amazement of his pupil, and, dropping his violin, rushed to a telescope, and apostrophised a certain star, saying how enraptured he was to see it again ("Retrospections," vol. ii. chap. ii. pp 60–62). Bernard took his lessons in Herschel's rooms, and tells us that "His … lodgings … then resembled an astronomer's much more than a musician's, being heaped up with globes, maps, telescopes, reflectors, etc., under which his piano was hid, and the violoncello, like a discarded favourite, skulked away in one corner" (*ibid.* p 58).

69 Mrs John Herschel, "Memoir and Correspondence of Caroline Herschel," chap. ii.

70 "I was constantly obliged to feed him by putting the victuals by bits into his mouth. This was once the case when, in order to finish a seven-foot mirror, he had not taken his hands from it for sixteen hours together" (Mrs John Herschel, "Memoir and Correspondence of Caroline Herschel," chap. ii. pp 36–7).

71 "Now a very busy winter was commencing, for my brother had engaged himself to conduct the oratorios conjointly with Rauzzini, and he had made himself answerable for the payment of the engaged performers, for his credit ever stood high in the opinion of every one he had to deal with" (*ibid.* p 42).

XI

The Transformation of Bath in the Nineteenth Century

Miss Austen's novels have shown us Bath at the dawn of the nineteenth century, a noisy, animated Bath, more frequented and crowded, perhaps, than at any other period, but, by reason of this very excess of popularity and prosperity, on the way to lose certain of its distinctive characteristics.[1] The city of pleasure had extended its circle of attraction too far; rapid and easy means of communication and the diffusion of wealth had thrown it open to the crowd. In this universal afflux the more refined section of society began to feel ill at ease. As long as they had dominated by members in the Assembly Rooms and the Pump Room, or reigned by the prestige of their rank, they had accepted the inevitable promiscuity with a good grace, smiled at certain intrusions, and even admitted to their acquaintance on occasion those who accounted it such an honour to be allowed to approach them respectfully. Under the new conditions, this company found itself submerged by the other; less tolerant than of yore, and jealously insisting upon distinctions that were fast disappearing,[2] it tended to secede from the throng, and form a coterie apart. Social community ceased; in such a numerous population, each fraction was important enough to be self-sufficing, and Bath was reconstructed in separate compartments. Various societies came to sojourn simultaneously in a town so well adapted for refined pleasure, and consecrated by tradition to holiday pastime. But there was no longer, or, to be exact, there was soon no longer to be, any Bath society. The clearest indication of this change was given by the gradual decline of those public amusements with which Nash had consolidated his empire, and welded together a hundred diverse elements. They were replaced in the favour of the fashionable world by private arid exclusive gatherings, which had been very unusual in former times, and were even forbidden during the reign of the autocrat.[3]

If the Pump Room and the Assembly Rooms[4] were still thronged (as Dickens describes them to have been), it was no longer with the aristocratic company of former days. These persons appeared only occasionally, visiting them chiefly from curiosity, and holding them and their frequenters in contempt.[5]

It became a more serious matter when this contempt, by a natural process of extension, was directed against Bath itself. Miss Austen and Dickens bear witness, each in characteristic fashion, to the decline of its ancient prestige; travellers also recognised the fact with surprise,[6] but the most curious and explicit document I have met with in this connection is a long article, or rather a series of two articles, which appeared in 1824–1825 in the "Album," a London periodical, under the title: "The Bath Man."[7] The anonymous author, who professes to be a Bath man, denounces, mercilessly and unreservedly, the false elegance, the affected or insolent manners, which, he declares, are supposed by the inhabitants of Bath to represent the extreme of good breeding, though they are laughed at in London. He further gives a comical account of the mortifications that await the man who brings the education and manners of Bath with him to the metropolis. Making due allowance for obvious exaggerations, this diatribe shows us none the less how greatly opinion had changed in respect of what was once the capital of fashion: "What a world of contempt," declares the author, "is conveyed in that little word *Bath,* when applied to some unfortunate, by one who claims any kindred or connexion with the great city."[8] In vain, "knowing the holy horror with which every man and woman of fashion in town regards a Bath man," did the poor denizen of that city try to mend his manners, and model them upon those of London. "The stain of the place was upon him, and he could not wash it out." Should he, by some humiliating subterfuge, attempt to conceal whence he came, "some pert peculiarity of manner has carried Bath upon the very face of it: some half-awkward, half-impudent speech, betraying the elegant city, or some ultra compliment, or extravagant flattery, has drawn forth the contemptuous observation, how *Bathish!*"

At a ball, when he invites a lady to dance, she not only refuses, but gives him the additional mortification of letting him hear her whisper to her neighbour: "If I had not known before he was a Bath man, I could have sworn it." All this, with a hundred similar humiliations, is related as a personal experience. In the author's judgment, there is no longer any affinity between the society of Bath and that of London: "They appeared a separate breed and distinct race of people." In the watering-place, "the men and women of the best set, though not generally vulgar, are at least a century behind the metropolitans in everything like proper style, dress, or fashion."[9]

It was the permanent population of Bath that was meant here ; but the immense increase in this, from 25,000 to 30,000 in the first quarter of the century,[10] instead of the 2000 or 3000 found there by Nash,[11] and the important part it now played, was one of the new features of the place, and one of the factors that made for the formation of distinct coteries. As the town is pleasant, cheerful, well-built, well-arranged, and amply provided with necessaries, as also it is possible to make a good figure in society, and keep up a position far more easily there than in London or the country, many persons followed the example of Miss Austen's Sir Walter Elliot; they chose it as a residence and settled there.[12]

As far back as 1779, Mrs Montagu had noted this permanent population as very different, or, at any rate, quite distinct from the other.[13]

One considerable section of it was formed by half-pay officers, who, having no previous local ties, chose Bath for their retreat on leaving the service.[14] Another, of clergymen of all ranks; and their choice sufficiently shows how much the character of the city had changed.[15]

A permanent local society was constituted by these newcomers and their families; a provincial town sprang up with the watering-place, a provincial town like any other, or only distinguished, if we are to believe the satirists, by certain absurdities born of a clumsy imitation of the capital. Here was a new reason in the fashionable world for keeping rigorously aloof in this transformed and invaded Bath, a new reason, added to certain external circumstances, for gradually withdrawing from it altogether.

External circumstances that had taken place in the first quarter of the nineteenth century were, in themselves, sufficient to draw away a large number of habitual visitors to Bath. These were the Peace of Amiens, the fall of Napoleon, and, as a consequence, the opening up of the Continent, and above all, the invention of railways, with all the incredible facility they offered to travellers. The position of Bath was greatly modified, to its detriment, by both these causes. A sojourn on the banks of the Avon ceased to be the almost classic *villegiatura,* the first and almost the only one that suggested itself, the one that was naturally, almost necessarily, associated with the idea of holidays and change of air. A hundred other places, hitherto inaccessible or unknown to the crowd, competed for the various groups which the old social attraction of Bath was gradually ceasing to muster there. To say nothing of rivals that had long remained obscure, like Cheltenham, but which became suddenly popular, as more rural and less commonplace,[16] Paris, Italy, the traditional goals of the English traveller, invited the British multitude.[17] The new-born lovers of wild and picturesque nature turned to the Alps, sung by Byron; the mountains of Scotland, extolled by Scott; the English Lakes; immortalised by Wordsworth. The recently created vogue of seaside resorts peopled the coast, and filled Brighton and Boulogne.[18]

Even the first and fundamental *clientèle* of Bath, the invalids, dwindled; delicate persons found the air of Torquay or Cannes milder; the German baths offered greater comfort, prices probably lower, and above all, a more complete change of air and habits, to sufferers.[19]

If these German resorts, Homburg and Baden, to which we may add Spa, replaced the ancient Bath that was disappearing, in the affections of the English generally, and not only in those of the invalids, it was because in many points they reproduced it with added splendour and on a larger scale. They had the same social brilliance, enhanced indeed by the fact that their visitors were not confined to the English aristocracy, but included that of every continental country. Play was high at these places, roulette and *trente-et-quarante* failing in no wise short of Nash's EO and faro. Finally, and this was by no means the least of all these attractions, morals were not severe, and the libertines of both sexes did not feel themselves supervised, as in England, by a public opinion that had become rigorous, and harassed by a press that revelled in the denunciation of scandals. Invalids, pleasure-seekers, gamblers, adventurers, gathered there as formerly on the banks of the Avon, and led a very similar life in surroundings that were much the same.[20] Let us turn from Bath, crystallising into a provincial town, its process of extinction enlivened by no traits of any interest,[21] and look towards Germany, to that "common garden of all Europe" as Michelet calls it,[22] to Baden, as Thackeray, for instance, has described it. What do we find here, slightly enlarged, a little less restricted, and much more international, but the Bath of former days?

"... The prettiest town," exclaims the novelist, "of all places where Pleasure has set up her tents; and where the gay, the melancholy, the 'idle or occupied, grave or naughty, come for amusement, or business, or relaxation; where London beauties, having danced and flirted all the season, may dance and flirt a little more; where well-dressed rogues from all quarters of the world assemble where wistful schemers conspire and prick cards down, and deeply meditate the infallible coup ... where even virtuous British ladies venture their little stakes, and draw up their winnings with trembling rakes, by the side of ladies who are not virtuous at all, no, not even by name; ... where you meet wonderful countesses and princesses, whose husbands are almost always absent on their vast estates ... while trains of suitors surround those wandering Penelopes their noble wives; Russian Boyars, Spanish grandees of the Order of the Fleece, Counts of France and Princes Polish and Italian innumerable, who perfume the gilded halls with their tobacco-smoke, and swear in all languages against the black and the red."[23] This is a trait which was never found in the English Spa. It was no international rendezvous, and although foreigners occasionally visited it, it never offered the spectacle of a little cosmopolitan world. All the rest, a painter of the eighteenth century might have included (and, as a fact, did include) in his portrait of Bath.

They would find a place, it may be said, not only in a picture of Bath or of Baden, but in that of a hundred other watering-places of all periods and all countries. Are not all these places very much alike? Do they not all reproduce the same mode of life? Assuredly, and I by no means deny the numerous analogies that unite all watering-places, and arise from essential conditions, analogies I have already mentioned in comparing the new-born English "baths" to French ones of the same period.[24] But as I said then, and as I think I have now shown, when we have admitted inevitable resemblances, the English watering-places of the eighteenth century, and Bath above all the rest, had a special character of their own. This character, one we shall look for in vain else where, lies in the fact that, for a hundred years and more, they were not merely places of healing and amusement, but national sanctuaries of breeding and fashion, *Conservatoires* of good manners; that, by attracting all in the three kingdoms who prided themselves on their refinement, they became the crucibles of social fusion; that finally, to the great advantage of letters, they set a marvellously instructive and varied spectacle before the eyes of one or two great observers. The origin of these towns was not fortuitous, neither was their social mission insignificant. A breath from France evoked them. They came into being just at the period when what is known as polite society began to constitute itself, arising outside the Court, yet modelling itself on the Court, and dominated more or less by its influence, at the period when, by virtue of a new phenomenon, a taste for the same refinements, a desire for the same cultivated pleasures, rather than equal rank and birth, began to bring persons together. Of this new society, they were not only the centres, but the colleges, so to speak, where it was organised, regulated and even disciplined Then, when circumstances had progressively multiplied this society to such an extent that its members were no longer isolated from it in any part of the United Kingdom and when too many of the profane had invaded the temple of elegance, they finally disappeared, together with the conditions that gave birth to them and upheld them. They played a very considerable part in the slow, but profound modification of English manners; in the midst of much frivolity, dissipation, and even vice, they helped to spread throughout the nation that refinement of manners which undoubtedly tends to refinement of mind and feeling, which is the preparation for these, and remains their ordinary accompaniment. They also threw down certain social barriers, brought about a desirable contact of individuals, and amalgamated various classes hitherto ignorant one of another in a general atmosphere of good fellowship. These results were far from insignificant. Even had they been less important, had they remained mere subjects of curious inquiry, they would not be unworthy of passing examination from students of the history or English manners. If we wish to know a society, it cannot but be interesting to see where and how it takes its pleasures.

1 See above, chap. vii. pp 175–177.

2 In 1822 (and perhaps for some time before this) all official recognition of rank in public places had been abolished:

No seats for peeresses are now appointed,
But rank and titles are all disjointed.
And ev'ry upstart whom great Nash had humbled
With dukes and princes, counts and lords is jumbled ...
("A Summer in Bath," p 21).

The author adds:

The consequence is plain—they will not come.
But are to all their private friends at home.

A defender of Bath says, about the same time: "A few years ago Bath was divided into a great many sets, but now I think they may be all resolved into two; the good and the bad ... [The good] is not open, as many imagine, to every aspirant after fashion ... It does not hold out its arm to every person of large fortune and low family. It does not always court the honour arid patronage of those who have some little rank and less reputation. It is not always deaf to the suggestions of morality and good feeling—nor does it (as it has often been accused of doing) press into its service every man who wears pantaloons" ("Album," 1823, p 180).

3 See "Jane Austen," quoted above, chap. vii. p 176, and *cf* "Wonders of a Week in Bath," Monday (1811), pp 10, 19, 22, 43. A local historian, Warner, notes this change and all its significance; he also shows why, the rigid discipline established by Nash could not be maintained by his successors: "Acting upon the great principle of congregating the devotees of fashionable amusement, regularly and frequently, into one brilliant focus, he had discountenanced all private parties and select *coteries:* and the daily and nightly attendance at the public rooms formed as integral a part of the business and duty of Bath visitors as their diurnal operation of eating and drinking ... From the moment of *Beau Nash's* quitting the scene of his power and pride those corruptions and relaxations (which first sap, and then crumble, the mightiest states) crept insensibly into his formal and elaborate system of public punctilio; and the fear of violating the law that prohibited the domestic rout, and enforced a regular attendance at the public assemblies in which he had presided, gradually evaporated ... Late dinners began by little and little to interfere with the regular early attendance at the Upper and Lower Rooms: and fatal 'at homes' on the ball nights, to prevent that attendance altogether ... Taste and fashion now no longer checked, chose for solace and display, the private rather than the public arena" ("Literary Recollections," vol. ii. chap. xiii. pp 3–8).

4 The sole survivor of these establishments, that is to say the Upper Rooms. As early as 1820, Warner tells us that they had been stricken by an incurable decline, and were dragging on a precarious existence ("Literary Recollections," vol. ii. chap. xiii.).

5 "If it be Thursday night, the Rooms are generally looked into, but it is hardly advisable to join oneself to the *herd* who are dancing there" ("The Album," 1825, p 182). It is true, that in a retort made to this article, the following lines are to be found: " ... Among the herd, a few weeks since ... no less than eighteen ladies ... bore honourable designations as relatives of nobility: and amongst the gazers upon the herd were Lord Liverpool and several other Nobles and their Ladies, who did not think themselves contaminated by the air of the *Upper Rooms*, nor their daughters degraded by dancing with the 'herd' there assembled" ("Remarks on the Bath Man," by a Man of the World, pp 20–21).

6 "Bath is deserted by Fashion after having served as its temple. Its old-world elegance reminded sue of the graces of those superannuated fops who find, in place of admires and imitators, very indifferent and even somewhat incredulous spectators." (Custine, "Mémoires et Voyages," p 452 [1822].)

7 "The Bath Man" (nos. vii. and viii. January 1824, and April 1825; the two numbers form volume iv. of the publication).

8 "The Album," vol. iv. p 173.

9 On this point, as on others, the author of "Remarks on the Bath Man" defends his city, and roundly lays all the impertinences endured by the Bath man to his personal account. This was a skilful thrust, and he was perhaps right, but it is curious that be should have thought a formal reply necessary. It should be noted further that the editor of the "London Review" came voluntarily to the support of his contributor: "Ourselves have been in Bath during the last month, and have witnessed the commotion the first part of this paper has caused there with a mixture of merriment,

sorrow, and disgust ... Why ... we ask, is Bath to be exempt from ridicule, which, as all its sensible inhabitants and visitors will allow, contains more folly and is more open to ridicule, than any other town of its size in his Majesty's dominions?" ("The Album," p 413, editor's note at the head of the second article).

10 Mainwaring gives the total as 34,163 for the year 1801 ("Annals of Bath," p 11).

11 See above, chap. i. pp 18–19, and *cf* chap. x. p 254, *note* 6.

12 See above, chap. vii. p 176, *cf* this statement in the "Bath Man": "My father had come to live entirely at Bath for the same reason that most people do—because they cannot afford to live in London or the country" ("The Album," 1825, p 175).

13 "There are many people established at Bath who were once of the public and busy world, so they retain a certain politeness of manners and vivacity of mind one cannot find in many country towns. All contracted society, where there are no great objects of pursuit, must in time grow a little narrow and *un peu fade*; but then there is an addition of company by people who come to the waters, from all the active parts of life, and they throw a vivacity into conversation which we must not expect from persons whose chief object was the *odd trick* or a *sans prendre* ... The ladies, as is usual in little societies, are some of them a little gossiping and apt to find fault with the cap, the gown, the manner, or the under standings of their neighbours. But that does not much concern the water-drinkers, who, not being resident, are not the object of this envy; and I must say, they are all very obliging to strangers " (letter to Mrs Robinson, June 18, 1779, in Doran, "A Lady of the Last Century," chap. x. pp 248–49.) *Cf* "A Tour thro' Great Britain," ed. of 1778: "Bath is now become of very great extent, from the great increase of new buildings, as it is not only a place of occasional resort for health or pleasure, but the perpetual residence of many people of fashion and fortune" (vol. ii. p 232). Taking instances only from among literary people and their families, we have seen the following settling in Bath, for reasons unconnected with health or calling: Anstey, Thomas de Quincey's mother, Jane Austen's parents, Beckford, Landor. Madame d'Arblay; among other persons mentioned in the course of this work, we may further instance Mrs Thrale and Quin.

14 They had begun to do so in Smollett's time ("Humphry Clinker," Matthew Bramble, May 5), and still continue the practice. *Cf* Earle, "Bath Ancient and Modern," chap. xi. p 252.

15 "Bath ... seems to have been much frequented in those days by clergymen retiring from work" (Leigh, "Memoirs of Jane Austen"). The ecclesiastics Smollett noticed in great numbers in Bath ("Humphry Clinker," letter from Jeremy Melford, May 17), seem, on the contrary, to have been birds of passage. The religious spirit, however, developed very considerably in the city in the first part of the nineteenth century. In 1841, the author of a pamphlet called "The Decline and Fall of Bath" virulently accuses the clergy of having ruined the town by their preaching: "Nothing thrives in Bath nowadays but preaching and praying ... Yes, my dear Jack, the parsons have completely got the whip hand of the good people of Bath" (p 9). Many persons note the decorum verging on austerity that reigned in the city in the first decade. A private letter of 1810, comparing Bath and Brighton, says: "We think the society of a more moral tone, at all events it is more staid and steady, though by no means dull"

("The Bath Archives, a Selection from the Letters of Sir George Jackson," vol. i. p 171). A French traveller says in 1811 that

"Bath is a sort of great convent ... peopled by superannuated celibates of both sexes, but especially women" (Simond, "Voyage d'un Français en Angleterre," vol. i. p 22).

16 Such at least is the cause to which I attribute the sudden and transient popularity of this town. Custine, in 1822, calls it "the Spa of England," and says it had "succeeded Bath, which is no longer fashionable "Mémoires et Voyages," p 448; *cf* also Ducos, "Itinéraire et Souvenirs d'Angleterre et d'Ecosse," vol. iv. pp 233–7. These expressions are much too, strong, at least if we remember the Bath of the eighteenth century. Cheltenham, even during its few years of splendour, never played a part or held a position in any way comparable to hers. But it is true that it attracted a brilliant concourse for, several years. Thackeray takes several of his characters there in "Vanity Fair" (chapters xii. and xvii.).

17 As regards Paris and France, *cf* Babeau, "Les Anglais en France après la Paix d'Amiens." So many of them left descriptions of their travels, that they must have come in considerable numbers (see the Bibliography at the beginning of this volume). Every one knows also that the events of 1815 brought a whole military and aristocratic colony to Paris, besides the ordinary curious traveller.

18 Cowper denounced them as early as 1782:

"Your prudent grandmammas, ye modern belles,
Content with Bristol, Bath, and Tunbridge Wells,
When health required it, would consent to roam,
Else more attach'd to pleasure found at home.
But now alike, gay widow, virgin, wife,
Ingenious to diversify dull life,
In coaches, chaises, caravans and hoys,
Fly to the coast for daily, nightly joys,
And all impatient of dry land agree
With one consent to rush into the sea."
(Cowper—"Retirement.")

19 Medical treatment had also been considerably modified. In the eighteenth century, the Bath waters seem to have been considered a kind of panacea.

20 The reputation for immorality which the Continent has in England may very possibly date from the time when loose-living Englishmen first took to seeking their equivocal pleasures on the other side of the Channel. This reputation, as far as France is concerned, appears to be of comparatively recent date, for the reproaches addressed to us by our neighbours in the eighteenth century were of quite a different order, servility, frivolity, and affectation being the grounds of accusation. At the beginning of the nineteenth century, it was even held to be ill-deserved by a number of writers, who formed a favourable opinion of French morals (see, for instance, Birkbeck, "Notes on a Journey through France" (1814), p 102; Lady Morgan, "France," book iii. (1817); Mrs Trollope, "Paris and the Parisians" (1836), vol. ii. chap. vi. pp 37–8); whereas the opposite opinion, at least where I have encountered it, relates more especially to the revolutionary period, and that immediately after it (quotations in

Babeau, "Les Anglais en France après la Paix d'Amiens" (pp 78–9), and in "La France et Paris sous le Directoire," by the same author, pp 272 and 281. In 1822, however, a licentious work by D. Carey lays the scene of certain unedifying adventures in our capital. English opinion seems, at any rate, to have been formed irrespective of English writers. Mrs Trollope, who combats it, speaks of the French as a nation "whose morality is considered as so much less strict than our own" ("Paris and the Parisians," vol. ii. chap. vi. p 37), and after attacking this prejudice, she declares very justly: "I do very strongly suspect that many of the pictures of French depravity which have been brought home to us by our travellers, have been made after sketches taken in scenes and circles to which the introductions I so strongly recommend to my countrywomen could by no possibility lead them" (*ibid.* p 38). The English forgot that the "scenes and circles" alluded to by the writer had obtained in their own midst very recently, and openly, especially in their watering-places. They were accordingly scandalised, some honestly so, others verbally, when they encountered them elsewhere.

21 This extinction was complete about 1840. (*cf* Earle, "Bath Ancient and Modern," p 253, and Warner, "Literary Recollections," vol. ii. chap. i.) An article that appeared in *Blackwood's Magazine* last year notes the complete abandonment of all the English watering-places (p 789), and preaches a return to the old methods of Nash (organisation of pleasures, authority conferred on a Master of the Ceremonies), etc.

22 "La France devant l'Europe," p 84.

23 "The Newcomes," chap. xxvii. *Cf* other passages in the same chapter, and also Tourguénief's novel, "Smoke."

24 See above, chap. i. p 20.

Appendix

A Ballad of Bath[1]

(See chap. viii, p. 221)

Like a queen enchanted that may not laugh nor weep,
Glad at heart and guarded from change and care like ours,
Girt about with beauty by days and nights that creep
Soft as breathless ripples that softly shorewards sweep,
Lies the lovely city whose grace no grief deflowers.
Age and grey forgetfulness, time that shifts and veers,
Touch not thee, our fairest, whose charm no rival nears,
Hailed as England's Florence of one whose praise gives grace,
Landor, once thy lover, a name that love reveres:
Dawn and noon and sunset are one before thy face.

Dawn whereof we know not, and noon whose fruit we reap,
Garnered up in record of years that fell like flowers,
Sunset liker sunrise along the shining steep
Whence thy fair face lightens, and where thy soft springs leap,
Crown at once and gird thee with grace of guardian powers.
Loved of men beloved of us, souls that fame inspheres,
All thine air hath music for him who dreams and hears;
Voices mixed of multitudes, feet of friends that pace,
Witness why for ever, if heaven's face clouds or clears,
Dawn and noon and sunset are one before thy face.

Peace has here found harbourage mild as very sleep
Not the hills and waters, fields and wildwood bowers,

Smile or speak more tenderly, clothed with peace more deep,
Here than memory whispers of days our memories keep
Fast with love and laughter and dreams of withered hours.
Bright were these with blossoms of old, and thought endears
Still the fair soft phantoms that pass with smiles or tears,
Sweet as roseleaves hoarded and dried wherein we trace
Still the soul and spirit of sense that lives and cheers.
Dawn and noon and sunset are one before thy face.

City lulled asleep by the chime of passing years,
Sweeter smiles thy rest than the radiance round thy peers;
Only love and lovely remembrance here have place.
Time on thee lies lighter than music on men's ears;
Dawn and noon and sunset are one before thy face.

[1] Inserted by kind permission of Mr Swinburne.

Bibliography

Ainsworth, William. "Beau Nash; or, Bath in the Eighteenth Century." London: 1879(?). 3 vols.

"Album, The." Vol. IV. London: January-July, 1825.

"Amusemens des Eaux de Spa." By Charles Louis Baron de Pollnitz. Amsterdam: 1734. 2 vols.

Andrews, Miles Peter. "The Bath Picture; or, a slight Sketch of Bath and its Beauties in 1771."

Angelo, Henry. "Reminiscences." London: 1830. 2 vols.

Anstey, Christopher. "The New Bath Guide; or, the Memoirs of the B-r-n-d Family." A new edition by J. Britton. Embellished with engravings by G. Cruikshank. London: 1832.

"Poetical Works ... with some Account of the Life and Writings of the Author by his son, John Anstey, Esq." London: 1808.

See "Inkle," "An Election Ball."

See "Journey of Dr. Robert Bongout."

See New Bath Guide.

Arblay, Madame d'. "Diary and Letters." With notes by W. C. Ward. London: 1890–91. 3 vols.

See Burney (Fanny).

Aristaenetus. "The Love Epistles." Translated from the Greek into English Metre by Halhed and Sheridan. London: 1771.

Armstrong, Sir Walter. "Gainsborough and his Place in English Art." London: 1898.

Ashton, John. "History of Gambling in England." London 1898.

Asmodeo [Sheridan]. "Clio's Protest." "The Rival Beauties." nd. [1771].

Athenaeum. London: 1828 and following years.

Austen, Jane. "Letters." Edited by Lord Brabourne. London: 1884. 2 vols.

"Northanger Abbey." London Bentley, nd.

"Persuasion." London: Bentley, nd.

de B. [Moreau de Brazey]. "Le Guide d'Angleterre, ou relation curieuse du voyage de M. de B." Amsterdam: 1744.

Babeau, Albert. "Les Anglais en France après la paix d'Amiens. Impressions de Sir John Carr." Paris: 1898.

"La France et Paris sous le Directoire." Paris: 1886.

Baccios, Andreas. "De Thermis, Lacubus, Fluminibus et Balneis totius Orbis." Venetiis: 1571.

"Bagatelle, or the Bath Anniversary." A Poem in three Parts. London: 1782.

Baker, David Erskine. "Biographia Dramatica." Continued by J. Reed and brought down to the Year 1811 by Stephen Jones. London: 1812. 3 vols.

Baker, Thomas. "Tunbridge Walks."

Barbey d'Aurevilly, J. A. "Du Dandysme et de G. Brummell." Caen: 1845.

"Bath": a Poem in three Parts: I. "Bath, the Beloved of Venus." II. "Bath, hated by Mercury." III. "Bath, rescued by Minerva." Bath: 1793. (Bath Reference Library.)

"Bath, a Simile. Bath, a Conversation Piece. Bath, a Medley. Preceded by a Prologue to the Critics; succeeded by a rhapsody on the Death of Mr Garrick." London: 1779.

"Bath: its Beauties and Amusements." By G. Ellis. Second Edition. Bath: 1777.

"Bath Anecdotes and Characters." By the Genius Loci. London: 1782.

"Bath, Bristol, Tunbridge and Epsom Miscellany," The Containing Poems, Tales, Songs, Epigrams, Lampoons, Satires, Panegyricks, Amours, Intrigues, etc. London: 1725.

"*Bath Chronicle*," The. From 1757.

"Bath Comedians," The. A Poem in two Cantos. London: 1753. British Museum, 1162, i. II [I].

"Bath Contest," The. Bath: 1769.

"Bath Intrigues: in Four Letters to a Friend in London." London 1725. (Bath Reference Library.)

"Bath Miscellany for the Year 1740," The. Wrote by the Gentlemen and Ladies of that Place. Containing all the Lampoons, Satyrs, Panegyrics, etc., for that Year. Bath: 1741.

Bayly, Thomas. "Rough Sketches of Bath, and other Poems." Fifth Edition. 1820.

See "Epistles from Bath."

Beckford, William. "Vathek." Lausanne: 1787.

Beijame, Alexandre. "Le Public et les Hommes de Lettres en Angleterre." Paris: 1881.

"Belles of Bath, The; with a Satire on the Prevailing Passions and a Model for Emulation." Number I. Bath: 1782. (Bath Reference Library.)

"Bemerkungen eines Reisenden durch Deutschland, Frankreich, England und Holland in Briefen an seine Freunde." By J. F. C. Grimm. Altenburg: 1775. 3 vols.

Bernard, John. "Retrospections of the Stage." London: 1830. 2 vols.

Besant, Walter, and Rice, James. "The Chaplain of the Fleet." London: 1890.

Bickerstaff, Isaac. *See The Spectator.*

"Biographical Magazine, The, or complete historical Library." 4 vols. London: 1776.

Birkbeck, Morris. "Notes on a Journey through France." London: 1814.

Blackwood's Magazine. 1840.

Boaden, James. "Memoirs of Mrs Siddons, interspersed with Anecdotes of Authors and Actors." London: 1893.

Boswell, James. "Life of Samuel Johnson, LLD, together with the Journal of a Tour to the Hebrides." A New Edition. by A. Napier. London: 1884. 5 vols.

Brazey, Moreau de. *See* de B.

Brereton, Jane. "Poems on several Occasions." London: 1744. 2 vols.

Bristol, Earl of. *See* Hervey, John.

"Bristol and Bath Magazine, The: or, weekly Miscellany." Containing selected Beauties from all the new publications, etc. Bristol: nd. [1782–1783].

British Critic. 1827–1843.

Brome, James. "Travels over England, Scotland and Wales." London: 1700.

Brown, Thomas, the Elder. "Bath." A Satirical Novel. Second Edition. London: 1818. 3 vols.

Bulwer Lytton. "Paul Clifford." 1830.

Bunbury (Caricature). A Long Minuet as danced at Bath. [1787].

Burke, Edmund. "Correspondence." Edited by Charles Fitzwilliam and Sir Richard Bourke. London: 1844. 4 vols.

Burnard, F. C. "Ixion, or the Man at the Wheel" (Lacy's Acting Edition of Plays, vol. 60). London: nd.

Burney, Fanny. "Evelina; or, a Young Lady's Introduction to the World." 1778. 3 vols. Burr, Thomas Benge. "The History of Tunbridge Wells." London: 1766.

Byron, Lord. "Don Juan." 1819–1824.

Calvert, Walter. "Bath Table Talk." Being a Collection of Anecdotes of Bath ... First Series. Bath: 1887.

Camden, William. "Britannia, sive florentissimorum regnorum, Angliae, Scotiae, Hiberiae, et insularum adiacentium ex intima antiquitate Chronographica Descriptio." Londini: 1586.

Campbell, Thomas. "Life of Mrs Siddons." London: 1834. 2 vols.

Campbell, John, Lord. "Lives of the Lord Chancellors and Keepers of the Great Seal of England." London: 1845–1869. 8 vols.

Castle, Agnes and Egertorn "The Bath Comedy." London: 1900.

Chandler, Mrs Mary. *See* "A Description of Bath."

Chantreau. "Voyage dans les trois Royaumes d'Angleterre, d'Ecosse et d'Irlande, fait en 1788 et 1789." Paris: 1792.

Chappuzeau. "La Muse enjouée, ou le Théâtre comique." Lyon: 1674.

"Characters at the Hot Well, Bristol; in September and at Bath, in October, 1723." London: 1724.

Chatham, Earl of. "Letters written to his nephew Thomas Pitt, afterwards Lord Camelford." A New Edition. London: 1810. *See* Pitt, William.

Chaucer, Geoffrey. Complete Works. Edited by the Rev. Walter W. Skeat. Oxford: Clarendon Press, 1894. 6 vols.

Cheakhill, Sir Joseph. "The Cross-Bath Guide, being the Correspondence of a Respectable Family." London: 1815.

Chesterfield, Philip Dormer Stanhope, Earl of. "Letters to his Son, Philip Stanhope, Esq." London: 1774. 2 vols.

"Letters." Edited by Lord Mahon. 5 vols. London: 1845.

"Letters." Edited by F. Bradshaw. 3 vols. London: 1892.

"Miscellaneous Works." To which are prefixed Memoirs of his Life. By M. Maty. London: 1777. 2 vols.

Chevrillon, André. "Sydney Smith et la Renaissance des Idées libérales en Angleterre." Paris: 1894.

"Cheyne's, Dr., own Account of himself and of his Writings faithfully extracted from his various Works." London: 1743.

Clarke, James Stanier, and MacArthur, John. "The Life of Admiral Lord Nelson." London: 1809. 2 vols.

Claromontius, Carolus. "De Aere, Locis et Aquis terrae Angliae." Londini: 1672.

Clément. "Les cinq années littéraires." La Haye: vols. 1754.

Coleridge, Samuel Taylor. "Poetical Works."

Collier, John Payne. "Memoirs of E. Alleyn." London: 1841.

Colvin, Sydney. "Landor." London: 1881.

"Comforts of Bath, The." Designed and etched by Rowlandson with Versification by Christopher Anstey, Esq. Bath: 1858. [Reproduction of a series of drawings published in 1798.]

Contemporary Review. 1889.

Conway, William Martin. "The Artistic Development of Reynolds and Gainsborough." London: 1886.

Cottle, Joseph. "Reminiscences of Samuel Taylor Coleridge and Robert Southey." London 1847.

"Court Tales: or, a History of the Present Nobility." To which is added, A Compleat Key by J Oldmixion. London: 1717.

Cowper, William. "Poems." London: 1782. 2 vols.

Cowper, Mary, Countess. "Diary, 1714–1720." London: 1764.

Cunningham, Allan. "The Lives of the Most Eminent British Painters." Revised Edition. London: 1879. 3 vols.

Custine, A de. "Mémoires et Voyages, ou Lettres écrites à diverses époques, pendant des courses en Suisse, en Calabre, en Angleterre et en Ecosse." Paris: 1830. 2 vols.

Dancourt. "Les Eaux de Bourbon." Comédie. Paris: 1697.

Davies, Thomas. See "A Genuine Account of the Life of Mr J. Henderson."

Davis, Charles E. "Ancient Landmarks of Bath." Bath: 1864.

Deane, Mary. "Mr Zinzan Of Bath, or Seen in an old Mirror." A Novel. London: 1891.

"Decline and Fall of Bath, The; or, the private Correspondence of Capt. Smallarms and T. Broadlands, Esq." Second Edition. Bath: nd. [1841]. (Bath Reference Library.) Defoe, Daniel. *See* "The Fortunes and Misfortunes of the Famous Moll Flanders." *See* "A Gentleman" and "A Tour thro' Great Britain."

Delany, Mary Granville, Mrs. "Autobiography and Correspondence." London: 1861. 3 vols.

Delesalle, Georges. "Dictionnaire argot-français et français-argot." Paris: 1896.

Delvau, Alfred. "Dictionnaire de la langue verte." Nouvelle édition conforme à la dernière revue par l'auteur. Avec un supplément par Gustave Fustier. Paris: nd.

De Quincey, Thomas. "Collected Writings." London: Black, 1896. 14 vols.

"Derrick's Jests; or, the Wits' Chronicle." Containing a pleasing Variety of Repartees, Puns, Bon-Mots, and other species of Wit and Humour, Which passed between Samuel Derricks Esq.; late Master of the Ceremonies at Bath, and other Persons distinguished for their Wit and Humour. Also a Collection of Poetical Pieces on Various Subjects by Mr Derrick and Others … London and Bath: 1769.

Derrick, Samuel. "Letters written from Leverpoole, Chester, Corke, the Lake of Killarney, Dublin, Tunbridge Wells, and Bath." Dublin: 1767.

"Description of Bath, A." A Poem. By Mary Chandler. London: 1734.

Deyverdun, G. See "Mémoires Littéraires de la Grande Bretagne."

Dhautel. *See* "Dictionnaire du bas-langage."

Dickens, Charles. "Bleak House." 1853.

"The Posthumous Papers of the Pickwick Club." London: 1837.

"Dictionary of Musicians, A. Second Edition. London: 1827. 2 vols.

"Dictionary of National Biography." Edited by Leslie Stephen.

"Dictionnaire du bas-langage. By Dhautel. Paris: 1808. 2 vols.

Diderot. "OEuvres complètes, revues." By J. Assézat et M. Tourneux. Paris: 1876. 20 vols.

Dilke, Charles Wentworth "Papers of a Critic." London: 1875. 2 vols.

"Diseases of Bath, The." A Satire Unadorn'd with a Frontispiece. London: 1737.

Disraeli, Benjamin. "Tales and Sketches." London: 1891.

Disraeli, Isaac. *See* "Quarrels Of Authors."

Dobson, Austin. "Fielding." London: 1883; Rev. ed., New York, 1900.

"Life of O. Goldsmith." London: 1888.

Doran, John. "A Lady of the Last Century (Mrs Elizabeth Montagu), illustrated in her unpublished Letters." London: 1873.

Dowden, Edward. "Life of Percy Bysshe Shelley." London: 1886. 2 vols.

"Drawings from Living Models taken at Bath." London: nd. [1785].

"Dream, A: or the Force of Fancy." A Poem containing Characters of the Company now at the Bath." London: 1719. (B. M., 164, k. 38.).

Ducos, M. *See* "Itinéraire et Souvenirs."

Durfey, "The Bath, or the Western Lass." London: 1701.

Earle, John. "A Guide to the Knowledge of Bath ancient and modern." London: 1864.

Ellis, George. *See* "Bath: its Beauties," etc.

English Illustrated Magazine, 1883, *sqq*.

"Englishwoman, An." [Lady Miller.] Letters from Italy, describing the Manners, Customs, Antiquities, etc., of that Country. London: 1776. 3 vols. Second Edition. 1777. 2 vols.

"Euphrosyne: or, Amusements on the Road of Life." By the Author of "The Spiritual Quixote." R. Graves. Third Edition, London: 1783.

"Faint Sketch of the Life, Character, and Manners of the late Mr Nash, A." Bath, nd.

"Festoon, The: a Collection of Epigrams, ancient and modern." By R. Graves. London: 1766.

Fétis, J. J. "Biographie universelle des Musiciens et Bibliographie générale de la Musique." Second Edition. Paris: 8 vols.

Fielding, Henry. "Miscellanies." London: 1743. 3 vols.

"Complete Works." London: 1762.

"Works." Edited by Leslie Stephen. London: 1882. 10 vols.

Fiennes, Celia. *See* "Through England on a Side-saddle," etc.

Fitzgerald, Percy. "The History of Pickwick" London: 1891.

"The Life of Laurence Sterne." London: 1864. 2 vols.

"The Lives of the Sheridans." London: 1886. 2 vols.

Fleming, F. *See* "Life and Extraordinary Adventures of Timothy Ginnadrake."

"Foreigner's Guide, The: or, a necessary and instructive Companion, etc." Fourth Edition. London: 1763.

Forster, John. "The Life of Charles Dickens." Thirteenth Edition. London: 1873.

"The Life and Adventures of Oliver Goldsmith." London: 1848.

"Fortunes and Misfortunes of the Famous Moll Flanders, The." By Daniel Defoe. London: 1721.

Freeman. "The Thermal Baths of Bath." London: 1888.

Fulcher, G. W. "Life of Thomas Gainsborough." London: 1886.

Garrick, David. "Private Correspondence." London: 1831. 2 vols.

"General Account of Tunbridge Wells, and its Environs: historical and descriptive." London: 1771.

Genest, John. "Some Account of the English Stage, from the Restoration in 1660 to 1830." Bath and London: 1832. 10 vols.

Genius Loci. See "Bath Anecdotes and Characters."

Gentleman, A. (Daniel Defoe). "A Tour thro' the Whole Island of Great Britain." London: 1724–1727. 3 vols. Ditto, Third Edition: 1742, 4 vols.; ditto, Fourth Edition: 1748 4 vols.; ditto, Fifth Edition: 1753; ditto, Sixth Edition: 1762,4 vols.

See "A Tour."

"*Gentleman's Magazine, The*, or *Monthly Intelligencer*." London: 1731–1833. Ditto, Entirely new Series: 1868, *sqq*.

"Genuine Account, A, of the Life and Theatrical Transactions of Mr John Henderson." London: 1826.

Geoffroi de Monmouth. *See* "Gottfried von Monmouth."

Gibbon, Edward. "Private Letters." Edited by Rowland E. Prothero. London 1896. 2 vols. *See* "Mémoires Litteraires de la Grand-Bretagne."

Godwin, Mary. "Frankenstein."

Goldsmith, Oliver. "Works" (The Globe Edition). London, nd. "Works," a new Edition by W. Gibbs. London: 1885–6. 5 vols. *See* "Life of Richard Nash."

Gottfried von Monmouth. "Historia Regum Britanniae,"," herausgegeben von San-Marte. Halle: 1854.

Goudar, A de. *See* "Histoire des Grecs."

Graves, Richard. "The Triflers." To which are added the "Rout, or a Sketch of modern Manners"; and the "Farmer's Son," a moral Tale. London: 1806. *See* "Euphrosyne."

Graves, Richard. *See* "Festoon." *See* "Recollections of some Particulars." *See* "The Spiritual Quixote." Gray, Thomas. "Works, with critical notes," etc. By John Mitford. London: 1816. 2 vols.

Green, John Richard. "A Short History of the English People." London: 1885.

Grein, C. "Bibliothek der angel sachsischen Poesie." Göttingen: 1857–1864. 4 vols.

Grimm, Johann Friedrich Carl. *See* "Bemerkungen."

Grove, George. "A Dictionary of Music and Musicians (A. D. 1450–1880"). London: 1880. 4 vols.

Guardian. 1713.

Guidott, Thomas. "A Discourse of the Bath." London: 1676. Ditto, 1725.

Halhed, N. B. See "Artistaenetus."

Hamilton, Antoine. "Memoires du Chevalier de Grammont."

"Handbook to Bath prepared on the Occasion of the Visit of the British Association." By various Authors. Edited by J. W. Morris. Bath: 1888.

Hannay, David. "Life of Tobias George Smollett." London: 1887.

Harington, Sir E. "A Schizzo on the Genius of Man, in which, among various Subjects, the Merit of … T. Barker, the celebrated young Painter of Bath, is particularly considered." Bath: 1793.

Hartley, David. "Observations on Man, his Frame, his Duty and his Expectations." London: 1749. 2 vols.

Hartmann, Dr. Hermann. "Ueber die Vorlagen zu Sheridans Rivals, eine Buellenuntersuchung." Colberg: 1888.

Hazlitt, W. Carew. "Memoirs of William Hazlitt." London: 1867. 2 vols.

Heard, William. "A Sentimental Journey to Bath, Bristol, and their Environs." A descriptive Poem. London: 1778.

Henderson, John. "Letters and Poems, with Anecdotes of his Life." By John Ireland. London: 1786.

Henley, Eden, afterwards Baron. "A Memoir of the Life of Robert Henley, Earl of Northington, Lord High Chancellor of England." London: 1831.

Herschel, Mrs John. "Memoir and Correspondence of Caroline Herschel." London: 1876.

Hervey, John, First Earl of Bristol. "Letter-books." Wells: 1894. 3 vols.

"L'Histoire des Grecs, ou de ceux qui corrigent la fortune au jeu." By A. de Goudar. Second Edition … La Haye: 1757.

Historical Manuscripts Commission. Eleventh Report. Appendix. Part I. London: 1887. Ditto, Twelfth Report. Appendix. Part III. London: 1889.

"Hobby-Horses," read at Bath Easton. London: 1780.

Hume, David. "Letters to William Strahan." Edited by G. Birkbeck Hill. Oxford: 1888.

Inkle [C. Anstey]. "An Election Ball." Bath: 1776.

"Intercepted Epistle from a Person in Bath to his Friend in London, An." Second Edition. Bath: 1815. (Bath Reference Library.)

Invalid, An. "The Register of Folly; or, Characters and Incidents at Bath and the Hot Wells in a Series of poetical Epistles." London: Bath, Bristol and Oxford: 1773.

Ireland, John. *See* John Henderson.

"Itinéraire et Souvenirs d'Angleterre et d'Ecosse, 1814–1826." By M. Ducos. Paris: 1834. 4 vols.

"Itinerarium Antonini Augusti." Ediderunt G. Parthey et M. Pinder. Berolini: 1848.

Jackson, Lady. "The Bath Archives." A further Selection from the Diaries and Letters of Sir George Jackson from 1809 to 1816. London: 1873. 2 vols.

Jerrold, Douglas. "Beau Nash; the King of Bath." A Comedy in three Acts. London: 1834.

Jesse, Captain. "The Life of George Brummell." Revised and Annotated Edition from the Author's own Interleaved Copy. London: 1886. 2 vols.

"Jests of Beau Nash, The, late Master of the Ceremonies at Bath.". Bath: 1763.

Johnson, Samuel. "Letters, collected and edited by George Birkbeck Hill." Oxford: 1892. 2 vols.

"Works," with notes. By Sir John Hawkins. London: 1787. 11 vols.

Johnsonus, Thomas. "Thermae Bathonicae, sive earum descriptio, vis, utendi tempus, modus, etc" Londini: 1634.

Jones, Dr. John. "The Bathes of Bathes Ayde." London: 1572.

Jorden, Ed. "A Discourse of Naturall Bathes and Minerall Waters." The Second Edition in many points enlarged. London: 1632.

"Journey of Dr. Robert Bongout and his Lady to Bath, The," performed in the year 177-. By C. Anstey. London: 1778.

"Journey through England, A." In familiar Letters from a Gentleman here to his Friend abroad. By I. Macky. London: 1714, 1722, 1729. 3 vols.

"Journey to Bath and Bristol, A." An Heroi-Comic and Geographical Poem. London, nd. (Bath Reference Library.)

Joyce, Herbert. "History of the Post Office." London: 1893.

Jusserand, J. J. "A French Ambassador at the Court of Charles the Second." Le Comte de Cominges. From his unpublished Correspondence. London: 1892.

Kelly, Michael. "Reminiscences." London: 1826. 2 vols.

Kennard, Mrs A. "Mrs Siddons." London: 1887.

Kenrick, William. "The Widow'd Wife." A Comedy. London: 1767.

Kilvert, Rev. Francis. "Memoirs of the Life and Writings of the Right Rev. Richard Hurd, DD." London: 1860. "Remains in Verse and Prose." Bath and London: 1866.

King, Austin J., and Watts, B. H. "The Municipal Records of Bath, 1189 to 1604." Published with the Approval of the Town Council and at the special Request of the Bath Literary Society. London and Bath [1885].

L., J. M. "The Bath Comedians." A Poem in Two Cantos. Written in Imitation of "Hudibras." London: 1753.

Lamb, Charles. "Essays of Elia."

Landor, Walter Savage. "Imaginary Conversations of Literary Men and Statesmen." Second Edition. London: 1826. 3 vols.

Larchey, Lorédan. "Dictionnaire historique d'argot." Tenth Edition. Paris: 1889.

Layamon. "Brut, a Chronicle of Britain." Published by Sir Frederic Madden. London: 1857. 3 vols.

Le Blanc. *See* "Lettres d'un Français."

Lecky, William E. H. "History of England in the Eighteenth Century." A New Edition. London: 1897. 7 vols.

Lefanu, Alicia. "Memoirs of the Life and Writings of Mrs Frances Sheridan." London: 1824.

Leigh, Austen. "A Memoir of Jane Austen." Second Edition. London: 1871.

Leland, John. "Commentarii de Scriptoribus Britannicus." Oxonli: 1719. 2 vols.
"Itinerary." The Second Edition. Oxford: 1745. 9 vols.

"Letter, A, from a Citizen of Bath to his Excellency Dr. R. at Tunbridg" (*sic*). Bath: 1705. (Bath Reference Library.)

"Lettres d'un Français." Par l'abbé Le Blanc. La Haye: 1745. 3 vols.

"Life and Extraordinary Adventures, The, the Perils and Critical Escapes of Timothy Ginnadrake." By F. Fleming. Bath: 3 vols. [the last dated 1771.]

"Life of Mr James Quin, The, Comedian, with the History of the Stage from his commencing Actor to his Retreat at Bath." London: 1887 [new edition of a work dated 1766].

"Life of Richard Nash, Esq., The." Extracted principally from his original Papers. By Oliver Goldsmith. London and Bath: 1762. Ditto. The Second Edition. London: 1762.

Lilly, John. "Dramatic Works." With notes by F. W. Fairholt. London; 1892. vols.

Lockhart, J. G. "Memoirs of the Life of Sir Walter Scott, Bart." A New Edition. Edinburgh: 1845.

London Evening Post. 1735 and following years.

London Gazette. 1665 and following years.

London Magazine and *Monthly Chronologer*. London: 1762. vol. xxxi.

Lucas, Theophilus. "Memoirs of the Lives, Intrigues, and Comical Adventures of the most famous Gamesters and celebrated Sharpers in the Reigns of Charles II, James II, William III, and Queen Anne." London: 1714.

Luxborough, Lady. "Letters written to William Shenstone." London: 1775.

Lyly. *See* Lilly.

Macaulay, Thomas Babington, Lord. "History of England." London: 1849–61. 5 vols.
Ditto. "Life and Works." Edinburgh Edition. London: 1898.

Macknight, Thomas. "History of the Life and Times of Edmund Burke." London: 1858. 3 vols.

Macky, J. *See* "A Journey through England."

Macmillan's Magazine. Edited by David Masson. Vol. iii. Cambridge: 1861.

Macready. "Reminiscences." Edited by Sir F. Pollock. London: 1875. 2 vols.

Madden, William. "The Bath Macaroni." With other Sketches from Nature. Bath: 1781. (Bath Reference Library.)

Mainwaring, Captain. "Annals of Bath, from the Year 1800 to the passing of the New Municipal Act." Bath: 1838.

Marshall, Emma. "Her Season in Bath." A Story of bygone Days. London: '1890.

Massinger, Philip. "Plays." With notes by W. Gifford. Second Edition. London: 1813. 4 vols.

Meehan, J. F. "Famous Houses of Bath and District." Bath: 1901.

"Member, A, of the Houses of Shirley and Hastings: The Life and Times of Selina, Countess of Huntingdon." London: 1839. 2 vols.

Mémoires littéraires de la Grande-Bretagne pour l'An 1767 [par Gibbon et Deyverdun]. Londres: 1768.

"Memoirs of the Life and Writings of Samuel Foote, Esq." [London, nd.]

"Merry Newes from Epsom Wells." London: 1663.

Michelet, Jules. "La France devant l'Europe." Florence: 1871.

Miller, Lady. *See* "An Englishwoman."

"Mirror, A, for Magistrates." Edited by Joseph Haslewood. London: 1815. 3 vols.

Misson, H. *See* de Ve, M.

Mitford, Mary Russell. "Our Village." Fourth Series. London: 1830.

"Modern Amours; or, a Secret History of the Adventures of some Persons of the first Rank." With a Key prefixed. London: 1733.

Montagu, Mrs Elizabeth. "Letters, published by Matthew Montagu, Esq." London: 1809. 4 vols.

Ditto. *See* Doran, J.

Montagu, Lady Mary Wortley. "Letters and Works." Edited by Lord Wharndiffe. London: 1837. 3 vols.

Montesquieu. "OEuvres complétes." Ed. Laboulaye. Paris: 1875–79. 7 vols.

Montpensier, Mile. de. "Memoires." Collationnés par Chéruel. Paris: 1859. 4 vols.

Moore, Frank Frankfort. "A Nest of Linnets." London: 1900.

Moore, Thomas. "Life of Lord Byron." London: 1854. 6 vols.

"Memoirs, Journal and Correspondence." Edited by Lord John Russell. London: 1853. 8 vols.

"Memoirs of the Life of the Right Honourable Richard Brinsley Sheridan." London: 1825.

Ditto. The Fourth Edition. London: 1826. 2 vols.

Ditto. The Fifth Edition. 1827.

Moreau de Brazey. *See* de B.

Morgan, Lady. *See* Owenson.

Morris, J. W. *See* "Handbook to Bath."

Murch, Jerom. "The Bath Physicians of former Times." A Paper read before the Bath Literary and Philosophical Association, October 20, 1882. Bath: 1882.

"Biographical Sketches of Bath Celebrities, Ancient and Modern, with some Fragments of Local History." Bath: 1893.

"Ralph Allen, and the English Post-Office." A Paper read before the Bath Literary and Philosophical Association. London and Bath: 1880.

"New Bath Guide; or, the Memoirs of the B—r— d Family, in a series of Poetical Epistles." By Christopher Anstey. Second Edition. Cambridge: 1766.

Neckam, Alexander. "De Natura Rerum libri duo." With the Poem of the same Author, "De Laudibus Divinae Sapientiae." Edited by Thomas Wright. London: 1863.

"New Foundling Hospital for Wit." Third Edition. London: 1771. 6 vols.

"New Prose Bath Guide for the Year 1778" by the Author of "A Year's Journey through France and Spain." Philip Thicknesse. London: 1778?

Newman, John Henry, Cardinal. "Essays, Critical and Historical." New Impression. London: 1901. 2 vols.

Nightingale, J. "Beauties of England and Wales." London: 1801–1815. 13 vols.

Notes and Queries. London: 1849, *sqq*.

Nouvelle Revue. Paris: 1876, *sqq*. Octogenarian. "Sheridan and his Times." London: 1859. 2 vols.

"Ode on an Evening View of the Crescent at Bath." London: 1783. (Bath Reference Library).

Odingsells, GabrieL "The Bath—Unmask'd." London: 1725.

An Officer. "Bath: an Adumbration." Bath: 1995. (Bath Reference Library.)

Oldmixion, J. See "Court Tales." Oliphant, Mrs "Sheridan." London: 1883.

"Omnium Gatherum; or, Bath Bristol, and Cheltenham Literary Repository." By Us Two. 7 numbers. Bath: 1814.

"On Novelty: and on Trifles and Triflers." Poetical Amusements at a Villa near Bath. Bath: 1778.

Orrery, John, Earl of. "Remarks on the Life and Writings of Dr Jonathan Swift." Second Edition. London: 1752.

Owenson, Lady Morgan. "France." London: 1817. "France in 1829–1830." London: 1830. 2 vols.

P. [R. Pugh]. "Bathoniensium et Aquisgranensium Thermarum Comparatio." Londini: 1676.

Pallet, Peter Paul [Richard Warner]. "Bath Characters; or, Sketches from Life." Second. Edition. London: 1808.

"Rebellion in Bath; or, the Battle of the Upper Rooms." An heroico-odico-tragico comic Poem in two Cantos. London: 1808.

Parke, W. T. "Musical Memoirs." London: 1830. 2 vols.

Pasquin, Anthony [John Williams]. "A Postscript to the New Bath Guide." A Poem. London: 1790.

Pavilion, Etienne. "OEuvres." Amsterdam: 1750.

Peach, R. E. M. "Bath, Old and New." A Handy Guide and a History. London: 1888.

"Historic Houses in Bath and their Associations." London: 1888.

"Life and Times of Ralph Allen." London: 1895.

"Street-Lore of Bath: a Record of Changes in the Highways and Byways of the City." London and Bath: 1893.

Peirce, Robert. "Bath Memoirs; or, Observations in Three and Forty Years Practice at the Bath, what Cures have been there Wrought, etc." Bristol: 1697.

Penley, Belville S. "The Bath Stage: a History of Dramatic Representations in Bath." London: 1892.

Pepys Samuel. "Diary." Edited by H. B. Wheatley. London: 1897. 10 vols.

"Person of Quality" [Thomas Rawlins]. "Tunbridge Wells." A Comedy. London: 1678.

Pindar, Peter [John Wolcot]. "The Bath Pump Room; or, a Sovereign Remedy for Low Spirits." A Poem. London: 1818.

Pindémonte, Ippolito. "Lettere inedite." Venezia: 1843.

Pitt, William, Lord Chatham. "Correspondence." London: 1828. 4 vols.

See Chatham, Earl of.

"Pleasures of Bath." Bristol: 1721

"Poetical Address to the Ladies at Bath." Bath: 1774. (Bath Reference Library.)

"Poetical Amusements at a Villa near Bath." The Second Edition. London: 1776–81. 4 vols.

"Poetical Epistles to the Author of the New Bath Guide." From a Genteel Family in —shire. Cambridge and London: 1767. (*British Museum*, 840, I. 16, 3.)

Pollnitz, de. *See* "Amusements des Eaux de Spa."

Polwhele, R. "Biographical Sketches in Cornwall." London: 1831. 3 vols.

Pope, Alexander. "The Dunciad."

"Moral Essays."

"One Thousand Seven Hundred and Thirty-Eight." A Dialogue something like Horace. London: Cowper, nd. 1738.

Ditto. Dublin. Reprinted by Gev. Faulkner. 1738.

"Works." London: 1740–49–53. 8 vols. (*British Museum*, 686, d. 16.)

"Works, together with the Commentary and Notes of Mr Warburton." London: 1757. 9 vols.

"Works." With Introduction and Notes by W. Elwin and W. J. Courthorpe. London: 1871–79. 10 vols.

"Pour et Contre, Le." Ouvrage périodique d'un gout nouveau par l'auteur des "Mémoires d'un Homme de Qualité" [l'abbé Prévost]. Paris: 1733–40. 20 vols.

P. P. "Iconism in Verse, with additional Sketches of several well-known Characters in and around Bath." Third and last Edition. Bristol: 1817. (Bath Reference Library.) Pratt, Samuel. "Harvest Home." London: 1805. 3 vols.

Prévost, l'Abbé. *See* "Pour et Contre," and "Suite des Mémoires et Aventures d'un Homme de Qualité."

"*Proceedings* of the Bath Natural History and Antiquarian Field Club." Bath: 1868, and following years.

Πτολεμαίος (Κλώδιος). Γεωγραφική ὑφήγησις … recognovit C. Mullerus. Parisiis: 1883.

Pugh, R. *See* P.

Q. in the Corner. "Epistles from Bath; or, Q.'s Letters to his Yorkshire Relations." By Q. in the Corner, author of "Rough Sketches of Bath" (T. Bayly?). Bath: 1817.

"Quarrels of Authors." By Isaac Disraeli. London: 1814. 4 vols.

Rae, W. Fraser. "Sheridan." A Biography. London: 1896. 2 vols.

Rake, Robert. "Bath." A Satire. Bath: 1819.

Rawlins, Thomas. *See* "A Person of Quality."

"Receipt to make a Bath-Easton Poet and to obtain a *Prize* from the *Vase*." Bath: 1777. (Bath Reference Library.)

"Recollections of some Particulars in the Life of Mr Shenstone." By Richard Graves. London: 1788.

Rees, Abraham. "The Cyclopaedia." London: 1819. 39 vols.

"Remarks on the 'Bath Man' by a Man of the World, intended as a Reply to an Essay on Bath Manners in No. of the *Album*." Bath: 1825. (Bath Reference Library.) Remusat, Charles de. "L'Angleterre au XVIII° siècle." Paris: 1865. 2 vols.

Richardson, Samuel. "Correspondence." London: 1804. 6 vols.

See "A Tour."

Rigaud, L. "Dictionnaire d'argot Moderne." Paris: 1881.

"Rivals, The." A Comedy. By R. B. Sheridan. London: 1775. (*British Museum*, 1346, f. 31.)

Roberts, William. "Memoirs of the Life and Correspondence of Mrs Hannah More." Second Edition. London: 1834. 4 vols.

Rochester, John Wilmot, Earl of. "Works." London: Tonson, 1714.

Rochester, Roscomon and Dorset, Earls of. "Works." Also those of the Dukes of Devonshire and Buckinghamshire. London: Goodcurl, 1735.

"Rod, A, for Tunbridge Beaus, bundl'd up at the Request of the Tunbridge Ladies to jerk Fools into more Wit, and Clowns into more Manners." A Burlesque Poem. London: 1701.

Rogers, S. "Poems on Various Occasions." Bath: 1782. 2 vols.

Rowlandson. *See* "The Comforts of Bath."

Ruffhead, O. "Life of Alexander Pope, Esq." London: 1769.

Russell, William C. "Representative Actors." London: 1869.

Saunders, Lloyd C. "Life of Richard Brinsley Sheridan." London.

Scarth, Harry Mingdern "Aquae Solis; or, Notices of Roman Bath." London: 1864.

Schimmelpenninck, A Mannery. "Life." Edited by Christiana C. Hankin. Third Edition. London: 1859.

Scott, Sir Walter. "St Ronan's Well." 1824.

"Sentence of Momus on the Poetical Amusements at a Villa near Bath." London: 1775. (Bath Reference Library.)

Seward, Anna. "A Poem to the Memory of Lady Miller." London: 1782.

Shadwell, Thomas. "Epsom Well A Comedy. London: 1673.

Sheridan, Mrs Frances. "A Journey to Bath." A Comedy. (*British Museum*, MSS 25, 975.)03 *See* Sheridan, R. B. "Plays." Edited by W. Fraser Rae.

Sheridan, Richard Brinsley. Comedies. "The Rivals" and "The School for Scandal" Edited by Brander Matthews. London: 1885.

Plays, now printed as he wrote them, and his mother's unpublished Comedy, "A Journey to Bath." Edited by W. Fraser Rae. London: 1902.

See "Aristaenetus."

See "Asmodeo."

See "The Rivals."

Sheridan, Thomas. "Life of Dr. Jonathan Swift." London: 1784.

Sidney, Sir Philip. "Correspondence of Sir Philip Sidney and Hubert Languet." Collected and translated from the Latin by S. A. Pears. London: 1845.

Simond, L. *See* "Voyage d'un Français en Angleterre."

Smithus, Thomas. "De Republica Anglorum." Libri II Lug duni Batavorum: CIↃIↃC XLI Smollett, Tobias. "The Adventures of Ferdinand Count Fathom."

"The Adventures of Peregrine Pickle." 1751.

"The Adventures of Roderick Random." 1748.

"An Essay on the External Use of Water." Third Edition. London: 1770. (Bath Reference, Library.)

"The Expedition of Humphry Clinker." London: 1671 (*sic*, for 1771). 3 vols.

Solinus, C. Julius. "Polyhistor." Biponti: CIↃIↃCCXCIV

"Some Memoirs of the Life of John Radcliffe, MD." London: 1715.

Southey, Robert. "The Life of Wesley and the Rise and Progress of Methodism." Second Edition. London: 1820. 2 vols.

"Life and Correspondence." Edited by his Son. London: 1849.

Spectator, The. London: 1711–14.

Spence, Rev. John. "Anecdotes, Observations and Characters of Books and Men." Collected from the Conversation of Mr Pope and other Eminent Persons of his Time." London: 1820.

Spenser. "The Faerie Queene."

"Spiritual Quixote, The; or, the Summer's Ramble of Mr Geoffry Wildgoose." A Comic Romance. London: 1773. 3 vols.

"Step to the Bath, A, with a Character of the Place." London: 1700.

Stephen, Sir Leslie. "Pope." New Edition. London: 1888.

See "Dictionary of National Biography."

Stone, Mrs "Chronicles of Fashion." London: 1845. 2 vols.

Suffolk, Henrietta, Countess of. "Letters to and from Henrietta, Countess of Suffolk, and her second Husband, the Hon. George Berkeley." London: 1824. 2 vols.

"Suite des Mémoires et Aventures d'un Homme de Qualité qui s'est retiré du Monde." By l'Abbé Prévost, whom *see.* Amsterdam: 1731.

"Summer in Bath, A." In a Series of Letters Descriptive of its Scenery, Machinery, Dresses, and Decorations. Sherborne: 1822.

Sutherland, Alexander. "Attempts to Revive Ancient Medical Doctrines." London: 1763.

Swallow, Dr. J. A. "Methodism in the Light of the English Literature of the last Century." Erlangen und Leipzig: 1895. (Munchener Beitrage zur romanischenund englischen Philologie, IX).

Swift, Jonathan. "Literary Correspondence." London: 1741.

"Prose Works." Edited by T. Scott. Vol. II, "Journal to Stella." London: 1897.

"Works." Arranged, with Notes, by Thomas Sheridan. London: 1784. 17 vols.

"Works." With Memoirs by Thomas Roscoe. London, Bohn: 1864. 2 vols.

Swinburne, Algernon Charles. "Poems and Ballads." Third Series. London: 1889.

T — (F.) "The Wonders of a Week at Bath in a Doggrell Address to the Honourable T. S." London: 1811.

Taine, H. "Histoire de la Littérature Anglaise." Sixième Edition. Paris: 1885–87. 5 vols.

Tarkington, Booth. "Monsieur Beaucaire: a Tale of Bath Life in the Eighteenth Century." London: 1901.

Tatler, The. By Isaac Bickerstaff. London: 1809–11.

Taylor, John. "Records of My Life." London: 1832. 2 vols.

Thackeray, William Makepeace. "The Four Georges." 1861.

"Vanity Fair." 1848.

"The Virginians: a Tale of the Last Century." 1858–59.

Thicknesse, Philip. "A Sketch of the Life and Paintings of Thomas Gainsborough." London: 1788.

"The Valetudinarian's Bath Guide; or, the Means of Obtaining Long Life and Health." Second Edition. London and Bath: 1780.

See "New Prose Bath Guide."

Thrale, Mrs "Letters To and From Johnson." London: 1788. 2 vols.

"Through England on a Side saddle in the Time of William and Mary, being the Diary of Celia Fiennes." London: 1888.

"Tour, A, through the whole Island of Great Britain, originally begun by D. Defoe, continued by the late Mr Richardson, and brought down to the Present Time by a Gentleman of Eminence in the Literary World." Seventh Edition. London: 1769. 4 vols.

Ditto. 1778.

Tourguénief, Ivan. "Fumée." Paris: 1868.

Trollope, Frances. "Paris and the Parisians in 1835." London: 1836. 2 vols.

"The Tradesman's and Traveller's Pocket Companion; or, the Bath and Bristol Guide." Second Edition. Bath: 1750?

"Tunbridge Walks; or, the Yeoman of Kent." A Comedy. By the Author of the Humour o' the Age (Thomas Barker). London: 1703.

Tunbridge Wells. *See* "A Person of Quality."

"Tunbridgiale." A Poem. Being a Description of Tunbridge in a Letter to a Friend at London. By the Author of "My Time, O ye Muses," etc. London: 1726.

"Tunbridgialla; or, Tunbridge Miscellanies for the Year 1733." London: 1733.

"Tunbrigalia; or, Tunbridge Miscellanies for the Year 1719." London: 1719.

"Tunbrigalia; or, the Tunbridge Miscellany for the Years 1737, 1738, 1739." Being a Curious

Collection of Miscellany Poems, etc., exhibited upon the Walks at Tunbridge Wells in the three last Years, by a Society of Gentlemen and Ladies. London and Westminster: 1840.
"Tunbrigalia; or, the Tunbridge Miscellany for the Year 1722." London: nd.
Tunstall, James. "Rambles about Bath and its Neighbourhood." London and Bath: 1847.
Turner, William. "A Book of the Natures and Properties as well of the Bathes in England as of the Bathes in Germanye and Italye." Collen (Cologne): 1562.
Universal Magazine of Knowledge and Pleasure. Vol. xxxi. London: 1762.
Urban, Sylvanus. *The Gentleman's Magazine*, or *Monthly Intelligencer.* London: 1731.
Us Two. *See* "Omnium Gatherum."
V., M. de (H. Misson). "Mémoires et Observations faites par un Voyageur en Angleterre." La Haye: 1698.
"Voyage d'un Français en Angleterre pendant les années 1810 et 1811." By L. Simond. Paris: 1817. 2 vols.
Wace. "Le Roman de Brut." Publié par Le Roux de Lincy. Rouen: 1836.
Walpole, Horace. "Catalogue of the Royal and Noble Authors." London: 1806. vols.
"Letters." Edited by Peter Cunningham. London: 1891. 9 vols.
Warburton, William. "A Sermon preached at the Abbey Church at Bath on Sunday, October 24, 1742." London: 1742.
"Works." London: 1788. 7 vols.
Ware, Mrs Hibbert. "The King of Bath; or, Life at a Spa in the Eighteenth Century." Second Edition. London: 1879.
Warner, Rebecca. "Original Letters from Richard Baxter, Matthew Prior, etc." Bath: 1817.
Warner, Richard. "An Illustration of the Roman Antiquities discovered at Bath." Bath: 1797.
"The History of Bath." Bath: 1801.
"Literary Recollections." London: 1830. 2 vols.
"A New Guide through Bath." Bath: 1811.
See "Pallet" (Peter-Paul).
"Water Poetry." A Collection of Verses written at several Public Places, most of them never published. London: nd.
Watkins, John. "Memoirs of the Public and Private Life of the Right Honourable Richard Brinsley Sheridan." London: 1817.
Watson, Rev. John S. "Life of William Warburton." London: 1863.
Weiss, R. B. "Sheridan als Lustspieldichter." Leipzig : 1888.
Wesley, John. "An Extract of the Reverend Mr John Wesley's Journal." London: 1805. 8 vols.
Whalley, Thomas Sedgwick. "Journals and Correspondence." London: 1863. 2 vols.
Wilkes, John. "Correspondence." Printed by J. Almon. London: 1805. 4 vols.
Williams, D. E. "Life and Correspondence of Sir Thomas Lawrence, Knight," London: 1831. 2 vols.
Williams, John. *See* "Pasquin."
"A Winter in Bath." By the Author of two popular Novels. London: 1807. 4 vols.
Wolcot, John. *See* Pindar, Peter. Wood, John. "A Description of Bath." Second Edition. London: 1749. 2 vols.
Ditto. Second *(sic)* Edition. London: 1765.
Wright, the Rev. G. N.. "The Historic Guide to Bath." Bath: 1864.
Wright, Robert. "The Life of Major-General James Wolfe." London: 1864.
Young, Edward. "Poetical Works." London, Bell: 1867. 2 vols.